# OpenVPN Cookbook

*Second Edition*

Discover over 90 practical and exciting recipes that leverage the power of OpenVPN 2.4 to help you obtain a reliable and secure VPN

**Jan Just Keijser**

**BIRMINGHAM - MUMBAI**

# OpenVPN Cookbook

*Second Edition*



First published: February 2011

Second edition: February 2017

Production reference: 1100217

Published by Packt Publishing Ltd.
Livery Place
35 Livery Street
Birmingham
B3 2PB, UK.

ISBN 978-1-78646-312-8

www.packtpub.com

# Credits

**Author**

Jan Just Keijser

**Reviewer**

Ralf Hildebrandt

**Commissioning Editor**

Pratik Shah

**Acquisition Editor**

Rahul Nair

**Content Development Editor**

Zeeyan Pinheiro

**Technical Editor**

Vivek Pala

**Copy Editor**

Pranjali Chury

**Project Coordinator**

Izzat Contractor

**Proofreader**

Safis Editing

**Indexer**

Tejal Soni

**Production Coordinator**

Melwyn D'sa

# About the Author

**Jan Just Keijser** is an open source professional from Utrecht, the Netherlands. He has a wide range of experience in IT, ranging from providing user support, system administration, and systems programming to network programming. He has worked for various IT companies since 1989. He was an active USENET contributor in the early 1990s and has been working mainly on Unix/Linux platforms since 1995.

Currently, he is employed as a senior scientific programmer in Amsterdam, the Netherlands, at Nikhef, the institute for subatomic physics from the Dutch Foundation for Fundamental Research on Matter (FOM). He works on multi-core and many-core computing systems and grid computing as well as smartcard applications. His open source interests include all types of virtual private networking, including IPSec, PPTP, and, of course, OpenVPN. In 2004, he discovered OpenVPN and has been using it ever since.

His first book was *OpenVPN 2 Cookbook* by Packt Publishing in 2011, followed by *Mastering OpenVPN*, also by Packt Publishing, in 2015.

# About the Reviewer

**Ralf Hildebrandt** is an active and well-known figure in the Postfix community. He's currently employed at Charite, Europe's largest university hospital. OpenVPN has successfully been used at Charite for over 10 years now on a multitude of client operating systems.

Together with Patrick Koetter, he has written the *Book of Postfix*.

# www.PacktPub.com

For support files and downloads related to your book, please visit www.PacktPub.com.

Did you know that Packt offers eBook versions of every book published, with PDF and ePub files available? You can upgrade to the eBook version at www.PacktPub.com and as a print book customer, you are entitled to a discount on the eBook copy. Get in touch with us at service@packtpub.com for more details.

At www.PacktPub.com, you can also read a collection of free technical articles, sign up for a range of free newsletters and receive exclusive discounts and offers on Packt books and eBooks.

https://www.packtpub.com/mapt

Get the most in-demand software skills with Mapt. Mapt gives you full access to all Packt books and video courses, as well as industry-leading tools to help you plan your personal development and advance your career.

## Why subscribe?

- Fully searchable across every book published by Packt
- Copy and paste, print, and bookmark content
- web browser

OpenVPN 2.4 [?]
has a feature to
obfuscate yr VPN traffic
called "tlscrypt"?

? diff .ovpn .conf

# Customer Feedback

Thanks for purchasing this Packt book. At Packt, quality is at the heart of our editorial process. To help us improve, please leave us an honest review on this book's Amazon page at `https://goo.gl/A3V0ND`.

If you'd like to join our team of regular reviewers, you can e-mail us at `customerreviews@packtpub.com`. We award our regular reviewers with free eBooks and videos in exchange for their valuable feedback. Help us be relentless in improving our products!

Notes

- Most configs are done on the server.conf file not client side
- Manually, uncomment this line #net.ipv4.ip_forward=1 from /etc/sysctl.conf (Edit is persistent)
  -- Do this for all configs & on client & server
  --- sysctl -w net.ipv4.ip_forward=1 doesn't work as suggested in book
  --- check it #sysctl -p
- Server side do: sudo iptables -t nat -I POSTROUTING -o eth0 -s 10.200.0.0/24 \
  -j MASQUERADE
  (pg. 55)
  (This needs to stay eth0)
- Run #traceroute 8.8.8.8 to make sure 1st hop is tunnel gateway ie 10.200.0.1
- Most .conf files are in /etc/openvpn/cookbook

- Topology "Subnet" param in server.conf is for newer versions of OpenVPN
- It gives each client 1 Ip as opposed to the legacy default "Net30" which gives 4 Ips for every client.

# Table of Contents

# Preface

OpenVPN is one of the world's most popular packages for setting up a Virtual Private Network (VPN). OpenVPN provides an extensible VPN framework that has been designed to ease site-specific customization, such as providing the capability to distribute a customized installation package to clients or supporting alternative authentication methods via OpenVPN's plugin module interface. It is widely used by many individuals and companies, and some service providers even offer OpenVPN access as a service to users in remote, unsecured environments.

This book provides you with many different recipes for setting up, monitoring, and troubleshooting an OpenVPN network. The author's experience in troubleshooting OpenVPN and networking configurations enables him to share his insights and solutions to help you get the most out of your OpenVPN setup.

## What this book covers

`Chapter 1`, *Point-to-Point Networks*, gives an introduction to configuring OpenVPN. The recipes are based on a point-to-point-style network, meaning that only a single client can connect at a time.

`Chapter 2`, *Client-Server IP-Only Networks*, introduces the reader to the most commonly-used deployment model for OpenVPN: a single server with multiple remote clients capable of routing IP traffic. This chapter provides the foundation for many of the recipes found in the other chapters.

`Chapter 3`, *Client-Server Ethernet-Style Networks*, covers another popular deployment model for OpenVPN: a single server with multiple clients, capable of routing Ethernet traffic. This includes non-IP traffic as well as bridging. You will also learn about the use of an external DHCP server and the use of the OpenVPN status file.

`Chapter 4`, *PKI, Certificates, and OpenSSL*, introduces you to the public key infrastructure (PKI) and X.509 certificates, which are used in OpenVPN. You will learn how to generate, manage, manipulate, and view certificates, and you will also learn about the interactions between OpenVPN and the OpenSSL libraries that it depends upon.

`Chapter 5`, *Scripting and Plugins*, covers the powerful scripting and plugin capabilities that OpenVPN offers. You will learn to use client-side scripting, which can be used to tail the connection process to the site-specific needs. You will also learn about server-side scripting and the use of OpenVPN plugins.

`Chapter 6`, *Troubleshooting OpenVPN - Configurations*, is all about troubleshooting OpenVPN misconfigurations. Some of the configuration directives used in this chapter have not been demonstrated before, so even if your setup is functioning properly, this chapter will still be insightful.

`Chapter 7`, *Troubleshooting OpenVPN - Routing*, gives an insight into troubleshooting routing problems when setting up a VPN using OpenVPN. You will learn how to detect, diagnose, and repair common routing issues.

`Chapter 8`, *Performance Tuning*, explains how you can optimize the performance of your OpenVPN setup. You will learn how to diagnose performance issues and how to tune OpenVPN's settings to speed up your VPN.

`Chapter 9`, *OS Integration*, covers the intricacies of integrating OpenVPN with the operating system it is run on. You will learn how to use OpenVPN on the most commonly used client operating systems: Linux, Mac OS X, and Windows.

`Chapter 10`, *Advanced Configuration*, goes deeper into the configuration options that OpenVPN has to offer. The recipes will cover both advanced server configurations, such as the use of a dynamic DNS, as well as the advanced client configuration, such as using a proxy server to connect to an OpenVPN server.

# What you need for this book

In order to get the most from this book, there are some expectations of prior knowledge and experience. It is assumed that the reader has a fair understanding of the system administration as well as knowledge of TCP/IP networking. Some knowledge on installing OpenVPN is required as well, for which you can refer to the book *Beginning OpenVPN 2.0.9*.

# Who this book is for

This book is for system administrators who have basic knowledge of OpenVPN and are eagerly waiting to build, secure, and manage VPNs using the latest version. This book assumes some prior knowledge of TCP/IP networking and OpenVPN. And to get the most out of this book, you must have network administration skills.

# Conventions

In this book, you will find a number of styles of text that distinguish between different kinds of information. Here are some examples of these styles, and an explanation of their meaning.

Code words in text are shown as follows: "Copy over the `tls-auth` secret key file from the `/etc/openvpn/cookbook/keys` directory."

A block of code is set as follows:

```
user  nobody
group nobody
persist-tun
persist-key
keepalive 10 60
ping-timer-rem
```

When we wish to draw your attention to a particular part of a code block, the relevant lines or items are set in bold:

```
secret secret.key 1
ifconfig 10.200.0.2 10.200.0.1
route 172.31.32.0 255.255.255.0

tun-ipv6
ifconfig-ipv6 2001:db8:100::2 2001:db8:100::1
```

Any command-line input or output is written as follows:

```
[root@server]# openvpn --genkey --secret secret.key
```

**New terms** and **important words** are shown in bold. Words that you see on the screen, in menus or dialog boxes for example, appear in the text like this: "Go to the **Network and Sharing Center** and observe that the TAP adapter is in the section **Public Network** and that it is not possible to change this."

Warnings or important notes appear in a box like this.

Tips and tricks appear like this.

# Reader feedback

Feedback from our readers is always welcome. Let us know what you think about this book—what you liked or disliked. Reader feedback is important for us as it helps us develop titles that you will really get the most out of.

To send us general feedback, simply e-mail `feedback@packtpub.com`, and mention the book's title in the subject of your message.

If there is a topic that you have expertise in and you are interested in either writing or contributing to a book, see our author guide at `www.packtpub.com/authors`.

# Customer support

Now that you are the proud owner of a Packt book, we have a number of things to help you to get the most from your purchase.

## Downloading the example code

You can download the example code files for this book from your account at `http://www.packtpub.com`. If you purchased this book elsewhere, you can visit `http://www.packtpub.com/support`and register to have the files e-mailed directly to you.

You can download the code files by following these steps:

1. Log in or register to our website using your e-mail address and password.
2. Hover the mouse pointer on the **SUPPORT** tab at the top.
3. Click on **Code Downloads & Errata**.
4. Enter the name of the book in the **Search** box.
5. Select the book for which you're looking to download the code files.
6. Choose from the drop-down menu where you purchased this book from.
7. Click on **Code Download**.

You can also download the code files by clicking on the **Code Files** button on the book's webpage at the Packt Publishing website. This page can be accessed by entering the book's name in the Search box. Please note that you need to be logged in to your Packt account.

Once the file is downloaded, please make sure that you unzip or extract the folder using the latest version of:

- WinRAR / 7-Zip for Windows
- Zipeg / iZip / UnRarX for Mac
- 7-Zip / PeaZip for Linux

The code bundle for the book is also hosted on GitHub at `https://github.com/PacktPublishing/openvpncookbook`. We also have other code bundles from our rich catalog of books and videos available at `https://github.com/PacktPublishing/`. Check them out!

# Errata

Although we have taken every care to ensure the accuracy of our content, mistakes do happen. If you find a mistake in one of our books—maybe a mistake in the text or the code—we would be grateful if you could report this to us. By doing so, you can save other readers from frustration and help us improve subsequent versions of this book. If you find any errata, please report them by visiting `http://www.packtpub.com/submit-errata`, selecting your book, clicking on the Errata Submission Form link, and entering the details of your errata. Once your errata are verified, your submission will be accepted and the errata will be uploaded to our website or added to any list of existing errata under the Errata section of that title.

To view the previously submitted errata, go to `https://www.packtpub.com/books/content/support`and enter the name of the book in the search field. The required information will appear under the Errata section.

# Piracy

Piracy of copyrighted material on the Internet is an ongoing problem across all media. At Packt, we take the protection of our copyright and licenses very seriously. If you come across any illegal copies of our works in any form on the Internet, please provide us with the location address or website name immediately so that we can pursue a remedy.

Please contact us at `copyright@packtpub.com` with a link to the suspected pirated material.

We appreciate your help in protecting our authors and our ability to bring you valuable content.

# Questions

If you have a problem with any aspect of this book, you can contact us at `questions@packtpub.com`, and we will do our best to address the problem.

# 1
# Point-to-Point Networks

In this chapter, we will cover the following:

- The shortest setup possible
- OpenVPN secret keys
- Multiple secret keys
- Plaintext tunnel
- Routing
- Configuration files versus the command line
- IP-less configurations
- Complete site-to-site setup
- Three-way routing
- Using IPv6

## Introduction

The recipes in this chapter will provide an introduction to configuring OpenVPN. They are based on a point-to-point type of network, meaning that only a single client can connect at a given time.

A point-to-point network is very useful when connecting to a small number of sites or clients. It is easier to set up, as no certificates or **public key infrastructure** (**PKI**) is required. Also, routing is slightly easier to configure as no client-specific configuration files containing `--iroute` statements are required.

The drawbacks of a point-to-point network are as follows:

- The lack of having perfect forward secrecy-a key compromise may result in a total disclosure of previous sessions
- The secret key must exist in plaintext form on each VPN peer

# The shortest setup possible

This recipe will explain the shortest setup possible when using OpenVPN. For this setup, you require two computers that are connected over a network (LAN or Internet). We will use both a TUN-style network and a TAP-style network and will focus on the differences between them. A TUN device is used mostly for VPN tunnels where only IP traffic is used. A TAP device allows all the Ethernet frames to be passed over the OpenVPN tunnel, hence providing support for non-IP based protocols, such as IPX and AppleTalk.

While this may seem useless at first glance, it can be very useful to quickly test whether OpenVPN can connect to a remote system.

# Getting ready

Install OpenVPN 2.3.9 or higher on two computers. Make sure the computers are connected over a network. For this recipe, the server computer was running CentOS 6 Linux and OpenVPN 2.3.9 and the client was running Windows 7 Pro 64bit and OpenVPN 2.3.10.

# How to do it...

Here are the steps that you need to follow:

1. Launch the server-side (listening) OpenVPN process for the TUN-style network:

```
[root@server]# openvpn --ifconfig 10.200.0.1 10.200.0.2 \
  --dev tun
```

The preceding command should be entered as a single line. The character \ is used to denote the fact that the command continues on the next line.

2. Then, launch the client-side OpenVPN process:

```
[WinClient] C:\>"\Program Files\OpenVPN\bin\openvpn.exe" \
    --ifconfig 10.200.0.2 10.200.0.1 --dev tun \
    --remote openvpnserver.example.com
```

The following screenshot shows how a connection is established:

```
[] OpenVPN 2.3.10 F4:EXIT F1:USR1 F2:USR2 F3:HUP
c:\Program Files\OpenVPN\bin>openvpn --ifconfig 10.200.0.2 10.200.0.1 --dev tun
  --remote openvpnserver.example.org
Sat Jan 09 18:44:52 2016 OpenVPN 2.3.10 x86_64-w64-mingw32 [SSL (OpenSSL)] [LZO]
 [PKCS11] [IPv6] built on Jan  4 2016
Sat Jan 09 18:44:52 2016 Windows version 6.1 (Windows 7)
Sat Jan 09 18:44:52 2016 library versions: OpenSSL 1.0.1q 3 Dec 2015, LZO 2.09
Sat Jan 09 18:44:52 2016 ******* WARNING *******: all encryption and authenticat
ion features disabled -- all data will be tunnelled as cleartext
Sat Jan 09 18:44:52 2016 do_ifconfig, tt->ipv6=0, tt->did_ifconfig_ipv6_setup=0
Sat Jan 09 18:44:52 2016 open_tun, tt->ipv6=0
Sat Jan 09 18:44:52 2016 TAP-WIN32 device [tun0] opened: \\.\Global\{0E837379-61
04-4D00-9417-EB5B6782543B}.tap
Sat Jan 09 18:44:52 2016 Notified TAP-Windows driver to set a DHCP IP/netmask of
 10.200.0.2/255.255.255.252 on interface {0E837379-6104-4D00-9417-EB5B6782543B}
[DHCP-serv: 10.200.0.1, lease-time: 31536000]
Sat Jan 09 18:44:53 2016 UDPv4 link local (bound): [undef]
Sat Jan 09 18:44:53 2016 UDPv4 link remote: [AF_INET]172.16.8.1:1194
Sat Jan 09 18:45:03 2016 Peer Connection Initiated with [AF_INET]172.16.8.1:1194

Sat Jan 09 18:45:09 2016 Initialization Sequence Completed
```

As soon as the connection is established, we can ping the other end of the tunnel.

3. Next, stop the tunnel by pressing the *F4* function key in the command window and restart both ends of the tunnel using the TAP device.
4. Launch the server-side (listening) OpenVPN process for the TAP-style network:

```
[root@server]# openvpn --ifconfig 10.200.0.1 255.255.255.0 \
  --dev tap
```

5. Then launch the client-side OpenVPN process:

```
            [WinClient] C:\>"
\Program Files\OpenVPN\bin\openvpn.exe" \
            --ifconfig 10.200.0.2 255.255.255.0 --dev tap \
            --remote openvpnserver.example.com
```

The connection will now be established and we can again ping the other end of the tunnel.

# How it works...

The server listens on UDP port `1194`, which is the OpenVPN default port for incoming connections. The client connects to the server on this port. After the initial handshake, the server configures the first available TUN device with the IP address `10.200.0.1` and it expects the remote end (the Peer address) to be `10.200.0.2`.

The client does the opposite: after the initial handshake, the first TUN or TAP-Win32 device is configured with the IP address `10.200.0.2`. It expects the remote end (the Peer address) to be `10.200.0.1`. After this, the VPN is established.

Notice the warning:
******* **WARNING** *******: **all encryption and authentication features disabled — all data will be tunnelled as cleartext**
Here, the data is not secure: all of the data that is sent over the VPN tunnel can be read!

# There's more...

Let's look at a couple of different scenarios and check whether they would modify the process.

## Using the TCP protocol

In the previous example, we chose the UDP protocol. It would not have made any difference if we had chosen the TCP protocol, provided that we had done that on the server side (the side without `--remote`) as well as the client side. The following is the code for doing this on the server side:

```
[root@server]# openvpn --ifconfig 10.200.0.1 10.200.0.2 \
    --dev tun --proto tcp-server
```

Here's the code for the client side:

```
[root@client]# openvpn --ifconfig 10.200.0.2 10.200.0.1 \
    --dev tun --proto tcp-client --remote openvpnserver.example.com
```

## Forwarding non-IP traffic over the tunnel

With the TAP-style interface, it is possible to run non-IP traffic over the tunnel. For example, if AppleTalk is configured correctly on both sides, we can query a remote host using the `aecho` command:

```
aecho openvpnserver
22 bytes from 65280.1: aep_seq=0. time=26. ms
22 bytes from 65280.1: aep_seq=1. time=26. ms
22 bytes from 65280.1: aep_seq=2. time=27. ms
```

A `tcpdump -nnel -i tap0` command shows that the type of traffic is indeed non-IP-based AppleTalk.

# OpenVPN secret keys

This recipe uses OpenVPN secret keys to secure the VPN tunnel. It is very similar to the previous recipe, but this time, we will use a shared secret key to encrypt the traffic between the client and the server.

## Getting ready

Install OpenVPN 2.3.9 or higher on two computers. Make sure the computers are connected over a network. For this recipe, the server computer was running CentOS 6 Linux and OpenVPN 2.3.9 and the client was running Windows 7 64 bit and OpenVPN 2.3.10.

## How to do it...

1. First, generate a secret key on the server (listener):

   ```
   [root@server]# openvpn --genkey --secret secret.key
   ```

2. Transfer this key to the client side over a secure channel (for example, using `scp`).
3. Next, launch the server-side (listening) OpenVPN process:

   ```
   [root@server]# openvpn --ifconfig 10.200.0.1 10.200.0.2 \
     --dev tun --secret secret.key
   ```

4. Then, launch the client-side OpenVPN process:

```
[WinClient] C:\>"\Program Files\OpenVPN\bin\openvpn.exe" \
  --ifconfig 10.200.0.2 10.200.0.1 \
  --dev tun --secret secret.key \
  --remote openvpnserver.example.com
```

The connection is now established, as shown in the following screenshot:

```
[] OpenVPN 2.3.10 F4:EXIT F1:USR1 F2:USR2 F3:HUP
Sat Jan 09 18:54:19 2016 SIGTERM[hard,] received, process exiting

c:\Program Files\OpenVPN\config>..\bin\openvpn --ifconfig 10.200.0.2 10.200.0.1
  --dev tun --remote openvpnserver.example.org --secret secret.key
Sat Jan 09 18:54:27 2016 OpenVPN 2.3.10 x86_64-w64-mingw32 [SSL (OpenSSL)] [LZO]
[PKCS11] [IPv6] built on Jan  4 2016
Sat Jan 09 18:54:27 2016 Windows version 6.1 (Windows 7)
Sat Jan 09 18:54:27 2016 library versions: OpenSSL 1.0.1q 3 Dec 2015, LZO 2.09
Sat Jan 09 18:54:27 2016 do_ifconfig, tt->ipv6=0, tt->did_ifconfig_ipv6_setup=0
Sat Jan 09 18:54:27 2016 open_tun, tt->ipv6=0
Sat Jan 09 18:54:27 2016 TAP-WIN32 device [tun0] opened: \\.\Global\{0E837379-610
4-4D00-9417-EB5B6782543B}.tap
Sat Jan 09 18:54:27 2016 Notified TAP-Windows driver to set a DHCP IP/netmask of
10.200.0.2/255.255.255.252 on interface {0E837379-6104-4D00-9417-EB5B6782543B} [D
HCP-serv: 10.200.0.1, lease-time: 31536000]
Sat Jan 09 18:54:27 2016 UDPv4 link local (bound): [undef]
Sat Jan 09 18:54:27 2016 UDPv4 link remote: [AF_INET]172.16.8.1:1194
Sat Jan 09 18:54:37 2016 Peer Connection Initiated with [AF_INET]172.16.8.1:1194
Sat Jan 09 18:54:45 2016 Initialization Sequence Completed
```

## How it works...

This example works exactly as the first one: the server listens to the incoming connections on UDP port `1194`. The client connects to the server on this port. After the initial handshake, the server configures the first available TUN device with the IP address `10.200.0.1` and it expects the remote end (Peer address) to be `10.200.0.2`. The client does the opposite.

## There's more...

By default, OpenVPN uses two symmetric keys when setting up a point-to-point connection:

- A cipher key to encrypt the contents of the packets being exchanged.
- An HMAC key to sign packets. When packets arrive that are not signed using the appropriate HMAC key, they are dropped immediately. This is the first line of defense against a "denial-of-service" attack.



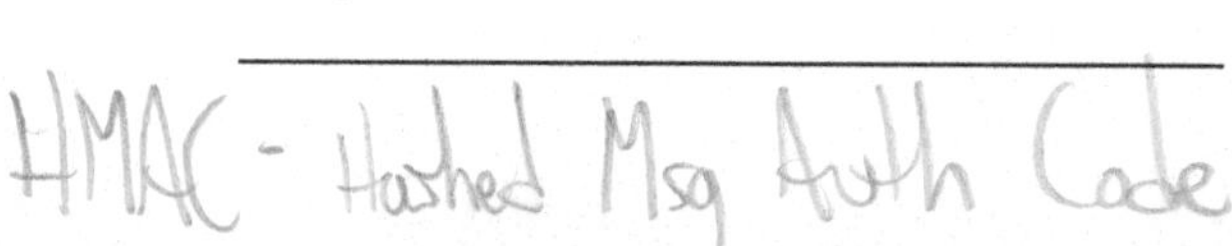

- The same set of keys are used on both ends and both keys are derived from the file specified using the `--secret` parameter.

An OpenVPN secret key file is formatted as follows:

```
#
# 2048 bit OpenVPN static key
#
-----BEGIN OpenVPN Static key V1-----
<16 lines of random bytes>
-----END OpenVPN Static key V1-----
```

From the random bytes, the OpenVPN Cipher and HMAC keys are derived. Note that these keys are the same for each session.

## See also

- The next recipe, *Multiple secret keys*, will explain the format of secret keys in detail

# Multiple secret keys

As stated in the previous recipe, OpenVPN uses two symmetric keys when setting up a point-to-point connection. However, it is also possible to use shared yet asymmetric keys in point-to-point mode. OpenVPN will use four keys in this case:

- A cipher key on the client side
- An HMAC key on the client side
- A cipher key on the server side
- An HMAC key on the server side

The same keying material is shared by both sides of the point-to-point connection, but the keys that are derived for encrypting and signing the data are different for each side. This recipe explains how to set up OpenVPN in this manner and how the keys can be made visible.

# Getting ready

For this recipe, we use the `secret.key` file from the previous recipe. Install OpenVPN 2.3.9 or higher on two computers. Make sure the computers are connected over a network. For this recipe, the server computer was running CentOS 6 Linux and OpenVPN 2.3.9 and the client was running Windows 7 64 bit and OpenVPN 2.3.10. We'll use the `secret.key` file from the *OpenVPN secret keys* recipe here.

# How to do it...

1. Launch the server-side (listening) OpenVPN process with an extra option to the `--secret` parameter and with more verbose logging:

```
[root@server]# openvpn \
  --ifconfig 10.200.0.1 10.200.0.2 \
  --dev tun --secret secret.key 0 \
  --verb 7
```

2. Then launch the client-side OpenVPN process:

```
[WinClient] C:\>"\Program Files\OpenVPN\bin\openvpn.exe" \
  --ifconfig 10.200.0.2 10.200.0.1 \
  --dev tun --secret secret.key 1\
  --remote openvpnserver \
  --verb 7
```

The connection will be established with a lot of debugging messages.

If we look through the server-side messages (searching for `crypt`), we can find the negotiated keys on the server side. Note that the output has been reformatted for clarity:

```
... Static Encrypt:
Cipher 'BF-CBC' initialized with 128 bit key
... Static Encrypt:
CIPHER KEY: 80797ddc 547fbdef 79eb353f 2a1f3d1f
... Static Encrypt:
Using 160 bit message hash 'SHA1' for HMAC authentication
... Static Encrypt:
HMAC KEY: c752f254 cc4ac230 83bd8daf 6141e73d 844764d8
... Static Decrypt:
Cipher 'BF-CBC' initialized with 128 bit key
... Static Decrypt:
CIPHER KEY: 8cf9abdd 371392b1 14b51523 25302c99
... Static Decrypt:
```

```
Using 160 bit message hash 'SHA1' for HMAC authentication
... Static Decrypt:
HMAC KEY: 39e06d8e 20c0d3c6 0f63b3e7 d94f35af bd744b27
```

On the client side, we will find the same keys but the "Encrypt" and "Decrypt" keys would have been reversed:

```
... Static Encrypt:
Cipher 'BF-CBC' initialized with 128 bit key
... Static Encrypt:
CIPHER KEY: 8cf9abdd 371392b1 14b51523 25302c99
... Static Encrypt:
Using 160 bit message hash 'SHA1' for HMAC authentication
... Static Encrypt:
HMAC KEY: 39e06d8e 20c0d3c6 0f63b3e7 d94f35af bd744b27
... Static Decrypt:
Cipher 'BF-CBC' initialized with 128 bit key
... Static Decrypt:
CIPHER KEY: 80797ddc 547fbdef 79eb353f 2a1f3d1f
... Static Decrypt:
Using 160 bit message hash 'SHA1' for HMAC authentication
... Static Decrypt:
HMAC KEY: c752f254 cc4ac230 83bd8daf 6141e73d 844764d8
```

If you look at the keys carefully, you will see that each one of them is mirrored on the client and the server side.

# How it works...

OpenVPN derives all the keys from the `static.key` file, provided there is enough entropy (randomness) in the file to reliably generate four keys. All the keys generated using the following will have enough entropy:

```
$ openvpn --genkey --secret secret.key
```

An OpenVPN static key file is 2,048 bits in size. The cipher keys are each 128 bits, whereas the HMAC keys are 160 bits each, for a total of 776 bits. This allows OpenVPN to easily generate four random keys from the static key file, even if a cipher is chosen that requires a larger initialization key.

## There's more...

The same secret key files are used in a client/server setup when the `tls-auth ta.key` parameter is used.

## See also

- The *Setting up the public and private keys* recipe from `Chapter 2`, *Client-server IP-only Networks*, in which the `tls-auth` key is generated in a very similar manner

# Plaintext tunnel

In the very first recipe, we created a tunnel in which the data traffic was not encrypted. To create a completely plain text tunnel, we also disable the HMAC authentication. This can be useful when debugging a bad connection, as all traffic over the tunnel can now easily be monitored. In this recipe, we will look at how to do this. This type of tunnel is also useful when doing performance measurements, as it is the least CPU-intensive tunnel that can be established.

## Getting ready

Install OpenVPN 2.3.9 or higher on two computers. Make sure the computers are connected over a network. For this recipe, the server computer was running CentOS 6 Linux and OpenVPN 2.3.9 and the client was running Fedora 22 Linux and OpenVPN 2.3.10.

As we are not using any encryption, no secret keys are needed.

## How to do it...

1. Launch the server-side (listening) OpenVPN process:

```
[root@server]# openvpn \
    --ifconfig 10.200.0.1 10.200.0.2 \
    --dev tun --auth none
```

2. Then launch the client-side OpenVPN process:

```
[root@client]# openvpn \
    --ifconfig 10.200.0.2 10.200.0.1 \
    --dev tun --auth none\
    --remote openvpnserver.example.com
```

3. The connection will be established with the following two warning messages as the output:

```
... ******* WARNING *******: null cipher specified, no encryption will be
used
... ******* WARNING *******: null MAC specified, no authentication will
be used
```

# How it works...

With this setup, absolutely no encryption is performed. All of the traffic that is sent over the tunnel is encapsulated in an OpenVPN packet and then sent as is.

# There's more...

To actually view the traffic, we can use `tcpdump`; follow these steps:

1. Set up the connection as outlined.
2. Start `tcpdump` and listen on the network interface, not the tunnel interface itself:

```
[root@client]# tcpdump -l -w - -i eth0 -s 0 host
openvpnserver | strings
```

3. Now, send some text across the tunnel, using something like `nc` (Netcat). First, launch `nc` on the server side:

```
[server]$ nc -l 31000
```

4. On the client side, launch the `nc` command in client mode and type `hello` and `goodbye`:

```
[client]$ nc 10.200.0.1 3100
  hello
  goodbye
```

5. In the `tcpdump` window, you should now see the following:

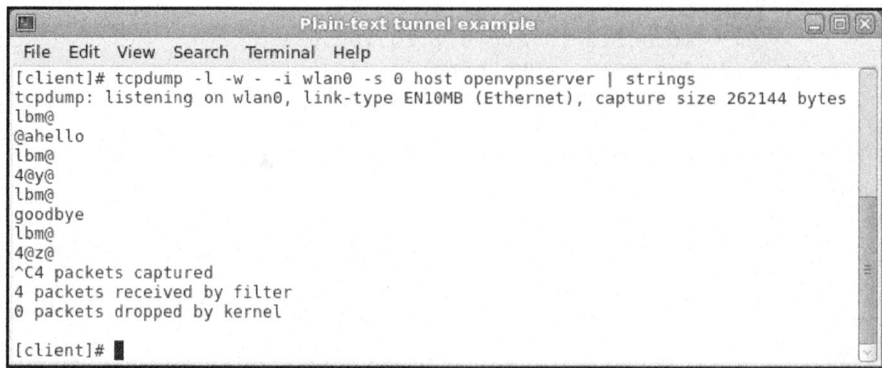


6. Press *Ctrl* + C to terminate `tcpdump` as well as `nc`.

# Routing

The point-to-point type of networks are great if you want to connect two networks together over a static, encrypted tunnel. If you only have a small number of endpoints (fewer than four), then routing is far easier than using a client/server setup as described in `Chapter 2`, *Client-server IP-only Networks*.

# Getting ready

For this recipe, we will use the following network layout:

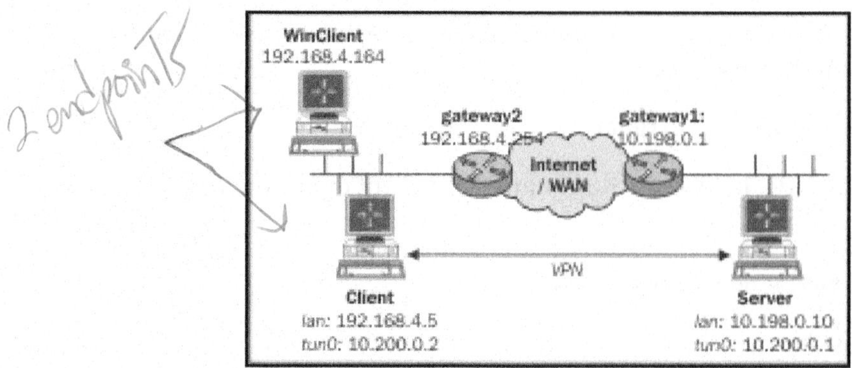

Install OpenVPN 2.3.9 or higher on two computers. Make sure the computers are connected over a network. For this recipe, the server computer was running CentOS 6 Linux and OpenVPN 2.3.9 and the client was running Windows 7 64 bit and OpenVPN 2.3.10. We'll use the `secret.key` file from the *OpenVPN secret keys* recipe here.

# How to do it...

1. First, establish the connection, but also make sure OpenVPN has daemonized itself:

```
[root@server]# openvpn \
  --ifconfig 10.200.0.1 10.200.0.2 \
  --dev tun --secret secret.key \
  --daemon --log /tmp/openvpnserver.log
```

2. Then, launch the client-side OpenVPN process:

```
[client]$ openvpn \
  --ifconfig 10.200.0.2 10.200.0.1 \
  --dev tun --secret secret.key \
  --remote openvpnserver \
  --daemon --log /tmp/openvpnclient.log
```

3. The connection is established:

```
[server]$ tail -1 /tmp/openvpnserver.log
     Initialization Sequence Completed
```

Now we add routing:

1. On the server side, we add a static route:

```
[root@server]# route add -net 192.168.4.0/24 gw 10.200.0.2
```

2. On the client side, we need to do two things:

   Make sure that you have the IP traffic forwarding enabled. On Linux, this can be achieved using the following:

```
[root@client]# sysctl -w net.ipv4.ip_forward=1
```

Note that this setting does not survive a reboot of the system.

On the Windows client on the client-side LAN, make sure there is a route back to the OpenVPN server:

```
C:> route add 10.200.0.0 mask 255.255.255.0 192.168.4.5
```

Here, `192.168.4.5` is the LAN IP address of the OpenVPN client.

3. From the server, we can now ping machines on the client LAN. First, ping the LAN IP of the OpenVPN client:

```
 [root@server]# ping -c 2 192.168.4.5
 PING 192.168.4.5 (192.168.4.5) 56(84) bytes of data.
 64 bytes from 192.168.4.5: icmp_seq=0 ttl=64 time=31.7 ms
 64 bytes from 192.168.4.5: icmp_seq=1 ttl=64 time=31.3 ms
--- 192.168.4.5 ping statistics ---
 2 packets transmitted, 2 received, 0% packet loss, time
 1000ms
rtt min/avg/max/mdev = 31.359/31.537/31.716/0.251 ms, pipe 2
```

4. Then, ping the LAN IP of a machine on the OpenVPN client LAN:

```
[root@server]# ping -c 2 192.168.4.164
[server]$ ping -c 2 192.168.4.164
PING 192.168.4.164 (192.168.4.164) 56(84) bytes of data.
64 bytes from 192.168.4.164: icmp_seq=0 ttl=63 time=31.9 ms
64 bytes from 192.168.4.164: icmp_seq=1 ttl=63 time=31.4 ms
--- 192.168.4.164 ping statistics ---
2 packets transmitted, 2 received, 0% packet loss, time
 1001ms
rtt min/avg/max/mdev = 31.486/31.737/31.989/0.308 ms, pipe 2
```

## How it works...

In our network setup, the LAN we want to reach is behind the OpenVPN client, so we have to add a route to the server:

```
[server]$ route add -net 192.168.4.0/24 gw 10.200.0.2
```

On the client side, we need to do two things:

- Make sure that the routing is enabled. If you want routing to remain enabled after a reboot, edit the `/etc/sysctl.cnf` file:

  ```
  net.ipv4.ip_forward = 1
  ```

- We also need to make sure that there is a route back to the OpenVPN server on the client LAN. This can be done by adding a route to the LAN gateway or by adding a static route to each of the machines on the client LAN. In this recipe, we added a route to a Windows client that is in the same LAN as the OpenVPN client:

  ```
  C:> route add 10.200.0.0 mask 255.255.255.0 192.168.4.5
  ```

Here, `192.168.4.5` is the LAN IP address of the OpenVPN client.

## There's more...

Let's discuss a bit about routing issues and how to automate the setup.

### Routing issues

On the OpenVPN users mailing list, a large number of the problems that are reported have something to do with routing issues. Most of them have little to do with OpenVPN itself, but more with understanding the routing and the flow of packets over the network. `Chapter 7`, *Troubleshooting OpenVPN – Routing*, provides some recipes to diagnose and fix the most common routing problems.

## Automating the setup

It is also possible to add the appropriate routes when the tunnel first comes up. This can be done using the `--route` statement:

```
[server]$ openvpn \
    --ifconfig 10.200.0.1 10.200.0.2 \
    --dev tun --secret secret.key \
    --daemon --log /var/log/openvpnserver-1.5.log \
    --route 192.168.4.0 255.255.255.0
```

Note that on the client LAN, the route back to the server still has to be set manually.

## See also

- The *Three-way routing* recipe, later on in this chapter, where a more complicated setup using three remote sites is explained
- `Chapter 7`, *Troubleshooting OpenVPN – Routing*

# Configuration files versus the command line

Most recipes in this book can be carried out without using configuration files. However, in most real-life cases, a configuration file is much easier to use than a lengthy command line. It is important to know that OpenVPN actually treats configuration file entries and command-line parameters identically. The only difference is that all command-line parameters start with a double dash (`--`) whereas the configuration file entries do not. This makes it very easy to overrule the configuration file entries using an extra command-line parameter.

## Getting ready

Install OpenVPN 2.3.9 or higher on two computers. Make sure the computers are connected over a network. For this recipe, the server computer was running CentOS 6 Linux and OpenVPN 2.3.9 and the client was running Windows 7 64 bit and OpenVPN 2.3.10. In this recipe, we'll use the `secret.key` file from the *OpenVPN secret keys* recipe.

# How to do it...

1. Create a configuration file based on an earlier recipe:

```
dev tun
port 1194
ifconfig 10.200.0.1 10.200.0.2
secret secret.key
remote openvpnserver.example.com
verb 3
```

2. Save this file as `example1-6-client.conf`.
3. Launch the server-side (listening) OpenVPN process on a non-standard port:

```
[root@server]# openvpn \
  --ifconfig 10.200.0.1 10.200.0.2 \
  --dev tun --secret secret.key \
  --port 11000
```

4. Then launch the client-side OpenVPN process and add an extra command-line parameter:

```
[WinClient] C:\>"\Program Files\OpenVPN\bin\openvpn.exe" \
  --config client.conf \
  --port 11000
```

The connection is established:

```
Jan 11 16:14:04 2016 UDPv4 link local (bound): [undef]
Jan 11 16:14:04 2016 UDPv4 link remote: [AF_INET]172.16.8.1:11000
Jan 11 16:14:06 2016 Peer Connection Initiated with
[AF_INET]172.16.8.1:11000
Jan 11 16:14:12 2016 TEST ROUTES: 0/0 succeeded len=0 ret=1 a=0 u/d=up
Jan 11 16:14:12 2016 Initialization Sequence Completed
```

# How it works...

The command line and the configuration file are read and parsed from left to right and top to bottom. This means that most options that are specified before the configuration file can be overruled by the entries in that file. Similarly, the options specified after the following directive overrule the entries in that file:

```
--config client.conf
```

Hence, the following option overruled the line "`port 1194`" from the configuration file:

```
--port 11000
```

However, some options can be specified multiple times, in which case, the first occurrence "wins." In such a case, it is also possible to specify the option before specifying the `--config` directive.

## There's more...

Here is another example that shows the importance of the ordering of the command-line parameters:

```
C:\>"\Program Files\OpenVPN\bin\openvpn.exe" \
    --verb 0 \
    --config client.conf \
    --port 11000
```

This produces the exact same connection log as shown before. The `verb 3` command from the `client.conf` configuration file overruled `--verb 0`, as specified on the command line. However, refer to the following command line:

```
C:\>"\Program Files\OpenVPN\bin\openvpn.exe" \
    --config client.conf \
    --port 11000 \
    --verb 0
```

Using this command line, the connection log will remain entirely empty, yet the VPN connection will be in functioning mode.

## Exceptions to the rule

Some of the newer features of OpenVPN deviate slightly from this principle, most notably the `<connection>` blocks and the inline certificates. Some people prefer to write the following command:

```
remote openvpnserver.example.com 1194
```

They prefer this instead of the following command:

```
port 1194
remote openvpnserver.example.com
```

The downside of this notation is that this is translated as a connection block by OpenVPN. For connection blocks, it is not possible to overrule the port using `--port 11000`.

# Complete site-to-site setup

In this recipe, we set up a complete site-to-site network, using most of the built-in security features that OpenVPN offers. It is intended as a "one-stop-shop" example of how to set up a point-to-point network.

## Getting ready

Install OpenVPN 2.3.9 or higher on two computers. Make sure the computers are connected over a network. For this recipe, the server computer was running CentOS 6 Linux and OpenVPN 2.3.9 and the client was running Fedora 22 Linux and OpenVPN 2.3.10. We'll use the `secret.key` file from the *OpenVPN secret keys* recipe here.

We will use the following network layout:

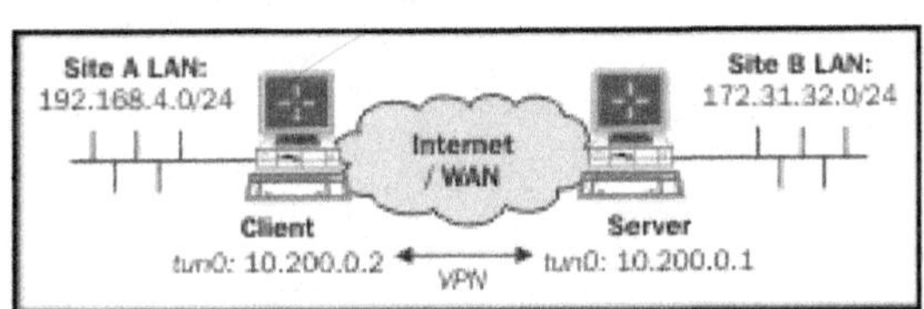


Make sure routing (IP forwarding) is configured on both the server and client.

## How to do it...

1. Create the server configuration file:

```
dev tun
proto udp
local  openvpnserver.example.com
lport  1194
remote openvpnclient.example.com
rport  1194

secret secret.key 0
ifconfig 10.200.0.1 10.200.0.2
```

```
route 192.168.4.0 255.255.255.0

user  nobody
group nobody  # use "group nogroup" on some distros
persist-tun
persist-key
keepalive 10 60
ping-timer-rem

verb 3
daemon
log-append /tmp/openvpn.log
```

2. Save it as `example1-7-server.conf`.
3. On the client side, create the configuration file:

```
dev tun
proto udp
local  openvpnclient.example.com
lport  1194
remote openvpnserver.example.com
rport  1194

secret secret.key 1
ifconfig 10.200.0.2 10.200.0.1
route 172.31.32.0 255.255.255.0

user  nobody
group nobody  # use "group nogroup" on some distros
persist-tun
persist-key
keepalive 10 60
ping-timer-rem

verb 3
daemon
log-append /tmp/openvpn.log
```

4. Save it as `example1-7-client.conf`.
5. Then start the tunnel on both ends. The following is for the server end:

```
[root@server]# openvpn --config example1-7-server.conf
```

Here's the code for the client end:

```
[root@client]# openvpn --config example1-7-client.conf
```

Now our site-to-site tunnel is established.

6. Check the log files on both the client and server to verify that the connection has been established.
7. After the connection comes up, the machines on the LANs behind both the end points can be reached over the OpenVPN tunnel. For example, when we ping a machine on the client-side LAN from the server, we will see the following:

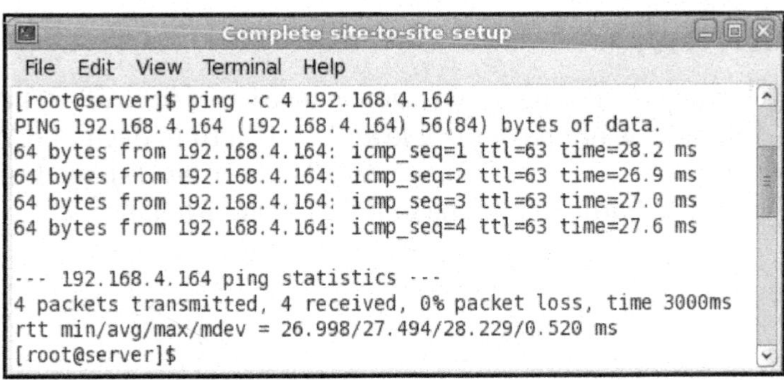

Complete site-to-site setup
File Edit View Terminal Help
[root@server]$ ping -c 4 192.168.4.164
PING 192.168.4.164 (192.168.4.164) 56(84) bytes of data.
64 bytes from 192.168.4.164: icmp_seq=1 ttl=63 time=28.2 ms
64 bytes from 192.168.4.164: icmp_seq=2 ttl=63 time=26.9 ms
64 bytes from 192.168.4.164: icmp_seq=3 ttl=63 time=27.0 ms
64 bytes from 192.168.4.164: icmp_seq=4 ttl=63 time=27.6 ms
--- 192.168.4.164 ping statistics ---
4 packets transmitted, 4 received, 0% packet loss, time 3000ms
rtt min/avg/max/mdev = 26.998/27.494/28.229/0.520 ms
[root@server]$


## How it works...

The client and server configuration files are very similar:

- The server listens only on one interface and one UDP port
- The server accepts connections only from a single IP address and port
- The client has these options mirrored

Here is the set of configuration options:

```
user  nobody
group nobody
persist-tun
persist-key
keepalive 10 60
ping-timer-rem
```

These options are used to make the connection more robust and secure, as follows:

The OpenVPN process runs as user `nobody` and group `nobody` after the initial connection is established. Even if somebody is able to take control of the OpenVPN process itself, he or she would still only be `nobody` and not `root`. Note that on some Linux distributions, `nogroup` is used instead.

The `persist-tun` and `persist-key` options are used to ensure that the connection comes back automatically if the underlying network is disrupted. These options are necessary when using `user nobody` and `group nobody` (or `group nogroup`).

The `keepalive` and `ping-timer-rem` options cause OpenVPN to send a periodic "ping" message over the tunnel to ensure that both ends of the tunnel remain up and running.

## There's more...

This point-to-point setup can also be used to evade restrictive firewalls. The data stream between the two endpoints is not recognizable and very hard to decipher. When OpenVPN is run in client/server (see `Chapter 2`, *Client-server IP-only Networks*), the traffic is recognizable as OpenVPN traffic due to the initial TLS handshake.

## See also

- The last recipe in this chapter, *Using IPv6*, which builds upon this recipe by adding support for IPv6 traffic
- `Chapter 7`, *Troubleshooting OpenVPN – Routing*, in which the most common routing issues are explained

# Three-way routing

For a small number (less than four) of fixed endpoints, a point-to-point setup is very flexible. In this recipe, we set up three OpenVPN tunnels between three sites, including routing between the endpoints. By setting up three tunnels, we create redundant routing so that all the sites are connected even if one of the tunnels is disrupted.

## Getting ready

Install OpenVPN 2.3.9 or higher on two computers. Make sure the computers are connected over a network. For this recipe, the server computer was running CentOS 6 Linux and OpenVPN 2.3.9 and the client was running Fedora 22 Linux and OpenVPN 2.3.10.

We will use the following network layout:

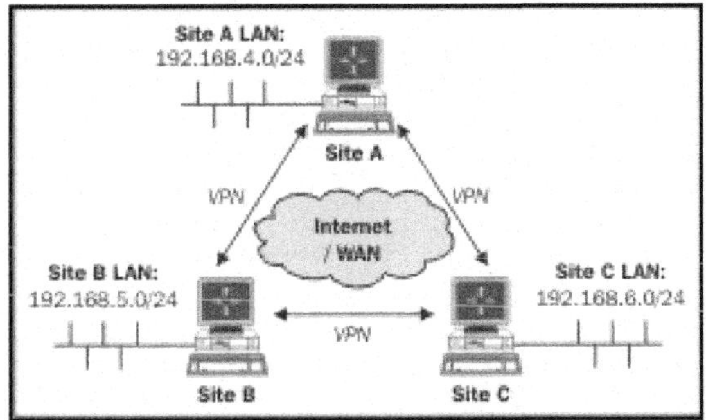


Make sure that the routing (IP forwarding) is configured on all the OpenVPN endpoints.

# How to do it...

1. We generate three static keys:

```
[root@siteA]# openvpn --genkey --secret AtoB.key
[root@siteA]# openvpn --genkey --secret AtoC.key
[root@siteA]# openvpn --genkey --secret BtoC.key
```

2. Transfer these keys to all the endpoints over a secure channel (for example, using `scp`).
3. Create the server (listener) configuration file named `example1-8-serverBtoA.conf`:

```
dev tun
proto udp
port  1194

secret AtoB.key 0
ifconfig 10.200.0.1 10.200.0.2

route 192.168.4.0 255.255.255.0 vpn_gateway 5
route 192.168.6.0 255.255.255.0 vpn_gateway 10
route-delay

keepalive 10 60
verb 3
```

4. Next, create an `example1-8-serverCtoA.conf` file:

```
dev tun
proto udp
port  1195

secret AtoC.key 0
ifconfig 10.200.0.5 10.200.0.6

route 192.168.4.0 255.255.255.0 vpn_gateway 5
route 192.168.5.0 255.255.255.0 vpn_gateway 10
route-delay

keepalive 10 60
verb 3
```

5. Also, create an `example1-8-serverBtoC.conf` file:

```
dev tun
proto udp
port  1196

secret BtoC.key 0
ifconfig 10.200.0.9 10.200.0.10

route 192.168.4.0 255.255.255.0 vpn_gateway 10
route 192.168.6.0 255.255.255.0 vpn_gateway 5
route-delay

keepalive 10 60
verb 3
```

6. Now, create the client (connector) configuration files, `example1-8-clientAtoB.conf`:

```
dev tun
proto udp
remote siteB
port  1194

secret AtoB.key 1
ifconfig 10.200.0.2 10.200.0.1

route 192.168.5.0 255.255.255.0 vpn_gateway 5
route 192.168.6.0 255.255.255.0 vpn_gateway 10
route-delay
```

```
keepalive 10 60
verb 3
```

7. Also, create an `example1-8-clientAtoC.conf` file:

```
dev tun
proto udp
remote siteC
port  1195

secret AtoC.key 1
ifconfig 10.200.0.6 10.200.0.5

route 192.168.5.0 255.255.255.0 vpn_gateway 10
route 192.168.6.0 255.255.255.0 vpn_gateway 5
route-delay

verb 3
```

8. And finally, create `example1-8-clientCtoB.conf`:

```
dev tun
proto udp
remote siteB
port  1196

secret BtoC.key 1
ifconfig 10.200.0.10 10.200.0.9

route 192.168.4.0 255.255.255.0 vpn_gateway 10
route 192.168.5.0 255.255.255.0 vpn_gateway 5
route-delay

keepalive 10 60
verb 3
```

First, we start all the listener tunnels:

```
[root@siteB]# openvpn --config example1-8-serverBtoA.conf
[root@siteB]# openvpn --config example1-8-serverBtoC.conf
[root@siteC]# openvpn --config example1-8-serverCtoA.conf
```

These are followed by the connector tunnels:

```
[root@siteA]# openvpn --config example1-8-clientAtoB.conf
[root@siteA]# openvpn --config example1-8-clientAtoC.conf
[root@siteC]# openvpn --config example1-8-clientCtoB.conf
```

And with that, our three-way site-to-site network is established.

## How it works...

It can be clearly seen that the number of configuration files gets out of hand too quickly. In principle, two tunnels would have been sufficient to connect three remote sites, but then there would have been no redundancy.

With the third tunnel and with the configuration options, there are always two routes available for each remote network:

```
route 192.168.5.0 255.255.255.0 vpn_gateway 5
route 192.168.6.0 255.255.255.0 vpn_gateway 10
route-delay
keepalive 10 60
```

For example, site A has two routes to site B (LAN `192.168.5.0/24`), as seen from the following routing table:

```
[siteA]$ ip route show
[...]
192.168.5.0/24 via 10.200.0.1 dev tun0  metric 5
192.168.5.0/24 via 10.200.0.5 dev tun1  metric 10
[...]
```

These are the two routes to site A:

- Via the "direct" tunnel to site B; this route has the lowest metric
- Via an indirect tunnel: first to site C and then to site B; this route has a higher metric and is not chosen until the first route is down

This setup has the advantage that if one tunnel fails, then after 60 seconds, the connection and its corresponding routes are dropped and restarted. The backup route to the other network then automatically takes over and all three sites can reach each other again.

When the direct tunnel is restored, the direct routes are also restored and the network traffic will automatically choose the best path to the remote site.

## There's more...

Let's discuss a bit about scalability and routing protocols.

## Scalability

In this recipe, we connect three remote sites. This results in six different configuration files that provide the limitations of the point-to-point setup. In general, to connect *n* number of possible sites with full redundancy, you will have *n * ( n – 1 )* configuration files. This is manageable for up to four sites, but after that, a server/multiple-client setup, as described in the next chapters, is much easier.

## Routing protocols

To increase the availability of the networks, it is better to run a routing protocol, such as RIPv2 or OSPF. Using a routing protocol, the failing routes are discovered much faster, resulting in less network downtime.

## See also

- `Chapter 7`, *Troubleshooting OpenVPN – Routing*, in which the most common routing issues are explained

# Using IPv6

In this recipe, we extend the complete site-to-site network recipe to include support for IPv6.

## Getting ready

Install OpenVPN 2.3.9 or higher on two computers. Make sure the computers are connected over a network. For this recipe, the server computer was running CentOS 6 Linux and OpenVPN 2.3.9 and the client was running Fedora 22 Linux and OpenVPN 2.3.10. We'll use the `secret.key` file from the *OpenVPN secret keys* recipe here.

We will use the following network layout:

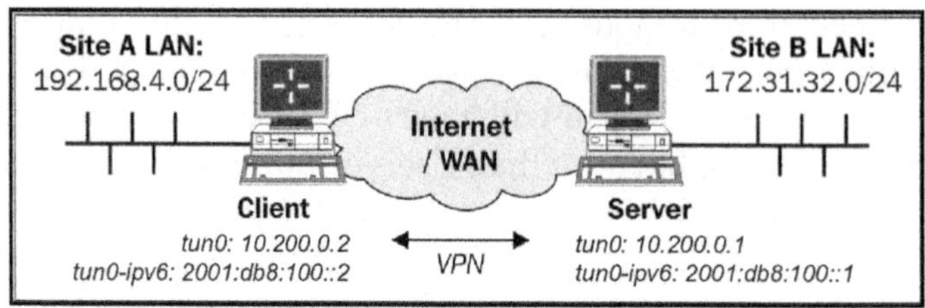


# How to do it...

1. Create the server configuration file:

```
dev tun
proto udp
local  openvpnserver.example.com
lport  1194
remote openvpnclient.example.com
rport  1194

secret secret.key 0
ifconfig 10.200.0.1 10.200.0.2
route 192.168.4.0 255.255.255.0

tun-ipv6
ifconfig-ipv6 2001:db8:100::1 2001:db8:100::2

user  nobody
group nobody  # use "group nogroup" on some distros
persist-tun
persist-key
keepalive 10 60
ping-timer-rem

verb 3
daemon
log-append /tmp/openvpn.log
```

2. Save it as `example1-9-server.conf`.

3. On the client side, create the configuration file:

```
dev tun
proto udp
local  openvpnclient.example.com
lport  1194
remote openvpnserver.example.com
rport  1194

secret secret.key 1
ifconfig 10.200.0.2 10.200.0.1
route 172.31.32.0 255.255.255.0

tun-ipv6
ifconfig-ipv6 2001:db8:100::2 2001:db8:100::1

user  nobody
group nobody  # use "group nogroup" on some distros
persist-tun
persist-key
keepalive 10 60
ping-timer-rem

verb 3
```

4. Save it as `example1-9-client.conf`.
5. Then start the tunnel on both ends The following is for the server end:

   ```
   [root@server]# openvpn --config example1-9-server.conf
   ```

   This is the code for the client end:

   ```
   [root@client]# openvpn --config example1-9-client.conf
   ```

   Now our site-to-site tunnel is established.

6. After the connection comes up, the machines on the LANs behind both end points can be reached over the OpenVPN tunnel. Notice that the client OpenVPN session is running in the foreground.

7. Next, ping the IPv6 address of the server endpoint to verify that IPv6 traffic over the tunnel is working:

```
[client]$ ping6 -c 4 2001:db8:100::1
PING 2001:db8:100::1(2001:db8:100::1) 56 data bytes
64 bytes from 2001:db8:100::1: icmp_seq=1 ttl=64 time=7.43 ms
64 bytes from 2001:db8:100::1: icmp_seq=2 ttl=64 time=7.54 ms
64 bytes from 2001:db8:100::1: icmp_seq=3 ttl=64 time=7.77 ms
64 bytes from 2001:db8:100::1: icmp_seq=4 ttl=64 time=7.42 ms
--- 2001:db8:100::1 ping statistics ---
4 packets transmitted, 4 received, 0% packet loss, time 3005ms
rtt min/avg/max/mdev = 7.425/7.546/7.778/0.177 ms
```

8. Finally, abort the client-side session by pressing *Ctrl* + *C*. The following screenshot lists the full client-side log:

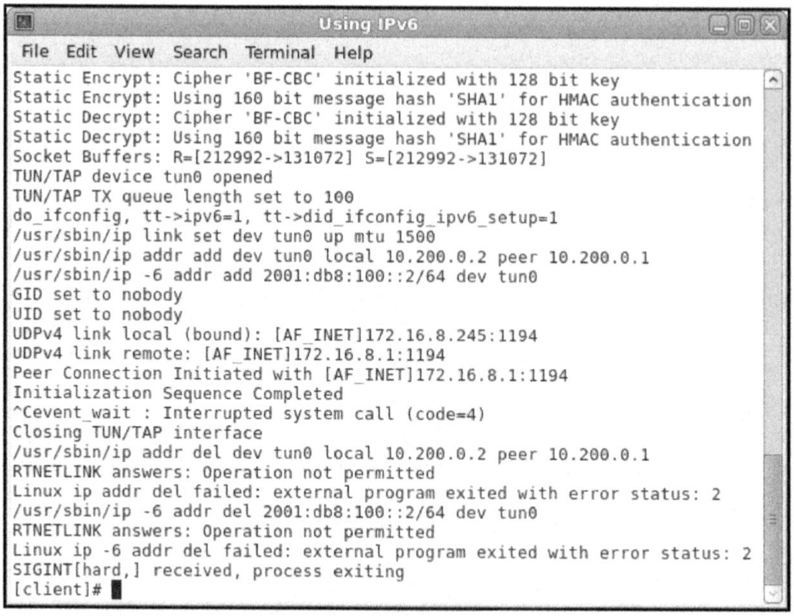

```
Using IPv6
File  Edit  View  Search  Terminal  Help
Static Encrypt: Cipher 'BF-CBC' initialized with 128 bit key
Static Encrypt: Using 160 bit message hash 'SHA1' for HMAC authentication
Static Decrypt: Cipher 'BF-CBC' initialized with 128 bit key
Static Decrypt: Using 160 bit message hash 'SHA1' for HMAC authentication
Socket Buffers: R=[212992->131072] S=[212992->131072]
TUN/TAP device tun0 opened
TUN/TAP TX queue length set to 100
do_ifconfig, tt->ipv6=1, tt->did_ifconfig_ipv6_setup=1
/usr/sbin/ip link set dev tun0 up mtu 1500
/usr/sbin/ip addr add dev tun0 local 10.200.0.2 peer 10.200.0.1
/usr/sbin/ip -6 addr add 2001:db8:100::2/64 dev tun0
GID set to nobody
UID set to nobody
UDPv4 link local (bound): [AF_INET]172.16.8.245:1194
UDPv4 link remote: [AF_INET]172.16.8.1:1194
Peer Connection Initiated with [AF_INET]172.16.8.1:1194
Initialization Sequence Completed
^Cevent_wait : Interrupted system call (code=4)
Closing TUN/TAP interface
/usr/sbin/ip addr del dev tun0 local 10.200.0.2 peer 10.200.0.1
RTNETLINK answers: Operation not permitted
Linux ip addr del failed: external program exited with error status: 2
/usr/sbin/ip -6 addr del 2001:db8:100::2/64 dev tun0
RTNETLINK answers: Operation not permitted
Linux ip -6 addr del failed: external program exited with error status: 2
SIGINT[hard,] received, process exiting
[client]#
```

## How it works...

Both client and server configuration files are very similar to the ones from the *Complete site-to-site setup* recipe, with the addition of the following two lines:

```
tun-ipv6
ifconfig-ipv6 2001:db8:100::2 2001:db8:100::1
```

This enables IPv6 support, next to the default IPv4 support.

Also, in the client configuration, the options `daemon` and `log-append` are not present, hence all of the OpenVPN output is sent to the screen and the process continues running in the foreground.

# There's more...

Let's talk a bit about log file errors and the IPv6-only tunnel.

## Log file errors

If we take a closer look at the client-side connection output, we will see a few error messages after pressing *Ctrl* + *C*, most notably the following:

```
RTNETLINK answers: operation not permitted
```

This is a side-effect when you use the `user nobody` option to protect an OpenVPN setup, and it often confuses new users. What happens is this:

OpenVPN starts as `root`, opens the appropriate `tun` device, and sets the right IPv4 and IPv6 addresses on this `tun` interface.

For extra security, OpenVPN then switches to `nobody`, dropping all the privileges associated with `root`.

When OpenVPN terminates (in our case, by pressing *Ctrl* + *C*), it closes the access to the `tun` device and tries to remove the IPv4 and IPv6 addresses assigned to that device. At this point, the error messages appear, as `nobody` is not allowed to perform these operations.

Upon termination of the OpenVPN process, the Linux kernel closes the `tun` device and all the configuration settings are removed.

In this case, these error messages are harmless, but in general, one should pay close attention to the warning and error messages that are printed by OpenVPN.

## IPv6-only tunnel

With OpenVPN 2.3, the IPv6-only tunnel is required to always enable IPv4 support. From OpenVPN 2.4 on, it is possible to set up an IPv6-only connection.

# See also

The recipe *Complete site-to-site setup*, earlier in this chapter, in which an IPv4-only site-to-site setup is explained in detail.

The last recipe of `Chapter 6`, *Troubleshooting OpenVPN – Configurations*, which explains how to interpret the OpenVPN log files in detail.

# 2

# Client-server IP-only Networks

In this chapter, we will cover the following topics:

- Setting up the public and private keys
- A simple configuration
- Server-side routing
- Adding IPv6 support
- Using `client-config-dir` files
- Routing – subnets on both sides
- Redirecting the default gateway
- Redirecting the IPv6 default gateway
- Using an `ifconfig-pool` block
- Using the status file
- The management interface
- Proxy-arp

## Introduction

The recipes in this chapter will cover the most commonly used deployment model for OpenVPN: a single server with multiple remote clients capable of routing IP traffic.

We will also look at several common routing configurations in addition to the use of the management interface at both the client and server side.

The last recipe of this chapter will show how it is possible to avoid the use of network bridges for most practical use cases.

As a routed TUN-style setup is the most commonly used deployment model, some of the sample configuration files presented in this chapter will be reused throughout the rest of the book. In particular, the configuration files such as `basic-udp-server.conf`, `basic-udp-client.conf`, `basic-tcp-server.conf`, and `basic-tcp-client.conf` from the *Server-side routing* recipe will be reused often, as well as the Windows client configuration files `basic-udp-client.ovpn` and `basic-tcp-client.ovpn` from the *Using an ifconfig-pool block* recipe.

# Setting up the public and private keys

Before we can set up a client/server VPN, we need to set up the public key infrastructure (PKI). The PKI comprises the certificate authority, the private keys, and the certificates (public keys) for both the client and server. We also need to generate a Diffie-Hellman parameter file, which is required for perfect forward secrecy.

To set up PKI, we make use of the `easy-rsa` scripts. These scripts were originally supplied with the OpenVPN distribution itself, but nowadays, they can also be downloaded and installed separately.

## Getting ready

The PKI needs to be set up on a trusted computer. This can be the same as the computer on which the OpenVPN server is run, but from a security point of view, it is best if the PKI is kept completely separate from the rest of the OpenVPN services. One option is to keep the PKI certificate authority (CA) key located on a separate external disk, which is attached only when required. Another option would be to keep the CA private key on a separate computer that is not hooked up to any network at all.

This recipe was done on Linux, but can also be done on a Mac OS machine. On Windows, the commands are very similar as well. The Linux `easy-rsa` scripts are meant to be run from a bash-like shell, so make sure you are not running csh/tcsh (UNIX shells).

# How to do it...

1. Create the directories for the PKI and copy over the `easy-rsa` distribution from your OpenVPN installation:

```
$ mkdir -m 700 -p /etc/openvpn/cookbook/keys
$ cd /etc/openvpn/cookbook
$ cp -drp /usr/share/easy-rsa/2.0/* .
```

Note that there is no need to run these commands as the `root` user, provided that the user is allowed to create the above directory path.

2. Next, we set up the `vars` file. Create a file containing the following:

```
export EASY_RSA=/etc/openvpn/cookbook
export OPENSSL="openssl"
export PKCS11TOOL="pkcs11-tool"
export GREP="grep"
export KEY_CONFIG=`$EASY_RSA/whichopensslcnf $EASY_RSA`
export KEY_DIR="$EASY_RSA/keys"
export PKCS11_MODULE_PATH="dummy"
export PKCS11_PIN="dummy"
export KEY_SIZE=2048
export CA_EXPIRE=3650
export KEY_EXPIRE=1000
export KEY_COUNTRY="US"
export KEY_PROVINCE=
export KEY_CITY=
export KEY_ORG="Cookbook 2.4"
export KEY_OU=
export KEY_CN=
export KEY_EMAIL="openvpn@example.com"
```

> Note that the `PKCS11_MODULE_PATH` and `PKCS11_PIN` entries are needed even if you are not using smart cards.
> Also note that some `KEY_` variables are set to an empty value. This is required for generating certificates in a batch, as we shall see later on.
> The default `KEY_SIZE` of 2048 bits is sufficiently secure for the next few years. A larger key size (4096 bits) is possible, but the tradeoff is a performance penalty. We shall generate a 4096 bit CA private key, as performance is not an issue here.
> Adjust the settings (`KEY_ORG`, `KEY_OU`, `KEY_EMAIL`) to reflect your organization. The meaning of these settings is explained in more details later.

3. Source the `vars` file and generate the CA private key and certificate, using a 4096-bit modulus. Choose a strong password for the CA certificate. After that, simply press the *Enter* key every time the script asks for input:

```
$ cd /etc/openvpn/cookbook
$ . ./vars
$ ./clean-all
$ KEY_SIZE=4096 ./build-ca --pass
```

Sample output is shown in the following screenshot:

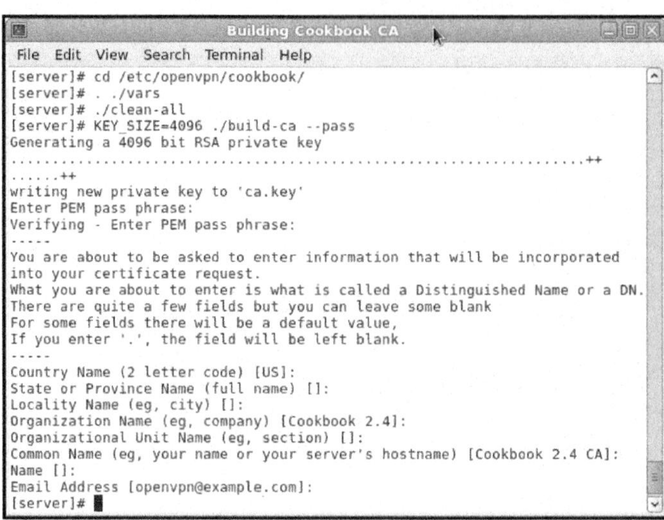
Building Cookbook CA
File Edit View Search Terminal Help
[server]# cd /etc/openvpn/cookbook/
[server]# . ./vars
[server]# ./clean-all
[server]# KEY_SIZE=4096 ./build-ca --pass
Generating a 4096 bit RSA private key
.................................................................++
......++
writing new private key to 'ca.key'
Enter PEM pass phrase:
Verifying - Enter PEM pass phrase:
-----
You are about to be asked to enter information that will be incorporated
into your certificate request.
What you are about to enter is what is called a Distinguished Name or a DN.
There are quite a few fields but you can leave some blank
For some fields there will be a default value,
If you enter '.', the field will be left blank.
-----
Country Name (2 letter code) [US]:
State or Province Name (full name) []:
Locality Name (eg, city) []:
Organization Name (eg, company) [Cookbook 2.4]:
Organizational Unit Name (eg, section) []:
Common Name (eg, your name or your server's hostname) [Cookbook 2.4 CA]:
Name []:
Email Address [openvpn@example.com]:
[server]#

4. Next, we build the server certificate. As we do not wish to include an e-mail address in every certificate, we now set the `KEY_EMAIL` variable to an empty value. When the script asks for input, press the *Enter* key. When the script asks for the CA private key (`ca.key`) password, enter the password for the CA certificate. Finally, when the script asks for a `[y/n]` answer, type `y`:

```
$ export KEY_EMAIL=
$ ./build-key-server openvpnserver
Generating a 2048 bit RSA private key

.............................................................
............................+++
..........................................+++
writing new private key to 'openvpnserver.key'
-----
You are about to be asked to enter information that will be
incorporated
into your certificate request.
What you are about to enter is what is called a Distinguished
Name or a DN.
There are quite a few fields but you can leave some blank
For some fields there will be a default value,
If you enter '.', the field will be left blank.
-----
Country Name (2 letter code) [US]:
State or Province Name (full name) []:
Locality Name (eg, city) []:
Organization Name (eg, company) [Cookbook 2.4]:
Organizational Unit Name (eg, section) []:
Common Name (eg, your name or your server's hostname)
[openvpnserver]:
    Name []:
    Email Address []:
Please enter the following 'extra' attributes
to be sent with your certificate request
A challenge password []:
An optional company name []:
Using configuration from /etc/openvpn/cookbook/openssl-
1.0.0.cnf
Enter pass phrase for /etc/openvpn/cookbook/keys/ca.key:
Check that the request matches the signature
Signature ok
The Subject's Distinguished Name is as follows
countryName             :PRINTABLE:'US'
organizationName        :PRINTABLE:'Cookbook 2.4'
commonName              :PRINTABLE:'openvpnserver'
Certificate is to be certified until Oct 13 17:49:24 2018 GMT
```

```
(1000 days)
Sign the certificate? [y/n]:y
1 out of 1 certificate requests certified, commit? [y/n]y
Write out database with 1 new entries
Data Base Updated
```

5. The first client certificate is generated in a batch. It is a very fast method for generating a client certificate, but it is not possible to set a password on the client's private key file. It is still required to enter the `ca.key` password:

```
$ ./build-key --batch client1
```

   Sample output is shown in the following screenshot:

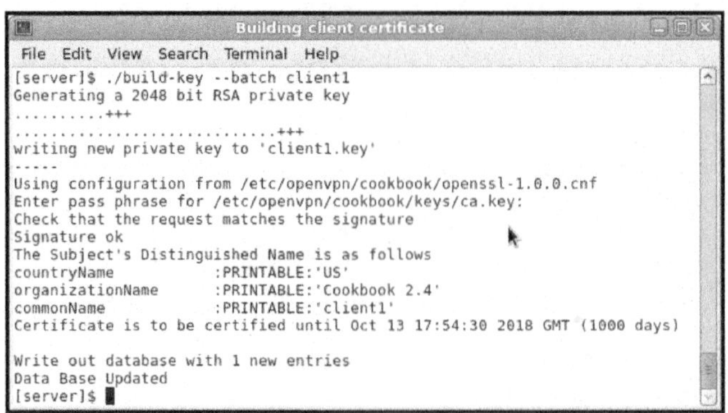


6. The second client certificate is generated with a password. Choose a strong password (but different from the CA certificate password!). The output is abbreviated for clarity:

```
$ ./build-key-pass --batch client2
Generating a 2048 bit RSA private key
............+++
...............+++
writing new private key to 'client2.key'
Enter PEM pass phrase:
Verifying - Enter PEM pass phrase:
-----
Using configuration from /etc/openvpn/cookbook/openssl-
1.0.0.cnf
Enter pass phrase for /etc/openvpn/cookbook/keys/ca.key:
Check that the request matches the signature
Signature ok
The Subject's Distinguished Name is as follows
countryName           :PRINTABLE:'US'
```

```
organizationName      :PRINTABLE:'Cookbook 2.4'
commonName            :PRINTABLE:'client2'
Certificate is to be certified until Oct 13 17:59:15 2018 GMT
(1000 days)
Write out database with 1 new entries
Data Base Updated
```

7. Next, build the Diffie-Hellman parameter file for the server:

```
Generating Diffie-Hellman parameters
File  Edit  View  Search  Terminal  Help
[server]$ ./build-dh
Generating DH parameters, 2048 bit long safe prime, generator 2
This is going to take a long time
.................................................................
....+.....................+......................................
.................................................................
.+............................++*++*
[server]$
```

8. And finally, generate the `tls-auth` key file:

```
$ openvpn --genkey --secret ta.key
```

# How it works...

The `easy-rsa` scripts are a handy set of wrapper scripts around some of the `openssl ca` commands. The `openssl ca` commands are commonly used to set up a PKI using X509 certificates. The `build-dh` script is a wrapper for the `openssl dh` command.

# There's more...

The `easy-rsa` scripts provide a full PKI setup, supporting different platforms and many settings. Some of these are outlined here.

## Using the easy-rsa scripts on Windows

To use the `easy-rsa` scripts on Windows, a command window (`cmd.exe`) is required and the starting `./` needs to be removed from all the commands, for example:

```
[Win]C:> vars
[Win]C:> clean-all
[Win]C:> build-ca
```

## Some notes on the different variables

The following variables are set in the `vars` file:

- `KEY_SIZE=2048`: This is the cipher strength for all private keys. The longer the key size is, the stronger the encryption. Unfortunately, it also makes the encryption process slower.
- `CA_EXPIRE=3650`: This gives the number of days the CA certificate is considered valid, thus translating to a period of 10 years. For a medium-secure setup, this is fine; however, if stronger security is required, this number needs to be lowered.
- `KEY_EXPIRE=1000`: This gives the number of days for which the client of the server certificate is considered valid, thus translating to a period of almost 3 years.
- `KEY_COUNTRY="US"`, `KEY_PROVINCE=`, `KEY_CITY=`, `KEY_ORG="Cookbook 2.4"`, `KEY_EMAIL=openvpn@example.com`: These variables are all used to form the certificate **Distinguished Name** (**DN**). None of them are required, but both OpenVPN and OpenSSL suggest using at least `KEY_COUNTRY` to indicate where a certificate was issued.

## See also

- See `Chapter 4`, *PKI, Certificates, and OpenSSL*, for a lengthier introduction to the `easy-rsa` scripts and the `openssl` commands

# A simple configuration

This recipe will demonstrate how to set up a connection in the client or server mode using certificates.

## Getting ready

Install OpenVPN 2.3.9 or higher on two computers. Make sure the computers are connected over a network. Set up the client and server certificates using the previous recipe. For this recipe, the server computer was running CentOS 6 Linux and OpenVPN 2.3.9 and the client was running Fedora 22 Linux and OpenVPN 2.3.10.

# How to do it...

1. Create the server configuration file:

```
proto udp
port 1194
dev tun
server 10.200.0.0 255.255.255.0

ca   /etc/openvpn/cookbook/ca.crt
cert /etc/openvpn/cookbook/server.crt
key  /etc/openvpn/cookbook/server.key
dh   /etc/openvpn/cookbook/dh2048.pem
```

   Then save it as `example2-2-server.conf`.

2. Copy over the public certificates and the server private key from the `/etc/openvpn/cookbook/keys` directory:

```
[server]$ cd /etc/openvpn/cookbook
[server]$ cp keys/ca.crt ca.crt
[server]$ cp keys/openvpnserver.crt server.crt
[server]$ cp keys/openvpnserver.key server.key
[server]$ cp keys/dh2048.pem dh2048.pem
```

Note that there is no need to run the preceding commands as user `root`, provided that write access to these directories has been given.

3. Start the server:

```
[root@server]# openvpn --config example2-2-server.conf
```

4. Next, create the client configuration file:

```
client
proto udp
remote openvpnserver.example.com
port 1194
dev tun
nobind

ca /etc/openvpn/cookbook/ca.crt
cert /etc/openvpn/cookbook/client1.crt
key /etc/openvpn/cookbook/client1.key
```

Then save it as `example2-2-client.conf`.

5. Transfer the files such as `ca.crt`, `client1.crt`, and `client1.key` to the client machine using a secure channel; for example, using the `scp` command:

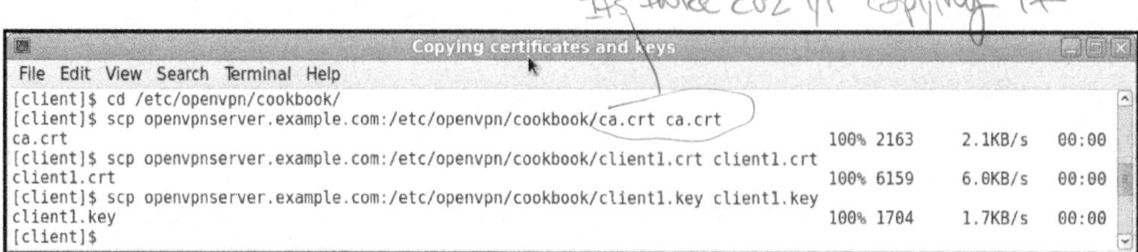


6. Then, start the client:

```
[root@client]# openvpn --config example2-2-client.conf
[...]
[openvpnserver] Peer Connection Initiated with
openvpnserver:1194
TUN/TAP device tun0 opened
/sbin/ip link set dev tun0 up mtu 1500
/sbin/ip addr add dev tun0 local 10.200.0.6 peer 10.200.0.5
Initialization Sequence Completed
```

After the connection is established, we can verify that it is working by pinging the server (notice the IP address):

```
[client]$ ping -c 2 10.200.0.1
PING 10.200.0.1 (10.200.0.1) 56(84) bytes of data.
64 bytes from 10.200.0.1: icmp_seq=1 ttl=64 time=30.6 ms
64 bytes from 10.200.0.1: icmp_seq=2 ttl=64 time=30.7 ms
```

# How it works...

When the server starts, it configures the first available TUN interface with the IP address `10.200.0.1` and with a fake remote address of `10.200.0.2`. After that, the server listens on the UDP port `1194` for incoming connections.

The client connects to the server on this port. After the initial TLS handshake, using both the client and server certificates, the client is assigned the IP address `10.200.0.6` (or rather the mini-network `10.200.0.4` – `10.200.0.7`). The client configures its first available TUN interface using this information, after which the VPN is established.

## There's more...

After the connection is established, you can query the `tun0` interface like this:

```
[client]$ /sbin/ifconfig tun0 | grep inet
```

Then, look for the following:

```
inet addr:10.200.0.6  P-t-P:10.200.0.5
```

The IP address `10.200.0.5` is a placeholder address and can never be reached. Starting with OpenVPN 2.1, it has also become possible to assign linear addresses to the clients that allow you to have more clients in the same range of IP addresses. This will be explained in the next recipe.

The first address is the VPN client address from a `/30` subnet, and the second address is the fake remote endpoint address. Each `/30` subnet has to start at a multiple of four, and the VPN client IP address is at the starting address plus two:

- `10.200.0.[0-3]`, the VPN IP is `10.200.0.1`. Normally, this block is for the OpenVPN server itself.
- `10.200.0.[4-7]`, the client IP is `10.200.0.6`. Normally, this block is for the first client to connect.
- `10.200.0.[8-11]`, `[12-15]`, `[16-19]`, and so on are used for consecutive clients.

Because of the `/30` subnet for each address, this topology mode is known as **net30**. It is still the default topology mode, but this will change in the near future.

# Server-side routing

This recipe will demonstrate how to set up server-side routing in client or server mode. With this setup, the OpenVPN client will be able to reach all the machines behind the OpenVPN server.

Compared to the previous recipe, this recipe contains extra settings that are often used in production environments including the use of `linear` addresses (`topology subnet`).

The configuration files used in this recipe are useful building blocks for other recipes throughout this book; therefore, they are named `basic-udp-server.conf`, `basic-udp-client.conf`, and so on.

## Getting ready

Install OpenVPN 2.3.9 or higher on two computers. Make sure the computers are connected over a network. Set up the client and server certificates using the previous recipe. For this recipe, the server computer was running CentOS 6 Linux and OpenVPN 2.3.9 and the client was running Fedora 20 Linux and OpenVPN 2.3.9.

We use the following network layout here:

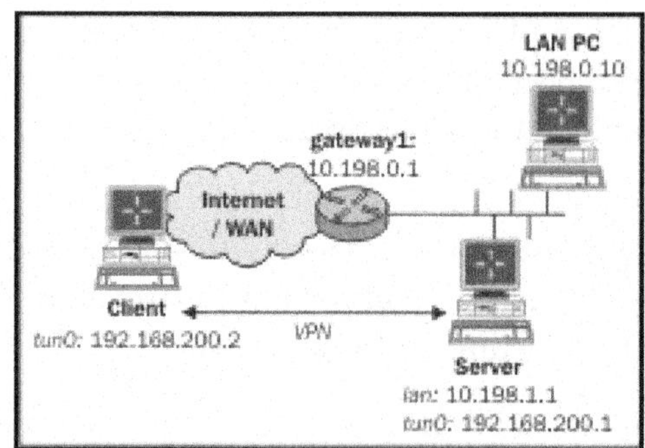


## How to do it...

1. Create the server configuration file:

```
proto udp
port 1194
dev tun
server 10.200.0.0 255.255.255.0

ca       /etc/openvpn/cookbook/ca.crt
cert     /etc/openvpn/cookbook/server.crt
key      /etc/openvpn/cookbook/server.key
dh       /etc/openvpn/cookbook/dh2048.pem
tls-auth /etc/openvpn/cookbook/ta.key 0

persist-key
persist-tun
keepalive 10 60

push "route 10.198.0.0 255.255.0.0"
topology subnet

user  nobody
```

```
group nobody   # use "group nogroup" on some distros

daemon
log-append /var/log/openvpn.log
```

Then save it as `basic-udp-server.conf`. Note that in some Linux distributions, the group `nogroup` is used instead of `nobody`.

2. Copy over the `tls-auth` secret key file from the `/etc/openvpn/cookbook/keys` directory:

   ```
   [root@server]# cp keys/ta.key ta.key
   ```

3. Then start the server:

   ```
   root@server]# openvpn --config basic-udp-server.conf
   ```

4. Make sure IP-traffic forwarding is enabled on the server:

   ```
   [root@server]# sysctl -w net.ipv4.ip_forward=1
   ```

5. Next, create the client configuration file:

   ```
   client
   proto udp
   remote openvpnserver.example.com
   port 1194
   dev tun
   nobind

   ca       /etc/openvpn/cookbook/ca.crt
   cert     /etc/openvpn/cookbook/client1.crt
   key      /etc/openvpn/cookbook/client1.key
   tls-auth /etc/openvpn/cookbook/ta.key 1

   remote-cert-tls server
   ```

   Save it as `basic-udp-client.conf`.

6. Transfer the `tls-auth` secret key file, `ta.key`, to the client machine using a secure channel, such as `scp`:

   ```
   [root@client]# scp \
       openvpnserver:/etc/openvpn/cookbook/keys/ta.key .
   ```

7. Start the client:

```
[root@client]# openvpn --config basic-udp-client.conf
OpenVPN 2.3.9 x86_64-redhat-linux-gnu [SSL (OpenSSL)] [LZO]
[EPOLL][PKCS11] [MH] [IPv6] built on Dec 16 2015
library versions: OpenSSL 1.0.1e-fips 11 Feb 2013, LZO 2.08
Control Channel Authentication: using
'/etc/openvpn/cookbook/ta.key' as a OpenVPN static key file
UDPv4 link local: [undef]
UDPv4 link remote: [AF_INET]openvpnserver:1194
[openvpnserver] Peer Connection Initiated with
[AF_INET]openvpnserver:1194
TUN/TAP device tun0 opened
do_ifconfig, tt->ipv6=0, tt->did_ifconfig_ipv6_setup=0
/usr/sbin/ip link set dev tun0 up mtu 1500
/usr/sbin/ip addr add dev tun0 10.200.0.2/24 broadcast
10.200.0.255
Initialization Sequence Completed
```

8. Add a route to the server-side gateway, `gateway1`, so that all VPN traffic is sent back to the VPN server. In this recipe, we use a router that understands a Linux `ip route` like syntax:

```
[gateway1]> ip route add 10.200.0.0/24 via 10.198.1.1
```

After the VPN is established, verify that we are able to ping a machine on the remote server LAN:

```
[client]$ ping -c 2 10.198.0.10
PING 10.198.0.10 (10.198.0.10) 56(84) bytes of data.
64 bytes from 10.198.0.10: icmp_seq=1 ttl=63 time=31.1 ms
64 bytes from 10.198.0.10: icmp_seq=2 ttl=63 time=30.0 ms
```

# How it works...

The server starts and configures the first available TUN interface with the IP address `10.200.0.1`. With the directive `topology subnet`, the fake remote address is also 10.200.0.1. After that, the server listens on the UDP port `1194` for incoming connections. For security reasons, the OpenVPN process switches to user and group `nobody`. Even if a remote attacker was able to compromise the OpenVPN process, the security breach would be contained to the user `nobody` instead of the user `root`. When the `user` and `group` directives are used, it is wise to add the following as well:

```
persist-key
persist-tun
```

Otherwise, OpenVPN will not be able to restart itself correctly.

Another security measure is the use of the following on the server side (and `ta.key 1` on the client side):

```
tls-auth /etc/openvpn/cookbook/ta.key 0
```

This prevents the server from being overloaded by a so-called **Distributed Denial of Service** (**DDoS**) attack, as OpenVPN will just ignore those packets immediately if the HMAC is not correct.

The following directive sets up a `keepalive` timer on both the client and the server side:

```
keepalive 10 60
```

Every 10 seconds, a packet is sent from the server to the client side and vice versa to ensure that the VPN tunnel is still up and running. If no reply is received after 60 seconds on the client side, the VPN connection is automatically restarted. On the server side, the timeout period is multiplied by two; hence the server will restart the VPN connection if no reply is received after 120 seconds.

Finally, the following directives are very commonly used in a production setup, where the OpenVPN process continues to run in the background (daemonizes itself) after the operator logs out:

```
daemon
log-append /var/log/openvpn.log
```

All output of the OpenVPN process is appended to the log file, `/var/log/openvpn.log`. You can use the `tail -f` command to monitor the output of the OpenVPN process.

The client connects to the server. After the initial TLS handshake, using both the client and server certificates, the client is assigned the IP address `10.200.0.2`. The client configures its first available TUN interface using this information and updates its routing table so that traffic for the server-side Site B's LAN is tunneled over the VPN.

# There's more...

As the example files used in this recipe are reused later on, it is useful to explain a bit more about the options used.

## Linear addresses

After the connection is established, you can query the `tun0` interface like this:

```
[client]$ /sbin/ifconfig tun0 | grep inet
```

Then, look for the following:

```
inet addr:10.200.0.2  P-t-P:10.200.0.2
```

This is caused by the `topology subnet` directive, which is something new in OpenVPN 2.1. This directive tells OpenVPN to assign only a single IP address to each client. With OpenVPN 2.0, the minimum number of IP addresses per client is four (as we can see in the previous recipe).

## Using the TCP protocol

In the previous example, we chose the UDP protocol. The configuration files in this recipe can easily be converted to use the TCP protocol by changing the following line:

```
proto udp
```

It should be changed to the following:

```
proto tcp
```

This should be done in both the client and server configuration files. Save these files as `basic-tcp-server.conf` and `basic-tcp-client.conf` for future use:

```
$ cd /etc/openvpn/cookbook
$ sed 's/proto udp/proto tcp' basic-udp-server.conf \
    > basic-tcp-server.conf
$ sed 's/proto udp/proto tcp/' basic-udp-client.conf \
    > basic-tcp-client.conf
```

## Server certificates and ns-cert-type server

On the client side, the `remote-cert-tls server` directive is often used in combination with a server certificate that is built using the following:

```
$ build-key-server
```

This is done in order to prevent man-in-the-middle attacks. The idea is that a client will refuse to connect to a server that does not have a special server certificate. By doing this, it is no longer possible for a malicious client to pose as a server. This option also supports certificates with explicit key usage and extended key usage, based on the RFC 3280 TLS rules.

Older versions of OpenVPN used the `ns-cert-type server` directive. This option is still supported, but it will be deprecated in a future version of OpenVPN.

## Masquerading

In this recipe, the gateway on the server-side LAN is configured with an extra route for the VPN traffic. Sometimes, this is not possible, in which case, the Linux `iptables` command can be used to set up masquerading:

```
[root@server]# iptables -t nat -I POSTROUTING -o eth0 \
    -s 10.200.0.0/24 -j MASQUERADE
```

This instructs the Linux kernel to rewrite all traffic that is coming from the subnet `10.200.0.0/24` (that is, our OpenVPN subnet) and that is leaving the Ethernet interface `eth0`. Each of these packets has its source address rewritten so that it appears as if it's coming from the OpenVPN server itself and not from the OpenVPN client.
The `iptables` module keeps track of these rewritten packets so that when a return packet is received, the reverse is done and the packets are forwarded back to the OpenVPN client again. This is an easy method to enable routing to work, but there is a drawback when many clients are used, as it is no longer possible to distinguish traffic on Site B's LAN if it is coming from the OpenVPN server itself, from client1 via the VPN tunnel, or from clientN via the VPN tunnel.

# Adding IPv6 support

Support for IPv6 addresses is relatively new in OpenVPN. As IPv6 addresses are now being used more and more by companies and Internet Service Providers, this recipe provides a setup for using IPv6 for tunnel endpoints as well as using it inside the tunnel.

## Getting ready

This recipe is a continuation of the previous one. Install OpenVPN 2.3.9 or higher on two computers. Make sure the computers are connected over a network. Set up the client and server certificates using the previous recipe. For this recipe, the server computer was running CentOS 6 Linux and OpenVPN 2.3.9 and the client was running Fedora 20 Linux and OpenVPN 2.3.9. Keep the configuration file, `basic-udp-server.conf`, from the previous recipe at hand as well as the client configuration file, `basic-udp-client.conf`.

## How to do it...

1. Modify the server configuration file, `basic-udp-server.conf`, by adding a line:

   ```
   server-ipv6 2001:db8:100::0/112
   ```

   Then save it as `example2-4-server.conf`.

2. Start the server:

   ```
   [root@server]# openvpn --config example2-4-server.conf
   [...]
   do_ifconfig, tt->ipv6=1, tt->did_ifconfig_ipv6_setup=1
   /sbin/ip link set dev tun0 up mtu 1500
   /sbin/ip addr add dev tun0 10.200.0.1/24 broadcast
   10.200.0.255
   /sbin/ip -6 addr add 2001:db8:100::1/112 dev tun0
   [...]
   ```

3. Start the client using the configuration file from the previous recipe:

   ```
   [root@client]# openvpn --config basic-udp-client.conf
   [...]
   [openvpnserver] Peer Connection Initiated with
   [AF_INET]openvpnserver:1194
   TUN/TAP device tun0 opened
   do_ifconfig, tt->ipv6=1, tt->did_ifconfig_ipv6_setup=1
   /usr/sbin/ip link set dev tun0 up mtu 1500
   /usr/sbin/ip addr add dev tun0 10.200.0.2/24 broadcast
   10.200.0.255
   /usr/sbin/ip -6 addr add 2001:db8:100::1000/112 dev tun0
   Initialization Sequence Completed
   ```

The output showing that OpenVPN has configured an IPv6 address is shown in boldface.

4. Verify that we can reach the server using the `ping6` command:

```
[client]$   ping6 -c 4  2001:db8:100::
PING 2001:db8:100::1(2001:db8:100::1) 56 data bytes
64 bytes from 2001:db8:100::1: icmp_seq=1 ttl=64 time=9.01 ms
64 bytes from 2001:db8:100::1: icmp_seq=2 ttl=64 time=10.8 ms
64 bytes from 2001:db8:100::1: icmp_seq=3 ttl=64 time=9.42 ms
64 bytes from 2001:db8:100::1: icmp_seq=4 ttl=64 time=8.36 ms
--- 2001:db8:100::1 ping statistics ---
4 packets transmitted, 4 received, 0% packet loss, time
3004ms
rtt min/avg/max/mdev = 8.364/9.409/10.832/0.904 ms
```

## How it works...

IPv6 support in OpenVPN works almost exactly like IPv4. The addressing format is different and most options need an extra `-ipv6` suffix.

## There's more...

There are a couple of useful tricks to keep in mind when using client configuration files. Some of these tricks are explained here.

### IPv6 endpoints

If the server `openvpnserver.example.com` resolves to an IPv6 address and the client has a valid IPv6 address, then the connection can be automatically established using IPv6. This is achieved by changing the `proto udp` line in both client and server configurations to `proto udp6`. It is then also possible to specify an IPv6 address for the server, using the following command:

```
remote 2001:db8:120:e120:225:90ff:fec0:3ed1
```

Note that even with `proto udp6` in the server configuration file, IPv4 clients can still connect.

## IPv6-only setup

Even with OpenVPN 2.4, it is not yet possible to set up an IPv6-only VPN. You must always supply an (bogus) IPv4 address range for the VPN IP space. However, with OpenVPN 2.4, it is possible to set up an OpenVPN server that will accept requests only from IPv6-enabled clients. A new flag for the `bind` directive was added for this:

```
proto udp6
bind ipv6only
```

# Using client-config-dir files

In a setup where a single server can handle many clients, it is sometimes necessary to set per-client options that overrule the global options. The `client-config-dir` option is very useful for this. It allows the administrator to assign a specific IP address to a client; to push specific options, such as compression and DNS server, to a client; or to temporarily disable a client altogether.

## Getting ready

This recipe is a continuation of the previous one. Install OpenVPN 2.3.9 or higher on two computers. Make sure the computers are connected over a network. Set up the client and server certificates using the previous recipe. For this recipe, the server computer was running CentOS 6 Linux and OpenVPN 2.3.9 and the client was running Fedora 20 Linux and OpenVPN 2.3.9. Keep the server configuration file, `basic-udp-server.conf`, at hand along with the client configuration file, `basic-udp-client.conf`, from the *Server-side routing* recipe.

## How to do it...

1. Modify the server configuration file, `basic-udp-server.conf`, by adding a line:

   ```
   client-config-dir /etc/openvpn/cookbook/clients
   ```

   Then save it as `example2-5-server.conf`.

2. Next, create the directory for the `client-config` files and place a file in there with the name of the client certificate. This file needs to contain a single line with the IP address for the client listed twice:

```
[root@server]# mkdir -m 755 /etc/openvpn/cookbook/clients
[root@server]# cd /etc/openvpn/cookbook/clients
[root@server]# echo "ifconfig-push 10.200.0.7 10.200.0.7" \
   > client1
```

3. This name can be retrieved from the client certificate file using the following:

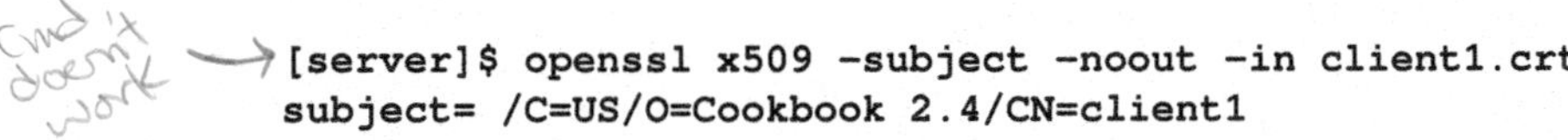

```
[server]$ openssl x509 -subject -noout -in client1.crt
subject= /C=US/O=Cookbook 2.4/CN=client1
```

4. Start the server:

```
[root@server]# openvpn --config example2-5-server.conf
```

5. Start the client using the configuration file from the previous recipe:

```
[root@client]# openvpn --config basic-udp-client.conf
[...]
[openvpnserver] Peer Connection Initiated with
[AF_INET]openvpnserver:1194
TUN/TAP device tun0 opened
do_ifconfig, tt->ipv6=0, tt->did_ifconfig_ipv6_setup=0
/usr/sbin/ip link set dev tun0 up mtu 1500
/usr/sbin/ip addr add dev tun0 10.200.0.7/24 broadcast
10.200.0.255
Initialization Sequence Completed
```

## How it works...

When a client connects to the server with its certificate and with the certificate's common name `client1`, the OpenVPN server checks whether there is a corresponding client configuration file (also known as a CCD file) in the `client-config-dir` directory. If it exists, it is read in as an extra set of options for that particular client. In this recipe, we use it to assign a specific IP address to a client (although there are more flexible ways to do that). The client is now always assigned the IP address `10.200.0.7`.

The client configuration file contains a single line, `ifconfig-push 10.200.0.7 10.200.0.7`, which instructs the OpenVPN server to push the client IP address `10.200.0.7` to this particular client. The IP address needs to be listed twice, which is mostly due to the legacy of `topology net30` mode.

In this mode, which is still the default in OpenVPN 2.3, a remote endpoint address is always needed and it needs to be within a /30 network range of the client's VPN IP address. In `topology subnet` mode, it suffices to list the client's VPN IP address twice, or to list the client's VPN IP address followed by a netmask.

# There's more...

There are a couple of useful tricks to keep in mind when using client configuration files. Some of these tricks are explained here.

## The default configuration file

If the following conditions are met, then the `DEFAULT` file is read and processed instead:

- A `client-config-dir` directive is specified
- There is no matching client file for the client's certificate in that directory
- A file called `DEFAULT` does exist in that directory

Please note that this name is case-sensitive.

## Troubleshooting

Troubleshooting configuration problems with CCD files is a recurring topic on the OpenVPN mailing lists. The most common configuration errors are as follows:

- Always specify the full path in the `client-config-dir` directive
- Make sure the directory is accessible and the CCD file, is readable to the user which is used to run OpenVPN (`nobody` or `openvpn` in most cases)
- Make sure that the right filename is used for the CCD file, without any extensions

## Options allowed in a client-config-dir file

The following configuration options are allowed in a CCD file:

- `push`: This option is used for pushing DNS servers, WINS servers, routes, and so on
- `push-reset`: This option is used to overrule global push options
- `iroute`: This option is used for routing client subnets to the server

- `ifconfig-push`: This option is used for assigning a specific IP address, as done in this recipe
- `disable`: This option is used for temporarily disabling a client altogether
- `config`: This option is used for including another configuration file

# Routing – subnets on both sides

This recipe will demonstrate how to set up server-side and client-side routing in client/server mode. With this setup, the OpenVPN client will be able to reach all the machines behind the OpenVPN server, and the server will be able to reach all the machines behind the client.

## Getting ready

This recipe uses the PKI files created in the first recipe of this chapter. Install OpenVPN 2.3.9 or higher on two computers. Make sure the computers are connected over a network. For this recipe, the server computer was running CentOS 6 Linux and OpenVPN 2.3.9 and the client was running Fedora 20 Linux and OpenVPN 2.3.9. Keep the server configuration file, `basic-udp-server.conf`, handy along with the client configuration file, `basic-udp-client.conf`, from the *Server-side routing* recipe.

We use the following network layout:

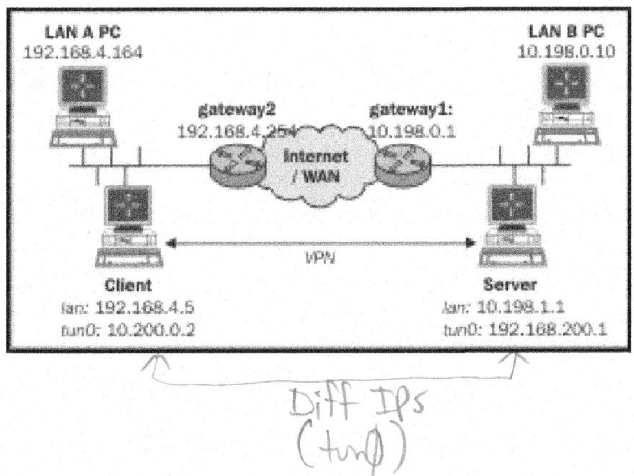

# How to do it...

1. Modify the server configuration file, `basic-udp-server.conf`, by adding these lines:

   ```
   client-config-dir /etc/openvpn/cookbook/clients
   route 192.168.4.0 255.255.255.0 10.200.0.1
   ```

   Then save it as `example2-6-server.conf`.

2. Next, create the directory for the client configuration files:

   ```
   [root@server]# mkdir -m 755 /etc/openvpn/cookbook/clients
   ```

3. Place a file in this directory with the name of the client certificate. This file will contain a single line:

   ```
   iroute 192.168.4.0 255.255.255.0
   ```

   The name of the client certificate can be retrieved from the client certificate file using the following command:

   ```
   $ openssl x509 -subject -noout -in client1.crt
   subject= /C=US/O=Cookbook 2.4/CN=client1
   ```

   Thus, for this recipe, the client configuration file needs to be named `client1`, without an extension.

4. Start the server:

   ```
   [root@server]# openvpn --config example2-6-server.conf
   ```

5. Start the client:

   ```
   [root@client]# openvpn --config basic-udp-client.conf
   ```

6. After the VPN is established, we need to set up routing on both sides. Enable the IP traffic forwarding feature on the server:

   ```
   [root@server]# sysctl -w net.ipv4.ip_forward=1
   ```

7. Add a route to LAN B's Gateway to point to the OpenVPN server itself:

   ```
   [siteB-gw]> ip route add 192.168.4.0/24 via 10.198.1.1
   [siteB-gw]> ip route add 10.200.0.0/24 via 10.198.1.1
   ```

Here, `10.198.1.1` is the LAN IP address of the OpenVPN server used in this recipe.

8. Now set up routing on the client side:

```
[client]$ sysctl -w net.ipv4.ip_forward=1
```

9. And similarly, add a route for the LAN A Gateway:

```
[siteA-gw]> ip route add 10.198.0.0/16 via 192.168.4.5
[siteA-gw]> ip route add 10.200.0.0/24 via 192.168.4.5
```

Here, `192.168.4.5` is the LAN IP address of the OpenVPN client used in this recipe.

10. Now, we verify that we can ping a machine on the remote server LAN:

```
[client]$ ping -c 2 10.198.0.10
PING 10.198.0.10 (10.198.0.10) 56(84) bytes of data.
64 bytes from 10.198.0.10: icmp_seq=1 ttl=63 time=31.1 ms
64 bytes from 10.198.0.10: icmp_seq=2 ttl=63 time=30.0 ms
```

We verify the same vice versa:

```
[server]$ ping -c 2 192.168.4.164
PING 192.168.4.164 (192.168.4.164) 56(84) bytes of data.
64 bytes from 192.168.4.164: icmp_seq=1 ttl=64 time=30.2 ms
64 bytes from 192.168.4.164: icmp_seq=2 ttl=64 time=29.7 ms
```

## How it works...

When a client connects to the server with its certificate and with the certificate's common name, `client1`, the OpenVPN server reads the client configuration file (also known as a CCD file) in the `client-config-dir` directory. The following directive in this file tells the OpenVPN server that the subnet `192.168.4.0/24` is reachable through the client `client1`:

```
iroute 192.168.4.0 255.255.255.0
```

This directive has nothing to do with a kernel routing table and is only used internally by the OpenVPN server process.

The following server directive is used by OpenVPN to configure the routing table of the operating system so that all of the traffic intended for the subnet `192.168.4.0/24` is forwarded to the interface with the IP address `10.200.0.1`, which is the VPN IP of the server:

```
route 192.168.4.0 255.255.255.0 10.200.0.1
```

With the appropriate routing set up on both ends, site-to-site routing is now possible.

## There's more...

When routing client-side traffic to and from multiple clients, there are several caveats to be aware of.

### Masquerading

We could have used masquerading on both ends as well, but with multiple clients it becomes very hard to keep track of the network traffic.

### Client-to-client subnet routing

If another VPN client needs to reach the subnet `192.168.4.0/24` behind client `client1`, the server configuration file needs to be extended with the following:

```
push "route 192.168.4.0 255.255.255.0"
```

This instructs all clients that subnet `192.168.4.0/24` is reachable through the VPN tunnel, except for client `client1`. The client `client1` itself is excluded due to the matching `iroute` entry.

### No route statements in a CCD file

Note that you cannot use the route directive inside a CCD file. This is a long-standing missing feature of OpenVPN. It is possible to achieve similar behavior using a `learn-address` script, as we will learn in `Chapter 5`, *Scripting and Plugins*.

## See also

- The *Complete site-to-site setup* recipe from `Chapter 1`, *Point-to-Point Networks*, where it is explained how to connect two remote LANs via a VPN tunnel using a point-to-point setup
- The *Using a learn-address script* recipe from `Chapter 5`, *Scripting and Plugins*, where it is explained how to use a `learn-address` script to dynamically set and remove server-side routes

# Redirecting the default gateway

A very common use of a VPN is to route all of the traffic over a secure tunnel. This allows one to safely access a network or even the Internet itself from within a hostile environment (for example, a poorly protected, but properly trojaned Internet cafeteria).

In this recipe, we will set up OpenVPN to do exactly this. This recipe is very similar to the *Server-side routing* recipe, but there are some pitfalls when redirecting all of the traffic over a VPN tunnel.

## Getting ready

The network layout used in this recipe is the same as in the *Server-side routing* recipe.

This recipe uses the PKI files created in the first recipe of this chapter. Install OpenVPN 2.3.9 or higher on two computers. Make sure the computers are connected over a network. For this recipe, the server computer was running CentOS 6 Linux and OpenVPN 2.3.9 and the client was running Fedora 20 Linux and OpenVPN 2.3.9. Keep the server configuration file, `basic-udp-server.conf`, at hand along with the client configuration file, `basic-udp-client.conf`, from the *Server-side routing* recipe.

## How to do it...

1. Create the server configuration file by adding a line to the `basic-udp-server.conf` file:

```
push "redirect-gateway def1"
```

Save it as `example2-7-server.conf`.

2. Start the server:

```
[root@server]# openvpn --config example2-7-server.conf
```

3. In another server terminal, enable IP-traffic forwarding:

```
[root@server]# sysctl -w net.ipv4.ip_forward=1
```

4. Start the client:

```
[root@client]# openvpn --config basic-udp-client.conf
```

You will observe something like this:

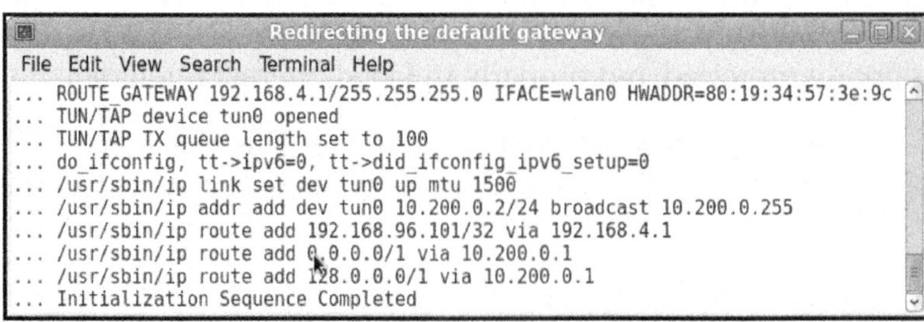

Redirecting the default gateway
File Edit View Search Terminal Help
... ROUTE_GATEWAY 192.168.4.1/255.255.255.0 IFACE=wlan0 HWADDR=80:19:34:57:3e:9c
... TUN/TAP device tun0 opened
... TUN/TAP TX queue length set to 100
... do_ifconfig, tt->ipv6=0, tt->did_ifconfig_ipv6_setup=0
... /usr/sbin/ip link set dev tun0 up mtu 1500
... /usr/sbin/ip addr add dev tun0 10.200.0.2/24 broadcast 10.200.0.255
... /usr/sbin/ip route add 192.168.96.101/32 via 192.168.4.1
... /usr/sbin/ip route add 0.0.0.0/1 via 10.200.0.1
... /usr/sbin/ip route add 128.0.0.0/1 via 10.200.0.1
... Initialization Sequence Completed


5. After the VPN is established, verify that all of the traffic is going over the tunnel:

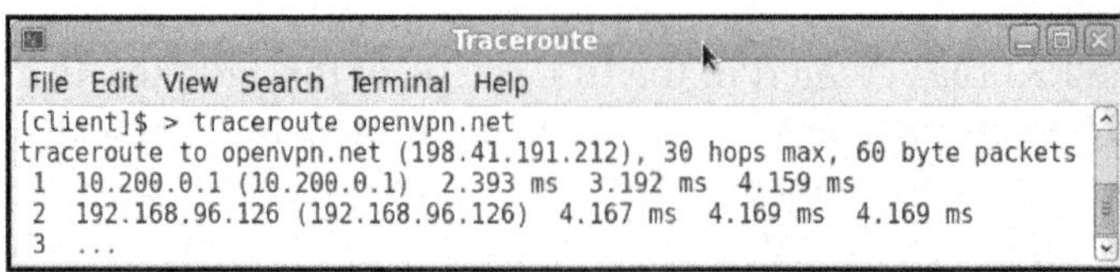

Traceroute
File Edit View Search Terminal Help
[client]$ > traceroute openvpn.net
traceroute to openvpn.net (198.41.191.212), 30 hops max, 60 byte packets
1 10.200.0.1 (10.200.0.1) 2.393 ms 3.192 ms 4.159 ms
2 192.168.96.126 (192.168.96.126) 4.167 ms 4.169 ms 4.169 ms
3 ...


The first address in the `traceroute` output is the address of the OpenVPN server, hence all of the traffic is routed over the tunnel.

## How it works...

When the client connects to the OpenVPN server, a special redirect statement is pushed out by the server to the OpenVPN client:

```
push "redirect-gateway def1"
```

The configuration option def1 tells the OpenVPN client to add three routes to the client operating system:

```
192.168.96.101 via 192.168.4.1 dev eth0
0.0.0.0/1 via 10.200.0.1 dev tun0
128.0.0.0/1 via 10.200.0.1 dev tun0
```

The first route is an explicit route from the client to the OpenVPN server via the LAN interface. This route is needed as otherwise all the traffic for the OpenVPN server itself would go through the tunnel.

The other two routes are a clever trick to overrule the default route so that all of the traffic is sent through the tunnel instead of to the default LAN gateway. The existing default route to the LAN gateway is not deleted due to the def1 parameter.

# There's more...

There are many parameters and flags related to the redirect-gateway directive. A subset of these parameters is listed here as well as some other special use cases.

## Redirect-gateway parameters

Originally, OpenVPN supported only the following directive:

```
push "redirect-gateway"
```

This is used to delete the original default route and replace it with a route to the OpenVPN server. This may seem like a clean solution, but in some cases, OpenVPN was unable to determine the existing default route. This often happened to clients connecting through mobile connections. This also used to create routing lockups, where all of the traffic was routed through the tunnel, including the packets sent by the OpenVPN client itself.

With the current version of OpenVPN, there are several flags for the redirect-gateway directive:

- local: This flag tells OpenVPN to not set a direct route from the client to the server. It is useful only if the client and server are in the same LAN, such as when securing wireless networks.
- block-local: This flag instructs OpenVPN to block all of the network access to the LAN after the VPN tunnel is established. This is achieved by routing all of the LAN traffic into the tunnel itself, except for the traffic to the OpenVPN server itself.

- `bypass-dhcp`: This flag adds a direct route to the local DHCP server. If the local DHCP server is on a separate subnet, this will ensure that the DHCP addresses assigned to the non-VPN interfaces will continue to be refreshed. This option is picked up automatically by a Windows client. On other operating systems, a plugin or script is required.
- `bypass-dns`: This flag adds a direct route to the local DNS server. In large-scale networks, the DNS server is often not found on the local subnet that the client is connected to. If the route to this DNS server is altered to go through the VPN tunnel after the client has connected, this will cause, at the very least, a serious performance penalty. More likely, the entire DNS server will become unreachable. It is picked up by a Windows client automatically and requires a plugin or script on other operating systems.
- `!ipv4`: This flag was added in OpenVPN 2.4 and it instructs OpenVPN to not redirect any IPv4 traffic over the VPN tunnel. It is useful only in combination with the flag `ipv6`. We will go into detail more in the next recipe.
- `ipv6`: This flag was added in OpenVPN 2.4 and it instructs OpenVPN to also redirect all IPv6 traffic over the VPN tunnel. We will go into more detail in the next recipe.

## The redirect-private option

Apart from the `redirect-gateway` directive, OpenVPN has a second, comparatively less well-known, option called `redirect-private`. This option takes the same parameters as the `redirect-gateway` directive, but it instructs OpenVPN to make no changes to the default routes at all. It is used most often in combination with the `bypass-dhcp`, `bypass-dns`, `ipv6`, and `block-local` flags.

## Split tunneling

In some cases, the `redirect-gateway` parameter is a bit too restrictive. You might want to add a few routes to local networks and route all other traffic over the VPN tunnel. The OpenVPN `route` directive has a few special parameters for this:

- `net_gateway`: This is a special gateway representing the LAN gateway address that OpenVPN determined when starting. For example, to add a direct route to the LAN `192.168.4.0/24`, you would add the following to the client configuration file:

```
route 192.168.4.0 255.255.255.0 net_gateway
```

- `vpn_gateway`: This is a special gateway representing the VPN gateway address. If you want to add a route that explicitly sends traffic for a particular subnet over the VPN tunnel, overruling any local routes, you would add the following option:

```
route 10.198.0.0 255.255.0.0 vpn_gateway
```

## See also

- The *Server-side routing* recipe, where the basic steps of setting up server-side routing is explained

# Redirecting the IPv6 default gateway

With the advent of IPv6 networks, it is becoming increasingly important to be able to set up a VPN that will secure both IPv4 and IPv6 traffic. If only IPv4 traffic is secured over a VPN tunnel, then it is still possible for traffic to leak out over IPv6. In this recipe, we will set up OpenVPN to secure all IPv6 traffic as well. Support for this was added in OpenVPN 2.4.

## Getting ready

The network layout used in this recipe is the same as in the *Server-side routing* recipe.

This recipe uses the PKI files created in the first recipe of this chapter. Install OpenVPN 2.4 or higher on two computers. Make sure the computers are connected over a network. For this recipe, the server computer was running CentOS 6 Linux and OpenVPN 2.4 and the client was running Fedora 20 Linux and OpenVPN 2.4. For the server, keep the IPv6 configuration file, `example2-4-server.conf`, from the *Adding IPv6 support* recipe at hand. For the client, keep the configuration file, `basic-udp-client.conf`, from the *Server-side routing* recipe at hand.

# How to do it...

1. Create the server configuration file by adding a line to the `example2-4-server.conf` file:

   ```
   push "redirect-gateway ipv6 !ipv4"
   ```

   Save it as `example2-8-server.conf`.

2. Start the server:

   ```
   [root@server]# openvpn --config example2-8-server.conf
   ```

3. In another server terminal, enable IP-traffic forwarding:

   ```
   [root@server]# sysctl -w net.ipv6.conf.all.forwarding=1
   ```

4. Start the client:

   ```
   [root@client]# openvpn --config basic-udp-client.conf
   [...]
   add_route_ipv6(::/3 -> 2001:db8:100::1 metric -1) dev tun1
   add_route_ipv6(2000::/4 -> 2001:db8:100::1 metric -1) dev
   tun1
   add_route_ipv6(3000::/4 -> 2001:db8:100::1 metric -1) dev
   tun1
   add_route_ipv6(fc00::/7 -> 2001:db8:100::1 metric -1) dev
   tun1
   Initialization Sequence Completed
   ```

# How it works...

When the client connects to the OpenVPN server, a special redirect statement is pushed out by the server to the OpenVPN client:

```
push "redirect-gateway ipv6 !ipv4"
```

The configuration flag `ipv6` tells the OpenVPN client to redirect all of the IPv6 traffic over the tunnel, by adding three routes to the client operating system:

```
2000::/4
3000::/4
fc00::/4
```

This effectively redirects all of the IPv6 traffic over the VPN tunnel.

The second flag `!ipv4`, tells the OpenVPN client to not redirect IPv4 traffic. This was added to this example to demonstrate that it is also possible to redirect IPv6 traffic only.

## There's more...

It is possible to achieve the same behavior by adding the following lines to the server configuration file:

```
push "route-ipv6 2000::/4"
push "route-ipv6 3000::/4"
push "route-ipv6 fc00::/4"
```

This is supported in OpenVPN 2.3 as well. However, there is a very important caveat to this: if the IPv6 address of the server is in the same range as any of the preceding addresses, then this setup will fail, as all of the traffic for the preceding IPv6 networks will be redirected over the tunnel. To overcome this problem, the flag `ipv6` was introduced in OpenVPN 2.4.

# Using an ifconfig-pool block

In this recipe, we will use an `ifconfig-pool` block to separate regular VPN clients from administrative VPN clients. This makes it easier to set up different firewall rules for administrative users.

## Getting ready

This recipe uses the PKI files created in the first recipe of this chapter. Install OpenVPN 2.3.9 or higher on two computers. Make sure the computers are connected over a network. For this recipe, the server computer was running CentOS 6 Linux and OpenVPN 2.3.9 and the regular VPN client was running Windows 7 64 bit and OpenVPN 2.3.11 and was assigned to the `192.168.200.0` network. The VPN client Admin was running Fedora 20 Linux and OpenVPN 2.3.9 and was on the `192.168.202.0` network. Keep the client configuration file, `basic-udp-client.conf`, from the *Server-side routing* recipe at hand.

We use the following network layout:

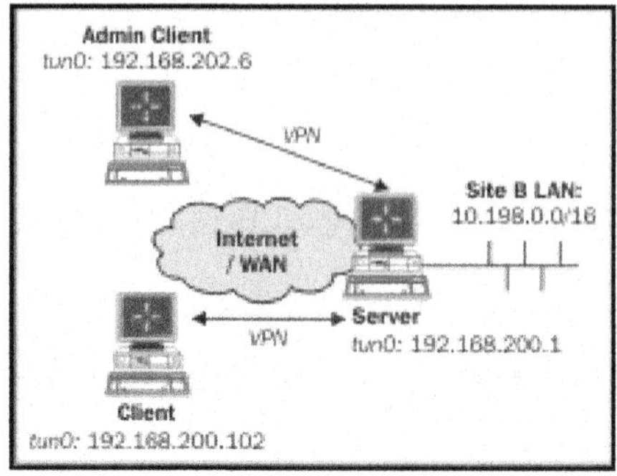


# How to do it...

1. Create the server configuration file:

```
proto udp
port 1194
dev tun

mode server
ifconfig 192.168.200.1 255.255.255.0
ifconfig-pool 192.168.200.100 192.168.200.120
route 192.168.200.0 255.255.248.0 192.168.200.1
push "route 192.168.200.1"
push "route 192.168.200.0 255.255.248.0"

ca       /etc/openvpn/cookbook/ca.crt
cert     /etc/openvpn/cookbook/server.crt
key      /etc/openvpn/cookbook/server.key
dh       /etc/openvpn/cookbook/dh2048.pem
tls-auth /etc/openvpn/cookbook/ta.key 0

persist-key
persist-tun
keepalive 10 60

topology subnet
push "topology subnet"

user  nobody
group nobody  # use "group nogroup" on some distros
```

```
daemon
log-append /var/log/openvpn.log

client-config-dir /etc/openvpn/cookbook/clients
```

Then save it as `example2-9-server.conf`.

2. Start the server:

```
[root@server]# openvpn --config example2-9-server.conf
```

3. The administrative VPN client will be assigned a special IP address using a client-configuration file:

```
[root@server]# mkdir -m 755 /etc/openvpn/cookbook/clients
[root@server]# cd /etc/openvpn/cookbook/clients
[root@server]# echo "ifconfig-push 192.168.202.6
192.168.202.6" \
  > client1
```

Note that the client VPN address is listed twice. This is not a typo; for more details on this, refer to the previous recipe.

4. Note that the `clients` directory needs to be world-readable, as the OpenVPN server process will run as user `nobody` after starting up.
5. Next, start the Linux client using the configuration file from the earlier recipe:

```
[root@AdminClient]# openvpn --config basic-udp-client.conf
[...]
[openvpnserver] Peer Connection Initiated with
openvpnserver:1194
TUN/TAP device tun0 opened
do_ifconfig, tt->ipv6=0, tt->did_ifconfig_ipv6_setup=0
/usr/sbin/ip link set dev tun0 up mtu 1500
/usr/sbin/ip addr add dev tun0 192.168.202.6/24 broadcast
192.168.200.255
Initialization Sequence Completed
```

The IP address that is assigned to the administrative client is highlighted for clarity.

6. Create a configuration file for the Windows client:

```
client
proto udp
remote openvpnserver.example.com
port 1194
```

```
dev tun
nobind

ca       "c:/program files/openvpn/config/ca.crt"
cert     "c:/program files/openvpn/config/client2.crt"
key      "c:/program files/openvpn/config/client2.key"
tls-auth "c:/program files/openvpn/config/ta.key" 1

remote-cert-tls server
```

7. Then save it as `basic-udp-client.ovpn`.

Note the use of the forward slash (/), which is easier to use than the backslash (\), as the backslash needs to be repeated twice each time.

8. Transfer the `ca.crt`, `client2.crt`, and `client2.key` files along with the `tls-auth` secret key file, `ta.key`, to the Windows machine using a secure channel, such as `winscp` or the PuTTY `pscp` command-line tool.
9. Start the Windows client using the OpenVPN GUI:

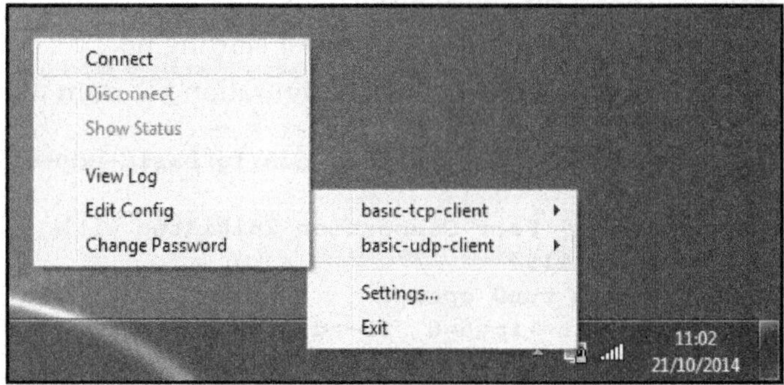

Remember that this client's private key file is protected using a password or passphrase. After both the clients are connected, we verify that they can ping each other and the server (assuming that no firewalls are blocking access).

10. On the Admin Client:

```
[AdminClient]$ ping 192.168.200.1
[AdminClient]$ ping 192.168.200.102
```

11. And on the regular client:

```
[WinClient]C:> ping 192.168.200.1
[WinClient]C:> ping 192.168.202.6
```

# How it works...

A server configuration file normally uses the following directive to configure a range of IP addresses for the clients:

```
server 192.168.200.0 255.255.255.0
```

This directive is internally expanded to the following:

```
mode server
tls-server

ifconfig 192.168.200.1 192.168.200.2
ifconfig-pool 192.168.200.4 192.168.200.251
route 192.168.200.0 255.255.255.0
push "route 192.168.200.1"
if (topology==subnet) push "topology subnet"
```

So, by not using the `server` directive, but by specifying our own `ifconfig-pool` range, we can override this behavior. We then use a CCD file to assign an IP address to the administrative client, which falls outside of the `ifconfig-pool` range. By using the appropriate `route` and `push "route"` statements, we ensure that all clients are able to ping each other.

Note that we also need to explicitly push the topology in this case, as this is no longer done automatically by the `server` directive.

# There's more..

There are many details to consider when setting up the default configuration files.

## Configuration files on Windows

The OpenVPN GUI application on Windows always starts in the directory:

```
C:\Program Files\OpenVPN\config
```

Or, `C:\Program Files(x86)\...` when using the 32-bit version of OpenVPN on 64-bit versions of Windows. Thus, the directory paths in the `basic-udp-client.ovpn` configuration file can be omitted:

```
ca        ca.crt
cert      client2.crt
key       client2.key
tls-auth ta.key 1
```

## Client-to-client access

With this setup, the VPN clients can connect to each other even though we did not make use of the following directive in the server-side configuration:

```
client-to-client
```

This is possible due to the `route` and `push "route"` statements in the server configuration file. The advantage of not using `client-to-client` is that it is still possible to filter out unwanted traffic using `iptables` or another firewalling solution.

If there is no need for the administrative clients to connect to the regular VPN clients (or vice versa), then the netmask can be adjusted to:

```
route 192.168.200.0 255.255.255.0
push "route 192.168.200.0 255.255.255.0"
```

Now, the networks are completely separated.

## Using the TCP protocol

In this example, we chose the UDP protocol. The client configuration file in this recipe can easily be converted to use TCP protocol by changing the line:

```
proto udp
```

Change it to the following:

```
proto tcp
```

Save this file as `basic-tcp-client.ovpn` for future use.

# Using the status file

OpenVPN offers several options to monitor the clients connected to a server. The most commonly used method is using a status file. This recipe will show how to use and read the OpenVPN's status file.

# Getting ready

The network layout used in this recipe is the same as in the *Server-side routing* recipe. This recipe uses the PKI files created in the first recipe of this chapter. Install OpenVPN 2.3.9 or higher on two computers. Make sure the computers are connected over a network. For this recipe, the server computer was running CentOS 6 Linux and OpenVPN 2.3.9. The first client was running Fedora 20 Linux and OpenVPN 2.3.9. The second client was running Windows 7 64 bit and OpenVPN 2.3.11. For the Linux server, keep the server configuration file `basic-udp-server.conf` from the *Server-side routing* recipe at hand. For the Linux client, keep the client configuration file `basic-udp-client.conf` from the same recipe at hand. For the Windows client, keep the corresponding client configuration file, `basic-udp-client.ovpn`, from the previous recipe at hand.

# How to do it...

1. Create the server configuration file by adding a line to the `basic-udp-server.conf` file:

   ```
   status /var/log/openvpn.status
   ```

Save it as `example2-10-server.conf`.

2. Start the server:

```
[root@server]# openvpn --config example2-10-server.conf
```

3. First, start the Linux client:

```
[root@client1]# openvpn --config basic-udp-client.conf
```

4. After the VPN is established, list the contents of the `openvpn.status` file:

```
[root@server]# cat /var/log/openvpn.status
```

A sample output is shown in the following screenshot:

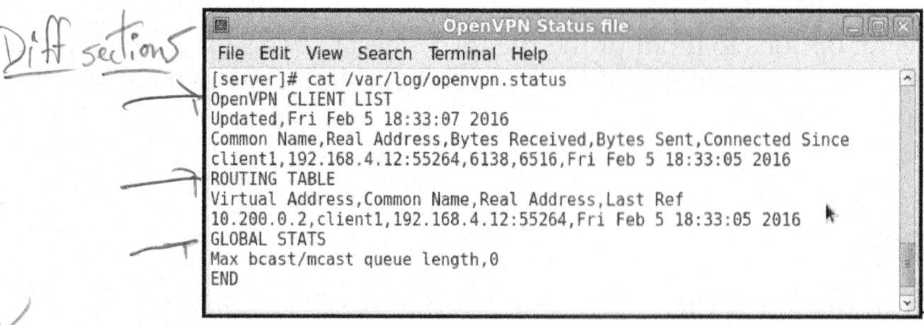
OpenVPN Status file
File Edit View Search Terminal Help
[server]# cat /var/log/openvpn.status
OpenVPN CLIENT LIST
Updated,Fri Feb 5 18:33:07 2016
Common Name,Real Address,Bytes Received,Bytes Sent,Connected Since
client1,192.168.4.12:55264,6138,6516,Fri Feb 5 18:33:05 2016
ROUTING TABLE
Virtual Address,Common Name,Real Address,Last Ref
10.200.0.2,client1,192.168.4.12:55264,Fri Feb 5 18:33:05 2016
GLOBAL STATS
Max bcast/mcast queue length,0
END

5. Transfer the `ca.crt`, `client2.crt`, and `client2.key` files along with the `tls-auth` secret key file, `ta.key`, to the Windows machine using a secure channel, such as `winscp` or PuTTY's `pscp` command-line tool.
6. Start the Windows client on the command line:

```
[WinClient2]C:> cd \program files\openvpn\config
[WinClient2]C:> ..\bin\openvpn --config basic-udp-
client.ovpn
```

Remember that this client's private key file is protected using a password or passphrase.

7. List the contents of the status file again on the server:

```
[root@server]# cat /var/log/openvpn.status
```

A sample output is shown in the following screenshot:

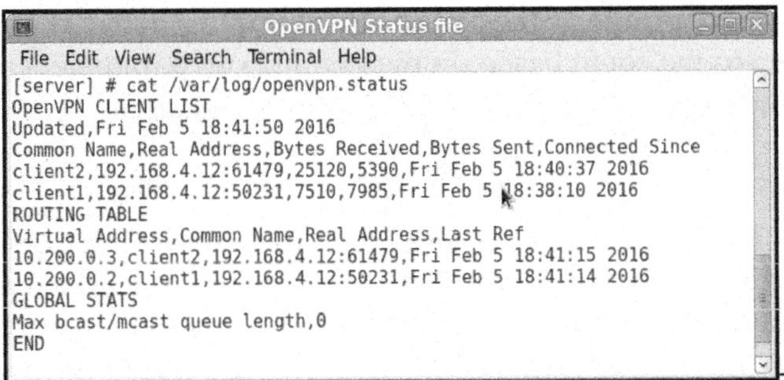
OpenVPN Status file
File Edit View Search Terminal Help
[server] # cat /var/log/openvpn.status
OpenVPN CLIENT LIST
Updated,Fri Feb 5 18:41:50 2016
Common Name,Real Address,Bytes Received,Bytes Sent,Connected Since
client2,192.168.4.12:61479,25120,5390,Fri Feb 5 18:40:37 2016
client1,192.168.4.12:50231,7510,7985,Fri Feb 5 18:38:10 2016
ROUTING TABLE
Virtual Address,Common Name,Real Address,Last Ref
10.200.0.3,client2,192.168.4.12:61479,Fri Feb 5 18:41:15 2016
10.200.0.2,client1,192.168.4.12:50231,Fri Feb 5 18:41:14 2016
GLOBAL STATS
Max bcast/mcast queue length,0
END

# How it works...

Each time a client connects to the OpenVPN server, the status file is updated with the connection information. The **OpenVPN CLIENTLIST** and **ROUTING TABLE** tables are the most interesting ones, as they provide the following information:

- Which clients are connected
- From which IP address the clients are connecting
- The number of bytes each client has received and transferred
- The time at which the client connected

In addition, the routing table also shows which networks are routed to each client.

# There's more...

There are three things to keep in mind when using status files:

## Status parameters

The `status` directive takes two parameters:

- The filename of the status file.
- Optionally, the refresh frequency for updating the status file. The default value of 60 seconds should suffice for most situations.

# Disconnecting clients

Note that when a client disconnects the status file, it is not updated immediately. OpenVPN first tries to reconnect to the client based on the `keepalive` parameters in the server configuration file. The server configuration file in this recipe uses:

```
keepalive 10 60
```

This tells the server that it will ping the client every 10 seconds. If it does not get a response after 60 seconds * 2, the connection is restarted. The OpenVPN server will double the value of the second argument. The server will also tell the client to ping every 10 seconds and to restart the connection after 60 seconds if it does not get any response.

# Explicit-exit-notify

One of the lesser-known options of OpenVPN is the following directive:

```
explicit-exit-notify [N]
```

This can be set on the client side so that when the client disconnects, it will send an explicit **OCC_EXIT** message to the server (if at all possible). This will speed up the removal of disconnected clients. The optional parameter N indicates the number of times the message will be sent. By default, only a single **OCC_EXIT** message is sent, which can cause problems as the UDP protocol does not guarantee the delivery of packets.

# The management interface

This recipe shows how an OpenVPN client is managed using the management interface from the server side.

# Getting ready

The network layout used in this recipe is the same as in the *Server-side routing* recipe. This recipe uses the PKI files created in the first recipe of this chapter. For this recipe, the server computer was running CentOS 6 Linux and OpenVPN 2.3.9. The client was running Windows 7 64 bit and OpenVPN 2.3.10. For the server, keep the server configuration file, `basic-udp-server.conf`, from the *Server-side routing* recipe at hand. For the Windows client, keep the corresponding client configuration file, `basic-udp-client.ovpn`, from the previous recipe at hand.

# How to do it...

1. Start the server using the default server configuration file:

```
[root@server]# openvpn --config basic-udp-server.conf
```

2. Create a configuration file for the Windows client by adding a line to the `basic-udp-client.ovpn` file:

```
management tunnel 23000 stdin
```

   Save it as `example2-11.ovpn`.

3. Transfer the `ca.crt`, `client2.crt`, and `client2.key` files along with the `tls-auth` secret key file, `ta.key`, to the Windows machine using a secure channel, such as `winscp` or the PuTTY `pscp` command-line tool.
4. The OpenVPN GUI does not support this particular configuration of the management interface. Therefore, we start the Windows client on the command line:

```
[WinClient]C:> cd \program files\openvpn\config
[WinClient]C:> ..\bin\openvpn --config example2-11.ovpn
```

   The OpenVPN client will now ask for a password for the management interface. Pick a good password. After that, it will ask for the private key passphrase.

5. After the VPN is established, we can connect from the server to the management interface of the OpenVPN client using the telnet program on the server:

```
[server]$ telnet 10.200.0.3 23000
Trying 10.200.0.3...
Connected to 10.200.0.3.
Escape character is '^]'.
ENTER PASSWORD:
SUCCESS: password is correct
>INFO:OpenVPN Management Interface Version 1 -- type 'help'
for more info
status
OpenVPN STATISTICS
Updated,Fri Feb 5 18:22:31 2016
TUN/TAP read bytes,21849
TUN/TAP write bytes,451
TCP/UDP read bytes,6571
TCP/UDP write bytes,30172
```

```
Auth read bytes,707
TAP-WIN32 driver status,"(null)"
END
signal SIGTERM
```

6. Use *Ctrl + ]* or quit to exit the `telnet` program.

# How it works...

When the OpenVPN client connects to the server, a special management interface is set up using the directive:

```
management tunnel 23000 stdin
```

It has the following parameters:

- The `tunnel` parameter to bind the management interface to the VPN tunnel itself. This is useful for testing purposes and some advanced client setups. On the server side, it is best to always specify `127.0.0.1` for the management IP.
- The port `23000` on which the management interface will be listening.
- The last parameter is the password file or the special keyword `stdin` to indicate that the management interface password will be specified when OpenVPN starts up. Note that this password is completely unrelated to the private key passphrases or any other user management passwords that OpenVPN uses.

After the management interface comes up, the server operator can connect to it using telnet and can query the client. The client can type the following:

```
signal SIGTERM
```

This effectively shuts itself down as if the user has stopped it! This shows how important it is to protect the management interface and its password.

# There's more...

The management interface can also be run on the OpenVPN server itself. In that case, it is possible to list the connected clients, disconnect them, or perform a variety of other OpenVPN administrative tasks.

It is expected that the management interface will become more important in future versions of OpenVPN, both on the client and the server side, as the preferred method for programmatically interacting with the OpenVPN software.

## See Also

- The *Management interface* recipe in `Chapter 3`, *Client-server Ethernet-style Networks*, explains the use of the server-side management interface in more detail

# Proxy ARP

In this recipe, we will use the `proxy-arp` feature of the Linux kernel to make the VPN clients appear as part of the server-side LAN. This eliminates the need to use bridging, which is desirable in most cases.

## Getting ready

This recipe uses the PKI files created in the first recipe of this chapter. For this recipe, the server computer was running CentOS 6 Linux and OpenVPN 2.3.9. The client was running Windows 7 64 bit and OpenVPN 2.3.10. For the server, keep the server configuration file, `basic-udp-server.conf`, from the *Server-side routing* recipe at hand. For the Windows client, keep the corresponding client configuration file, `basic-udp-client.ovpn`, from the *Using an ifconfig-pool block* recipe at hand.

We use the following network layout:

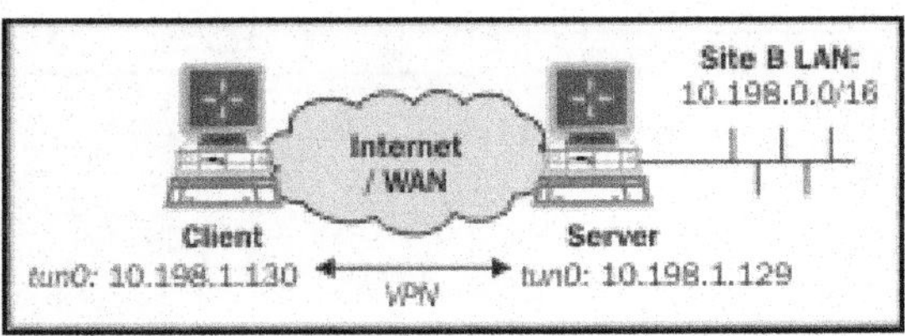

# How to do it...

1. Create the server config file by adding the following lines to the `basic-udp-server.conf` file:

   ```
   script-security 2
   client-connect    /etc/openvpn/cookbook/proxyarp-connect.sh
   client-disconnect /etc/openvpn/cookbook/proxyarp-disconnect.sh
   ```

   Save it as `example2-12-server.conf`.

2. Create the `proxyarp-connect.sh` script:

   ```
   #!/bin/bash
   /sbin/arp -i eth0  -Ds $ifconfig_pool_remote_ip eth0 pub
   ```

   Then create the `proxyarp-disconnect.sh` script:

   ```
   #!/bin/bash
   /sbin/arp -i eth0  -d $ifconfig_pool_remote_ip
   ```

3. Make sure that both the scripts are executable:

   ```
   [root@server]# cd /etc/openvpn/cookbook
   [root@server]# chmod 755 proxyarp-connect.sh
   [root@server]# chmod 755 proxyarp-disconnect.sh
   ```

4. Start the server:

   ```
   [root@server]# openvpn --config example2-12-server.conf
   ```

5. Then, start the Windows client using the OpenVPN GUI:

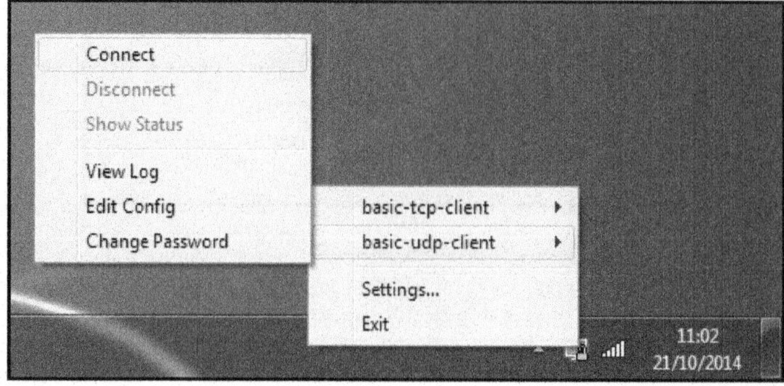

After a client has successfully connected, the `arp` table on the OpenVPN server will have a new entry:

```
10.198.1.130 * * MP eth0
```

From a machine on the server-side LAN, we can now ping the VPN client:

```
[siteBclient]C:> ping 10.198.1.130
```

Note that no special routing is required on Site B's LAN. The VPN client truly appears as being on the LAN itself.

## How it works...

The `proxy-arp` feature is supported by most UNIX and Linux kernels. It is used most often for connecting dial-in clients to a LAN, and nowadays, also by ADSL and cable Internet providers. When the OpenVPN client connects, an IP address is borrowed from Site B's LAN range. This IP address is assigned to the OpenVPN client. At the same time, a special ARP entry is made on the OpenVPN server to tell the rest of the network that the OpenVPN server acts as a proxy for `10.198.1.130`. This means that when another machine on Site B's LAN wants to know where to find the host with `10.198.1.130`, then the OpenVPN server will respond (with its own MAC address).

## There's more...

A `proxy-arp` setup has its own set of applications as well as challenges. Some of them are listed here:

### TAP-style networks

The `proxy-arp` feature can also be used in a TAP-style network. In combination with an external DHCP server, it provides almost the same functionality as that of an Ethernet bridging solution without the drawbacks of Ethernet bridging itself.

### User nobody

Note that in this example we did not use:

```
user nobody
group nobody
```

We did this because it would have prevented the `proxyarp-*` scripts from working. In order to execute the `/sbin/arp` command, root privileges are required. Therefore, it is not possible to switch to user `nobody` after the OpenVPN server has started. Alternatively, one can configure `sudo` access to the `/sbin/arp` command to circumvent this.

## Broadcast traffic might not always work

Sending broadcast traffic over a network where `proxy-arp` is used is tricky. For most purposes (for example, Windows Network Neighborhood browsing), `proxy-arp` will work. For some applications that require all the clients to be a member of a full broadcast domain, using `proxy-arp` might not suffice. In that case, Ethernet bridging is a better solution.

# See also

- The *Checking broadcast and non-IP traffic* recipe from `Chapter 3`, *Client-server Ethernet-style Networks*

# 3

# Client-server Ethernet-style Networks

In this chapter, we will cover the following topics:

- Simple configuration – non-bridged
- Enabling client-to-client traffic
- Bridging – Linux
- Bridging – Windows
- Checking broadcast and non-IP traffic
- An external DHCP
- Using the status file
- The management interface
- Integrating IPv6 into TAP-style networks

## Introduction

The recipes in this chapter will cover the deployment model of a single server with multiple remote clients capable of forwarding Ethernet traffic.

We will look at several common configurations, including bridging, the use of an external DHCP server, and also the use of the `OpenVPN` status file. Please note that bridging should only be used as a last resort. Most of the functionality provided by bridging can be achieved through other methods. Moreover, there are many disadvantages to using bridging, especially in terms of performance and security.

# Simple configuration – non-bridged

This recipe will demonstrate how to set up a TAP-based connection in client or server mode using certificates. It also uses masquerading to allow the OpenVPN clients to reach all the machines behind the OpenVPN server. The advantage of masquerading is that with it, no special routes are needed on the server LAN. Masquerading for OpenVPN servers is available only on the Linux and UNIX variants. This recipe is similar to the *Server-side routing* recipe from the previous chapter.

## Getting ready

Set up the client and server certificates using the first recipe from `Chapter 2`, *Client-server IP-only Networks*. For this recipe, both the server computer and the client computer were running CentOS 6 Linux and OpenVPN 2.3.10.

We use the following network layout:

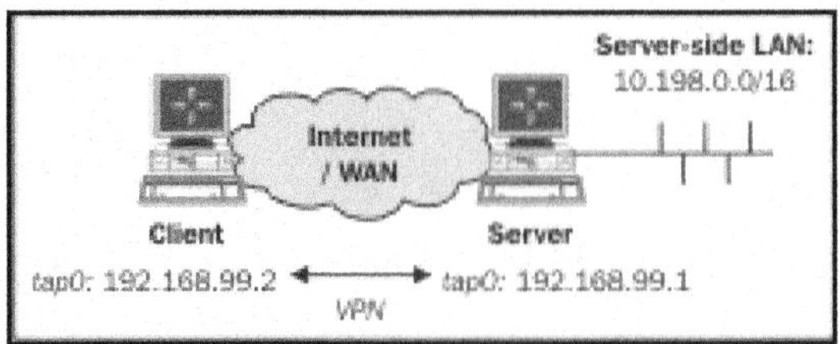


## How to do it...

1. Create the server configuration file:

```
tls-server
proto udp
port 1194
dev tap

server 192.168.99.0 255.255.255.0

tls-auth /etc/openvpn/cookbook/ta.key 0
ca       /etc/openvpn/cookbook/ca.crt
cert     /etc/openvpn/cookbook/server.crt
key      /etc/openvpn/cookbook/server.key
dh       /etc/openvpn/cookbook/dh2048.pem
```

```
persist-key
persist-tun
keepalive 10 60

push "route 10.198.0.0 255.255.0.0"

user  nobody
group nobody   # use "group nogroup" on some distros

daemon
log-append /var/log/openvpn.log
```

Save it as `example-3-1-server.conf`. Note that on some Linux distributions, the group `nogroup` is used instead of `nobody`.

2. Start the server:

```
[root@server]# openvpn --config example3-1-server.conf
```

3. Set up IP forwarding and an `iptables` masquerading rule:

```
[root@server]# sysctl -w net.ipv4.ip_forward=1
[root@server]# iptables -t nat -I POSTROUTING -i tap+ -o eth0 \
   -s 192.168.99.0/24 -j MASQUERADE
```

4. Next, create the client configuration file:

```
client
proto udp
remote openvpnserver.example.com
port 1194
dev tap
nobind

remote-cert-tls server
tls-auth /etc/openvpn/cookbook/ta.key 1
ca   /etc/openvpn/cookbook/ca.crt
cert /etc/openvpn/cookbook/client1.crt
key  /etc/openvpn/cookbook/client1.key
```

Save it as `example-3-1-client.conf`.

5. Start the client:

```
[root@client]# openvpn --config example3-1-client.conf
```

The output generated is shown as follows:

```
Example 3-1
File Edit View Search Terminal Help
[root@client]# openvpn --config example3-1-client.conf
Tue Mar  1 12:23:28 2016 OpenVPN 2.3.10 x86_64-redhat-linux-gnu [SSL (OpenSSL)] [LZO] [EPOLL] [PKCS11]
 [MH] [IPv6] built on Jan  4 2016
Tue Mar  1 12:23:28 2016 library versions: OpenSSL 1.0.1e-fips 11 Feb 2013, LZO 2.03
Tue Mar  1 12:23:28 2016 Control Channel Authentication: using '/etc/openvpn/cookbook/ta.key' as a Ope
nVPN static key file
Tue Mar  1 12:23:28 2016 UDPv4 link local: [undef]
Tue Mar  1 12:23:28 2016 UDPv4 link remote: [AF_INET]194.171.96.101:1194
Tue Mar  1 12:23:28 2016 [openvpnserver] Peer Connection Initiated with [AF_INET]194.171.96.101:1194
Tue Mar  1 12:23:30 2016 TUN/TAP device tap0 opened
Tue Mar  1 12:23:30 2016 do_ifconfig, tt->ipv6=0, tt->did_ifconfig_ipv6_setup=0
Tue Mar  1 12:23:30 2016 /sbin/ip link set dev tap0 up mtu 1500
Tue Mar  1 12:23:30 2016 /sbin/ip addr add dev tap0 192.168.99.2/24 broadcast 192.168.99.255
Tue Mar  1 12:23:30 2016 Initialization Sequence Completed

[root@client]#
```

6. After the connection is established, we can verify that it is working. First, we ping the server:

```
[client]$ ping -c 2 192.168.99.1
PING 192.168.99.1 (192.168.99.1) 56(84) bytes of data.
64 bytes from 192.168.99.1: icmp_seq=1 ttl=64 time=25.3 ms
64 bytes from 192.168.99.1: icmp_seq=2 ttl=64 time=25.2 ms
```

Second, we ping a host on the server-side LAN:

```
[client]$ ping -c 2 10.198.0.1
PING 10.198.0.1 (10.198.0.1) 56(84) bytes of data.
64 bytes from 10.198.0.1: icmp_seq=1 ttl=63 time=29.2 ms
64 bytes from 10.198.0.1: icmp_seq=2 ttl=63 time=25.3 ms
```

# How it works...

When the server starts, it configures the first available TAP interface with the IP address `192.168.99.1`. After that, the server listens on the UDP port 1194 for incoming connections, which serves as an OpenVPN default.

The client connects to the server on this port. After the initial TLS handshake using both the client and server certificates, the client is assigned the IP address `192.168.99.2`. The client configures its first available TAP interface using this information; after this, the VPN is established.

Apart from the OpenVPN configuration, this recipe also uses an `iptables` command to enable the client to reach Site B's LAN without having to set up additional routes on Site B's LAN gateway. The following command instructs the Linux kernel to rewrite all of the traffic coming from the subnet `192.168.99.0/24` (which is our OpenVPN subnet) and that is leaving the Ethernet interface `eth0`:

```
[root@server]# iptables -t nat -I POSTROUTING -i tap+ -o eth0 \
-s 192.168.99.0/24 -j MASQUERADE
```

Each of these packets has its source address rewritten so that it appears as if it is coming from the OpenVPN server itself instead of coming from the OpenVPN client. The `iptables` module keeps track of these rewritten packets so that when a return packet is received, the reverse is done and the packets are forwarded back to the OpenVPN client again. This is an easy method to enable routing to work, but there is a drawback when many clients are used: it would not be possible to distinguish traffic on Site B's LAN if it is coming from the OpenVPN server itself, from client1via the VPN tunnel or from clientN via the VPN tunnel.

# There's more...

There are a few things to keep in mind when setting up a TAP-style network.

## Differences between TUN and TAP

The differences between this setup and the *Server-side routing* recipe of the previous chapter are minimal. There are a few subtle differences, however, which can lead to unforeseen effects if you are not aware of them:

- When using a TAP adapter, the full Ethernet frame is encapsulated. This causes a slightly larger overhead.
- All the machines that are connected to a TAP-style network form a single broadcast domain. The effects of this will become clearer in the next recipe.
- If bridging is needed, a TAP-style tunnel is required.

## Using the TCP protocol

In this example, we chose the UDP protocol. The configuration files in this recipe can be easily converted to use the TCP protocol by changing the following line:

```
proto udp
```

Change this to:

```
proto tcp
```

Do this in both the client and server configuration files.

The UDP protocol normally gives optimal performance, but some routers and firewalls have problems forwarding UDP traffic. In such cases, the TCP protocol often does work.

## Making IP forwarding permanent

On most Linux systems, the proper way to permanently set up IP forwarding is as follows:

- Add the following line to the `/etc/sysctl.con` file:

  ```
  net.ipv4.ip_forward=1
  ```

- Reload the `sysctl.conf` file using:

  ```
  [root@server]# sysctl -p
  ```

## See also

- The *Server-side routing* recipe from `Chapter 2`, *Client-server IP-only Networks*, in which a basic TUN-style setup is explained

# Enabling client-to-client traffic

This recipe is a continuation of the previous recipe. It will demonstrate how to set up a TAP-based connection in client or server mode using certificates. Using the `client-to-client` directive, it will also enable different OpenVPN clients to contact each other. For TAP-based networks, this leads to some important side effects.

# Getting ready

We use the following network layout:

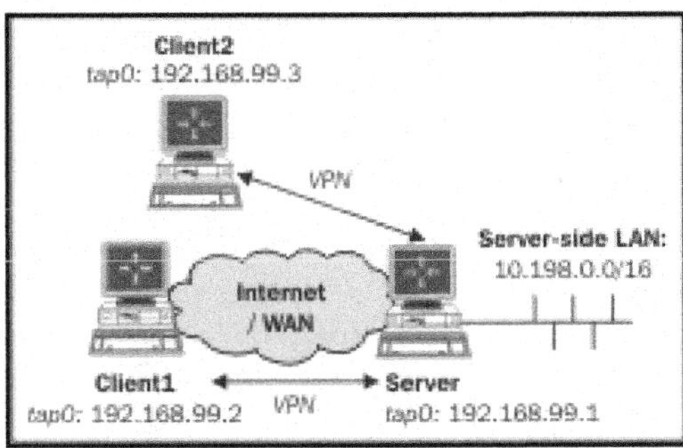


Set up the client and server certificates using the first recipe from `Chapter 2`, *Client-server IP-only Networks*.

For this recipe, the server was running CentOS 6 Linux and OpenVPN 2.3.10; both clients were running Windows 7 64 bit and OpenVPN 2.3.10. For the server, keep the configuration file `example3-1-server.conf` from the previous recipe at hand.

# How to do it...

1. Create the server configuration file by adding a line to the `example3-1-server.conf` file:

   ```
   client-to-client
   ```

   Save it as `example-3-2-server.conf`.

2. Start the server:

   ```
   [root@server]# openvpn --config example3-2-server.conf
   ```

3. Set up IP forwarding and an `iptables` masquerading rule:

   ```
   [root@server]# sysctl -w net.ipv4.ip_forward=1
   [root@server]# iptables -t nat -I POSTROUTING -i tap+ -o eth0 \
    -s 192.168.99.0/24 -j MASQUERADE
   ```

4. Next, create the client configuration file for the first client:

```
client
proto udp
remote openvpnserver.example.com
port 1194

dev tap
nobind

remote-cert-tls server
tls-auth "c:/program files/openvpn/config/ta.key" 1
ca       "c:/program files/openvpn/config/ca.crt"
cert     "c:/program files/openvpn/config/client1.crt"
key      "c:/program files/openvpn/config/client1.key"

verb 5
```

   Save it as `example-3-2-client1.ovpn`.

5. Similarly, for the second client, create the configuration file:

```
client
proto udp
remote openvpnserver.example.com
port 1194

dev tap
nobind

remote-cert-tls server
tls-auth "c:/program files/openvpn/config/ta.key" 1
ca       "c:/program files/openvpn/config/ca.crt"
cert     "c:/program files/openvpn/config/client2.crt"
key      "c:/program files/openvpn/config/client2.key"


verb 5
```

   Save it as `example-3-2-client2.ovpn`.

6. Start the Windows clients, one from the command line:

```
[WinClient1]C:> cd \program files\openvpn\config
[WinClient1]C:> ..\bin\openvpn --config example3-2-
client1.ovpn
```

   Start Client2 using the OpenVPN GUI:

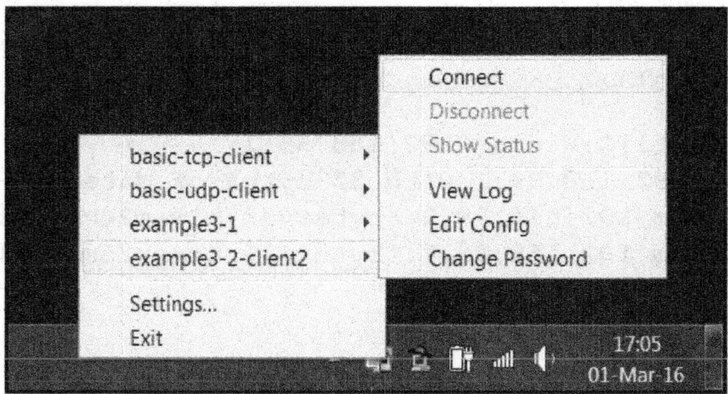


As the private key file `client2.key` is protected using a passphrase, we will be prompted for it:

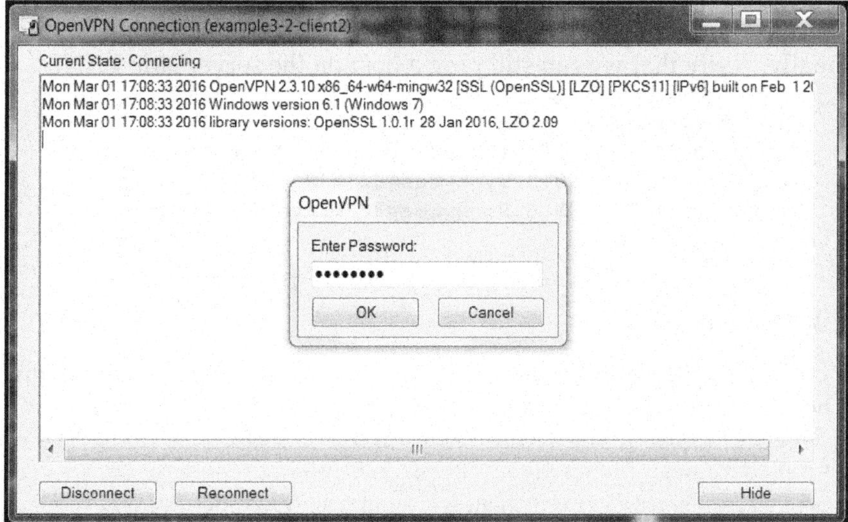


7. After the connection is established, the GUI window will disappear and a balloon will pop up:

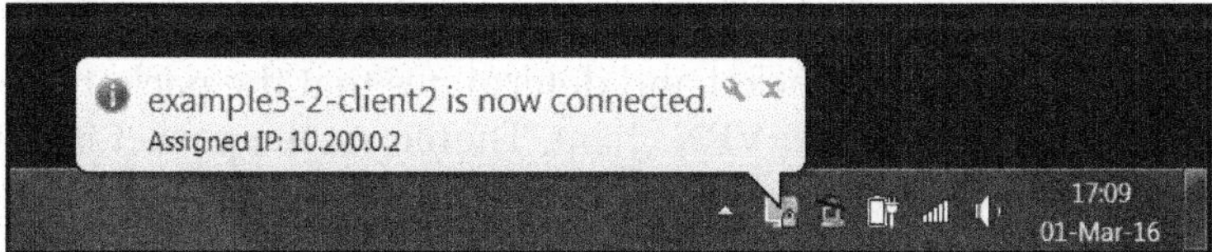

We can now verify that the VPN connection is working by doing this. First, ping the server:

```
[WinClient1]C:> ping 192.168.99.1
Pinging 192.168.99.1 with 32 bytes of data:
Reply from 192.168.99.1: bytes=32 time=24ms TTL=64
Reply from 192.168.99.1: bytes=32 time=25ms TTL=64
```

Then, ping the second client:

```
[WinClient1]C:> ping 192.168.99.3
Pinging 192.168.99.3 with 32 bytes of data:
Reply from 192.168.99.3: bytes=32 time=49ms TTL=128
Reply from 192.168.99.3: bytes=32 time=50ms TTL=128
```

Notice the higher round-trip time.

8. Finally, verify that we can still ping a host on the server-side LAN:

```
[WinClient1]C:\> ping -c 2 10.198.0.9
Pinging 10.198.0.9 with 32 bytes of data:
Reply from 10.198.0.9: bytes=32 time=25ms TTL=63
Reply from 10.198.0.9: bytes=32 time=25ms TTL=63
```

## How it works...

Both clients connect to the OpenVPN server in the regular manner. The following directive is all that is needed for the clients to see each other:

```
client-to-client
```

Communication between the clients will still pass through the OpenVPN server, which explains the higher round-trip time for the ICMP packets. The flow of an ICMP (`ping`) echo and reply is as follows:

1. The OpenVPN client encrypts the packet and forwards it to the server over a secure link.
2. The server decrypts the packet and determines that the packet needs to be forwarded to another OpenVPN client. Therefore, the packet is not forwarded to the kernel-routing modules, but is encrypted again and is forwarded to the second client.
3. The second client receives the packet, decrypts it, and sends a reply back to the server over the secure link.

4. The server decrypts the reply packet and determines that the packet needs to be forwarded to the first client. Therefore, the packet is not forwarded to the kernel-routing modules but is encrypted again and is forwarded to the original client.

# There's more...

As always, there are some caveats to watch out for.

## Broadcast traffic may affect scalability

All machines that are connected to a TAP-style network form a single broadcast domain. When `client-to-client` is enabled, this means that all of the broadcast traffic from all the clients is forwarded to all other clients. Wireshark running on `client2` indeed shows a lot of broadcast packets from `client1`, all of which passed through the OpenVPN server. This can lead to a scalability problem when a large number of clients are connected.

## Filtering traffic

In the current version of OpenVPN, it is not possible to filter the traffic between VPN clients when the `client-to-client` directive is used. OpenVPN does have the capability for a filtering plugin, but this plugin is not maintained and requires extensive configuration.

A second method of filtering traffic between clients is to use the system's routing tables, in combination with a Linux kernel flag, `proxy_arp_pvlan`. This flag is available in modern Linux kernels (2.6.34+ or kernels with back-ported options). This flag instructs the Linux kernel to resend the ARP request back out of the same interface from where it came. It is exactly this flag that is needed for client-to-client traffic to work without using the `client-to-client` directive. Thus, in order to filter traffic, we first enable client-to-client traffic in tap mode by setting this flag:

```
# echo 1 > /proc/sys/net/ipv4/conf/tap0/proxy_arp_pvlan
```

We can then use `iptables` command to filter traffic between clients.

## TUN-style networks

The `client-to-client` directive can also be used in TUN-style networks. It works in exactly the same manner as in this recipe, except that the OpenVPN clients do not form a single broadcast domain.

# Bridging – Linux

This recipe will demonstrate how to set up a bridged OpenVPN server. In this mode, the local network and the VPN network are bridged, which means that all of the traffic from one network is forwarded to the other and vice versa.

This setup is often used to securely connect remote clients to a Windows-based LAN, but it is quite hard to get it right. In almost all cases, it suffices to use a TUN-style network with a local WINS server on the OpenVPN server itself. A bridged VPN does have its advantages, as will become apparent in the next few recipes.

However, there are also disadvantages to using bridging, especially in terms of performance: the performance of a bridged 100 Mbps Ethernet adapter is about half the performance of a non-bridged adapter.

## Getting ready

We use the following network layout:

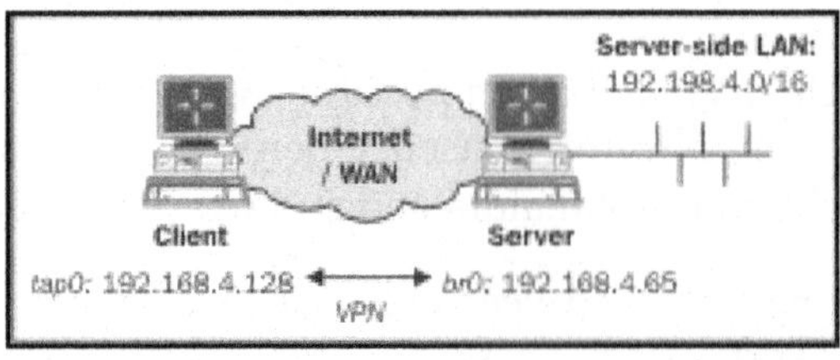


Set up the client and server certificates using the first recipe from `Chapter 2`, *Client-server IP-only networks*. For this recipe, the server was running CentOS 6 Linux and OpenVPN 2.3.10. The client computer was running Windows 7 64 bit and OpenVPN 2.3.10. For the client, keep the client configuration file `example3-2-client2.ovpn` at hand.

## How to do it...

1. Create the server configuration file:

```
proto udp
port 1194
dev tap0 ## the '0' is extremely important
server-bridge 192.168.4.65 255.255.255.0 192.168.4.128
192.168.4.200
```

```
push "route 192.168.4.0 255.255.255.0"
tls-auth /etc/openvpn/cookbook/ta.key 0
ca       /etc/openvpn/cookbook/ca.crt
cert     /etc/openvpn/cookbook/server.crt
key      /etc/openvpn/cookbook/server.key
dh       /etc/openvpn/cookbook/dh2048.pem
persist-key
persist-tun
keepalive 10 60
user  nobody
group nobody  # use "group nogroup" on some distros
daemon
log-append /var/log/openvpn.log
```

Save it as `example-3-3-server.conf`.

2. Next, create a script to start the network bridge:

```
#!/bin/bash

br="br0"
tap="tap0"

eth="eth0"
eth_ip="192.168.4.65"
eth_netmask="255.255.255.0"
eth_broadcast="192.168.4.255"

openvpn --mktun --dev $tap

brctl addbr $br
brctl addif $br $eth
brctl addif $br $tap
ifconfig $tap 0.0.0.0 promisc up
ifconfig $eth 0.0.0.0 promisc up
ifconfig $br $eth_ip netmask $eth_netmask \
broadcast $eth_broadcast
```

Save this script as `example3-3-bridge-start` file.

3. Similarly, use a script to stop the Ethernet bridge:

```
#!/bin/bash

br="br0"
tap="tap0"

ifconfig $br down
```

```
brctl delbr $br
openvpn --rmtun --dev $tap
```

Save this script as `example3-3-bridge-stop` file. These scripts are based on the `bridge-start` and `bridge-stop` examples, which are part of the OpenVPN distribution.

4. Create the network bridge and verify that it is working:

```
[root@server]# bash example3-3-bridge-start
TUN/TAP device tap0 opened
Persist state set to: ON
[root@server]# brctl show
bridge name bridge id         STP enabled interfaces
br0         8000.00219bd2d422 no          eth0
             tap0
```

5. Start the OpenVPN server:

```
[root@server]# openvpn --config example3-3-server.conf
```

6. Start the client:

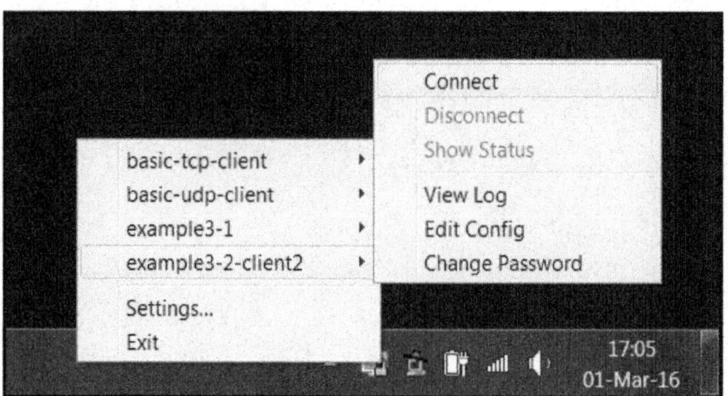


7. Check the assigned VPN address:

```
[WinClient]C:> ipconfig /all
[...]
Ethernet adapter tun0:
Connection-specific DNS Suffix  . :
Description . . . . . . . . . . . : TAP-Win32 Adapter V9
Physical Address. . . . . . . . . : 00-FF-17-82-55-DB
Dhcp Enabled. . . . . . . . . . . : Yes
Autoconfiguration Enabled . . . . : Yes
IP Address. . . . . . . . . . . . : 192.168.4.128
```

```
Subnet Mask . . . . . . . . . . . . : 255.255.255.0
Default Gateway . . . . . . . . . . :
DHCP Server . . . . . . . . . . . . : 192.168.4.0
```

8. Now, verify that we can ping a machine on the remote server LAN:

```
[WinClient]C:> ping 192.168.4.164
Pinging 192.168.4.164 with 32 bytes of data:
Reply from 192.168.4.164: bytes=32 time=3ms TTL=64
Reply from 192.168.4.164: bytes=32 time=1ms TTL=64
Reply from 192.168.4.164: bytes=32 time=1ms TTL=64
Reply from 192.168.4.164: bytes=32 time<1ms TTL=64
```

9. Remember to tear down the network bridge after stopping the OpenVPN server:

```
[root@server]# bash example3-3-bridge-stop
TUN/TAP device tap0 opened
Persist state set to: OFF
```

# How it works...

The `bridge-start` script forges a bond between two network adapters: on the one side, the LAN adapter `eth0`, and on the other side, the VPN adapter `tap0`. The main property of a network bridge is that all of the traffic is copied from one side to the other and vice versa. This allows us to set up a VPN where the client almost truly becomes a part of the server-side LAN.

The downside of a bridged network is the increased overhead and the performance penalty on the OpenVPN server itself: if there is a lot of broadcast traffic from many clients on either side, the bridge can become overloaded.

# There's more...

## Fixed addresses and the default gateway

In this recipe, the OpenVPN server is assigned a fixed address on the server LAN, as is done most often for a bridged interface. The difficulty with assigning a dynamic address to a network bridge is that it is not clear from which network the dynamic address should be chosen. This also enables us to specify a fixed server-bridge address in the server configuration file.

When using bridges, it is also important to check that the default route is available after the bridge is started. In most setups, `eth0` is assigned a dynamic address, including a default gateway. When the `bridge-start` script is executed, `br0` is assigned a fixed address, but as a side effect, the default gateway is often lost.

### Name resolution

One of the difficulties in setting up a bridged network in the proper fashion is related to name resolution. OpenVPN only does Ethernet (Layer2) or IP-based routing. Setting up a proper name resolution system (for example, a Domain Controller and/or a WINS server in a Windows network) can be tricky in a bridged environment as well.

## See also

- The next recipe in this chapter, in which bridging on a Windows server is explained

# Bridging- Windows

This recipe will demonstrate how to set up a bridged OpenVPN server on Windows. Bridging on Windows is slightly different from Linux or UNIX, but the concept is the same.

This recipe is very similar to the previous recipe, apart from the different methods used to set up bridging.

## Getting ready

Set up the client and server certificates using the first recipe from `Chapter 2`, *Client-server IP-only networks*.

For this recipe, the server computer was running Windows 7 64 bit and OpenVPN 2.3.10. The client computer was running Fedora 20 Linux and OpenVPN 2.3.10. For the Linux client, keep the client configuration file `example3-1-client.conf` at hand.

We use the following network layout:

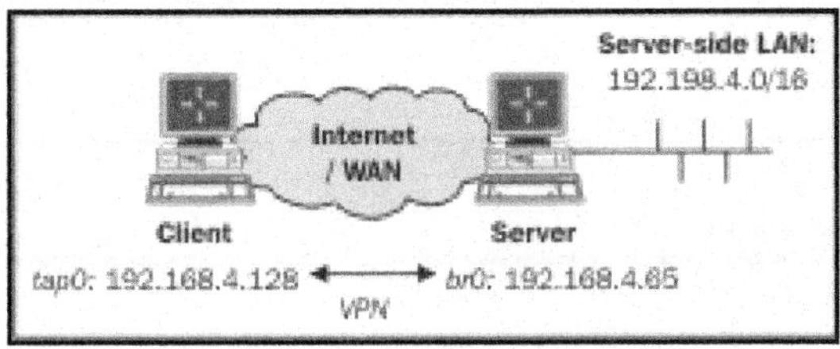


# How to do it...

1. Create the server configuration file:

```
proto udp
port 1194
dev tap
dev-node tapbridge

server-bridge 192.168.3.15 255.255.255.0 192.168.3.128
192.168.3.250

dh       "c:/program files/openvpn/config/dh2048.pem"
tls-auth "c:/program files/openvpn/config/ta.key" 0
ca       "c:/program files/openvpn/config/ca.crt"
cert     "c:/program files/openvpn/config/server.crt"
key      "c:/program files/openvpn/config/server.key"

push "route 192.168.3.0 255.255.255.0"

persist-key
persist-tun
keepalive 10 60
```

   Save it as `example-3-4-server.conf`.

2. Next, create the network bridge:
   - Go to **Network and Sharing Center** and **Change adapter settings**.
   - Rename the `TAP-Win` adapter as `tapbridge` by right-clicking on it and selecting **Rename**. On the test computer used, the Ethernet adapter connected to the LAN was renamed to `eth0`.

- Select the two adapters that need to be bridged by pressing the *Ctrl* key and clicking on each adapter, then right-clicking and selecting **Bridge Connections**:

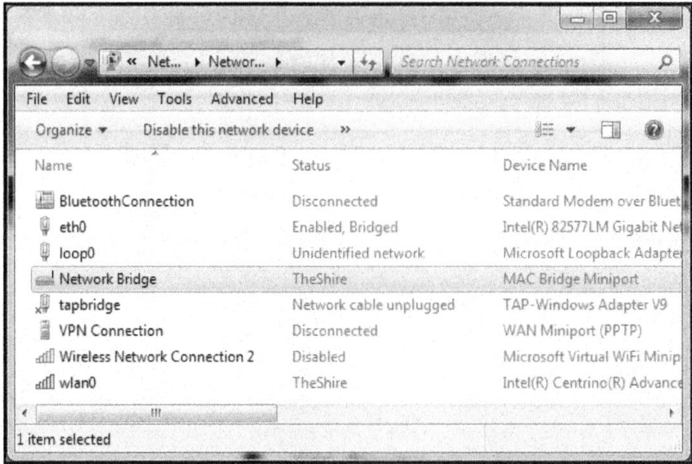


This will create a new bridge adapter icon in the control panel, usually named **Network Bridge (...)**.

3. The network bridge is now ready to be configured:

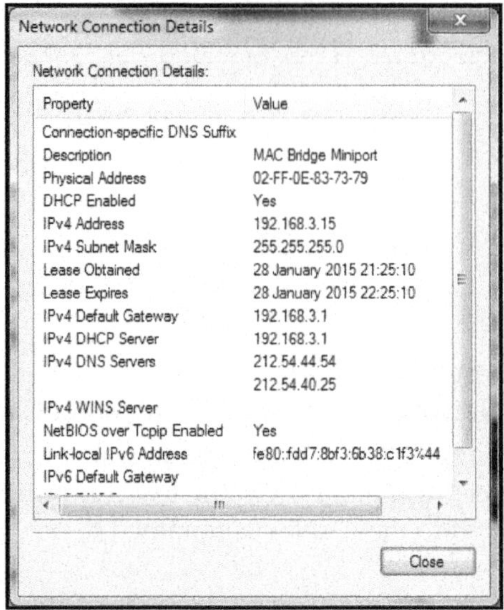

4. In a command window, verify that the bridge is configured correctly:

```
[winserver]C:> netsh interface ip show address "Network
Bridge"
Configuration for interface "Network Bridge"
DHCP enabled:                      No
IP Address:                        192.168.3.15
SubnetMask:                        255.255.255.0
Default Gateway:                   192.168.3.1
GatewayMetric:                     5
InterfaceMetric:                   0
```

5. Start the OpenVPN server:

```
[winserver]C:> cd \program files\openvpn\config
[winserver]C:> ..\bin\openvpn --config example3-4-server.ovpn
```

6. The Windows firewall will pop up a security warning. Allow OpenVPN access to the VPN:

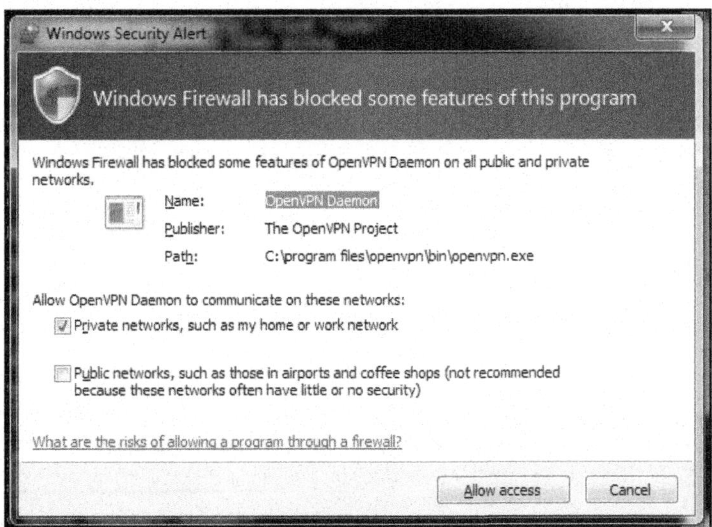


7. Start the client:

```
[root@client]# openvpn --config example3-1-client.conf
```

8. Now, check the assigned VPN address and verify that we can ping a machine on the remote server LAN:

```
[client]$ /sbin/ifconfig tap1
tap1  Link encap:Ethernet  HWaddr A2:F4:E2:41:05:BF
  inet addr:192.168.3.128  Bcast:192.168.3.255
  Mask:255.255.255.0
[...]
[client]$ ping -c 2 192.168.3.1
PING 192.168.3.1 (192.168.3.1) 56(84) bytes of data.
64 bytes from 192.168.3.1: icmp_seq=1 ttl=128 time=24.0 ms
64 bytes from 192.168.3.1: icmp_seq=2 ttl=128 time=26.0 ms
```

## How it works...

Apart from the way the bridge is created and configured, this recipe is very similar to the previous one. The one thing to keep in mind is how the adapter is selected in the server configuration file:

```
dev tap
dev-node tapbridge
```

On Linux and other UNIX variants, this could be achieved using a single line:

```
dev tap0
```

But the naming scheme for the TAP adapters on Windows is different. To overcome this, the `dev-node` directive needs to be added.

## See also

- The previous recipe, where bridging on Linux is explained

# Checking broadcast and non-IP traffic

The main reason for a bridged setup is to create a single broadcast domain for all the clients connected, both via the VPN and via a regular network connection.

Another reason is the ability to route or forward non-IP based traffic, such as the older Novell IPX and Appletalk protocols.

This recipe focuses on the use of tools such as `tcpdump` and `wireshark` to detect whether the broadcast domain is functioning and if non-IP traffic is flowing in the correct manner.

# Getting ready

For this recipe, we use the setup from the *Bridging – Linux* recipe of this chapter. We use the following network layout:

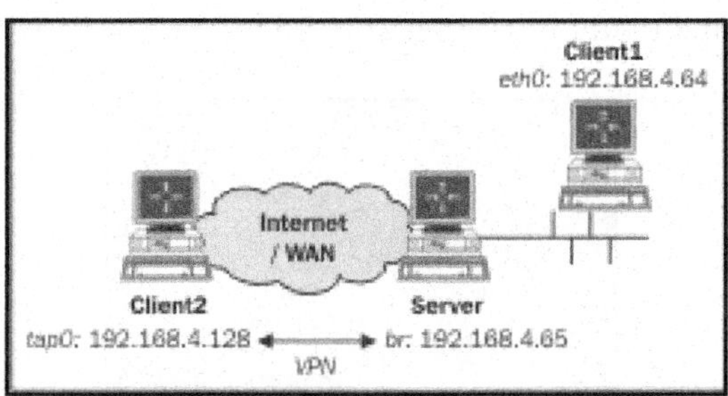


For this recipe, the server computer was running CentOS 6 Linux and OpenVPN 2.3.9. For the server, keep the server configuration file `example3-3-server.conf` from the *Bridging – Linux* recipe ready. The first client computer was running Windows 7 64 bit and OpenVPN 2.3.10 and was in the same LAN segment as the OpenVPN server. The second client was running Windows XP and OpenVPN 2.1.1. For this client, keep the client configuration file `example3-2-client2.ovpn` from the *Enabling client-to-client traffic* recipe at hand.

Make sure that the AppleTalk and IPX protocols are installed on both the Windows machines. Bind the protocols to the Local Area Network adapters (this is the default setting).

# How to do it...

1. Create the network bridge and verify that it is working:

```
[root@server]# bash example3-3-bridge-start
TUN/TAP device tap0 opened
Persist state set to: ON
[root@server]# brctl show
bridge name bridge id         STP enabled interfaces
br0         8000.00219bd2d422 no          eth0
                                          tap0
```

2. Start the OpenVPN server:

```
[root@server]# openvpn --config example3-3-server.conf
```

3. Start the OpenVPN clients:

```
[WinClient1]C:> cd \program files\openvpn\config
[WinClient1]C:> ..\bin\openvpn --config example3-2-
client2.ovpn
```

   Start Client 2 using the OpenVPN GUI:

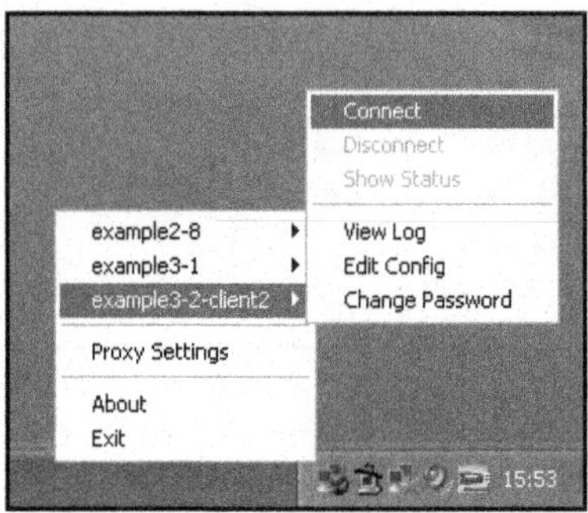


   In this recipe, the Windows 7 client was assigned `192.168.4.64`. The Windows XP client was assigned `192.168.4.128`.

4. After the client has successfully connected, we first check for ARP messages. On the server, run the `tcpdump` command and listen for traffic on the bridge interface `br0`:

```
Example 3-5
File Edit View Terminal Tabs Help
[server]# tcpdump -nnel -i br0 arp
listening on br0, link-type EN10MB (Ethernet), capture size 65535 bytes
[...] ARP, Request who-has 192.168.4.64 tell 192.168.4.254,
[...] ARP, Request who-has 192.168.4.1 tell 192.168.4.254,
[...] ARP, Request who-has 192.168.4.65 tell 192.168.4.254,
[...] ARP, Reply 192.168.4.65 is-at 00:21:9b:d2:d4:22,
[...] ARP, Request who-has 192.168.4.128 tell 192.168.4.254,
[...] ARP, Reply 192.168.4.128 is-at 00:ff:17:82:55:db,
[server]#
```

In this output, `192.168.4.254` is the address of the server-side gateway. So the gateway is asking for ARP information and the ARP replies are coming from both the OpenVPN server and the OpenVPN client itself. This can only happen if the ARP request is forwarded over the bridge to the OpenVPN client.

5. Next, on the Windows 7 client, check for the broadcast traffic coming from the Windows XP client. For this, we use Wireshark. Wireshark is available for both Linux and Windows. Configure it to capture all of the traffic from the Ethernet adapter. Here's an example of it:

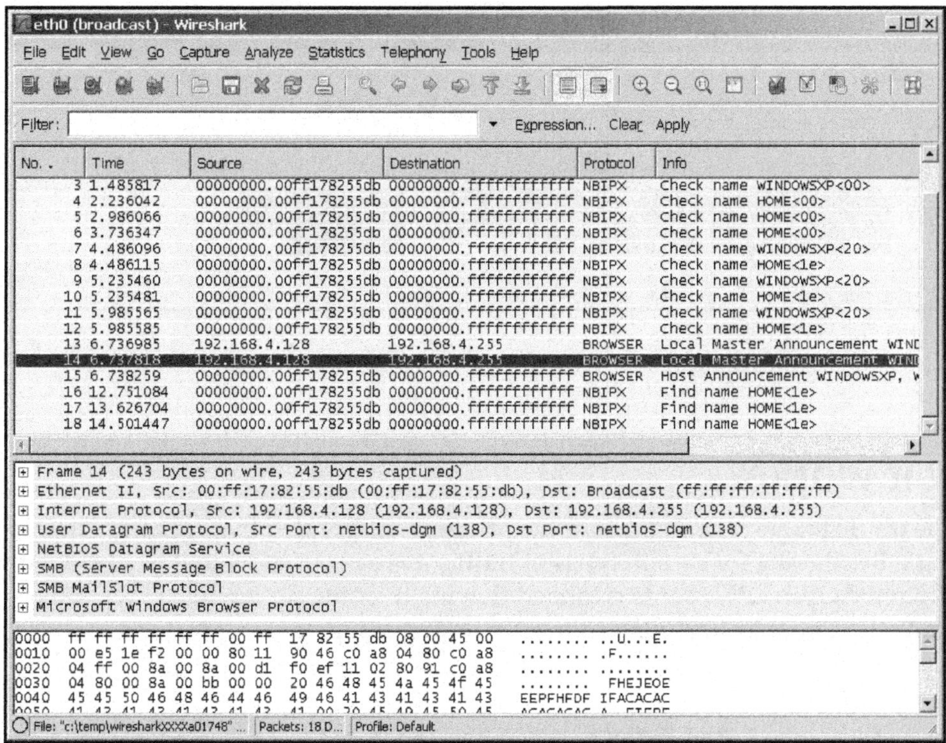


In this output, we see a lot of Netbios broadcast traffic when the OpenVPN client first connects to the network.

6. As a final example, we look for IPX traffic:

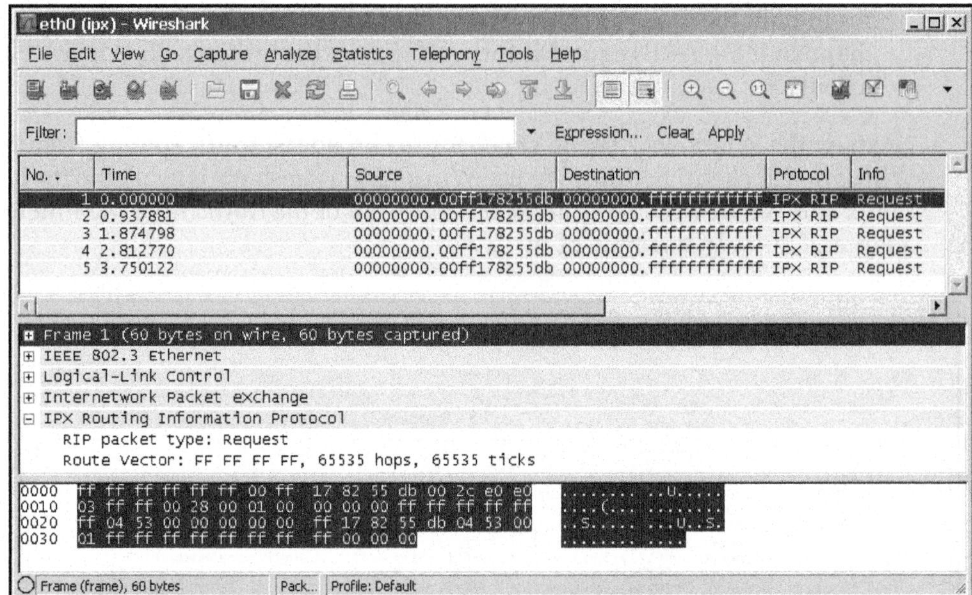


This shows that non-IP traffic is also forwarded over the bridge.

## How it works...

All of the traffic that is forwarded over the bridge is intercepted by programs such as Wireshark. By filtering for certain types of traffic, it is easy to show that in a bridged setup, traffic from the OpenVPN clients is indeed flowing over the server-side LAN. This is very important when troubleshooting an almost-working setup.

# An external DHCP server

In this recipe, we will configure a bridged OpenVPN server so that it uses an external DHCP server to assign addresses to the OpenVPN clients to further increase the integration of remote clients with the clients already present on the server-side LAN.

# Getting ready

We use the following network layout:

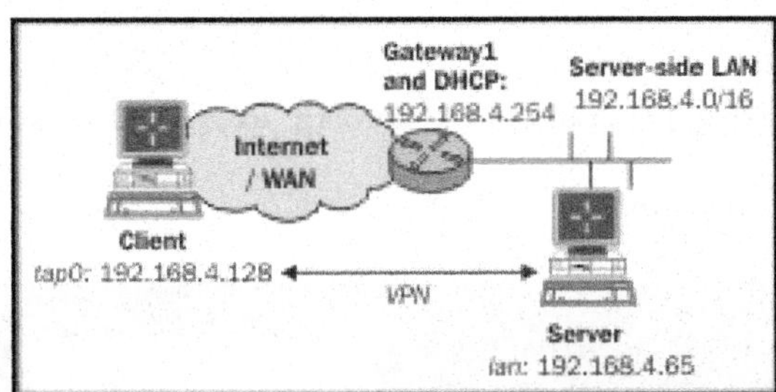


Set up the client and server certificates using the first recipe from `Chapter 2`, *Client-server IP-only Networks*. For this recipe, the server computer was running CentOS 6 Linux and OpenVPN 2.3.10. The client was running Windows 7 64 bit and OpenVPN 2.3.10. For this client, keep the client configuration file `example3-2-client2.ovpn` from the *Enabling client-to-client traffic* recipe at hand.

# How to do it...

1. Create the server configuration file:

```
proto udp
port 1194
dev tap0

server-bridge
push "route 0.0.0.0 255.255.255.255 net_gateway"

tls-auth /etc/openvpn/cookbook/ta.key 0
ca       /etc/openvpn/cookbook/ca.crt
cert     /etc/openvpn/cookbook/server.crt
key      /etc/openvpn/cookbook/server.key
dh       /etc/openvpn/cookbook/dh2048.pem

persist-key
persist-tun
keepalive 10 60

user  nobody
group nobody  # use "group nogroup" on some distros
```

```
daemon
log-append /var/log/openvpn.log
```

2. Save it as `example3-6-server.conf`.
3. Start the server:

```
[root@server]# openvpn --config example3-6-server.conf
```

4. Start the Windows client:

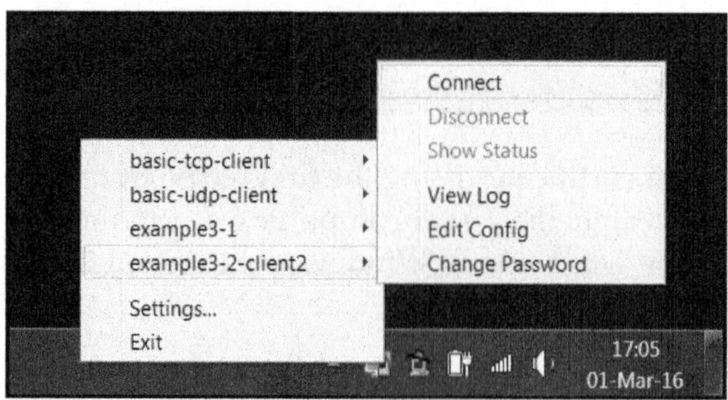


5. After the VPN connection is established, verify the IP address and the routing tables:

```
[WinClient]C:> ipconfig /all
[...]
Ethernet adapter tapwin32-0
Connection-specific DNS Suffix  . : lan
Description . . . . . . . . . . . : TAP-Win32 Adapter V9
Physical Address. . . . . . . . . : 00-FF-17-82-55-DB
Dhcp Enabled. . . . . . . . . . . : Yes
Autoconfiguration Enabled . . . . : Yes
IP Address. . . . . . . . . . . . : 192.168.4.66
Subnet Mask . . . . . . . . . . . : 255.255.255.0
Default Gateway . . . . . . . . . : 192.168.4.254
DHCP Server . . . . . . . . . . . : 192.168.4.254
DNS Servers . . . . . . . . . . . : 192.168.4.254
[...]
[WinClient]C:> netstat -rn
[...]
0.0.0.0  0.0.0.0         192.168.3.1    192.168.3.22  10
0.0.0.0  255.255.255.255 192.168.3.1    192.168.3.22   1
0.0.0.0  0.0.0.0         192.168.4.254 192.168.4.66   1
Default Gateway:        192.168.3.1
[...]
```

6. And finally, check that we can reach other hosts in the server-side LAN:

```
[WinClient]C:> ping 192.168.4.64
Pinging 192.168.4.64 with 32 bytes of data:
Reply from 192.168.4.64: bytes=32 time=3ms TTL=64
Reply from 192.168.4.64: bytes=32 time=1ms TTL=64
Reply from 192.168.4.64: bytes=32 time=1ms TTL=64
Reply from 192.168.4.64: bytes=32 time<1ms TTL=64
```

# How it works...

Here is the server directive:

```
server-bridge
```

Without any parameters, this directive instructs OpenVPN to not allocate a pool of IP addresses for the clients. So, all of the incoming DHCP requests from the clients are forwarded out over the bridge. The DHCP server on the server-side LAN then replies with an IP address.

The tricky part here is that the DHCP server almost always also returns a default gateway, which will be the LAN gateway. If a remote client sets its default gateway to the gateway of the LAN, funny things will happen, as in most cases the direct route to the OpenVPN server will be lost.

The following directive instructs the OpenVPN client to add an explicit default route via the `net_gateway`, which is always the LAN gateway at the client side:

```
push "route 0.0.0.0 255.255.255.255 net_gateway"
```

For Windows clients, this trick works and the default gateway remains intact.

For Linux clients, it is easier to tweak the `dhclient` and `network-scripts` settings. However, this is distribution-dependent.

With the default gateway intact, the OpenVPN client is properly assigned an address from the DHCP server on the server side.

# There's more...

When using an external DHCP setup, keep in mind the following.

## DHCP server configuration

The proper solution is to configure the DHCP server such that DHCP requests from the VPN clients do not get a default gateway assigned. This adds a burden to the administration of the server-side DHCP server.

In this case, it also makes sense to explicitly set a unique MAC address in each client configuration file using the following, for example:

```
lladdr CA:C6:F8:FB:EB:3B
```

On Linux, the MAC address is computed randomly when the TAP interface comes up, so each time the OpenVPN client is stopped and started, a new IP address is allocated. It is also possible to create a permanently fixed, static MAC address by using the system configuration scripts to bring up the TAP device before OpenVPN is started.

## DHCP relay

It is also possible to use an external DHCP server without using bridging. If the TAP adapter is configured before OpenVPN is started and the server configuration file from this recipe is used, then an external DHCP server can be used using the Linux `dhrelay` command:

```
[root@server]# dhrelay -i tap0 -i eth0
```

Make sure to list both the TAP adapter and the Ethernet adapter to which the external DHCP server is connected. By combining this with a `proxy-arp` script (see the *Proxy ARP* recipe from `Chapter 2`, *Client-server IP-only Networks*), it eliminates the need to use bridging in most cases.

## Tweaking /etc/sysconfig/network-scripts

On RedHat, Fedora, and OpenSuSE-based systems, the TAP adapter is brought up using a script `/etc/sysconfig/network-scripts/ifup-tap0` and the following command:

```
[root@client]# /sbin/ifup tap0
```

By adding the line to the `/etc/sysconfig/network-scripts/ifup-tap0` file, the `dhclient` script ignores the gateway that is assigned from the DHCP server:

```
GATEWAYDEV=eth0
```

A similar hack can be developed for Debian/Ubuntu-based systems.

# Using the status file

OpenVPN offers several options to monitor the clients connected to a server. The most commonly used method is using a status file. This recipe will show how to use and read the OpenVPN status file. We will also focus on some subtleties of the status file in a TAP-style setup.

## Getting ready

Set up the client and server certificates using the first recipe from `Chapter 2`, *Client-server IP-only Networks*. For this recipe, the server computer was running CentOS 6 Linux and OpenVPN 2.3.10. The first client was running Fedora 20 Linux and OpenVPN 2.3.10. The second client was running Windows 7 64 bit and OpenVPN 2.3.10. For the Linux client, keep the client configuration file `example3-1-client.conf` at hand. For the Windows client, keep the client configuration file `example3-2-client2.ovpn` at hand.

## How to do it...

1. Create the server configuration file by adding a line to the `example3-1-server.conf.` file:

   ```
   status /var/log/openvpn.status
   ```

   Save it as `example3-7-server.conf.`

2. Start the server:

   ```
   [root@server]# openvpn --config example3-7-server.conf
   ```

3. First, start the Linux client using the configuration file from the earlier recipe and ping a host on the remote network:

   ```
   [root@client1]# openvpn --config example3-1-client.conf
   [root@client1]# ping 10.198.0.1
   ```

4. After the VPN is established, list the contents of the `openvpn.status` file (as user root):

```
[root@server]# cat /var/log/openvpn.status
OpenVPN CLIENT LIST
Updated,Wed Mar  2 17:34:39 2016
Common Name,Real Address,Bytes Received,Bytes Sent,Connected
Since
client1,192.168.4.65:50183,10024,10159,Wed Mar 2 17:26:48
2016
ROUTING TABLE
Virtual Address,Common Name,Real Address,Last Ref
5e:52:73:5c:6a:ce,client1,192.168.4.65:50183,Wed Mar 2
17:27:06 2016
GLOBAL STATS
Max bcast/mcast queue length,1
END
```

5. Start the Windows client:

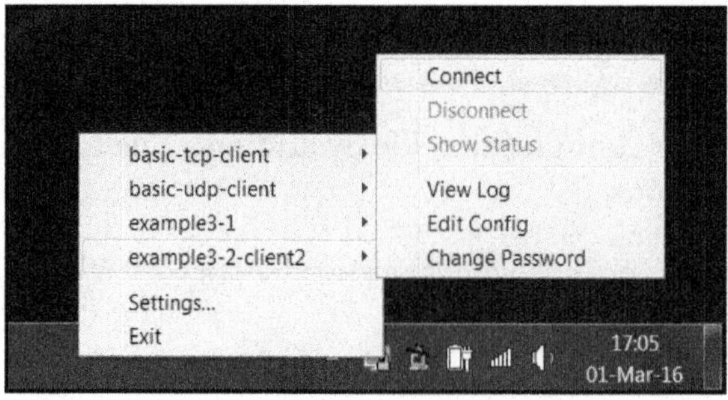


6. Ping a host on the remote network:

```
[WinClient2]C:> ping 10.198.0.1
```

7. List the contents of the status file again on the server:

```
[root@server]# cat /var/log/openvpn.status
  OpenVPN CLIENT LIST
Updated,Wed Mar  2 17:40:22 2016
Common Name,Real Address,Bytes Received,Bytes Sent,Connected
Since
client1,192.168.4.65:50183,10024,10159,Wed Mar  2 17:27:08
2016
client2,192.168.4.64:50186,18055,9726,Wed Mar  2 17:26:48
2016
```

```
  ROUTING TABLE
Virtual Address,Common Name,Real Address,Last Ref
5e:52:73:5c:6a:ce,client1,192.168.4.65:50183,Wed Mar  2
17:27:06 2016
00:ff:17:82:55:db,client2,192.168.4.64:50186,Wed Mar  2
17:27:16 2016
GLOBAL STATS
Max bcast/mcast queue length,1
END
```

# How it works...

Each time a client connects to the OpenVPN server, the status file is updated with the connection information. The **OPENVPN CLIENTLIST** and **ROUTING TABLE** tables are the most interesting tables, as they show the following:

- Which clients are connected
- From which IP address the clients are connecting
- The number of bytes each client has received and transferred
- The time at which the client connected

The routing table also shows which networks are routed to each client. This routing table is filled when clients start sending traffic that needs to be routed. The `ping` commands in the recipe were used to trigger the routing table entries.

# There's more...

When comparing this example with a TUN-style setup there are many similarities but also some differences:

## Difference with TUN-style networks

The major difference in the status file when using a TAP-style network compared to a TUN-style network (see the *Using the status file* recipe from `Chapter 2`, *Client-server IP-only Networks*) is in the **ROUTING TABLE**. The recipe from the previous chapter shows this:

```
10.200.0.2,client1,192.168.4.65:56764,<Date>
```

Whereas, in this recipe, we see the following:

```
5e:52:73:5c:6a:ce,client1,192.168.4.65:50183,<Date>
```

The address `5e:52:73:5c:6a:ce` is the randomly chosen MAC address of the tap adapter on the `client1` machine.

## Disconnecting clients

Note that when a client disconnects, the status file is not updated immediately. OpenVPN first tries to reconnect to the client based on the `keepalive` parameters in the server configuration file. The server configuration file in this recipe uses this:

```
keepalive 10 60
```

This tells the server that it will ping the client every 10th second. The OpenVPN server will double the second argument: if it does not get a response after 2 * 60 seconds, the connection is restarted. The server will also tell the client to ping the server every 10 seconds and to restart the connection after 60 seconds if it does not get any response.

If the client explicitly closes the connection using the `explicit-exit-notify` directive or when a TCP-based setup is used, the server does not wait for ping responses from the client.

## See also

- The *Using the status file* recipe from `Chapter 2`, *Client-server IP-only Networks*, which explains how the status file can be configured and used for IP-only style networks

# The management interface

This recipe shows how OpenVPN can be managed using the management interface on the server.

## Getting ready

Set up the client and server certificates using the first recipe from `Chapter 2`, *Client-server IP-only Networks*.

For this recipe, the server computer was running CentOS 6 Linux and OpenVPN 2.3.10. The first client was running Fedora 20 Linux and OpenVPN 2.3.10. The second client was running Windows 7 64 bit and OpenVPN 2.3.10.

For the server, keep the configuration file `example3-1-server.conf` from the first recipe of this chapter at hand. For the Linux client, keep the client configuration file `example3-1-client.conf` from the first recipe of this chapter at hand. For the Windows client, keep the client configuration file `example3-2-client2.ovpn` from the *Enabling client-to-client traffic* recipe at hand.

We use the following network layout:

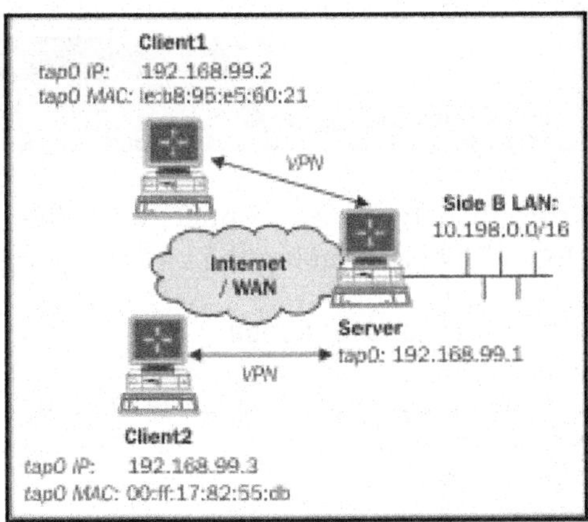


# How to do it...

1. Create the server configuration file by adding a line to the `example3-1-server.conf` file:

```
management tunnel 23000 stdin
```

2. Save it as `example3-8-server.conf`.
3. Start the server:

```
[root@server]# openvpn --config example3-8-server.conf
```

The OpenVPN server will now first ask for a password for the management interface.

4. Start the clients using the configuration files from the earlier recipe:

```
[root@client1]# openvpn --config example3-1-client.conf
```

5. Start the Windows client as well:

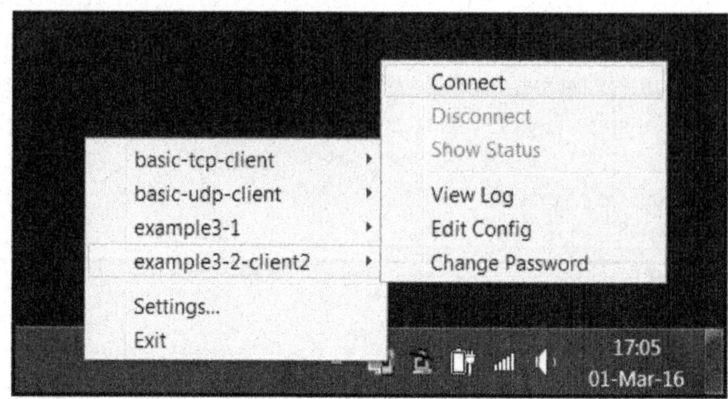


6. After the VPN is established, we can connect from the server to the management interface of the OpenVPN client using the `telnet` program:

```
[server]$ telnet 127.0.0.1 23000
Trying 127.0.0.1...
Connected to localhost.localdomain (127.0.0.1).
Escape character is '^]'.
ENTER PASSWORD:cookbook
SUCCESS: password is correct
>INFO:OpenVPN Management Interface Version 1 -- type 'help' for
more info
status
OpenVPN CLIENT LIST
Updated,Wed Mar  2 17:57:07 2016
Common Name,Real Address,Bytes Received,Bytes Sent,Connected
Since
client1,192.168.4.64:50209,7851,8095,Wed Mar  2 17:56:08 2016
client2,192.168.4.5:50212,11696,7447,Wed Mar  2 17:56:45 2016
ROUTING TABLE
Virtual Address,Common Name,Real Address,Last Ref
00:ff:17:82:55:db,client2,192.168.4.5:50212,Wed Mar  2 17:56:49
2016
1e:b8:95:e5:60:21,client1,192.168.4.64:50209,Wed Mar  2
17:56:53 2016
GLOBAL STATS
Max bcast/mcast queue length,1
END
```

Note that it looks exactly like the status file from the previous recipe.

7. It is also possible to disconnect a client:

```
kill client2
SUCCESS: common name 'client2' found, 1 client(s) killed

status
OpenVPN CLIENT LIST
Updated,Wed Mar  2 17:58:51 2016
Common Name,Real Address,Bytes Received,Bytes Sent,Connected
Since
client1,192.168.4.64:50209,8381,8625,Wed Mar  2 17:56:08 2016
ROUTING TABLE
Virtual Address,Common Name,Real Address,Last Ref
1e:b8:95:e5:60:21,client1,192.168.4.64:50209,Wed Mar  2
17:56:53 2016
GLOBAL STATS
Max bcast/mcast queue length,1
END
```

8. Use *Ctrl + ]* or exit to exit the telnet program.

# How it works...

When the OpenVPN server starts, a special management interface is set up using the directive:

```
management 127.0.0.1 23000 stdin
```

The interface is set up with these parameters:

- The IP `127.0.0.1` to bind the management interface to localhost only.
- The port `23000` on which the management interface will be listening.
- The last parameter is the password file or the special keyword `stdin` to indicate that the management interface password will be specified when OpenVPN starts up. Note that this password is completely unrelated to the private key passphrases or any other user management passwords that OpenVPN uses.

After the management interface comes up, the server operator can connect to it using `telnet` and can query the server. By typing the following, the operator can disconnect a client:

```
kill <clientcommonname>
```

Note that if the OpenVPN client is configured to reconnect automatically, it will do so after a few minutes.

When comparing the output of the management interface's `status` command with the status file output shown in the *Using the status file* recipe from `Chapter 2`, *Client-server IP-only Networks*, the major difference is the fact that here, the clients' MAC addresses are listed instead of the VPN IP addresses. The OpenVPN does not even need to know the clients' IP addresses, as they can be assigned by an external DHCP server.

## There's more...

The management interface can also be run on the OpenVPN clients. See the *Management interface* recipe in `Chapter 2`, *Client-server IP-only Networks.*

It is expected that the management interface will become more important in future versions of OpenVPN, both on the client and the server side, as the preferred method to programmatically interact with the OpenVPN software.

## See also

- *The Management interface* recipe from `Chapter 2`, *Client-server IP-only Networks*, in which the client-side management interface is explained
- The *Using the status file* recipe from `Chapter 2`, *Client-server IP-only Networks*, where the details of the status file for a TUN-style network are explained

# Integrating IPv6 into TAP-style networks

For the final recipe of this chapter, we will show how to integrate IPv6 settings into TAP-style networks. TAP-style networks have had support for IPv6 traffic longer than TUN-style networks, as a TAP-style network provides an Ethernet-like layer. This layer is capable of transporting almost any kind of network protocol, including IPv6. In OpenVPN 2.3, better IPv6 support was added so that an OpenVPN server could provide a DHCP pool with IPv6 addresses. In this recipe, we will show just how to do that.

# Getting ready

Set up the client and server certificates using the first recipe from `Chapter 2`, *Client-server IP-only Networks*. For this recipe, both the server computer and the client computer were running CentOS 6 Linux and OpenVPN 2.3.10. For the server, keep the configuration file `example3-1-server.conf` from the first recipe of this chapter at hand. For the client, keep the client configuration file `example3-1-client.conf` from the first recipe of this chapter at hand.

We use the following network layout:

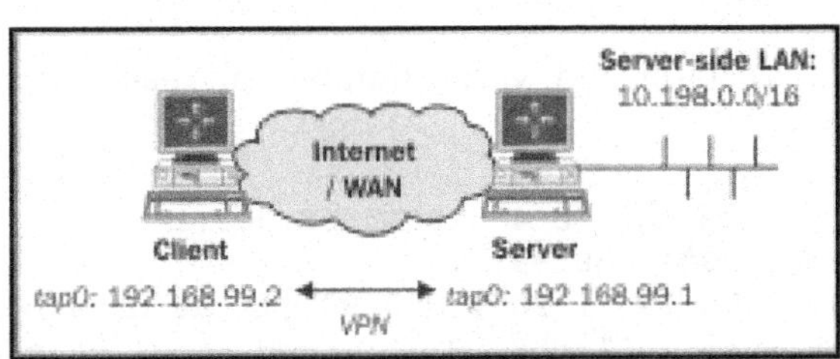


# How to do it...

1. Modify the server configuration file, `example3-1-server.conf`, by adding a line:

```
server-ipv6 2001:db8:99::0/112
```

2. Save it as `example3-9-server.conf`.
3. Start the server:

```
[root@server]# openvpn --config example3-9-server.conf
```

4. Start the client:

```
[root@client1]# openvpn --config example3-1-client.conf \
                            --suppress-timestamps
OpenVPN 2.3.10 x86_64-redhat-linux-gnu [SSL (OpenSSL)] [LZO]
[EPOLL] [PKCS11] [MH] [IPv6] built on Jan  4 2016
library versions: OpenSSL 1.0.1e-fips 11 Feb 2013, LZO 2.03
Control Channel Authentication: using
'/etc/openvpn/cookbook/ta.key' as a OpenVPN static key file
UDPv4 link local: [undef]
UDPv4 link remote: [AF_INET]openvpnserver:1194
```

```
[openvpnserver] Peer Connection Initiated with
[AF_INET]openvpnserver:1194
TUN/TAP device tap0 opened
do_ifconfig, tt->ipv6=1, tt->did_ifconfig_ipv6_setup=1
/sbin/ip link set dev tap0 up mtu 1500
/sbin/ip addr add dev tap0 192.168.99.2/24 broadcast
192.168.99.255
/sbin/ip -6 addr add 2001:db8:99::1000/112 dev tap0
Initialization Sequence Completed
```

Note that we have suppressed timestamps in the log file using the command-line directive `--suppress-timestamps`.

5. After the VPN is established, verify that we can reach the server using the `ping6` command:

```
[client]$   ping6 -c 4  2001:db8:99::1
ping6 -c 4 2001:db8:99::1
PING 2001:db8:99::1(2001:db8:99::1) 56 data bytes
64 bytes from 2001:db8:99::1: icmp_seq=1 ttl=64 time=0.620 ms
64 bytes from 2001:db8:99::1: icmp_seq=2 ttl=64 time=0.630 ms
64 bytes from 2001:db8:99::1: icmp_seq=3 ttl=64 time=0.631 ms
64 bytes from 2001:db8:99::1: icmp_seq=4 ttl=64 time=0.627 ms
--- 2001:db8:99::1 ping statistics ---
4 packets transmitted, 4 received, 0% packet loss, time
3000ms
rtt min/avg/max/mdev = 0.620/0.627/0.631/0.004 ms
```

## How it works...

IPv6 support for TAP-style networks is nearly identical to IPv6 support for TUN-style networks. By adding a single line to the server configuration file, we provide IPv6 addresses to the connecting VPN clients:

```
server-ipv6 2001:db8:99::0/112
```

The same directives, ending in `-ip6`, which apply to TUN-based setups, also apply to TAP-style networks.

# There's more...

The firewall rules for IPv6 traffic are slightly different from the firewall rules for IPv4 traffic. Also, with TAP-style networks, it is often useful to allow all incoming and outgoing traffic on the `tap+` adapter range. This can be especially helpful when debugging a non-working setup:

```
# iptables -I INPUT -i tap+ -j ACCEPT
# iptables -I OUTPUT -o tap+ -j ACCEPT
# ip6tables -I INPUT -i tap+ -j ACCEPT
# ip6tables -I OUTPUT -o tap+ -j ACCEPT
# iptables -I FORWARD -i tap+ -j ACCEPT
# iptables -I FORWARD -o tap+ -j ACCEPT
# ip6tables -I FORWARD -i tap+ -j ACCEPT
# ip6tables -I FORWARD -o tap+ -j ACCEPT
```

Note that such rules should be used for debugging purposes only.

# See also

- The *Adding IPv6 support* recipe from `Chapter 2`, *Client-server IP-only Networks*, in which IPv6 support is added to a very similar TUN-style setup

# 4

# PKI, Certificates, and OpenSSL

In this chapter, we will cover:

- Certificate generation
- OpenSSL tricks: x509, pkcs12, verify output
- Revoking certificates
- The use of CRLs
- Checking expired/revoked certificates
- Intermediary CAs
- Multiple CAs: stacking, using the `capath` directive
- Determining which crypto library is used
- Crypto features of OpenSSL and PolarSSL
- Pushing ciphers
- Elliptic curve support

## Introduction

This chapter is a small detour into the public key infrastructures (PKIs), certificates, and `openssl` commands. The primary purpose of the recipes in this chapter is to show how the certificates, which are used in OpenVPN, can be generated, managed, viewed, and what kind of interactions exist between OpenSSL and OpenVPN.

# Certificate generation

This recipe will demonstrate how to create and sign a certificate request using plain `openssl` commands. This is slightly different from using the `easy-rsa` scripts, but very instructive.

## Getting ready

Set up the `easy-rsa` certificate environment using the first recipe from `Chapter 2`, *Client-server IP-only Networks*, by sourcing the `vars` file. This recipe was performed on a computer running Fedora 22 Linux but it can easily be run on Windows or MacOS. Note that the `easy-rsa` package can be downloaded independently of OpenVPN itself.

## How to do it...

Before we can use plain `openssl` commands to generate and sign a request, there are a few environment variables that need to be set. These variables are not set in the `vars` file by default.

1. Add the missing environment variables:

   ```
   $ cd /etc/openvpn/cookbook
   $ . ./vars
   $ export KEY_CN=
   $ export KEY_OU=
   $ export KEY_NAME=
   $ export OPENSSL_CONF=/etc/openvpn/cookbook/openssl-
   1.0.0.cnf
   ```

   Note that the `openssl-1.0.0.cnf` file is part of the easy-rsa distribution and should already be present in the directory `/etc/openvpn/cookbook`.

2. Next, we generate the certificate request without a password. This is achieved by adding the option `-nodes` to the `openssl req` command:

   ```
       $ openssl req -nodes -newkey rsa:2048 -new -out client.req \
         -subj "/C=NL/O=Cookbook/CN=MyClient"
   Generating a 2048 bit RSA private key
   .......................................++++++
   ............++++++
   writing new private key to 'privkey.pem'
   -----
   ```

3. Finally, we sign the certificate request using the Certificate Authority private key:

```
   $ openssl ca -in client.req -out client.crt
Using configuration from /etc/openvpn/cookbook/openssl.cnf
Enter pass phrase for /etc/openvpn/cookbook/keys/ca.key:
[enter CA key password]
Check that the request matches the signature
Signature ok
The Subject's Distinguished Name is as follows
countryName           :PRINTABLE:'NL'
organizationName      :PRINTABLE:'Cookbook'
commonName            :PRINTABLE:'MyClient'
Certificate is to be certified until Apr 20 15:08:25 2026 GMT
(3650 days)
Sign the certificate? [y/n]:y
1 out of 1 certificate requests certified, commit? [y/n]y
Write out database with 1 new entries
Data Base Updated
```

## How it works...

The first step is always to generate a private key. In this recipe, we generate a private key without a password, which is not really secure. A certificate request is signed using the private key to prove that the certificate request and the private key belong together. The `openssl req` command generates both the private key and the certificate requests in one go.

The second step is to sign the certificate request using the private key of the **Certificate Authority** (**CA**). This results in an X.509 certificate file, which can be used in OpenVPN.

A copy of the (public) X.509 certificate is also stored in the `/etc/openvpn/cookbook/keys` directory. This copy is important if the certificate needs to be revoked later on, so do not remove it from that directory.

## There's more...

It is also possible to generate a private key protected by a password ("pass phrase" in OpenSSL terms). In order to generate such a private key, simply remove the `-nodes` command line parameter:

```
$ openssl req -newkey rsa:1024 -new -out client.req \
    -subj "/C=NL/O=Cookbook/CN=MyClient"
```

The OpenSSL command will now ask for a passphrase:

```
Enter PEM pass phrase:
Verifying - Enter PEM pass phrase:
```

## See also

- The *Setting up the public and private keys* recipe from `Chapter 2`, *Client-server IP-only Networks*, where the initial setup of the PKI using the `easy-rsa` scripts is explained

# OpenSSL tricks – x509, pkcs12, verify output

The OpenSSL commands may seem daunting at first, but there are a lot of useful commands in the OpenSSL toolbox for viewing and managing X.509 certificates and private keys. This recipe will show how to use a few of those commands.

## Getting ready

Set up the `easy-rsa` certificate environment using the first recipe from `Chapter 2`, *Client-server IP-only Networks*, by sourcing the `vars` file. This recipe was performed on a computer running Fedora 22 Linux but it can easily be run on Windows or MacOS.

## How to do it...

For this recipe, we need to perform the following steps:

1. To view the subject and expiry date of a given certificate, type:

```
$ cd /etc/openvpn/cookbook/keys
$ openssl x509 -subject -enddate -noout -in client1.crt
  subject= /C=US/O=Cookbook 2.4/CN=client1
notAfter=Oct 13 17:54:30 2018 GMT
```

2. To export a certificate and private key in `PKCS12` format:

```
$ openssl pkcs12 -export -in client1.crt \
  -inkey client1.key -out client1.p12
   Enter Export Password:[Choose a strong password]
```

```
    Verifying - Enter Export Password:[Type the password again]
$ chmod 600 client1.p12
```

Note that the `chmod 600` ensures that the PKCS12 file is readable only by the user.

3. Verify the purpose of a given certificate:

```
$ openssl verify -purpose sslclient -CAfile ca.crt client1.crt
 client1.crt: OK
```

4. Notice the error if we select the wrong purpose (`sslclient` versus `sslserver`):

```
$ openssl verify -purpose sslclient -CAfile ca.crt server.crt
  server.crt: C = US, O = Cookbook 2.4, CN = openvpnserver
  error 26 at 0 depth lookup:unsupported certificate purpose
  OK
```

5. Change the password (passphrase) of a certificate:

```
$ openssl rsa -in client2.key -aes256 -out newclient.key
  Enter pass phrase for client2.key:[old password]
  writing RSA key
  Enter PEM pass phrase:[new password]
  Verifying - Enter PEM pass phrase:[new password]
```

# How it works...

The OpenSSL toolkit consists of a wide range of commands to generate, manipulate, and view X.509 certificates and their corresponding private keys. The commands in this chapter are but a small subset of the available commands. On Linux and UNIX systems, you can use `openssl -h` and the manual pages for `x509`, `pkcs12`, and `req` for more details. The manual pages are also available online at `http://www.openssl.org/docs/apps/openssl.html`.

Click on the OpenSSL commands lower down in the list of all commands for direct pointers.

# Revoking certificates

A common task when managing a PKI is to revoke certificates that are no longer needed or that have been compromised. This recipe demonstrates how certificates can be revoked using the `easy-rsa` script and how OpenVPN can be configured to make use of a **Certificate Revocation List** (**CRL**).

## Getting ready

Set up the client and server certificates using the first recipe from `Chapter 2`, *Client-server IP-only Networks*. This recipe was performed on a computer running CentOS 6 Linux, but it can easily be run on Windows or Mac OS.

## How to do it...

1. First, we generate a certificate:

```
$ cd /etc/openvpn/cookbook
$ . ./vars
$ ./build-key client4
[...]
```

2. Then, we immediately revoke it:

```
$ ./revoke-full client4
Using configuration from /etc/openvpn/cookbook/openssl-
1.0.0.cnf
Enter pass phrase for /etc/openvpn/cookbook/keys/ca.key:
Revoking Certificate 06.
Data Base Updated
Using configuration from /etc/openvpn/cookbook/openssl-
1.0.0.cnf
Enter pass phrase for /etc/openvpn/cookbook/keys/ca.key:
client4.crt: C = US, O = Cookbook 2.4, CN = client4
error 23 at 0 depth lookup:certificate revoked
```

3. This will also update the CRL list. The CRL can be viewed using the command:

```
$ openssl crl -text -noout -in keys/crl.pem
Certificate Revocation List (CRL):
        Version 1 (0x0)
    Signature Algorithm: sha256WithRSAEncryption
```

```
            Issuer: /C=US/O=Cookbook 2.4/CN=Cookbook 2.4
            CA/emailAddress=openvpn@example.com
            Last Update: Apr 22 15:54:10 2016 GMT
            Next Update: May 22 15:54:10 2016 GMT
    Revoked Certificates:
        Serial Number: 06
            Revocation Date: Apr 22 15:54:08 2016 GMT
        Signature Algorithm: sha256WithRSAEncryption
             12:8a:f0:b4:3e:aa:5b:a1:13:64:41:c7:0b:46:ef:00:99:50:
             6b:72:b8:2e:ff:93:eb:9b:7e:63:9e:8d:78:63:e8:96:44:30:
             5b:eb:3d:4a:a4:2a:36:1e:8c:c6:cd:11:63:b1:d5:88:31:46:
```

# How it works...

A CRL contains a list of certificate serial numbers that have been revoked. Each serial number can be handed out by a CA only once, so this serial number is unique to this particular CA. The CRL is signed using the CA's private key, ensuring that the CRL is indeed issued by the appropriate party.

# There's more...

The question “what exactly is needed to revoke a certificate” is often asked, so the following section goes a bit deeper into this.

## What is needed to revoke a certificate

In order to revoke a certificate, the certificate subject (“DN”) is required as well as the certificate serial number. If a certificate is lost, then it is simply not possible to revoke it. This shows how important it is to do proper PKI management, including backing up the certificates that have been handed out to users.

# See also

- The next recipe, *The use of CRLs*
- The recipe later in this chapter, *Multiple CA's: stacking, using the -capath directive*

# The use of CRLs

This recipe shows how to configure OpenVPN to use a CRL. It uses the CRL created in the previous recipe. This recipe is an extension of the recipe *Routing: masquerading* in `Chapter 2`, *Client-server IP-only Networks,* in the sense that the server and client configuration files are almost identical.

## Getting ready

Set up the client and server certificates using the first recipe from `Chapter 2`, *Client-server IP-only Networks*. Generate the CRL using the previous recipe. For this recipe, the server computer was running CentOS 6 Linux and OpenVPN 2.3.10. The client was running Fedora 22 Linux and OpenVPN 2.3.10. Keep the server configuration file `basic-udp-server.conf` from the *Server-side routing* recipe in `Chapter 2`, *Client-server IP-only Networks*.

## How to do it...

1. Copy the generated CRL to a more public directory:

```
[root@server]# cd /etc/openvpn/cookbook
[root@server]# cp keys/crl.pem .
```

2. Modify the server config file `basic-udp-server.conf` by adding the lines:

```
crl-verify /etc/openvpn/cookbook/crl.pem
```

   Save it as `example4-6-server.conf`.

3. Start the server:

```
[root@server]# openvpn --config example4-6-server.conf
```

4. Next, create the client configuration file:

```
client
proto udp
remote openvpnserver.example.com
port 1194
dev tun
nobind
```

```
remote-cert-tls server
tls-auth /etc/openvpn/cookbook/ta.key 1
ca       /etc/openvpn/cookbook/ca.crt
cert     /etc/openvpn/cookbook/client4.crt
key      /etc/openvpn/cookbook/client4.key
```

And save it as `example4-6-client.conf`.

5. Finally, start the client:

```
[root@client]# openvpn --config example4-6-client.conf
```

The client will not be able to connect but instead, the server log file shows:

```
[...] TLS_ERROR: BIO read tls_read_plaintext error: error:140890B2:SSL
      routines:SSL3_GET_CLIENT_CERTIFICATE:no certificate returned
[...] TLS Error: TLS object -> incoming plaintext read error
[...] TLS Error: TLS handshake failed
```

This rather cryptic message proves that the client is not allowed to connect because the certificate is not valid.

# How it works...

Each time a client connects to the OpenVPN server, the CRL is checked to see whether the client certificate is listed. If it is, the OpenVPN server simply refuses to accept the client certificate and the connection will not be established.

# There's more...

Generating a CRL is one thing and keeping it up-to-date is another. It is very important to ensure that the CRL is kept up-to-date. For this purpose, it is best to set up a cron job that updates the server CRL file overnight. There is an outstanding bug in OpenVPN related to CRL updates: each time a client connects, the OpenVPN server tries to access the CRL file. If the file is not present or not accessible, then the OpenVPN server process aborts with an error. The proper behavior would be to temporarily refuse access to the clients but unfortunately, this is not the case.

## See also

- The recipe later in this chapter, *Multiple CAs: stacking, using the -capath directive*, in which a more advanced use of CA and CRL is explained

# Checking expired/revoked certificates

The goal of this recipe is to give an insight into some of the internals of the OpenSSL CA commands. We will show how a certificate's status is changed from "Valid" to "Revoked", or "Expired".

## Getting ready

Set up the client and server certificates using the first recipe from `Chapter 2`, *Client-server IP-only Networks*. This recipe was performed on a computer running CentOS 6 Linux but it can easily be run on Windows or Mac OS.

## How to do it...

1. Before we can use plain `openssl` commands, there are a few environment variables that need to be set. These variables are not set in the `vars` file by default:

```
$ cd /etc/openvpn/cookbook
$ . ./vars
$ export KEY_NAME=
$ export OPENSSL_CONF=/etc/openvpn/cookbook/openssl-1.0.0.cnf
```

2. Now, we can query the status of a certificate using its serial number:

```
$ cd keys
$ openssl x509 -serial -noout -in server.crt
serial=01
$ openssl ca -status 01
Using configuration from /etc/openvpn/cookbook/openssl-
1.0.0.cnf
01=Valid (V)
```

This shows that our OpenVPN server certificate is still valid.

3. The certificate we revoked in the *Revoking certificates* recipe, shows the following:

```
$ openssl x509 -serial -noout -in client4.crt
serial=06
$ openssl ca -status 06
Using configuration from /etc/openvpn/cookbook/openssl-
1.0.0.cnf
08=Revoked (R)
```

4. If we look at the file `index.txt` in the `/etc/openvpn/cookbook/keys` directory, we see:

```
V 181013174924Z              01  unknown   .../CN=openvpnserver
R 190117155337Z 160422155408Z  06  unknown   .../CN=client4
```

5. Next, we modify this file using a normal text editor and replace the `R` with an `E` and we blank out the third field `160422155408Z` with spaces. This field is the timestamp when the certificate was revoked. The second line now becomes:

```
E  190117155337Z                    08 unknown .../CN=client4
```

6. Now, if we check the status again we get:

```
$ openssl ca -status 06
Using configuration from /etc/openvpn/cookbook/openssl-
1.0.0.cnf
08=Expired (E)
```

   If we generate the CRL again, we see that the certificate has been "un-revoked":

```
  $ openssl ca -gencrl -out crl.pem
  $ openssl crl -text -noout -in crl.pem  | head -8
Certificate Revocation List (CRL):
        Version 1 (0x0)
    Signature Algorithm: sha256WithRSAEncryption
        Issuer: /C=US/O=Cookbook 2.4/CN=Cookbook 2.4
        CA/emailAddress=openvpn@example.com
        Last Update: Apr 26 15:02:01 2016 GMT
        Next Update: May 26 15:02:01 2016 GMT
No Revoked Certificates.
    Signature Algorithm: sha256WithRSAEncryption
```

## How it works...

The OpenSSL `ca` command generates its CRL by looking at the `index.txt` file. Each line that starts with an `R` is added to the CRL, after which the CRL is cryptographically signed using the CA private key.

By changing the status of a revoked certificate to `E` or even `V` we can unrevoke a certificate.

## There's more...

In this recipe, we changed a certificate from `Revoked` to `Expired`. This will allow the client from the previous recipe to connect again to the server, as the certificate is still valid. The main reason to change a certificate from `Valid` to `Expired` in the `indext.txt` file is to allow us to generate and hand out a new certificate using the exact same name.

# Intermediary CAs

This recipe shows how to set up an intermediary CA and how to configure OpenVPN to make use of an intermediary CA. The OpenVPN `easy-rsa` scripts also include functionality to set up an intermediary CA. The advantage of an intermediary CA (or sub CA) is that the top-level CA (also known as the root CA) can be guarded more closely. The intermediary CAs can be distributed to the people responsible for generating the server and client certificates.

## Getting ready

Set up the client and server certificates using the first recipe from `Chapter 2`, *Client-server IP-only Networks*. This recipe was performed on a computer running CentOS 6 Linux but it can easily be run on Windows or Mac OS.

## How to do it...

1. First, we create the intermediary CA certificate:

```
$ cd /etc/openvpn/cookbook/
$ . ./vars
$ ./build-inter IntermediateCA
```

2. Verify that this certificate can indeed act as a Certificate Authority:

```
$ openssl x509 -text -noout -in keys/IntermediateCA.crt \
  | grep -C 1 CA
            X509v3 Basic Constraints:
                CA:TRUE
    Signature Algorithm: sha1WithRSAEncryption
```

3. Next, we create a new `keys` directory for our intermediary CA (the current directory is still `/etc/openvpn/cookbook`):

```
$ mkdir -m 700 -p IntermediateCA/keys
$ cp [a-z]* IntermediateCA
$ cd IntermediateCA
```

4. Edit the `vars` file in the new directory and change the `EASY_RSA` line to:

```
export EASY_RSA=/etc/openvpn/cookbook/IntermediateCA
```

5. Source this new `vars` file and set up the `keys` directory:

```
$ . ./vars
$ ./clean-all
$ cp ../keys/IntermediateCA.crt keys/ca.crt
$ cp ../keys/IntermediateCA.key keys/ca.key
```

6. Now we are ready to create our first intermediary certificate:

```
$ ./build-key IntermediateClient
```

7. Verify that the certificate has the new Intermediary CA as its issuer:

```
$ openssl x509 -subject -issuer -noout -in
keys/IntermediateClient.crt
   subject= /C=US/O=Cookbook 2.4/CN=IntermediateClient
   issuer= /C=US/O=Cookbook 2.4/CN=subCA/emailAddress=...
```

8. And finally, we verify that the certificate is indeed a valid certificate. In order to do this we need to "stack" the root CA (public) certificate and the intermediary CA certificate into a single file:

```
$ cd /etc/openvpn/cookbook
$ cat keys/ca.crt IntermediateCA/keys/ca.crt > ca+subca.pem
$ cp IntermediateCA/keys/IntermediateClient.{crt,key} .
$ openssl verify -CAfile ca+subca.pem IntermediateClient.crt
IntermediateClient.crt: OK
```

## How it works...

The intermediary CA certificate has the "right" to act as a certificate authority, meaning that it can sign new certificates itself. The intermediary CA needs a directory structure for this, which is very similar to the root CA directory structure. First, we set up this directory structure and then we copy over all the necessary files. After that we create a client certificate and verify that it is a valid certificate. In order to perform this validation, the entire certificate chain from the root-level CA to the intermediary CA to the client certificate need to be present. This is why the root CA public certificate and the intermediary CA public certificate are stacked into a single file. This single file is then used to perform the entire certificate chain validation.

## There's more...

Certificates that have been issued by an intermediary CA also need to be revoked by the same CA. This means that with multiple CAs you will also have to use multiple CRLs. Fortunately, CRLs can be stacked just like CA certificates: concatenate the files together using the `cat` command, as will be explained in the next recipe.

# Multiple CAs – stacking, using the capath directive

The goal of this recipe is to create an OpenVPN setup where the client certificates are signed by a "client-only" CA and the server certificate is signed by a different "server-only" CA. This provides an extra level of operational security, where one person is allowed to create only client certificates, whereas another is allowed to generate only a server certificate. This ensures that the client and server certificates can never be mixed for a Man-in-the-Middle attack.

## Getting ready

Set up the server certificate using the first recipe from `Chapter 2`, *Client-server IP-only Networks*. Use the client certificate and the intermediary CA certificate from the previous recipe. For this recipe, the server computer was running CentOS 6 Linux and OpenVPN 2.3.10. The client was running Fedora 22 Linux and OpenVPN 2.3.10.

# How to do it...

1. Create the server configuration file:

```
tls-server
proto udp
port 1194
dev tun

server 192.168.200.0 255.255.255.0

ca       /etc/openvpn/cookbook/ca+subca.pem
cert     /etc/openvpn/cookbook/server.crt
key      /etc/openvpn/cookbook/server.key
dh       /etc/openvpn/cookbook/dh1024.pem
tls-auth /etc/openvpn/cookbook/ta.key 0

persist-key
persist-tun
keepalive 10 60

user  nobody
group nobody

daemon
log-append /var/log/openvpn.log
```

   Save it as `example4-9-server.conf`.

2. Start the server:

```
[root@server]# openvpn --config example4-9-server.conf
```

3. Next, create the client configuration file:

```
client
proto udp
remote openvpnserver.example.com
port 1194

dev tun
nobind

tls-auth /etc/openvpn/cookbook/ta.key 1
ca       /etc/openvpn/cookbook/ca.crt
cert     /etc/openvpn/cookbook/IntermediateClient.crt
key      /etc/openvpn/cookbook/IntermediateClient.key
```

Save it as `example4-9-client.conf`. Note that we did not specify the `ca+subca.pem` file in the client configuration.

4. Start the client:

```
[root@client]# openvpn --config example4-9-client.conf
```

5. In the server log files, you can now see the client connecting using the certificate that was created by the Intermediary CA:

```
... openvpnclient:49283 [IntermediateClient] Peer Connection
Initiated with openvpnclient:49283
```

## How it works...

When the client connects to the server, the client (public) certificate is sent to the server for verification. The server needs to have access to the full certificate chain in order to do the verification; therefore, we stack the root CA certificate and the intermediary CA (or sub-CA) certificate together. This allows the client to connect to the server.

Vice versa, when the client connects, the server (public) certificate is also sent to the client. As the server certificate was originally signed by the root CA, we do not need to specify the full certificate stack here.

Note that if we had forgotten to specify the `ca+subca.pem` file in the OpenVPN server configuration file, we would have received an error:

```
openvpnclient:49286 VERIFY ERROR: depth=0, error=unable to get local issuer
certificate: C=US, O=Cookbook 2.4, CN=IntermediateClient
```

## There's more...

Apart from stacking the CA certificates, it is also possible to stack the CRLs or to use an entirely different mechanism to support multiple CA certificates and their corresponding CRLs.

## Using the –capath directive

Another way to include multiple CAs and CRLs in the OpenVPN server configuration is to use the following directive:

```
capath /etc/openvpn/cookbook/ca-dir
```

This directory needs to contain all CA certificates and CRLs using a special naming convention:

- All CA certificates must have a name equal to the hash of the CA certificate, and must end with `.0`
- All CRLs must have a name equal to the hash of the CA certificate, and must end with `.r0`

For our root CA and intermediary CA, we can achieve this using the following commands:

```
$ cd /etc/openvpn/cookbook
$ mkdir ca-dir
$ openssl x509 -hash -noout -in keys/ca.crt
bcd54da9
```

This hexadecimal number `bcd54da9` is the hash of the root CA certificate:

```
$ cp keys/ca.crt  ca-dir/bcd54da9.0
$ cp keys/crl.pem ca-dir/bcd54da9.r0
```

Similarly, for the intermediary CA certificate:

```
$ openssl x509 -hash -noout -in IntermediateCA/keys/ca.crt
1f5e4734
$ cp IntermediateCA/keys/ca.crt  ca-dir/1f5e4734.0
$ cp IntermediateCA/keys/crl.pem ca-dir/1f5e4734.r0
```

When using many different CA certificates and corresponding CRLs, this method is far easier to manage than the "stacked" files.

# Determining the crypto library to be used

Starting with OpenVPN 2.3, it became possible to build OpenVPN using either the OpenSSL cryptographic library or the PolarSSL library. The PolarSSL library is nowadays known as "mbedTLS". The PolarSSL library is used in the OpenVPN Connect apps for both Android and iOS, but the library can be used on all other supported platforms as well.

The goal of this recipe is to show how to determine which cryptographic library is used, including the run-time version number.

# Getting ready

Set up the server certificate using the first recipe from `Chapter 2`, *Client-server IP-only Networks*. Use the client certificate and the intermediary CA certificate from the previous recipe. For this recipe, the computer was running Fedora 22 Linux and OpenVPN 2.3.10, built both for OpenSSL and for PolarSSL. Keep the server configuration file `basic-udp-server.conf` from the *Server-side routing* recipe in `Chapter 2`, *Client-server IP-only Networks*.

# How to do it...

1. Start the regular version of OpenVPN using the standard configuration file:

```
[root@server]# openvpn --config  basic-udp-server.conf
```

2. Check the first few lines of the server log file:

```
    OpenVPN 2.3.10 x86_64-redhat-linux-gnu [SSL (OpenSSL)] [LZO]
[EPOLL] [PKCS11] [MH] [IPv6] built on Jan  4 2016

    library versions: OpenSSL 1.0.1e-fips 11 Feb 2013, LZO 2.08
```

3. Stop the server by killing the `openvpn` process.
4. Next, change the system's `LD_LIBRARY_PATH` to point to a more recent version of OpenSSL:

```
[root@server]# export LD_LIBRARY_PATH=..../openssl-1.0.1s
[root@server]# openvpn --config  basic-udp-server.conf
```

5. Check the first few lines of the server log file:

```
    OpenVPN 2.3.10 x86_64-redhat-linux-gnu [SSL (OpenSSL)] [LZO]
 [EPOLL] [PKCS11] [MH] [IPv6] built on Jan  4 2016

    library versions: OpenSSL 1.0.1s  1 Mar 2016, LZO 2.08
```

6. Again, stop the server by killing the `openvpn` process.

7. Switch to the PolarSSL-built version of OpenVPN and start the server again:

```
[root@server]# .../openvpn-2.3.10polarssl/openvpn --config
basic-udp-server.conf
```

8. Check the first few lines of the server log file:

```
    OpenVPN 2.3.10 x86_64-unknown-linux-gnu [SSL (PolarSSL)] [LZO]
[EPOLL] [MH] [IPv6] built on Apr 27 2016

    library versions: PolarSSL 1.3.16, LZO 2.08
```

# How it works...

When OpenVPN starts the cryptographics libraries are loaded and initialized. At this point, the library's version string is retrieved and printed. By using different builds of the crypto libraries we see that only the few first lines of the server logfile alter.

# There's more...

The type and build of cryptographics library used determine some of the more advanced features of OpenVPN, as we will see in the next few recipes. The library version string provides vital information for debugging a non-working setup, as we will see in `Chapter 6`, *Troubleshooting OpenVPN – Configurations*.

# See also

- The next recipe, in which the differences between the cryptographic libraries is explained
- The *How to read the OpenVPN log files* recipe, from `Chapter 6`, *Troubleshooting OpenVPN – Configurations*, which shows in detail how to read the OpenVPN log files

# Crypto features of OpenSSL and PolarSSL

As stated in the previous recipe, it has been possible to build OpenVPN using either the OpenSSL cryptographic library or the PolarSSL library since version 2.3. In this recipe, we will show what some of the key differences between the two cryptographic libraries are.

## Getting ready

Set up the server certificate using the first recipe from `Chapter 2`, *Client-server IP-only Networks*. Use the client certificate and the intermediary CA certificate from the previous recipe. For this recipe, the computer was running Fedora 22 Linux and OpenVPN 2.3.10, built both for OpenSSL and for PolarSSL.

## How to do it...

1. Start the regular version of OpenVPN with the `--show-ciphers` option:

   ```
   [root@server]# openvpn --show-ciphers
   ```

2. OpenVPN will now list all available ciphers, which can easily exceed 50 ciphers for OpenSSL 1.0+. The most common ciphers are:

   ```
   BF-CBC 128 bit default key (variable)
   BF-CFB 128 bit default key (variable) (TLS client/server...)
   BF-OFB 128 bit default key (variable) (TLS client/server...)
   AES-128-CBC 128 bit default key (fixed)
   AES-128-OFB 128 bit default key (fixed) (TLS client...)
   AES-128-CFB 128 bit default key (fixed) (TLS client...)
   AES-256-CBC 256 bit default key (fixed)
   AES-256-OFB 256 bit default key (fixed) (TLS client...)
   AES-256-CFB 256 bit default key (fixed) (TLS client...)
   AES-128-CFB1 128 bit default key (fixed) (TLS client...)
   AES-192-CFB1 192 bit default key (fixed) (TLS client...)
   AES-256-CFB1 256 bit default key (fixed) (TLS client...)
   AES-128-CFB8 128 bit default key (fixed) (TLS client...)
   AES-192-CFB8 192 bit default key (fixed) (TLS client...)
   AES-256-CFB8 256 bit default key (fixed) (TLS client...)
   ```

3. Next, switch to the PolarSSL-built version of OpenVPN and re-run the same command:

```
[root@server]# .../openvpn-2.3.10polarssl/openvpn --show-
ciphers
```

4. The list of ciphers now is:

```
AES-128-CBC 128 bit default key
AES-192-CBC 192 bit default key
AES-256-CBC 256 bit default key
BF-CBC 128 bit default key
CAMELLIA-128-CBC 128 bit default key
CAMELLIA-192-CBC 192 bit default key
CAMELLIA-256-CBC 256 bit default key
DES-CBC 64 bit default key
DES-EDE-CBC 128 bit default key
DES-EDE3-CBC 192 bit default key
```

5. Start the regular version of OpenVPN with the `--show-digests` option:

```
[root@server]# openvpn --show-digests
```

6. OpenVPN will now list all available HMAC algorithms, which can be specified using the `--auth` option. This list can easily exceed 25 entries, therefore only the most commonly used are printed:

```
MD5 128 bit digest size
SHA 160 bit digest size
RIPEMD160 160 bit digest size
ecdsa-with-SHA1 160 bit digest size
SHA224 224 bit digest size
SHA256 256 bit digest size
SHA384 384 bit digest size
SHA512 512 bit digest size
```

7. Next, switch to the PolarSSL-built version of OpenVPN and re-run the same command:

```
[root@server]# .../openvpn-2.3.10polarssl/openvpn --show-
digests
```

8. The list of HMAC algorithms now is:

```
SHA512 512 bit default key
SHA384 384 bit default key
SHA256 256 bit default key
```

```
SHA224 224 bit default key
SHA1 160 bit default key
RIPEMD160 160 bit default key
MD5 128 bit default key
```

# How it works...

When OpenVPN starts the cryptographics libraries are loaded and initialized. Only at that point are the available encryption algorithms and HMAC algorithms known. Both OpenSSL and PolarSSL provide a mechanism for retrieving the list of available algorithms, which OpenVPN uses for both the `--show-ciphers` and the `--show-digests` options.

This recipe shows that the PolarSSL/mbed-TLS library does not support all of the algorithms that OpenSSL does. When you need to support a PolarSSL-built version of OpenVPN (like the OpenVPN Connect clients for Android and iOS) then you can use only ciphers or digests (`--auth` parameter) which are supported by both crypto libraries.

# There's more...

Apart from the data channel cipher and HMAC algorithms, there is one more set of available algorithms that can be listed. This is the set of TLS algorithms that can be used for encrypting and authenticating the control channel. In order to list the set of TLS parameters, use the following command:

```
openvpn --show-tls
```

## AEAD Ciphers

Starting with OpenVPN 2.4, a new set of ciphers is supported. These ciphers are known as **AEAD** ciphers, which stands for **Authenticated Encryption with Associated Data**. These ciphers combine encryption with authentication, thereby removing the need for a separate HMAC algorithm and thus providing increased performance. Both OpenSSL 1.0+ and mbed-TLS 1.3+ support these ciphers. With OpenVPN 2.4+, the list of ciphers will include:

- AES-128-GCM
- AES-192-GCM
- AES-256-GCM

## Encryption speed

Another major difference between OpenSSL and PolarSSL is the encryption/decryption speed of the algorithms. OpenSSL included hand-tuned assembly routines for maximum encryption speed, especially for the AES algorithms on newer Intel CPUs. However, the encryption speed is not the most important factor when determining the throughput of an OpenVPN network, as we will see in `Chapter 8`, *Performance Tuning*.

# Pushing ciphers

Another new feature of OpenVPN 2.4+ is the ability to "push" a cipher or HMAC algorithm from the server to the client. This makes it much easier to switch encryption or HMAC authentication algorithms, provided that all clients are using OpenVPN 2.4. This recipe provides a setup for explicitly pushing a cipher, as well as an explanation of the new cipher negotiation protocol.

## Getting ready

This recipe uses the PKI files created in the first recipe from `Chapter 2`, *Client-server IP-only Networks*. For this recipe, the server computer was running CentOS 6 Linux and OpenVPN 2.4.0. The client was running Fedora 22 Linux and OpenVPN 2.4.0. For the server, keep the server configuration file `basic-udp-server.conf` from the *Server-side routing* recipe in `Chapter 2`, *Client-server IP-only Networks*. For the Windows client, keep the corresponding client configuration file `basic-udp-client.ovpn`, from the *Using an ifconfig-pool block* recipe in `Chapter 2`, *Client-server IP-only Networks*.

## How to do it...

1. Modify the server configuration file, `basic-udp-server.conf`, by adding the following lines:

   ```
   cipher aes-256-gcm
   push "cipher aes-256-gcm"
   ```

   Then save it as `example4-10-server.conf`.

2. Start the server:

   ```
   [root@server]# openvpn --config example4-10-server.conf
   ```

3. Start the client using the "standard" configuration file but with verbose logging:

```
    [root@client]# openvpn --config basic-udp-client.conf --
    verb 4
Data Channel Encrypt: Cipher 'BF-CBC' initialized with 128 bit
key
Data Channel Encrypt: Using 160 bit message hash 'SHA1' for
HMAC authentication
Data Channel Decrypt: Cipher 'BF-CBC' initialized with 128 bit
key
Data Channel Decrypt: Using 160 bit message hash 'SHA1' for
HMAC authentication
Control Channel: TLSv1.2, cipher TLSv1/SSLv3 ECDHE-RSA-AES256-
GCM-SHA384, 2048 bit RSA
[...]
OPTIONS IMPORT: data channel crypto options modified
[...]
Data Channel Encrypt: Cipher 'AES-256-GCM' initialized with 256
bit key
Data Channel Decrypt: Cipher 'AES-256-GCM' initialized with 256
bit key
```

   The output showing that OpenVPN is now using an AES-256 cipher is shown in bold face.

4. Verify that we can reach the server using the `ping` command:

```
      [client]$   ping -c 4  10.200.0.1
PING 10.200.0.1 (10.200.0.1) 56(84) bytes of data.
64 bytes from 10.200.0.1: icmp_seq=1 ttl=64 time=9.23 ms
64 bytes from 10.200.0.1: icmp_seq=2 ttl=64 time=8.78 ms
64 bytes from 10.200.0.1: icmp_seq=3 ttl=64 time=10.0 ms
64 bytes from 10.200.0.1: icmp_seq=4 ttl=64 time=9.00 ms
--- 10.200.0.1 ping statistics ---
4 packets transmitted, 4 received, 0% packet loss, time 3004ms
rtt min/avg/max/mdev = 8.780/9.259/10.022/0.468 ms
```

# How it works...

Pushing a cipher is now just as simple as pushing other OpenVPN options. Versions prior to 2.4 did not support this, however. This allows VPN administrators to change the encryption parameters used without having to modify all (remote) client configuration files.

# There's more...

Starting with OpenVPN 2.4 a new cipher negotiation protocol is introduced. At startup, the client and server will check whether both sides support the new GCM encryption protocols. The strongest cipher from this list is then chosen as the cipher. If no match is found, then OpenVPN reverts to the default BlowFish (BF-CBC) cipher, to ensure backward compatibility.

This feature can be tuned using the new directives `ncp-ciphers` and `disable-ncp`. The first directive specifies the list of ciphers to negotiate, whereas the second directive turns off cipher negotiation altogether.

When explicitly pushing a cipher from the server to the client you can only specify a cipher from the NCP cipher list. The default NCP cipher list is AES-256-GCM:AES-128-CGM:BF-CBC.

```
ccp-ciphers
push "auth SHA512"
```

## Future enhancements

It is expected that future enhancements of this new feature will be:

- A separate control channel HMAC algorithm so that you can switch the data channel algorithm independently
- The ability to set a "per-client" encryption cipher, allowing you to support different ciphers for different platforms and clients

# Elliptic curve support

In version 2.4 of OpenVPN support was added for using **elliptic curve** (**EC**) certificates instead of the more common RSA type certificates. **Elliptic curve cryptography** (**ECC**) provides a fast method for encrypting and authenticating a secure connection, but are not widely used yet. In part, this is due to some patenting issues. As most modern OpenSSL libraries provide ECC support, however, OpenVPN can also use EC certificates. The main advantage of ECC is that you can provide smaller keys to achieve the same level of security than with the more common RSA and DSA type encryption. This will result in a better VPN performance without sacrificing security. As we will see in this recipe, OpenVPN's control channel can be authenticated using an EC algorithm. The data channel is still authenticated using a non-EC HMAC algorithm, such as SHA1.

## Getting ready

For this recipe, the server computer was running CentOS 6 Linux and OpenVPN 2.4.0. The client was running Fedora 22 Linux and OpenVPN 2.4.0.

## How to do it...

1. We first need to generate a new EC-based Certificate Authority:

```
$ export KEY_CN=
$ export KEY_OU=
$ export KEY_NAME=
$ export OPENSSL_CONF=/etc/openvpn/cookbook/openssl-
1.0.0.cnf
$ openssl ecparam -out cakey_temp.pem \
    -name sect571k1 -text -genkey
$ openssl ec -in cakey_temp.pem -out ec-ca.key -aes256
$ openssl req -new -x509 -out ec-ca.crt -key ec-ca.key
    -days 3650 -sha512 -extensions v3_ca
    -subj "/C=US/O=Cookbook 2.4/CN=Elliptic Curve CA"
```

   This will result in an `ec-ca.crt` and `ec-ca.key` file using the `sect571k1` elliptic curve that we will use to sign the EC-based client and server certificates.

2. Next, generate the new EC server certificate:

```
$ openssl req -nodes -sha512 -newkey ec:ec-ca.crt
    -new -days 400 -out ec-server.req
    -keyout ec-server.key
    -subj "/C=US/O=Cookbook 2.4/CN=ecserver"
$ chmod 600 ec-server.key
$ openssl x509 -req
   -extfile $OPENSSL_CONF
   -extensions server
   -out ec-server.crt -sha512 -CA ec-ca.crt
   -CAkey ec-ca.key  -in ec-server.req
   -set_serial $RANDOM
```

   This will result in an `ec-server.crt` and `ec-server.key` file.

3. Similarly, generate the new EC client certificate:

```
$ openssl req -nodes -sha512
   -newkey ec:ec-ca.crt
```

```
        -new -days 400
        -out ec-client.req -keyout ec-client.key
        -subj "/C=US/O=Cookbook 2.4/CN=ecclient"
    $ chmod 600 ec-client.key
    $ openssl x509 -req -extfile $OPENSSL_CONF
        -extensions usr_cert
        -out ec-client.crt -sha512 -CA ec-ca.crt
        -CAkey ec-ca.key -in ec-client.req
        -set_serial $RANDOM
```

This will result in an `ec-client.crt` and `ec-client.key` file.

4. Create the server configuration file:

```
proto udp
port 1194
dev tun
server 10.200.0.0 255.255.255.0

ca   /etc/openvpn/cookbook/ec-ca.crt
cert /etc/openvpn/cookbook/ec-server.crt
key  /etc/openvpn/cookbook/ec-server.key
dh   /etc/openvpn/cookbook/dh2048.pem
```

Save it as `example4-11-server.conf`.

5. Start the server:

```
[root@server]# openvpn --config example4-11-server.conf
```

6. Next, create the client configuration file:

```
client
proto udp
remote openvpnserver.example.com
port 1194
dev tun
nobind

ca /etc/openvpn/cookbook/ec-ca.crt
cert /etc/openvpn/cookbook/ec-client.crt
key /etc/openvpn/cookbook/ec-client.key
verb 4
```

Then save it as `example4-11-client.conf`.

7. Transfer the files such as `ec-ca.crt`, `ec-client.crt`, and `ec-client.key` to the client machine using a secure channel.
8. Finally, start the client:

```
[root@client]# openvpn --config example4-11-client.conf
```

   And observe the chosen control channel cipher:

```
Control Channel: TLSv1.2, cipher TLSv1/SSLv3 ECDHE-ECDSA-
AES256-GCM-SHA384
```

   This shows that the control channel is protected using an ECDSA-based cipher.

## How it works...

By generating an EC-based Certificate Authority and by using EC-based certificates OpenVPN can now support elliptic curve cryptography on the control channel. The data channel is still protected using the default cipher BF-CBC (Blowfish) and the default HMAC algorithm SHA1.

It should be noted that with RSA-based certificates the control channel cipher looks remarkably similar:

```
Control Channel: TLSv1.2, cipher TLSv1/SSLv3 ECDHE-RSA-AES256-GCM-SHA384,
2048 bit RSA
```

It is not the “ECDHE” part which proves that ECC is used, but “ECDSA”.

## There's more...

It is also possible to choose different ECDH “curves”. This is done by first listing the available ECDH curves on the OpenVPN server:

```
[root@server]# openvpn --show-curves
Available Elliptic curves:
[...]
secp112r1
secp112r2
secp521r1
prime192v1
prime192v2
[...]
```

And then by adding the option to the server configuration file:

```
ecdh-curve secp521r1
```

## Elliptic curve support

Not all Linux distributions provide an OpenSSL library that supports elliptic curve cryptography out of the box. Notably RedHat-based and RedHat-derived distributions, such as RedHat Enterprise Linux, CentOS and Fedora explicitly disable ECC support. RedHat cites patent issues as the reason, but the "default" OpenSSL library ships with full ECC support.

As the Linux distributions used throughout this book are CentOS and Fedora, a custom build of the OpenSSL 1.0.2 library was made especially for this recipe.

# 5

# Scripting and Plugins

In this chapter, we will cover the following recipes:

- Using a client-side up/down script
- Using a `client-connect` script
- Using a `learn-address` script
- Using a `tls-verify` script
- Using an `auth-user-pass-verify` script
- Script order
- Script security and logging
- Scripting and IPv6
- Using the `down-root` plugin
- Using the PAM authentication plugin

## Introduction

One of the most powerful features of OpenVPN is its scripting capability and the ability to extend OpenVPN itself through the use of plugins. Using client-side scripting, the connection process can be tailored to the site-specific needs, such as setting up advanced routing options, adding firewall rules or mapping network drives. With server-side scripting, it is possible to assign a custom IP address to different clients, or to extend the authentication process by adding an extra username and password check. Plugins are very useful when integrating OpenVPN authentication into existing authentication frameworks, such as PAM, LDAP, or even Active Directory.

In this chapter, the focus will be on scripting, both at the client side and at the server side, and on a few often-used plugins.

# Using a client-side up/down script

In this recipe, we will use very simple `up` and `down` scripts on the client side to show how OpenVPN calls these scripts. By logging messages to a file, as well as the environment variables, we can easily see which information OpenVPN provides to the `up` and `down` scripts.

## Getting ready

Set up the client and server certificates using the *Setting up the public and private keys* recipe from `Chapter 2`, *Client-server IP-only Networks*. For this recipe, the server computer was running Fedora 22 Linux and OpenVPN 2.3.10. The client was running Windows 7 64 bit and OpenVPN 2.3.10. Keep the server configuration file, `basic-udp-server.conf`, from the *Server-side routing* recipe, from `Chapter 2`, *Client-server IP-only Networks*.

## How to do it...

1. Start the server:

```
[root@server]# openvpn --config basic-udp-server.conf
```

2. Create the client configuration file:

```
client
proto udp
remote openvpnserver.example.com
port 1194
dev tun
nobind

ca       "c:/program files/openvpn/config/ca.crt"
cert     "c:/program files/openvpn/config/client2.crt"
key      "c:/program files/openvpn/config/client2.key"
tls-auth "c:/program files/openvpn/config/ta.key"" 1

remote-cert-tls server
script-security 2
up   "c:\\program\ files\\openvpn\\scripts\\updown.bat"
down "c:\\program\ files\\openvpn\\scripts\\updown.bat"
```

Save the file as `example5-1.ovpn`. Note the backslashes: when specifying the `ca`, `cert`, `key`, and `tls-auth` directives, forward slashes can be used, but not for the `up` and `down` scripts!

3. Next, on the Windows client, create the batch file `updown.bat` batch file in the `C:\Program Files\OpenVPN\scripts` directory:

```
@echo off
echo === BEGIN '%script_type%' script === >>
c:\temp\openvpn.log
echo Script name: [%0] >> c:\temp\openvpn.log
echo Command line argument 1: [%1] >> c:\temp\openvpn.log
echo Command line argument 2: [%2] >> c:\temp\openvpn.log
echo Command line argument 3: [%3] >> c:\temp\openvpn.log
echo Command line argument 4: [%4] >> c:\temp\openvpn.log
echo Command line argument 5: [%5] >> c:\temp\openvpn.log
echo Command line argument 6: [%6] >> c:\temp\openvpn.log
echo Command line argument 7: [%7] >> c:\temp\openvpn.log
echo Command line argument 8: [%8] >> c:\temp\openvpn.log
echo Command line argument 9: [%9] >> c:\temp\openvpn.log
set >> c:\temp\openvpn.log
echo === END '%script_type%' script === >>
c:\temp\openvpn.log
```

4. Finally, start the OpenVPN client:

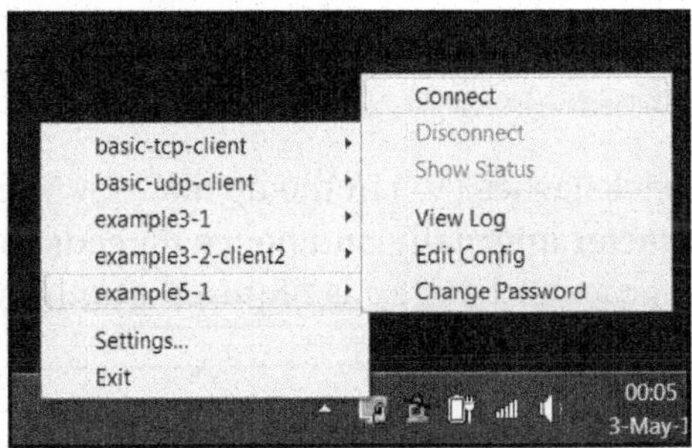


After the client successfully connects to the OpenVPN server, the `c:\temp\openvpn.log` log file will contain an output similar to the following:

```
=== BEGIN 'up' script ===
Script name: ["c:\program files\openvpn\scripts\updown.bat"]
Command line argument 1: [Local Area Connection 2]
Command line argument 2: [1500]
Command line argument 3: [1541]
Command line argument 4: [10.200.0.2]
```

```
Command line argument 5: [255.255.255.0]

Command line argument 6: [init]
Command line argument 7: []
Command line argument 8: []
Command line argument 9: []
...
script_type=up
[dump of environment variables]
...
=== END 'up' script ===
```

When the client disconnects from the server, the script is called again, with the exact same command-line parameters, but now the `script_type` is set to `down`.

Note that the first command-line argument contains the name of the `TUN` device. On Linux and Mac OS systems, this will generally be `tun0` or `tun1`, but on Windows platforms, it is the actual name of the TAP-Win32 adapter.

# How it works...

After the initial connection is made with the OpenVPN server, but before the VPN is fully established, the OpenVPN client calls the `up` script. If the `up` script returns with an exit code not equal to zero, the connection sequence is aborted.

Similarly, when the connection is shut down the `down` script is executed after the VPN connection has been stopped.

Note the use of the double backslashes (\\) in the `up` and `down` directives: OpenVPN translates the backslash character internally and hence it needs to be specified twice. The backslash between `c:\\program` and `files` is required as otherwise OpenVPN cannot find the `up` and `down` scripts without it.

# There's more...

In this section, we will see some more advanced tricks when using the `up` and `down` scripts, including a sample script to verify the remote hostname of a VPN server.

## Environment variables

The script used in this recipe merely writes out all the environment variables to a file. These environment variables contain useful information about the remote server, such as the `common_name` certificate. An extension to this script would be to check whether the `common_name` certificate matches the remote hostname. The IP address of the remote hostname is available as `trusted_ip`.

## Calling the down script before the connection terminates

The `down` script is executed after the actual connection to the OpenVPN server has been stopped. It is also possible to execute the script during the disconnect phase before the connection to the server is dropped. To do this, add the following directive to the client configuration file:

```
down-pre
```

## Advanced – verify the remote hostname

A more advanced usage of an `up` script would be to verify that the remote hostname matches the remote IP address, similar to the way that a web browser verifies the address of secure websites. On Linux systems, this can easily be done using a shell script as an `up` script:

```
#!/bin/bash

# reverse DNS lookup
server_name=`host $untrusted_ip | \
  sed -n 's/.*name pointer \(.*\)\./\1/p'
if [ "$server_name" != "$common_name" ]
then
    echo "Server certificate does not match hostname."
    echo "Aborting"
    exit 1
fi
```

But on Windows, this is trickier to achieve without resorting to tools such as PowerShell or Cygwin.

# Using a client-connect script

This recipe will demonstrate how to set up a client-connect script that gets executed on the server side when a new client connects. Similarly, we can specify a `client-disconnect` script that is executed when a client disconnects from the server. Client-connect and client-disconnect scripts can be used for several purposes:

- Extra authentication
- Opening and closing firewall ports
- Assigning specific IP address to special clients
- Writing out connection-specific configuration lines for a client

In this recipe, we will use a client-connect script to disable client access to the client with a `client2` certificate between 10 p.m. (or 22:00 hours) and 6 a.m. During other hours, a static IP is assigned to this client.

## Getting ready

Install OpenVPN 2.3 or higher on two computers. Make sure that the computers are connected over a network. Set up the client and server certificates using the first recipe from `Chapter 2`, *Client-server IP-only Networks*. For this recipe, the server computer was running Fedora 22 Linux and OpenVPN 2.3.10. The client was running Windows 7 64 bit and OpenVPN 2.3.10. Keep the server configuration file, `basic-udp-server.conf`, from the *Server-side routing* recipe, from `Chapter 2`, *Client-server IP-only Networks*, at hand. For the client, keep the client configuration file, `basic-udp-client.ovpn`, from the *Using an ifconfig-pool block* recipe from `Chapter 2`, *Client-server IP-only Networks*, at hand.

## How to do it...

1. Append the following lines to the `basic-udp-server.conf` server configuration file:

   ```
   script-security 2
   client-connect    /etc/openvpn/cookbook/example5-2-connect.sh
   ```

2. Save it as `example5-2-server.conf`.

3. Next, create the connect script:

```
#!/bin/bash

if [ "x$common_name" = "xclient2" ]
then
  hour= /bin/date +"%H"
  if [ $hour -lt 6 -o $hour -gt 22 ]
  then
    echo "disable" > $1
  else
    echo "ifconfig-push 10.200.0.200 255.255.255.0"
  fi
fi
```

4. Save this file as `example5-2-connect.sh`.
5. Make sure that the script is executable:

```
[root@server]# chmod 755 example5-2-connect.sh
```

6. Start the server:

```
[root@server]# openvpn --config example5-2-server.conf
```

7. Start the OpenVPN client:

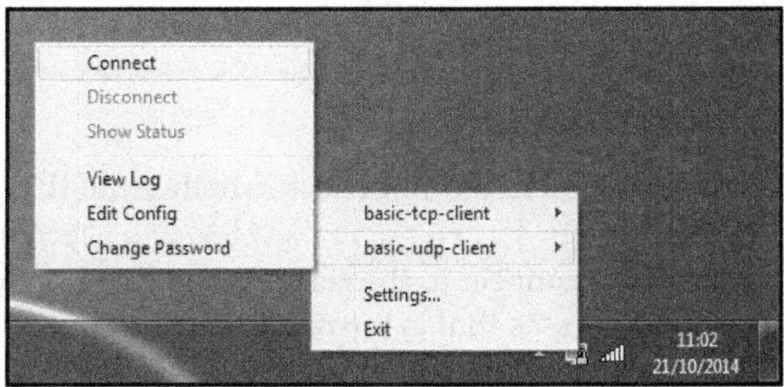


8. If the client is started after 6 am and before 10 p.m., the connection will be established successfully. Otherwise, the client log file will show lines similar to the following:

```
us=70083 SENT CONTROL [openvpnserver]: 'PUSH_REQUEST'
(status=1)
```

Also, the server log will more clearly state the reason for the connection refusal:

```
client2/192.168.3.22:57870 MULTI: client has been rejected due
to 'disable' directive
```

# How it works...

When a client connects, the OpenVPN server executes the `client-connect` script with several environment variable sets that are related to the client connecting. The script writes out two lines to the connect-specific configuration file, which is passed as the first and only parameter to the `client-connect` script. This configuration file is then processed by the OpenVPN server as if it's a normal configuration file. The two possible lines that we use are `disable` and `ifconfig-push 10.200.0.200 255.255.255.0`.

The first option disables a client from connecting. The second option pushes a pre-defined IP to the client.

# There's more...

In this section, we focus on `client-disconnect` and the many environment variables that are available to all OpenVPN scripts.

## Pitfall in using ifconfig-push

The `client-connect` script used here did not check whether the IP address that was assigned using the `ifconfig-push 10.200.0.200 255.255.255.0` command was actually available. If many clients connect to the server, then this IP address will also be assigned from the pool of IP addresses that is formed as a result of the `server 10.200.0.0 255.255.255.0` statement.

When assigning static IP addresses to a client, it is best to assign them from a special subnet.

## The client-disconnect scripts

A `client-disconnect` script can be specified using the following:

```
client-disconnect /etc/openvpn/cookbook/disconnect.sh
```

This script is executed when the client disconnects from the server. Be aware that when a client first disconnects and `explicit-exit-notify` is not specified on the client side, then the OpenVPN server will first try to reconnect several times to the client. If a client does not respond after several attempts, then the `client-disconnect` script will be executed. Depending on the server configuration, this might be several minutes after the client has actually disconnected. When using TCP connections, it is not needed to specify `explicit-exit-notify`, as the client is disconnected immediately when the TCP connection stops.

## Environment variables

There is a multitude of environment variables available inside a client-connect and client-disconnect script. It is very instructive to write a `client-connect` script that does a little more than the following:

```
#!/bin.bash
env >> /tmp/log
```

Also, similar to the `up` and `down` script, is the `script_type` environment variable that contains the type of script as configured in the server configuration file. This gives the server administrator the option to write a single script for both `client-connect` and `client-disconnect`.

## Absolute paths

Note that an absolute path is used for the script. Relative paths are allowed, but especially for the OpenVPN server, it is more secure to use absolute paths. Assuming that the OpenVPN server is always started in the same directory is a bad security practice. An alternative is to use the following:

```
cd /etc/openvpn/cookcook
client-connect example5-2-connect.sh
```

# Using a learn-address script

This recipe will demonstrate how to set up a `learn-address` script that is executed on the server side when there is a change in the address of a connecting client. Learn-address scripts can be used to dynamically set up firewalling rules for specific clients or to adjust routing tables.

In this recipe, we will use a `learn-address` script to open up a firewall and to set up masquerading for a client. When the client disconnects, the firewall is closed again and the `iptables` masquerading rule is removed.

# Getting ready

Install OpenVPN 2.3 or higher on two computers. Make sure that the computers are connected over a network. Set up the client and server certificates using the first recipe from `Chapter 2`, *Client-server IP-only Networks*. For this recipe, the server computer was running Fedora 22 Linux and OpenVPN 2.3.10, and the client was running Windows 7 64 bit and OpenVPN 2.3.10. For the client, keep the client configuration file, `basic-udp-client.ovpn`, from the *Using an ifconfig-pool block* recipe, from `Chapter 2`, *Client-server IP-only Networks*.

# How to do it...

1. Create the server configuration file:

```
proto udp
port 1194
dev tun

server 10.200.0.0 255.255.255.0

ca       /etc/openvpn/cookbook/ca.crt
cert     /etc/openvpn/cookbook/server.crt
key      /etc/openvpn/cookbook/server.key
dh       /etc/openvpn/cookbook/dh2048.pem
tls-auth /etc/openvpn/cookbook/ta.key 0

persist-key
persist-tun
keepalive 10 60

topology subnet

daemon
log-append /var/log/openvpn.log
script-security 2
learn-address /etc/openvpn/cookbook/example5-3-learn-address.sh
push "redirect-gateway def1"
```

2. Save it as `example5-3-server.conf`. Note that this server configuration file does not have the lines `user nobody` and `group nobody` (nor `group nogroup`).

3. Next, create the `learn-address` script:

```
#!/bin/bash

# $1 = action (add, update, delete)
# $2 = IP or MAC
# $3 = client_common name

if [ "$1" = "add" ]
then
    /sbin/iptables -I FORWARD -i tun0 -s $2 -j ACCEPT
    /sbin/iptables -I FORWARD -o tun0 -d $2 -j ACCEPT
    /sbin/iptables -t nat -I POSTROUTING -s $2 -o wlan0 -j
    MASQUERADE
elif [ "$1" = "delete" ]
then
    /sbin/iptables -D FORWARD -i tun0 -s $2 -j ACCEPT
    /sbin/iptables -D FORWARD -o tun0 -d $2 -j ACCEPT
    /sbin/iptables -t nat -D POSTROUTING -s $2 -o wlan0 -j
    MASQUERADE
fi
```

4. Save this file as `example5-3-learn-address.sh`.
5. Make sure that the script is executable and start the OpenVPN server:

```
[root@server]# chmod 755 example5-3-learn-address.sh
[root@server]# openvpn --config example5-3-server.conf
```

6. Start the client using the Windows GUI using the basic configuration file:

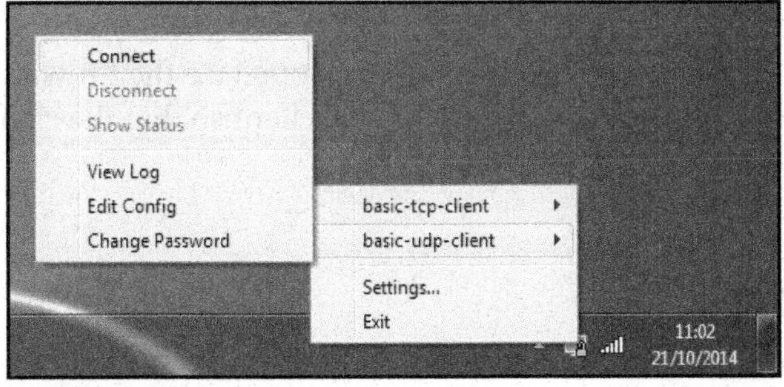

7. After the client connects to the server, check the `iptables` firewall rules on the server:

```
[root@server]# iptables -L FORWARD -n -v
Chain FORWARD (policy ACCEPT 4612K packets, 1761M bytes)
 pkts bytes target     prot opt in     out     source
destination
    0     0 ACCEPT     all  --  *      tun0    0.0.0.0/0
10.200.0.2
    0     0 ACCEPT     all  --  tun0   *       10.200.0.2
0.0.0.0/0
```

```
[root@server]# iptables -t nat -L POSTROUTING -n -v
Chain POSTROUTING (policy ACCEPT 336K packets, 20M bytes)
 pkts bytes target     prot opt in     out     source
destination
    0     0 MASQUERADE  all  --  *      wlan0   10.200.0.2
0.0.0.0/0
```

8. Disconnect the client, wait for a few minutes, and then verify that the `iptables` rules have been removed.

# How it works...

When a client connects to the OpenVPN server or disconnects from it, the OpenVPN server executes the `learn-address` script with several command-line arguments:

- `$1`: Action (add, update, delete).
- `$2`: IP or MAC. For tun-based networks, this is the client IP address. For tap-based networks, this is the client (virtual) MAC address.
- `$3`: `client_common` name.

In this recipe, the `learn-address` script is used to open up the firewall for the connecting client and to set up the masquerading rules for the client so that the clients can reach the other machines on the server-side LAN.

# There's more...

In the following section, some details of the use of the `user nobody` directive and the `update` action of the `learn-address` script are given.

## User nobody

As stated earlier, this server configuration does not include the following lines:

```
user nobody
group nobody
```

Or, on some Linux distributions, it can be as follows:

```
group
nogroup
```

If we had added these lines, then the OpenVPN server process would be running as user `nobody`. This user does not have the required rights to open and close firewall ports using `iptables`, hence they were removed in this example.

## The update action

The `learn-address` script is also called when the OpenVPN server detects an address change on the client side. This can happen most often in a TAP-based network when an external DHCP server is used. The `learn-address` script can then adjust routing tables or firewalling rules based on the new client IP address, using the `update` action.

Another method to generate a `learn-address update` action is by triggering a soft-reset of the server; for example, by sending a USR1 signal to the server process. This will cause all clients to reconnect, this time triggering an `update` action.

# Using a tls-verify script

OpenVPN has several layers in which the credentials of a connecting client are verified. It is even possible to add a custom layer to the verification process by specifying a `tls-verify` script. In this recipe, we will demonstrate how such a script can be used to allow access only for a particular certificate.

# Getting ready

Install OpenVPN 2.3 or higher on two computers. Make sure that the computers are connected over a network. Set up the client and server certificates using the *Setting up the public and private keys* recipe from `Chapter 2`, *Client-server IP-only Networks*. For this recipe, the server computer was running Fedora 22 Linux and OpenVPN 2.3.10. The client was running Windows 7 64 bit and OpenVPN 2.3.10. For the client, keep the client configuration file, `basic-udp-client.ovpn`, from the *Using an ifconfig-pool block* recipe, from `Chapter 2`, *Client-server IP-only Networks* .

# How to do it...

1. Create the server configuration file:

```
proto udp
port 1194
dev tun

server 10.200.0.0 255.255.255.0

ca       /etc/openvpn/cookbook/ca.crt
cert     /etc/openvpn/cookbook/server.crt
key      /etc/openvpn/cookbook/server.key
dh       /etc/openvpn/cookbook/dh2048.pem
tls-auth /etc/openvpn/cookbook/ta.key 0

persist-key
persist-tun
keepalive 10 60

topology subnet

user  nobody
group nobody  # nogroup on some distros
daemon
log-append /var/log/openvpn.log

script-security 2
tls-verify /etc/openvpn/cookbook/example5-4-tls-verify.sh
```

2. Save it as `example5-4-server.conf`.

3. Next, create the `tls-verify` script:

```
#!/bin/bash

[ $# -lt 2 ] && exit 1

# if the depth is non-zero , continue processing
[ "$1" -ne 0 ] && exit 0

allowed_cns=`sed 's/ /_/g' $0.allowed`
for i in $allowed_cns
do
  [ "$2" = "$i" ] && exit 0
done
# catch-all
exit 1
```

4. Save this file as `example5-4-tls-verify.sh`.
5. Make sure that the script is executable:

```
[root@server]# chmod 755 example5-4-tls-verify.sh
```

6. Finally, create the list of allowed certificates:

```
[root@server]# echo "/C=US/O=Cookbook 2.4/CN=client1" > \
    /etc/openvpn/cookbook/example5-4-tls-verify.sh.allowed
```

   Note that this is a one-line command.

7. Start the OpenVPN server:

```
[root@server]# openvpn --config example5-4-server.conf
```

8. Start the client with the Windows GUI using the basic configuration file:

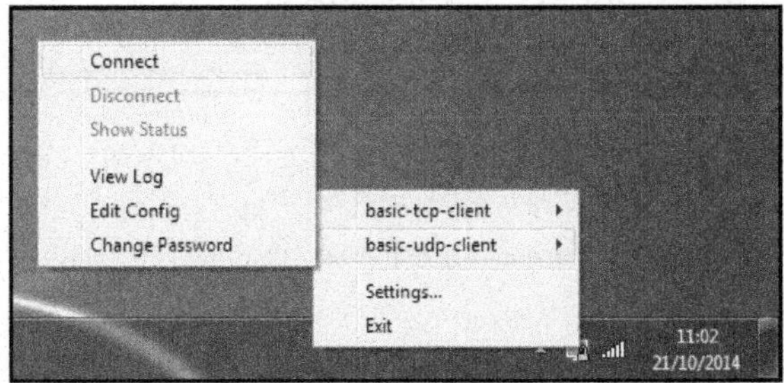


   The client should be able to connect normally.

9. Now, on the OpenVPN server, remove the `/etc/openvpn/cookbook/example5-4-tls-verify.sh.allowed` file and reconnect. This time the server log will show the following:

```
CN not found in /etc/openvpn/cookbook/example5-4-tls-
verify.sh.allowed, denying access
... openvpnclient1:9007 TLS_ERROR: BIO read tls_read_plaintext
error: error:140890B2:SSL
routines:SSL3_GET_CLIENT_CERTIFICATE:no certificate returned
... openvpnclient1:9007 TLS Error: TLS object -> incoming
plaintext read error
... openvpnclient1:9007 TLS Error: TLS handshake failed
```

   This means that the client is denied access by the OpenVPN server.

# How it works...

When a client connects to the OpenVPN server, the `tls-verify` script is executed several times to verify the entire certificate chain of the connecting client. In this recipe, we look for the end-user certificate, which is the equivalent of the `client1.crt` file. When this end-user certificate is found in the `example5-4-tls-verify.sh.allowed` file, the script returns `0`, indicating a successful verification. If it is not found, a message is printed to the OpenVPN log and the script returns `1`. The OpenVPN server then denies the access to this particular client.

# There's more...

In this recipe, we focus only on the end-user certificate using a simple lookup table. Of course, this could also have been achieved in many other ways (for example, by using a `client-config-dir` file). With a `tls-verify` script, it is also possible to disallow all the certificates from a particular certificate authority (CA).

In more complex setups, where client certificates can be signed by many different CAs, it is sometimes very useful to temporarily refuse access to all the certificates from a particular CA. For example, to deny access to all certificates that are signed with the CA certificate with the subject name "Cookbook 2.4 CA" from Chapter 2, *Client-server IP-only Networks*, the following script could be used:

```
#!/bin/bash

[ $# -lt 2 ] && exit 1
CA=`echo $2 | sed -n 's/.*\/CN=\(.*\)\/.*/\1/p'`
[ "$CA" = "Cookbook 2.4 CA" ] && exit 1
```

# Using an auth-user-pass-verify script

Other than certificates and private keys, OpenVPN also offers the option to use a username and password mechanism for verifying client access. In this recipe, we will demonstrate how to set up an `auth-user-pass-verify` script, which is executed on the server side when a client connects. This script can be used to look up a user in a database or file and can also be used to verify that the right password was specified.

## Getting ready

Install OpenVPN 2.3 or higher on two computers. Make sure that the computers are connected over a network. Set up the client and server certificates using the first recipe from Chapter 2, *Client-server IP-only Networks*. For this recipe, the server computer was running CentOS 6 Linux and OpenVPN 2.3.10, and the client was running Fedora 22 and OpenVPN 2.3.10. For the server, keep the server configuration file, `basic-udp-server.conf`, from the *Server-side routing* recipe, from Chapter 2, *Client-server IP-only Networks*.

## How to do it...

1. Append a line to the server configuration file, `basic-udp-server.conf`:

    ```
    script-security 2
    auth-user-pass-verify /etc/openvpn/cookbook/example5-5-aupv.sh
    via-file
    ```

    Note that the last line is a single line. Save it as `example5-5-server.conf`.

2. Create the `auth-user-pass-verify` script:

```
#!/bin/bash

# the username+password is stored in a temporary file
# pointed to by $1
username=`head -1 $1`
password=`tail -1 $1`

if grep "$username:$password" $0.passwd > /dev/null 2>&1
then
  exit 0
else
  if grep "$username" $0.passwd > /dev/null 2>&1
  then
    echo "auth-user-pass-verify: Wrong password entered for
           user '$username'"
  else
    echo "auth-user-pass-verify: Unknown user '$username'"
  fi
  exit 1
fi
```

3. Save it as `example5-5-aupv.sh`.
4. Set up a (very unsafe!) password file:

```
[server]$ cd /etc/openvpn/cookbook
[server]$ echo "cookbook:koobcook" > example5-5-
aupv.sh.passwd
```

5. Make sure that the `auth-user-pass-verify` script is executable, then start the server:

```
[root@server]#$ chmod 755 example5-5-aupv.sh
[root@server]# openvpn --config example5-5-server.conf
```

6. Next, create the client configuration file:

```
client
proto udp
remote openvpnserver.example.com
port 1194

dev tun
nobind

ca       /etc/openvpn/cookbook/ca.crt
```

```
cert     /etc/openvpn/cookbook/client1.crt
key      /etc/openvpn/cookbook/client1.key
tls-auth /etc/openvpn/cookbook/ta.key 1

remote-cert-tls server
auth-user-pass
```

7. Save it as `example5-5-client.conf`.
8. Start the client:

```
[root@client]# openvpn --config example5-5-client.conf
```

9. First, the OpenVPN client will ask for the username and password:

```
Enter Auth Username: cookbook
Enter Auth Password: koobcook
```

10. Then, if the correct password is entered, the connection is established as normal.
11. Next, try to reconnect using a different username:

```
Enter Auth Username: janjust
Enter Auth Password: whatever
```

12. The server log will now show the following:

```
auth-user-pass-verify: Unknown user 'janjust'
... openvpnclient:50834 TLS Auth Error: Auth Username/Password
verification failed for peer
```

And the client is now refused access.

# How it works...

The OpenVPN client first prompts the user for the Auth username and password. Note that the password is sent to the server over a secure channel, but the password itself is not hashed or encrypted. The server-side `auth-user-pass-verify` script is passed the username and password in a file on two lines. The script then looks up the username in its password file and verifies whether the right password was specified. If so, then the script exits with exit code 0, indicating success. Otherwise, the exit code of 1 is returned, causing the server to abort the client connection.

# There's more...

In the following section, we'll see some details about how a password can be specified and can be passed from the server to the `auth-user-pass-verify` script.

## Specifying the username and password in a file on the client

OpenVPN has the option to specify the username and password in a file on the client. For this, OpenVPN needs to be compiled with a special flag, which is enabled by default starting with OpenVPN 2.3.

Note that it is unsafe to allow the password to be stored on the client (in plaintext format!).

## Passing the password via environment variables

In this recipe, we used the following:

```
auth-user-pass-verify example5-5-aupv.sh via-file
```

This configured the OpenVPN server to pass the client-supplied username and password via a temporary file. This temporary file is accessible only to the server process, and hence, this is a safe mechanism to pass the encrypted password to the `auth-user-pass-verify` script.

It is also possible to pass the username and password to the `auth-user-pass-verify` script via environment variables:

```
auth-user-pass-verify example5-5-aupv.sh via-env
```

The advantage of this is that no extra files need to be created. The downside is that passing a password via plaintext and via the environment is slightly less secure: it is easier (but not easy!) to snoop the environment of another process than it is to read a secure file owned by another user.

# Script order

With all the possible scripts that can be configured on the OpenVPN server, it becomes important to determine the order in which these scripts are executed. In this recipe, we will find out what the order is, as well as the command-line parameters for each of these scripts.

# Getting ready

Install OpenVPN 2.3 or higher on two computers. Make sure that the computers are connected over a network. Set up the client and server certificates using the first recipe from `Chapter 2`, *Client-server IP-only Networks*. For this recipe, the server computer was running CentSO 6 Linux and OpenVPN 2.3.10., and the client was running Fedora 22 and OpenVPN 2.3.10. For the server, keep the server configuration file, `basic-udp-server.conf`, from the *Server-side routing* recipe, from `Chapter 2`, *Client-server IP-only Networks*. For the client, keep the client configuration file from the previous recipe at hand.

# How to do it...

1. Append the following lines to the server configuration file, `basic-udp-server.conf`:

```
script-security 2
cd /etc/openvpn/cookbook
up                   example5-6-script.sh
route-up             example5-6-script.sh
down                 example5-6-script.sh
client-connect       example5-7-script.sh
client-disconnect    example5-6-script.sh
learn-address        example5-6-script.sh
tls-verify           example5-6-script.sh
auth-user-pass-verify      example5-6-script.sh via-env
```

2. Save it as `example5-6-server.conf`.
3. Create the following script:

```
#!/bin/bash

exec >> /tmp/example5-6.log 2>&1
date +"%H:%M:%S: START $script_type script ==="
echo "argv = $0 $@"
echo "user = `id -un`/`id -gn`"
date +"%H:%M:%S: END $script_type script ==="
```

4. Save it as `example5-6-script.sh`.
5. Make sure that the script is executable and then start the server:

```
[root@server]# chmod 755 example5-6-script.sh
[root@server]# openvpn --config example5-6-server.conf
```

6. Next, start the client:

```
[root@client]# openvpn --config example5-5-client.conf
```

   The Auth username and password can be chosen arbitrarily, as they are not used.

7. After successfully connecting to the server, disconnect the client and wait for a few minutes until the server recognizes that the client has disconnected. Now, stop the OpenVPN server as well.

   A log file will be created in `/tmp/example5-6.log`, parts of which are shown here:

```
13:34:45: START up script ===
13:34:45: START route-up script ===
13:36:26: START tls-verify script ===
18:36:26: START tls-verify script ===
18:36:27: START user-pass-verify script ===
18:36:27: START client-connect script ===
18:36:27: START learn-address script ===
argv = example5-6-script.sh add 10.200.0.2 client1
18:37:14: START client-disconnect script ===
18:37:20: START learn-address script ===
argv = example5-6-script.sh delete 10.200.0.2
18:37:20: START down script ===
```

# How it works...

There are many script hooks built into OpenVPN. When the OpenVPN server starts up and when a client connects and then disconnects, these scripts are executed one by one. The order (for OpenVPN 2.3) is as follows:

- The `up` script as user `root`.
- The `route-up` script as user `root`; afterwards, root privileges are dropped and OpenVPN switches to the user `nobody` as specified in the server configuration.
- The `tls-verify` script. The CA certificate that was used to sign the client certificate is passed for verification.
- The `tls-verify` script. The client certificate itself is passed.
- The `user-pass-verify` script.
- The `client-connect` script.
- The `learn-address` script with the action, `add`.

At this point, the client has successfully established a VPN connection. Now, when the client disconnects:

- The `client-disconnect` script
- The `learn-address` script with the action, `delete`

And when the server shuts down:

- The `down` command; note that this is run as the user `nobody`!

## There's more...

When writing scripts, it is very important to keep the script execution time in mind. The design of OpenVPN 2 is very monolithic: everything (except plugins, which we will come to later in this chapter) is run under a single thread. This means that while a script is executing, the whole OpenVPN server is temporarily unavailable for all other clients: the routing of packets stops, other clients cannot connect or disconnect, and even the management interface will not respond. So, it is very important to ensure that all the server-side scripts execute very quickly.

This design flaw has been recognized, but it is not expected that there will be a major change until the arrival of OpenVPN 3.

# Script security and logging

One of the major differences between OpenVPN 2.0 and later versions is related to the security when running scripts. With OpenVPN 2.0, all scripts were executed using a `system` call and the entire set of server environment variables was passed to each script. Starting with OpenVPN 2.1, the `script-security` configuration directive is introduced and the default for executing scripts is now the `execv` call, which is more secure. Also, it is advisable to log output of your scripts for security reasons. With script logging output, including timestamps, it becomes much easier to track down problems and possible security incidents. Starting with OpenVPN 2.3, it is no longer possible to add the `system` option to the `script-security` configuration directive.

In this recipe, we will focus on the different options for the `script-security` configuration directive and on the methods to ease the logging of script output.

# Getting ready

Install OpenVPN 2.3 or higher on two computers. Make sure that the computers are connected over a network. Set up the client and server certificates using the first recipe from `Chapter 2`, *Client-server IP-only Networks*. For this recipe, the server computer was running CentSO 6 Linux and OpenVPN 2.3.10, and the client was running Fedora 22 and OpenVPN 2.3.10. For the server, keep the server configuration file, `basic-udp-server.conf`, from the *Server-side routing* recipe, from `Chapter 2`, *Client-server IP-only Networks*.

# How to do it...

1. Start the OpenVPN server using the configuration file from the *Using a client-side up/down script* recipe:

```
[root@server]# openvpn --config basic-udp-server.conf
```

2. Create the client configuration file:

```
client
proto udp
remote openvpnserver.example.com
port 1194

dev tun
nobind

ca       /etc/openvpn/cookbook/ca.crt
cert     /etc/openvpn/cookbook/client1.crt
key      /etc/openvpn/cookbook/client1.key
tls-auth /etc/openvpn/cookbook/ta.key 1

remote-cert-tls server
up "/etc/openvpn/cookbook/example5-7-up.sh arg1 arg2"
```

3. Save it as `example5-7-client.conf`. Notice the lack of the `script-security` directive.
4. Create the `up` script:

```
#!/bin/bash

exec >> /etc/openvpn/cookbook/example5-7.log 2>&1
date +"%H:%M:%S: START $script_type script ==="
echo "argv = [$0] [$1] [$2] [$3] [$4]"
```

```
pstree $PPID
date +"%H:%M:%S: END $script_type script ==="
```

5. Save it as `example5-7-up.sh` and make sure that it is executable.
6. Start the OpenVPN client:

```
[client]$ openvpn --config example5-7-client.conf
```

7. The client appears to connect successfully until the `up` script needs to be executed:

```
... /etc/openvpn/cookbook/example5-7-up.sh [arguments]
... WARNING: External program may not be called unless '--
script-security 2' or higher is enabled. See --help text or
man page for detailed info.
... WARNING: Failed running command (--up/--down): external
program fork failed
... Exiting due to fatal error
```

8. When we repeat the preceding with an extra command-line parameter, `--script-security 2`, the client can connect successfully:

```
[client]$ openvpn --config example5-7-client.conf  \
   --script-security 2
```

The `/etc/openvpn/cookbook/example5-7.log` log file now shows the following:

```
05:25:33: START up script ===
argv = [/etc/openvpn/cookbook/example5-7-up.sh] [argument1] [argument2]
[tun0] [1500]
openvpn---example5-7-up.s---pstree
05:25:33: END up script ===
```

If we repeat this preceding exercise using `--script-security 3`, we would get a similar output.

## How it works...

In order to execute the scripts on either the client or the server, the directive, `script-security 2` (or 3) must be specified; otherwise, OpenVPN 2.1 or higher will refuse to start. The following parameters can be specified for the `script-security` directive:

- `0`: This parameter specifies that no external programs can be called. This means that OpenVPN cannot successfully start up, except on Microsoft Windows under certain circumstances.
- `1`: This parameter specifies that only built-in external programs (such as `/sbin/ifconfig`, and `/sbin/ip` on Linux, and `netsh.exe`, and `route.exe` on Windows) can be called.
- `2`: This parameter specifies that built-ins and scripts can be called.
- `3`: This is the same as `2`, but now here, passwords can be passed to scripts via environment variables as well.

## There's more...

There are subtle differences between running scripts on Linux/NetBSD/Mac OS and on Windows. On Windows, the system call, `CreateProcess` , is used by default. This makes it impossible to pass extra parameters to some scripts, such as the `up` script, as the entire text enclosed with quotes after the `up` directive is considered as the name of the executable or script.

# Scripting and IPv6

Now that IPv6 addresses are more common, it is instructive to show how IPv6 addresses are passed from the server to client-side scripts. Basically, all environment variables that existed for IPv4 addresses also exist for IPv6, simply by appending or inserting `_ipv6` to the environment variable. In this recipe, we will show you how to process these environment variables.

## Getting ready

Install OpenVPN 2.3 or higher on two computers. Make sure that the computers are connected over a network. Set up the client and server certificates using the first recipe from `Chapter 2`, *Client-server IP-only Networks*. For this recipe, the server computer was running CentOS 6 Linux and OpenVPN 2.3.10., and the client was running Fedora 22 and OpenVPN 2.3.10. For the server, keep the server configuration file, `basic-udp-server.conf`, from the *Server-side routing* recipe, from `Chapter 2`, *Client-server IP-only Networks*.

## How to do it...

1. Append two lines to the server configuration file, `basic-udp-server.conf`:

```
push "route-ipv6 2001:610:120::111:0:1/96"
push "route-ipv6 2001:610:120::222:0:1/96"
```

2. Save it as `example5-8-server.conf`.
3. Start the server:

```
[root@server]# openvpn --config example5-8-server.conf
```

4. Next, create the client configuration file:

```
client
proto udp
remote openvpnserver.example.com
port 1194

dev tun
nobind

ca       /etc/openvpn/cookbook/ca.crt
cert     /etc/openvpn/cookbook/client1.crt
key      /etc/openvpn/cookbook/client1.key
tls-auth /etc/openvpn/cookbook/ta.key 1

remote-cert-tls server
script-security 2
up "/etc/openvpn/cookbook/example5-8.sh"

route-up "/etc/openvpn/cookbook/example5-8.sh"
```

5. Save it as `example5-8-client.conf`.
6. Create the following script:

```
#!/bin/bash

exec >> /tmp/example5-10.log 2>&1
date +"%H:%M:%S: START $script_type script ==="
export | grep ipv6
date +"%H:%M:%S: END $script_type script ==="
```

7. Save it as `example5-8-script.sh`.
8. Make sure that the `example5-8.sh` script is executable, and then start the client:

```
[root@client]# chmod 755 example5-8.sh
[root@client]# openvpn --config example5-8-client.conf
```

9. After the client has is connected, check the client-side log file, `/tmp/example5-8.log`:

```
16:19:58: START up script ===

declare -x ifconfig_ipv6_local="2001:610:120::200:0:1001"
declare -x ifconfig_ipv6_netbits="112"
declare -x ifconfig_ipv6_remote="2001:610:120::200:0:2"
declare -x route_ipv6_gateway_1="2001:610:120::200:0:2"
declare -x route_ipv6_gateway_2="2001:610:120::200:0:2"
declare -x route_ipv6_network_1="2001:610:120::111:0:1/96"
declare -x route_ipv6_network_2="2001:610:120::222:0:1/96"
16:19:58: END up script ===
16:19:58: START route-up script ===
declare -x ifconfig_ipv6_local="2001:610:120::200:0:1001"
declare -x ifconfig_ipv6_netbits="112"
declare -x ifconfig_ipv6_remote="2001:610:120::200:0:2"
declare -x route_ipv6_gateway_1="2001:610:120::200:0:2"
declare -x route_ipv6_gateway_2="2001:610:120::200:0:2"
declare -x route_ipv6_network_1="2001:610:120::111:0:1/96"
declare -x route_ipv6_network_2="2001:610:120::222:0:1/96"
16:19:58: END route-up script ===
```

## How it works...

The OpenVPN server assigns an IPv6 address to the client and also pushes out two IPv6 routes to the client using the `push "route-ipv6 ..."` directive. The client picks up these directives and passes them on to the `up` and `route-up` scripts. These scripts only show the environment variables that have `ipv6` in them, which gives a good overview of the IPv6 settings that are available to scripts and plugins.

## There's more...

Be careful when passing IPv6 routes to clients that contain the IPv6 address of the server itself–these routes can take precedence over an existing route to the server, causing the VPN connection to stall.

# Using the down-root plugin

OpenVPN supports a plugin architecture, where external plugins can be used to extend the functionality of OpenVPN. Plugins are special modules or libraries that adhere to the OpenVPN Plugin API. One of these plugins is the `down-root` plugin, which is available only on Linux. This allows the user to run specified commands as a user `root` plugin when OpenVPN shuts down. Normally, the OpenVPN process drops root privileges (if the `--user` directive is used) for security reasons. While this is a good security measure, it makes it difficult to undo some of the actions that an `up` script can perform, which is run as a user `root` plugin. For this, the `down-root` plugin was developed. This recipe will demonstrate how the `down-root` plugin can be used to remove a file that was created by an `up` script.

## Getting ready

Set up the client and server certificates using the *Setting up public and private keys* recipe from `Chapter 2`, *Client-server IP-only Networks*. For this recipe, the server computer was running CentOS 6 Linux and OpenVPN 2.3.10. No client computer was required.

# How to do it...

1. Create the server configuration file:

```
proto udp
port 1194
dev tun

server 10.200.0.0 255.255.255.0

ca       /etc/openvpn/cookbook/ca.crt
cert     /etc/openvpn/cookbook/server.crt
key      /etc/openvpn/cookbook/server.key
dh       /etc/openvpn/cookbook/dh2048.pem
tls-auth /etc/openvpn/cookbook/ta.key 0

persist-key
persist-tun
keepalive 10 60

topology subnet

user  nobody
group nobody  # nogroup on some distros

daemon
log-append /var/log/openvpn.log

script-security 2
cd /etc/openvpn/cookbook
up "example5-9.sh"
plugin /usr/lib64/openvpn/plugin/lib/openvpn-down-root.so
"./example5-9.sh --down"

suppress-timestamps
verb 5
```

2. Save it as `example5-9-server.conf`.
3. Next, create the `up` script, which we will also use for the `down-root` plugin:

```
#!/bin/sh
if [ "$script_type" = "up" ]
then
  touch /tmp/example5-9.tempfile
fi
if [ "$1" = "--down" ]
```

```
then
  rm /tmp/example5-9.tempfile
fi
```

4. Save it as `example5-9.sh` and make sure that it is executable.
5. Start the OpenVPN server:

   ```
   [root@server]# openvpn --config example5-9-server.conf
   ```

   The server log file will now show the following:

   ```
   PLUGIN_CALL: POST /usr/lib64/openvpn/plugin/lib/openvpn-down-
   root.so/PLUGIN_UP status=0
   example5-9.sh tun0 1500 1541 10.200.0.1 10.200.0.2 init
   ```

   This indicates the plugin has started. The fact that there were no error codes right after the `up` script was executed indicates that it ran successfully.

6. Verify that the `/tmp/example5-9.tempfile` file was created on the server.
7. Next, stop the server. The server log will now show the following:

   ```
   PLUGIN_CALL: POST /usr/lib64/openvpn/plugin/lib/openvpn-down-
   root.so/PLUGIN_DOWN status=0
   PLUGIN_CLOSE: /usr/lib64/openvpn/plugin/lib/openvpn-down-
   root.so
   ```

8. Verify that the `/tmp/example5-9.tempfile` file has been removed.

## How it works...

The `down-root` plugin is registered at system startup when the OpenVPN server process is still running with `root` privileges. Plugins are spawned off in a separate thread, meaning that when the main OpenVPN process drops its root privileges, the plugins will still have full `root` access. When OpenVPN shuts down, the plugin is called and it removes the file created by the user `root` plugin when the server started.

Here is an interesting part of the server log file is:

```
/sbin/ifconfig tun0 0.0.0.0
SIOCSIFADDR: Permission denied
SIOCSIFFLAGS: Permission denied
Linux ip addr del failed: external program exited with error status: 255
PLUGIN_CALL: POST /usr/lib64/openvpn/plugin/lib/openvpn-down-
root.so/PLUGIN_DOWN status=0
PLUGIN_CLOSE: /usr/lib64/openvpn/plugin/lib/openvpn-down-root.so
```

This indicates that the OpenVPN process was indeed not capable of running the command `/sbin/ifconfig tun0 0.0.0.0`, proving that `root` privileges had been successfully dropped. The plugin was then called, which did have `root` privileges, so that it could remove the root-owned file in `/tmp`.

Note that it is required to specify a path starting with `./` for the script that the plugin runs. If the leading `./` is not specified on Linux or Mac OS, then OpenVPN will not be able to find the script that the plugin needs to run, as the current directory (`.`) normally is not part of the PATH environment variable.

Also note that the `up` script is called with the `script_type` environment variable set but that this is not true for plugins. To overcome this, an extra parameter was added so that the same script could be used as both the `up` and `down-root` scripts.

# There's more...

Plugins are supported on Linux, Net/FreeBSD, and on Windows. The following script callbacks can be intercepted using a plugin:

- `up`
- `down`
- `route-up`
- `ipchange`
- `tls-verify`
- `auth-user-pass-verify`
- `client-connect`
- `client-disconnect`
- `learn-address`

## See also

- The next recipe, *Using the PAM authentication plugin*, which explains how to use an OpenVPN plugin to authenticate remote VPN clients

# Using the PAM authentication plugin

A very useful plugin for OpenVPN is a plugin to validate a username using the Linux/UNIX PAM authentication system. **PAM** stands for **pluggable authentication modules** and is a very modular system for allowing users access to system resources. It is used by most modern Linux and UNIX variants, offering a very flexible and extendible system for authenticating and authorizing users. In this recipe, we will use the PAM authentication plugin as a replacement of an `auth-user-pass-verify` script to validate a remote user's credentials against the system PAM configuration.

## Getting ready

Install OpenVPN 2.3 or higher on two computers. Make sure that the computers are connected over a network. Set up the client and server certificates using the first recipe from `Chapter 2`, *Client-server IP-only Networks*. For this recipe, the server computer was running CentOS 6 Linux and OpenVPN 2.3.11. The client was running Fedora 22 Linux and OpenVPN 2.3.11. For the client, keep the client configuration file, `example5-5-client.conf`, from the *Using an auth-user-pass-verify script* recipe at hand.

## How to do it...

1. Create the server configuration file:

```
proto udp
port 1194
dev tun

server 10.200.0.0 255.255.255.0

ca       /etc/openvpn/cookbook/ca.crt
cert     /etc/openvpn/cookbook/server.crt
key      /etc/openvpn/cookbook/server.key
dh       /etc/openvpn/cookbook/dh2048.pem
```

```
tls-auth /etc/openvpn/cookbook/ta.key 0

persist-key
persist-tun
keepalive 10 60

topology subnet

user  nobody
group nobody  # nogroup on some distros

daemon
log-append /var/log/openvpn.log

verb 5
suppress-timestamps

plugin /usr/lib64/openvpn/plugins/openvpn-plugin-auth-pam.so
"login login USERNAME password PASSWORD"
```

Note that the last line of the server configuration file is a single line. Save it as: `example5-10-server.conf`.

2. Start the OpenVPN server:

```
[root@server]# openvpn --config example5-10-server.conf
```

The server log file will now show:

```
AUTH-PAM: BACKGROUND: INIT service='login'
PLUGIN_INIT: POST /usr/lib64/openvpn/plugins/openvpn-plugin-
auth-pam.so '/usr/lib64/openvpn/plugins/openvpn-plugin-auth-
pam.so] [login] [login] [USERNAME] [password] [PASSWORD]'
intercepted=PLUGIN_AUTH_USER_PASS_VERIFY
```

This indicates that the PAM plugin successfully initialized in the background.

3. Start the OpenVPN client. OpenVPN will first prompt for the Auth username and password:

```
... OpenVPN 2.3.11 x86_64-redhat-linux-gnu [SSL (OpenSSL)]
[LZO] [EPOLL] [PKCS11] [MH] [IPv6] built on May 10 2016
... library versions: OpenSSL 1.0.1e-fips 11 Feb 2013, LZO 2.08
Enter Auth Username: ********
Enter Auth Password: ********
```

On the server used in this recipe, a special user `cookbook` was created. After typing in the username and password, the connection to the server is successfully established. The OpenVPN server log shows the following:

```
AUTH-PAM: BACKGROUND: received command code: 0
AUTH-PAM: BACKGROUND: USER: cookbook
AUTH-PAM: BACKGROUND: my_conv[0] query='login:' style=2
AUTH-PAM: BACKGROUND: name match found, query/match-string ['login:',
'login'] = 'USERNAME'
AUTH-PAM: BACKGROUND: my_conv[0] query='Password: ' style=1
AUTH-PAM: BACKGROUND: name match found, query/match-string ['Password: ',
'password'] = 'PASSWORD'
... 192.168.3.22:50887 PLUGIN_CALL: POST
/usr/lib64/openvpn/plugins/openvpn-plugin-auth-
pam.so/PLUGIN_AUTH_USER_PASS_VERIFY status=0
... 192.168.3.22:50887 TLS: Username/Password authentication succeeded for
username 'cookbook'
```

This shows that the user was successfully authenticated using PAM.

# How it works...

The PAM authentication plugin intercepts the `auth-user-pass-verify` callback. When the OpenVPN client connects and passes along the username and password, the plugin wakes up. It queries the PAM subsystem by looking at the `login` module (this is the first parameter for the `openvpn-auth-pam.so` file). The other parameters are used by the `auth-pam` plugin to know which input to expect from the PAM subsystem:

```
login USERNAME password PASSWORD
```

The PAM `login` subsystem will ask for the username by presenting the `login prompt` and will ask for the password by presenting the `password` prompt. The `auth-pam` plugin uses this information to know where to fill in the username (`USERNAME`) and password (`PASSWORD`).

After the user has been successfully authenticated by the PAM subsystem, the connection is established.

## There's more...

It would also have been possible to authenticate a user using an `auth-user-pass-verify` script, which queries the PAM subsystem. There are two major advantages to using the PAM plugin for this:

- It is not required to use the `script-security` directive at all.
- The plugin method is much faster and far more scalable. When many users try to connect to the OpenVPN server at the same time, the VPN performance would be greatly affected when using an `auth-user-pass-verify` script, as for each user connection, a separate process needs to be started, during which the OpenVPN's main thread is installed.

## See also

- The previous recipe, *Using the down-root plugin,* in which the basics of using OpenVPN plugins are explained

# 6
# Troubleshooting OpenVPN - Configurations

In this chapter, we will cover the following recipes:

- Cipher mismatches
- TUN versus TAP mismatches
- Compression mismatches
- Key mismatches
- Troubleshooting MTU and `tun-mtu` issues
- Troubleshooting network connectivity
- Troubleshooting `client-config-dir` issues
- Troubleshooting multiple `remote` issues
- Troubleshooting bridging issues
- How to read the OpenVPN log files

## Introduction

The topic of this chapter and the next is troubleshooting OpenVPN. This chapter will focus on troubleshooting OpenVPN misconfigurations, whereas the next chapter will focus on the all-too-common routing issues that occur when setting up a VPN.

The recipes in these chapters will therefore deal first with breaking things. We will then provide the tools on how to find and solve the configuration errors. Some of the configuration directives used in this chapter have not been demonstrated before, so even if you are not interested in breaking things, this chapter will still be insightful.

# Cipher mismatches

In this recipe, we will change the cryptographic ciphers that OpenVPN uses. Initially, we will change the cipher only on the client side, which will cause the initialization of the VPN connection to fail. The primary purpose of this recipe is to show the error messages that appear, not to explore the different types of ciphers that OpenVPN supports.

## Getting ready

Set up the client and server certificates using the first recipe from `Chapter 2`, *Client-server IP-only Networks*. For this recipe, the server computer was running CentOS 6 Linux and OpenVPN 2.3.11, and the client was running Windows 7 64 bit and OpenVPN 2.3.10. Keep the configuration file, `basic-udp-server.conf`, from the *Server-side routing* recipe from `Chapter 2`, *Client-server IP-only Networks*, as well as the client configuration file, `basic-udp-client.conf`.

## How to do it...

1. Start the server using the configuration file, `basic-udp-server.conf`:

```
[root@server]# openvpn --config basic-udp-server.conf
```

2. Next, create the client configuration file by appending a line to the `basic-udp-client.conf` file:

```
cipher CAST5-CBC
```

   Save it as `example6-1-client.conf`.

3. Start the client, after which the following message will appear in the client log:

```
[root@client]# openvpn --config example6-1-client.conf
... WARNING: 'cipher' is used inconsistently, local='cipher
CAST5-CBC'', remote='cipher BF-CBC''
... [openvpnserver] Peer Connection Initiated with server-
ip:1194
... TUN/TAP device tun0 opened
... /sbin/ip link set dev tun0 up mtu 1500
... /sbin/ip addr add dev tun0 10.200.0.2/24 broadcast
10.200.0.255
... Initialization Sequence Completed
```

```
... Authenticate/Decrypt packet error: cipher final failed
```

And, similarly, on the server side:

```
    ... client-ip:52461 WARNING: 'cipher' is used inconsistently,
local='cipher BF-CBC'', remote='cipher CAST5-CBC''
    ... client-ip:52461 [client1] Peer Connection Initiated with
client1:52461
    ... client1/client-ip:52461 Authenticate/Decrypt packet error:
    cipher final failed
    ... client1/client-ip:52461 Authenticate/Decrypt packet error:
    cipher final failed
```

The connection will not be successfully established, but it will also not be disconnected immediately.

## How it works...

During the connection phase, the client and the server negotiate several parameters needed to secure the connection. One of the most important parameters in this phase is the encryption cipher, which is used to encrypt and decrypt all the messages. If the client and server are using different ciphers, then they are simply not capable of talking to each other.

By adding the following configuration directive to the server configuration file, the client and the server can communicate again:

```
cipher CAST5-CBC
```

## There's more...

OpenVPN supports quite a few ciphers, although support for some of the ciphers is still experimental. To view the list of supported ciphers, type:

```
$ openvpn --show-ciphers
```

This will list all ciphers with both variables and fixed cipher length. The ciphers with variable cipher length are very well supported by OpenVPN, the others can sometimes lead to unpredictable results.

## Pushable ciphers

Starting with version 2.4, OpenVPN clients support the option to process a cipher pushed from the server to the client. Thus, if all clients are running OpenVPN 2.4 or later it becomes much easier to change the encryption cipher in an existing deployment.

# TUN versus TAP mismatches

A common mistake when setting up a VPN based on OpenVPN is the type of adapter that is used. If the server is configured to use a TUN-style network but a client is configured to use a TAP-style interface, then the VPN connection will fail. In this recipe, we will show what is typically seen when this common configuration error is made.

## Getting ready

Set up the client and server certificates using the first recipe from `Chapter 2`, *Client-server IP-only Networks*. For this recipe, the server computer was running CentOS 6 Linux and OpenVPN 2.3.11. The client was running Fedora 22 Linux and OpenVPN 2.3.11. Keep the configuration file, `basic-udp-server.conf`, from the *Server-side routing* recipe from `Chapter 2`, *Client-server IP-only Networks*.

## How to do it...

1. Start the server using the configuration file, `basic-udp-server.conf`:

```
[root@server]# openvpn --config basic-udp-server.conf
```

2. Next, create the client configuration:

```
client
proto udp
remote openvpnserver.example.com
port 1194

dev tap
nobind

remote-cert-tls server
tls-auth /etc/openvpn/cookbook/ta.key 1
ca       /etc/openvpn/cookbook/ca.crt
```

```
cert      /etc/openvpn/cookbook/client1.crt
key       /etc/openvpn/cookbook/client1.key
```

Save it as`example6-2-client.conf`.

3. Start the client:

```
[root@client]# openvpn --config example6-2-client.conf
```

The client log will show the following:

```
... WARNING: 'dev-type' is used inconsistently, local='dev-type
tap'', remote='dev-type tun''
... WARNING: 'link-mtu' is used inconsistently, local='link-mtu
1573'', remote='link-mtu 1541''
... WARNING: 'tun-mtu' is used inconsistently, local='tun-mtu
1532'', remote='tun-mtu 1500''
... [openvpnserver] Peer Connection Initiated with server-
ip:1194
... TUN/TAP device tap0 opened
... /sbin/ip link set dev tap0 up mtu 1500
... /sbin/ip addr add dev tap0 10.200.0.2/24 broadcast
10.200.0.255
... Initialization Sequence Completed
```

At this point, you can try pinging the server, but it will respond with an error:

```
[client]$ ping 10.200.0.1
PING 10.200.0.1 (10.200.0.1) 56(84) bytes of data.
From 10.200.0.2 icmp_seq=2 Destination Host Unreachable
From 10.200.0.2 icmp_seq=3 Destination Host Unreachable
From 10.200.0.2 icmp_seq=4 Destination Host Unreachable
```

# How it works...

A TUN-style interface offers a point-to-point connection over which only TCP/IP traffic can be tunneled. A TAP-style interface offers the equivalent of an Ethernet interface that includes extra headers. This allows a user to tunnel other types of traffic over the interface. When the client and the server are misconfigured, the expected packet size is different:

```
... WARNING: 'tun-mtu' is used inconsistently, local='tun-mtu 1532'',
remote='tun-mtu 1500''
```

This shows that each packet that is sent through a TAP-style interface is 32- bytes larger than the packets sent through a TUN-style interface.

By correcting the client configuration, this problem is resolved.

# Compression mismatches

OpenVPN supports on-the-fly compression of the traffic that is sent over the VPN tunnel. This can improve the performance over a slow network line, but it does add a little overhead. When transferring uncompressible data (such as ZIP files), the performance actually decreases slightly.

If the compression is enabled on the server but not on the client, then the VPN connection will fail.

# Getting ready

Set up the client and server certificates using the *Setting up public and private keys* recipe from `Chapter 2`, *Client-server IP-only Networks*. For this recipe, the server computer was running CentOS 6 Linux and OpenVPN 2.3.11. The client was running Fedora 22 Linux and OpenVPN 2.3.11. Keep the configuration file, `basic-udp-server.conf`, from the *Server-side routing* recipe from `Chapter 2`, *Client-server IP-only Networks*, as well as the client configuration file, `basic-udp-client.conf`, at hand.

# How to do it...

1. Append a line to the server configuration file, `basic-udp-server.conf`:

   ```
   comp-lzo
   ```

   Save it as `example6-3-server.conf`.

2. Start the server:

   ```
   [root@server]# openvpn --config example6-3-server.conf
   ```

3. Next, start the client:

   ```
   [root@client]# openvpn --config basic-udp-client.conf
   ```

The connection will initiate, but when data is sent over the VPN connection, the following messages will appear:

```
Initialization Sequence Completed
... write to TUN/TAP : Invalid argument (code=22)
... write to TUN/TAP : Invalid argument (code=22)
```

## How it works...

During the connection phase, no compression is used to transfer information between the client and the server. One of the parameters that is negotiated is the use of compression for the actual VPN payload. If there is a configuration mismatch between the client and the server, then both the sides will get confused by the traffic that the other side is sending.

This error can easily be fixed for all the clients by just adding another line:

```
push "comp-lzo"
```

# Key mismatches

OpenVPN offers extra protection for its TLS control channel in the form of HMAC keys. These keys are exactly the same as the static "secret" keys used in `Chapter 1`, *Point-to-Point Networks*, for point-to-point style networks. For multi-client style networks, this extra protection can be enabled using the `tls-auth` directive. If there is a mismatch between the client and the server related to this `tls-auth` key, then the VPN connection will fail to get initialized.

## Getting ready

Set up the client and server certificates using the first recipe from `Chapter 2`, *Client-server IP-only Networks*. For this recipe, the server computer was running CentOS 6 Linux and OpenVPN 2.3.11. The client was running Fedora 22 Linux and OpenVPN 2.3.11. Keep the configuration file, `basic-udp-server.conf`, from the *Server-side routing* recipe from `Chapter 2`, *Client-server IP-only Networks*.

# How to do it...

1. Start the server using the configuration file, `basic-udp-server.conf`:

```
[root@server]# openvpn --config basic-udp-server.conf
```

2. Next, create the client configuration:

```
client
proto udp
remote openvpnserver.example.com
port 1194

dev tun
nobind

remote-cert-tls server
tls-auth /etc/openvpn/cookbook/ta.key
ca       /etc/openvpn/cookbook/ca.crt
cert     /etc/openvpn/cookbook/client1.crt
key      /etc/openvpn/cookbook/client1.key
```

   Note the lack of the second parameter for `tls-auth`. Save it as `example6-4-client.conf` file.

3. Start the client:

```
[root@client]# openvpn --config example6-4-client.conf
```

   The client log will show no errors, but the connection will not be established either. In the server log we'll find the following:

```
... Initialization Sequence Completed
... Authenticate/Decrypt packet error: packet HMAC
authentication failed
... TLS Error: incoming packet authentication failed from
client-ip:54454
```

   This shows that the client, `client1`, is connecting using the wrong `tls-auth` parameter and the connection is refused.

## How it works...

At the very first phase of the connection initialization, the client and the server verify each other's HMAC keys. If an HMAC key is not configured correctly, then the initialization is aborted and the connection will fail to establish. As the OpenVPN server is not able to determine whether the client is simply misconfigured or whether a malicious client is trying to overload the server, the connection is simply dropped. This causes the client to keep listening for the traffic from the server until it eventually times out.

In this recipe, the misconfiguration consisted of the missing parameter `1` at the end of the configuration line:

```
tls-auth /etc/openvpn/cookbook/ta.key
```

The second parameter to the `tls-auth` directive is the direction of the key. Normally, the following convention is used:

- `0`: from server to client
- `1`: from client to server

This parameter causes OpenVPN to derive its HMAC keys from a different part of the `ta.key` file. If the client and server disagree on which parts the HMAC keys are derived from, the connection cannot be established. Similarly, when the client and server are deriving the HMAC keys from different `ta.key` files, the connection can also not be established.

## See also

- The *Multiple secret keys* recipe from `Chapter 1`, *Point-to-Point Networks*, in which the format and usage of the OpenVPN secret keys is explained in detail

# Troubleshooting MTU and tun-mtu issues

One of the more advanced features of OpenVPN is the ability to tune the network parameters of both the TUN (or TAP) adapter and the parameters of the encrypted link itself. This is a frequent cause of configuration mistakes, leading to low performance or even the inability to successfully transfer data across the VPN tunnel.

This recipe will show what happens if there is an MTU (Maximum Transfer Unit) mismatch between the client and the server and how this mismatch can cause the VPN tunnel to fail only under certain circumstances.

# Getting ready

Set up the client and server certificates using the first recipe from `Chapter 2`, *Client-server IP-only Networks*. For this recipe, the server computer was running CentOS 6 Linux and OpenVPN 2.3.11, and the client was running Fedora 22 Linux and OpenVPN 2.3.11. Keep the client configuration file, `basic-udp-client.conf`, handy along with the configuration file, `basic-udp-server.conf`, from the *Server-side routing* recipe, from `Chapter 2`, *Client-server IP-only Networks*, as well as the client configuration file `basic-udp-client.conf`.

# How to do it...

1. Start the server using the configuration file, `basic-udp-server.conf`:

```
[root@server]# openvpn --config basic-udp-server.conf
```

2. Next, create the client configuration file by appending a line to the `basic-udp-client.conf` file:

```
tun-mtu 1400
```

   Save it as `example6-5-client.conf`.

3. Start the client and look at the client log:

```
[root@client]# openvpn --config example6-5-client.conf
... WARNING: 'link-mtu' is used inconsistently, local='link-mtu
1441'', remote='link-mtu 1541''
... WARNING: 'tun-mtu' is used inconsistently, local='tun-mtu
1400'', remote='tun-mtu 1500''
... [openvpnserver] Peer Connection Initiated with server-
ip:1194
... TUN/TAP device tun0 opened
... /sbin/ip link set dev tun0 up mtu 1400
... /sbin/ip addr add dev tun0 10.200.0.2/24 broadcast
10.200.0.255
... Initialization Sequence Completed
```

There are a few warnings when the tunnel comes up, but the connection is initialized.

4. It is possible to send traffic over the link, which we can verify using the `ping` command:

```
[client]$ ping -c 2 10.200.0.1
PING 10.200.0.1 (10.200.0.1) 56(84) bytes of data.
64 bytes from 10.200.0.1: icmp_seq=1 ttl=64 time=30.6 ms
64 bytes from 10.200.0.1: icmp_seq=2 ttl=64 time=30.7 ms
```

5. However, consider when sending larger packets, for example:

```
[client]$ ping -s 1450 10.200.0.1
```

In such a case, the following messages appear in the client log file:

```
... Authenticate/Decrypt packet error: packet HMAC
authentication failed
... Authenticate/Decrypt packet error: packet HMAC
authentication failed
```

The same thing will happen if the client tries to download a large file.

## How it works...

The MTU determines how large packets can be that are sent over the tunnel without breaking up (fragmenting) the packet into multiple pieces. If the client and the server disagree on this MTU size, then the server will send packets to the client that are simply too large. This causes an HMAC failure (if `tls-auth` is used, as in this recipe) or the part of the packet that is too large is thrown away.

## There's more...

On the Windows platform, it is not easy to change the MTU setting for the Tap-Win32 adapter that OpenVPN uses. The `tun-mtu` directive can be specified but the Windows version of OpenVPN cannot alter the actual MTU setting, as Windows did not support this until Windows Vista. OpenVPN, however, does not yet have the capability of altering the MTU size on Windows.

## See also

- `Chapter 9`, *Performance Tuning*, which gives some hints and examples on how to optimize the `tun-mtu` directive

# Troubleshooting network connectivity

This recipe will focus on the type of log messages that are typically seen when the OpenVPN configurations are fine, but the network connectivity is not. In most cases, this is due to a firewall blocking access to either the server or the client. In this recipe, we explicitly block access to the server and then try to connect to it.

## Getting ready

Set up the client and server certificates using the first recipe from `Chapter 2`, *Client-server IP-only Networks*. For this recipe, the server computer was running CentOS 6 Linux and OpenVPN 2.3.11, and the client was running Fedora 22 Linux and OpenVPN 2.3.11. Keep the client configuration file, `basic-udp-client.conf`, handy along with the configuration file, `basic-udp-server.conf`, from the *Server-side routing* recipe from `Chapter 2`, *Client-server IP-only Networks*, as well as the client configuration file, `basic-udp-client.conf`.

## How to do it...

1. Start the server using the configuration file, `basic-udp-server.conf`:

   ```
   [root@server]# openvpn --config basic-udp-server.conf
   ```

2. On the server, explicitly block access to OpenVPN using `iptables`:

   ```
   [root@server]# iptables -I INPUT -p udp --dport 1194 -j DROP
   ```

3. Next, start the client using the configuration file, `basic-udp-client.conf`:

   ```
   [root@client]# openvpn --config basic-udp-client.conf
   ```

The client will try to connect the server using the UDP protocol. After a while, a timeout will occur because no traffic is getting through and the client will restart:

```
... TLS Error: TLS key negotiation failed to occur within 60
seconds (check your network connectivity)
... TLS Error: TLS handshake failed
... SIGUSR1[soft,tls-error] received, process restarting
```

Abort the client and stop the server.

## How it works...

When OpenVPN is configured to use the default UDP protocol, the client will wait for an answer from the server for 60 seconds. If no answer was received, the connection is restarted. As we are explicitly blocking UDP traffic, the timeout occurs and the client is never able to connect.

The amount of time for which the client waits for the connection to start is controlled using the following directive:

```
hand-window N
```

Here, `N` is the number of seconds to wait for the initial handshake to complete. The default value is 60 seconds.

Of course, the connection can be repaired by removing the firewall rule.

## There's more...

One of the major differences between the UDP protocol and the TCP protocol is the way connections are established: every TCP connection is started using a TCP handshake by both the client and the server. If the handshake fails, then the connection is not established. There is no need to wait for traffic coming back from the server, as the connection itself is dropped:

```
    ... Attempting to establish TCP connection with openvpnserver:1194
[nonblock]
    ... TCP: connect to openvpnserver:1194 failed, will try again in 5
seconds: Connection refused
```

# Troubleshooting client-config-dir issues

In this recipe, we will demonstrate how to troubleshoot issues related to the use of the `client-config-dir` directive. This directive can be used to specify a directory for so-called CCD files. CCD files can contain OpenVPN directives to assign a specific IP address to a client, based on the client's certificate. Experience has shown that it is easy to misconfigure this directive. In this recipe, we will make one of the common misconfigurations and then show how to troubleshoot it.

## Getting ready

Set up the client and server certificates using the first recipe from `Chapter 2`, *Client-server IP-only Networks*. For this recipe, the server computer was running CentOS 6 Linux and OpenVPN 2.3.11. The client was running Fedora 22 Linux and OpenVPN 2.3.11. Keep the client configuration file, `basic-udp-client.conf`, handy along with the configuration file, `basic-udp-server.conf`, from the *Server-side routing* recipe from `Chapter 2`, *Client-server IP-only Networks*, as well as the client configuration file, `basic-udp-client.conf`.

## How to do it...

1. Append the following lines to the configuration file, `basic-udp-server.conf`:

   ```
   client-config-dir /etc/openvpn/cookbook/clients
   ccd-exclusive
   ```

   Save it as `example6-7-server.conf`.

2. Make sure that the `/etc/openvpn/cookbook/clients` directory is accessible only to the root:

   ```
   [root@server]# chown root /etc/openvpn/cookbook/clients
   [root@server]# chmod 700  /etc/openvpn/cookbook/clients
   ```

3. Start the server:

   ```
   [root@server]# openvpn --config example6-7-server.conf
   ```

4. Next, start the client using the configuration file, `basic-udp-client.conf`:

   ```
   [root@client]# openvpn --config basic-udp-client.conf
   ```

Then, the client will fail to connect with the following message:

```
... [openvpnserver] Peer Connection Initiated with server-ip:1194
... AUTH: Received AUTH_FAILED control message
```

The server log file is a bit confusing: first; it mentions that there was a problem reading the CCD file, `client1`, but then it states that the client is connected:

```
... client-ip:45432 TLS Auth Error: --client-config-dir authentication
failed for common name 'client1'
file=''/etc/openvpn/cookbook/clients/client1''
... client-ip:45432 [client1] Peer Connection Initiated with client-
ip:45432
```

However, the VPN connection has not been properly initiated.

# How it works...

The following directives are used by the OpenVPN server to look in the `/etc/openvpn/cookbook/clients` directory for a CCD file with the name (CN) of the client certificate:

```
client-config-dir /etc/openvpn/cookbook/clients
ccd-exclusive
```

The purpose of the second directive, `ccd-exclusive`, is to only allow clients for which a CCD file is present. If a CCD file for a client is not present, the client will be denied access. The name of the client certificate is listed in the server log:

```
... client-ip:45432 TLS Auth Error: --client-config-dir authentication
failed for common name 'client1'
```

However, it can also be retrieved using the following:

```
openssl x509 -subject -noout -in client1.crt
```

Look for the first part starting with `/CN=` and convert all spaces to underscores.

The OpenVPN server process is running as user `nobody`. And because we have set very restrictive permissions on the `/etc/openvpn/cookbook/clients` directory, this user is not capable of reading any files in that directory. When the client with the `client1` certificate connects, the OpenVPN server is not capable of reading the CCD file (even though it might be there). Because of the `ccd-exclusive` directive, the client is then denied access.

# There's more...

In this section, we will explain how to increase the logging verbosity and what some of the most common `client-config-dir` mistakes are.

## More verbose logging

Increasing the verbosity of logging is often helpful when troubleshooting `client-config-dir` issues. With `verb 5` and the right permissions, you will see the following log file entries in the OpenVPN server log:

```
client1/client-ip:39814 OPTIONS IMPORT: reading client specific options
from: /etc/openvpn/cookbook/clients/client1
```

If this message is not present in the server log, then it is safe to assume that the CCD file has not been read.

## Other frequent client-config-dir mistakes

There are a few frequent `client-config-dir` mistakes:

- A non-absolute path is used to specify the `client-config-dir` directive, for example:

  ```
  client-config-dir clients
  ```

  This might work in some cases, but you have to be very careful when starting the server or when combining this with directives such as `--chroot` or `--cd`. Especially when the `--chroot` directive is used, all paths, including the absolute path, will be relative to the `chroot` path.

- The CCD file itself must be correctly named, without any extension. This typically tends to confuse Windows users. Look in the server log to see what the OpenVPN server thinks; the `/CN= name` is of the client certificate. Also, be aware that OpenVPN rewrites some characters of the `/CN= name`, such as spaces. For the full list of characters that will be remapped, refer to the manual page in the *String types and remapping* section.
- The CCD file and the full path to it must be readable to the user under which the OpenVPN server process is running (usually `nobody`).

## See also

- The *Using client-config-dir files* recipe from `Chapter 2`, *Client-server IP-only Networks*, which explains the basic usage of client configuration files

# Troubleshooting multiple remote issues

In this recipe, we will demonstrate how to troubleshoot issues related to the use of multiple `remote` directives. The ability to use multiple `remote` directives is one of the lesser well-known features of OpenVPN that has been available since version 2.2. It allows a user to specify multiple connection profiles to different hosts, different ports, and different protocols (for example, TCP versus UDP).

When using this directive, there is a pitfall to watch out for when specifying extra directives elsewhere in the configuration files, or on the command line. In this recipe, we will demonstrate what this pitfall is.

## Getting ready

Set up the client and server certificates using the first recipe from `Chapter 2`, *Client-server IP-only Networks*. For this recipe, the server computer was running CentOS 6 Linux and OpenVPN 2.3.11, and the client was running Fedora 22 Linux and OpenVPN 2.3.11. Keep the client configuration file, `basic-udp-client.conf`, handy along with the configuration file, `basic-udp-server.conf`, from the *Server-side routing* recipe from `Chapter 2`, *Client-server IP-only Networks*, as well as the client configuration file, `basic-udp-client.conf`.

## How to do it...

1. Start the server using the configuration file, `basic-udp-server.conf`:

```
[root@server]# openvpn --config basic-udp-server.conf
```

2. Next, create the client configuration:

```
client
remote openvpnserver.example.com 1195 udp
remote openvpnserver.example.com 1196 tcp
port 1194
```

```
dev tun
nobind

remote-cert-tls server
tls-auth /etc/openvpn/cookbook/ta.key 1
ca       /etc/openvpn/cookbook/ca.crt
cert     /etc/openvpn/cookbook/client1.crt
key      /etc/openvpn/cookbook/\client1.key
```

Note that we are specifying two connection profiles, one to the server using the UDP protocol, `port 1195`, and one using the TCP protocol, `port 1196`. However, we expect to overrule the port number using the line `port 1194`. Save this file as `example6-8-client.conf`.

3. Start the client:

```
[root@client]# openvpn --config example6-8-client.conf
```

Then, the client will fail to connect with a message:

```
... UDPv4 link local: [undef]
... UDPv4 link remote: [AF_INET]server-ip:1195
```

So, even though we explicitly stated `port 1194`, the client is still connecting using protocol UDP, port `1195`.

# How it works...

When you specify a remote connection entry using:

```
remote openvpnserver.example.com 1195 udp
```

OpenVPN transforms this internally into a connection profile. In general, connection profiles inherit settings from the global configuration. Anything specified inside a connection profile overrules whatever is specified globally, even if it is specified later in the configuration file, or on the command line. Thus, the line `port 1194` does not have any effect and the client attempts to connect using the first (default) `remote` connection profile, protocol UDP, and port `1195`.

To solve this issue, the port number needs to be modified in the `remote` line in the configuration file.

## There's more...

An alternative way to specify the `remote openvpnserver.example.com 1195 udp` is by using a connection block:

```
<connection>
    remote openvpnserver.example.com
    port 1195
    proto udp
</connection>
```

However, inside connection blocks, you can specify more directives, as we will see in the *Using connection blocks* recipe in `Chapter 10`, *Advanced Configuration*.

## See also

- The *Using connection blocks* recipe in `Chapter 10`, *Advanced Configuration*, which goes into detail into the usage of connection blocks

# Troubleshooting bridging issues

In this recipe, we will demonstrate how to troubleshoot a common issue related to bridging. OpenVPN bridging can be tricky to configure, as the warning and error messages can be confusing. In this recipe, we will make one of the common misconfigurations and then show how to troubleshoot it.

## Getting ready

Set up the client and server certificates using the first recipe from `Chapter 2`, *Client-server IP-only Networks*. For this recipe, the server computer was running CentOS 6 Linux and OpenVPN 2.3.11, and the client was running Fedora 22 Linux and OpenVPN 2.3.11. Keep the scripts, `example3-3-bridge-start` and `example3-3-bridge-stop`, from the *Bridging – Linux* recipe from `Chapter 3`, *Client-server Ethernet-style Networks*, handy along with the client configuration file, `example-3-2-client2.ovpn`, from the *Enabling client-to-client traffic* recipe, from `Chapter 3`, *Client-server Ethernet-style Networks*.

# How to do it...

1. Create the server configuration file:

```
proto udp
port 1194
dev tap
server-bridge 192.168.4.65 255.255.255.0 192.168.4.128
192.168.4.200
push "route 192.168.4.0 255.255.255.0"

tls-auth /etc/openvpn/cookbook/ta.key 0
ca       /etc/openvpn/cookbook/ca.crt
cert     /etc/openvpn/cookbook/server.crt
key      /etc/openvpn/cookbook/server.key
dh       /etc/openvpn/cookbook/dh2048.pem

persist-key
persist-tun
keepalive 10 60

user  nobody
group nobody  # use "group nogroup" on some distros

daemon
log-append /var/log/openvpn.log
```

   Note that we did not explicitly specify the adapter name (tap0). Save it as `example-6-9-server.conf`.

2. Create the network bridge and verify that it is working:

```
[root@server]# bash example3-3-bridge-start
  TUN/TAP device tap0 opened
  Persist state set to: ON
[root@server]# brctl show
  bridge name bridge id         STP enabled interfaces
  br0         8000.00219bd2d422 no          eth0
               tap0
```

3. Start the OpenVPN server:

```
[root@server]# openvpn --config example6-9-server.conf
```

4. Start the client:

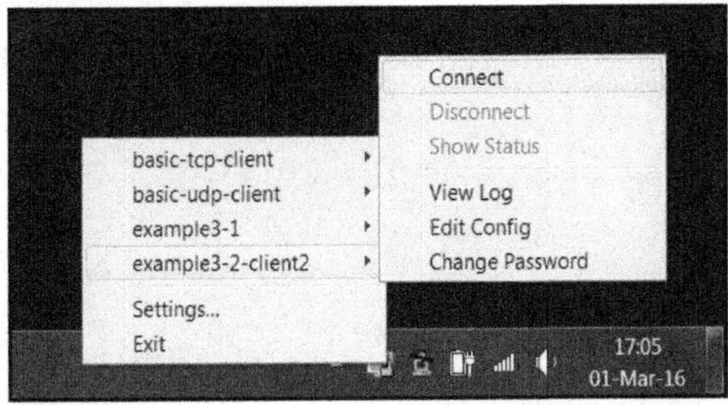


5. Now, try to reach the server:

```
[WinClient]C:> ping 192.168.4.65
```

Even though the connection is established, the client will fail to reach the server.

Remember to shut down the Ethernet bridge after stopping the OpenVPN server process.

# How it works...

The connection failures in this example are due to the fact that the OpenVPN server opened a new tap adapter at startup instead of connecting to the bridge. A hint is given in the server log file:

```
... TUN/TAP device tap1 opened
```

When checking the tap interfaces on the server, we see that there are now two tap interfaces:

```
[root@server]# ip addr show
...
39: br0: <BROADCAST,MULTICAST,UP,LOWER_UP> mtu 1500 qdisc noqueue
state UNKNOWN
    link/ether 00:25:90:c0:3e:d0 brd ff:ff:ff:ff:ff:ff
    inet 192.168.4.65/24 brd 192.168.4.255 scope global br0
    inet6 fe80::225:90ff:fec0:3ed0/64 scope link
       valid_lft forever preferred_lft forever
40: tap1: <BROADCAST,MULTICAST> mtu 1500 qdisc noop state DOWN qlen
100
    link/ether ae:9f:3e:ae:93:ba brd ff:ff:ff:ff:ff:ff
```

The second tap interface, `tap1`, is the one in use by OpenVPN, and it does not have an IP address assigned!

To solve this issue, the correct tap adapter needs to be specified in the server configuration file.

## See also

- The *Linux – bridging* recipe, from `Chapter 3`, *Client-server Ethernet-style Networks*, which explains in detail how to set up bridging on Linux in detail

# How to read the OpenVPN log files

Troubleshooting an OpenVPN setup often comes down to reading and interpreting the OpenVPN log file correctly. In this recipe, no new features of OpenVPN will be introduced, but a detailed walk-through of an OpenVPN log file will be given. The setup from the *Troubleshooting MTU and tun-mtu issues* recipe earlier in this chapter will be used as a starting point.

## Getting ready

Use the same setup as in the *Troubleshooting MTU and tun-mtu issues* recipe earlier in this chapter. For this recipe, the server computer was running CentOS 6 Linux and OpenVPN 2.3.11, and the client was running Fedora 22 Linux and OpenVPN 2.3.11. Keep the configuration file, `basic-udp-server.conf`, from the *Server-side routing* recipe from `Chapter 2`, *Client-server IP-only Networks*. For the client, keep the configuration file, `example6-5-client.conf`, from the *Troubleshooting MTU and tun-mtu issues* recipe at hand.

## How to do it...

1. Start the server using the configuration file, `basic-udp-server.conf`:

```
[root@server]# openvpn --config basic-udp-server.conf
```

2. Next, start the client with an increased verbosity setting and without timestamps in the log file:

   ```
   [root@client]# openvpn --config example6-5-client.conf \
     --verb 7 --suppress-timestamps
   ```

   The connection will initiate, but it will not be possible to send large packets.

3. Trigger an error by typing the following:

   ```
   [client]$ ping -c 1 10.200.0.1
   [client]$ ping -c 1 -s 1450 10.200.0.1
   ```

4. Abort the client. The log file will have become large quite quickly.
5. Open the log file using a text editor and browse through it. An explanation of the general structure of the log file is given in the next section.

## How it works...

The first part of the log file contains the configuration as specified in the configuration file and from the command-line parameters. This is the section starting with the following line:

```
Current Parameter Settings:
  config = 'example6-5-client.conf'
```

It ends with the following line:

```
OpenVPN 2.3.11 x86_64-redhat-linux-gnu [SSL (OpenSSL)] [LZO] [EPOLL]
[PKCS11] [MH] [IPv6] built on May 10 2016
```

This section is about 275 lines long depending on the configuration and it contains what OpenVPN thinks is the configuration. Check this section carefully to make sure that you agree.

The next interesting section is as follows:

```
Control Channel Authentication: using '/etc/openvpn/cookbook/ta.key' as a
OpenVPN static key file
Outgoing Control Channel Authentication: Using 160 bit message hash 'SHA1'
for HMAC authentication
Outgoing Control Channel Authentication: HMAC KEY: 51cc24c0 ...
Outgoing Control Channel Authentication: HMAC size=20 ... Incoming Control
Channel Authentication: Using 160 bit ...
Incoming Control Channel Authentication: HMAC KEY: 1c748f91 ...
Incoming Control Channel Authentication: HMAC size=20 ...
```

This part shows that a `tls-auth` key is read and used and that the two separate HMAC keys are derived. The keys are actually printed in the log file, so you can reference them with the output from the server log file. The server incoming key should be the same as the client outgoing key and vice versa. The misconfiguration from the *Key mismatches* recipe earlier in this chapter would have appeared here.

Right after this section is the warning that is the root cause of the misconfiguration from the *Troubleshooting MTU and tun-mtu issues* recipe earlier in this chapter:

```
WARNING: normally if you use --mssfix and/or --fragment, you should also
set --tun-mtu 1500 (currently it is 1400)
```

Log file messages starting with `WARNING` should always be given special attention to. In some cases, they can be ignored, but in this case, it was the root cause of the VPN connection not working properly.

After this warning comes a whole range of messages of the following form:

```
UDPv4 link remote: [AF_INET]server-ip:1194
UDPv4 WRITE [42] to [AF_INET]server-ip:1194: P_CONTROL_HARD_RESET_CLIENT_V2
kid=0 pid=[ #1 ] [ ] pid=0 DATA len=0
UDPv4 READ [54] from [AF_INET]server-ip:1194:
P_CONTROL_HARD_RESET_SERVER_V2 kid=0 pid=[ #1 ] [ 0 ] pid=0 DATA len=0
TLS: Initial packet from [AF_INET]server-ip:1194, sid=c483bcc9 a60cc834
PID_TEST [0] [TLS_AUTH-0] [] 0:0 1469290891:1 t=1469290891[0]
r=[0,64,15,0,1] sl=[0,0,64,528]
UDPv4 WRITE [50] to [AF_INET]server-ip:1194: P_ACK_V1 kid=0 pid=[ #2 ] [ 0
]
UDPv4 WRITE [249] to [AF_INET]server-ip:1194: P_CONTROL_V1 kid=0 pid=[ #3 ]
[ ] pid=1 DATA len=207
```

These messages are all part of the initial handshake between the client and the server to exchange configuration information, encryption keys, and other information for setting up the VPN connection. Right after this is another hint about the misconfiguration:

```
WARNING: 'link-mtu' is used inconsistently, local='link-mtu 1441',
remote='link-mtu 1541'
WARNING: 'tun-mtu' is used inconsistently, local='tun-mtu 1400',
remote='tun-mtu 1500'
```

We skip forward over a lot of `TLS_prf` messages to come to the end of the connection handshake:

```
Control Channel: TLSv1.2, cipher TLSv1/SSLv3 DHE-RSA-AES256-GCM-SHA384,
2048 bit RSA
[openvpnserver] Peer Connection Initiated with [AF_INET]server-ip:1194
```

At this point, the OpenVPN client has established the initial connection with the server and it is now ready to process the configuration directives pushed by the server, if any:

```
PUSH: Received control message: 'PUSH_REPLY,route-gateway
10.200.0.1,topology subnet,ping 10,ping-restart 60,ifconfig 10.200.0.2
255.255.255.0'
```

This is another important line to check for, as it shows what the server has actually pushed to the client. Verify that this actually matches what you thought the server should push.

After this, the local TUN adapter is opened and initialized and the first packets can begin to flow.

The first `ping` command worked fine, as we can see from this part:

```
TUN READ [84]
...
UDPv4 WRITE [125] to server-ip:1194: P_DATA_V1 kid=0 DATA len=124
UDPv4 READ [125] from server-ip:1194: P_DATA_V1 kid=0 DATA len=124
TLS: tls_pre_decrypt, key_id=0, IP=server-ip:1194
TUN WRITE [84]
```

The `TUN READ` is the ping command being read from the TUN interface, followed by a write over the encrypted channel to the remote server. Notice the difference in packet size: the packet sent over the encrypted tunnel is 125 bytes, which is 41- bytes larger than the original packet read from the TUN interface. This exactly matches the difference between the `link-mtu` and `tun-mtu` options as shown earlier in the log file.

Next comes the section where the `ping -s 1450` command breaks down. A `ping` of 1450 bytes cannot be read in one piece if the MTU of the interface is set to 1400, hence two `TUN READS` are necessary to capture all data:

```
TUN READ [1396]
...
UDPv4 WRITE [1437] to server-ip:1194: P_DATA_V1 kid=0 DATA len=1436
TUN READ [102]
...
UDPv4 WRITE [141] to server-ip:1194: P_DATA_V1 kid=0 DATA len=140
```

Notice that the data is actually sent as two separate packets to the server. This is perfectly normal behavior, as the packet needs to be fragmented. Calculation of the packet sizes versus the MTU sizes breaks down in this case, as the second packet is not a complete IP packet.

The server receives the large `ping` command and sends an equally large reply. As the server has an MTU setting of 1500, there is no need to fragment the data, so it arrives at the client as a single packet:

```
UDPv4 READ [1441] from server-ip:1194: P_DATA_V1 kid=0 DATA len=1440
TLS: tls_pre_decrypt, key_id=0, IP=server-ip:1194
Authenticate/Decrypt packet error: packet HMAC authentication failed
```

The client, however, is expecting a packet with a maximum size of 1400 bytes. It is not able to properly decode the larger packet and write out the `packet HMAC authentication failed` message.

Finally, when we abort the client, we see an `interrupted system call` message (in this case, *Ctrl* + *C* was used to abort the client, along with a range of clean-up messages before the client actually stops):

```
event_wait : Interrupted system call (code=4)
PID packet_id_free
...
TCP/UDP: Closing socket
Closing TUN/TAP interface
/sbin/ip addr del dev tun0 10.200.0.2/24
PID packet_id_free
SIGINT[hard,] received, process exiting
```

Consider that the client configuration had included this:

```
user nobody
```

Then, we would also have seen messages of this form:

```
SIOCSIFADDR: Permission denied
SIOCSIFFLAGS: Permission denied
Linux ip addr del failed: external program exited with error status: 255
```

In this case, these are harmless.

# There's more...

On UNIX-based operating systems, it is also possible to send the OpenVPN log output via `syslog`. This allows a system administrator to effectively manage a large set of computers using a single system logging interface. To send log messages via `syslog`, replace the directive `log-append` with the following:

```
syslog [name]
```

Here, `name` is an optional parameter to specify the name of the OpenVPN instance in the syslog log files. This is particularly useful if there are multiple instances of OpenVPN running on a single host, and they are all using `syslog` to log their output and error messages.

# 7

# Troubleshooting OpenVPN - Routing

In this chapter, we will cover the following troubleshooting topics:

- The missing return route
- Missing return routes when `iroute` is used
- All clients function except the OpenVPN endpoints
- Source routing
- Routing and permissions on Windows
- Unable to change Windows network location
- Troubleshooting client-to-client traffic routing
- Understanding the `MULTI: bad source` warnings
- Failure when redirecting the default gateway

## Introduction

The topic of this chapter and the previous one is troubleshooting the OpenVPN. This chapter focuses on the all-too-common routing issues that occur when setting up a VPN. As more than half of the questions asked on the `openvpn-users` mailing list can be traced back to routing issues, this chapter intends to provide answers to some of the more frequent routing misconfigurations.

The recipes in these chapters will therefore deal with first, breaking the things, and then, providing the tools for how to find and solve the configuration errors.

# The missing return route

After setting up OpenVPN successfully for the very first time, it is very common to misconfigure the network routes for the VPN. In this recipe, we will first set up a basic TUN-style VPN as is done in `Chapter 2`, *Client-server IP-only Networks*. At first, routing will not work until the right routes are added. The purpose of this recipe is to describe how to troubleshoot such a routing error.

## Getting ready

We use the following network layout:

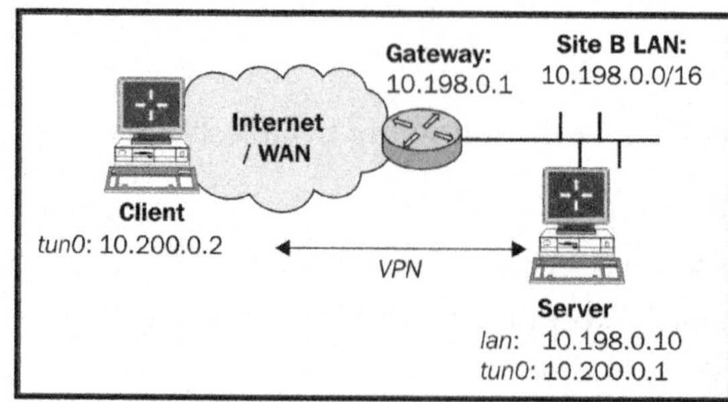


Set up the client and server certificates using the *Setting up the public and private keys* recipe from `Chapter 2`, *Client-server IP-only Networks*. For this recipe, the server computer was running CentOS 6 Linux and OpenVPN 2.3.11. The client was running Fedora 22 Linux and OpenVPN 2.3.11. Keep the configuration file `basic-udp-server.conf` from the *Server-side routing* recipe from `Chapter 2`, *Client-server IP-only Networks*, as well as the client configuration file `basic-udp-client.conf`.

## How to do it...

1. Start the server using the configuration file `basic-udp-server.conf`:

```
[root@server]# openvpn --config basic-udp-server.conf
```

2. Next, start the client:

```
[root@client]# openvpn --config basic-udp-client.conf
...
... Initialization Sequence Completed
```

3. At this point, it is possible to ping the remote VPN IP and all the interfaces that are on the VPN server themselves:

```
[client]$ ping -c 2 10.200.0.1
PING 10.200.0.1 (10.200.0.1) 56(84) bytes of data.
64 bytes from 10.200.0.1: icmp_seq=1 ttl=64 time=25.2 ms
64 bytes from 10.200.0.1: icmp_seq=2 ttl=64 time=25.1 ms
[client]$ ping -c 2 10.198.0.10
PING 10.198.0.10 (10.198.0.10) 56(84) bytes of data.
64 bytes from 10.198.0.10: icmp_seq=1 ttl=64 time=24.7 ms
64 bytes from 10.198.0.10: icmp_seq=2 ttl=64 time=25.0 ms
```

If either of these pings fails, then the VPN connection has not been established successfully and there is no need to continue.

4. If no routes have been added to the server-side gateway, then all other hosts on the remote `10.198.0.0/16` network will be unavailable:

```
[client]$ ping 10.198.0.1
PING 10.198.0.1 (10.198.0.1) 56(84) bytes of data.
^C
--- 10.198.0.1 ping statistics ---
1 packets transmitted, 0 received, 100% packet loss, time 764ms
```

5. If we add a route on the LAN gateway of the remote network to explicitly forward all the VPN traffic to the VPN server, then we can reach all machines on the remote LAN (like it was done in the *Server-side routing* recipe from `Chapter 2`, *Client-server IP-only Networks*):

```
[gateway]> ip route add 10.200.0.0/24 via 10.198.0.10
```

Here, `10.198.1.1` is the LAN IP address of the VPN server. In this case, the remote LAN gateway is running Linux. The exact syntax for adding a static route to the gateway will vary with the model and operating system of the gateway.

6. Now, all the machines are reachable:

```
[client]$ ping 10.198.0.1
PING 10.198.0.1 (10.198.0.1) 56(84) bytes of data.
64 bytes from 10.198.0.1: icmp_seq=1 ttl=63 time=27.1 ms
64 bytes from 10.198.0.1: icmp_seq=2 ttl=63 time=25.0 ms
```

# How it works...

When the VPN client attempts to make a connection to a host on the server-side LAN, packets are sent with a source and destination IP address:

- **Source IP** = `10.200.0.2`: This address is the VPN tunnel's IP address
- **Destination IP** = **IP**: This is the IP of the host we're trying to contact

The remote host will want to reply with a packet, with the source and destination IP addresses swapped. When the remote host wants to send the packet, it does not know where to send it to, as the address `10.200.0.2` is our private VPN address. It then forwards the packet to the LAN gateway. However, the LAN gateway also does not know where to return the packets to, and will forward them out to its default gateway. When the packets reach a router that is connected directly to the Internet, that router usually will decide to drop (throw away) the packets, causing the host to become unreachable.

By adding a route on the remote LAN gateway – telling it that all the traffic for the network `10.200.0.0/24` should be forwarded to the VPN server – the packets are sent back to the right machine. The VPN server will forward the packets back to the VPN client and the connection is established.

The step to ping the remote VPN endpoint first and then the server-LAN IP (`10.198.0.10`) may seem superfluous at first but these are crucial steps when troubleshooting routing issues. If these steps already fail, then there is no need to look at the missing routes.

# There's more...

In this section, we will focus on different solutions to the problem described in this recipe.

## Masquerading

A quick and dirty solution to the above issue is outlined in the *Server-side routing* recipe from `Chapter 2`, *Client-server IP-only Networks*. In the *There's More...* section of that recipe, masquerading (a form of NAT'ing) is used to make it appear as if all the traffic is coming from the OpenVPN server itself. This is perfect if you have no control over the remote LAN gateway, but it is not a very clean routing solution. Certain applications do not behave very well when NAT'ted. Also, from a security logging point of view, it is sometimes better to avoid NAT'ting, as you are mapping multiple IP addresses onto a single one, thereby losing information.

## Adding routes on the LAN hosts

Instead of adding a route to the remote LAN gateway, it is also possible to add a route on each of the remote LAN hosts that the VPN client needs to reach. This solution is perfect if the VPN client only needs to be able to reach a limited set of server-side hosts, but it does not scale very well.

## See also

- The *Server-side routing* recipe from `Chapter 2`, *Client-server IP-only Networks*, which contains the basic setup for routing the traffic from the server-side LAN

# Missing return routes when iroute is used

This recipe is a continuation of the previous one. After ensuring that a single VPN client can reach the server-side LAN, the next step is to make sure that other hosts behind the VPN client can reach the hosts on the server-side LAN.

In this recipe, we will first set up a VPN as is done in the *Routing: subnets on both sides* recipe from Chapter 2, *Client-Server IP-Only Networks*. If no return routes are set up, then the hosts on the client-side LAN will not be able to reach the hosts on the server-side LAN and vice versa. By adding the appropriate routes, the issue is resolved.

# Getting ready

We use the following network layout:

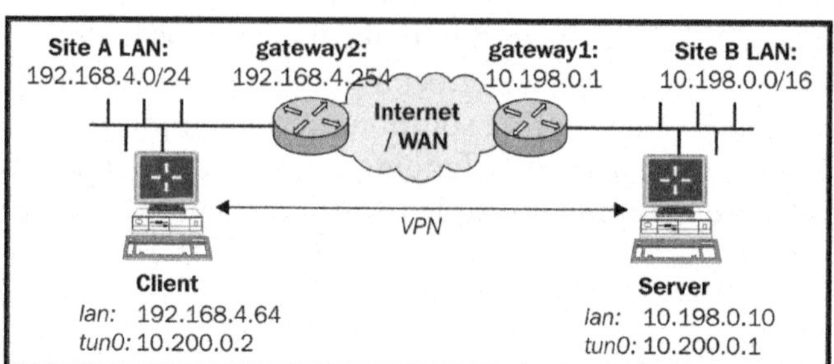


Set up the client and server certificates using the first recipe from `Chapter 2`, *Client-server IP-only Networks*. For this recipe, the server computer was running CentOS 6 Linux and OpenVPN 2.3.11. The client was running Fedora 22 Linux and OpenVPN 2.3.11. Keep the configuration file `example2-5-server.conf`, from the *Routing: subnets on both sides* recipe from `Chapter 2`, *Client-server IP-only Networks*, as well as the client configuration, `basic-udp-client.conf`, from the *Server-side routing* recipe from `Chapter 2`, *Client-server IP-only Networks*.

# How to do it...

1. Start the server:

```
[root@server]# openvpn --config example2-5-server.conf
```

2. Next, start the client:

```
[root@client]# openvpn --config basic-udp-client.conf
...
... Initialization Sequence Completed
```

3. At this point, it is possible to ping the remote VPN IP and all the interfaces that are on the VPN server itself, and vice versa:

```
[client]$ ping -c 2 10.200.0.1
PING 10.200.0.1 (10.200.0.1) 56(84) bytes of data.
64 bytes from 10.200.0.1: icmp_seq=1 ttl=64 time=25.2 ms
64 bytes from 10.200.0.1: icmp_seq=2 ttl=64 time=25.1 ms
[client]$ ping -c 2 10.198.0.10
PING 10.198.0.1 (10.198.0.10) 56(84) bytes of data.
64 bytes from 10.198.0.10: icmp_seq=1 ttl=64 time=24.7 ms
```

```
64 bytes from 10.198.0.10: icmp_seq=2 ttl=64 time=25.0 ms
[server]$ ping -c 2 10.200.0.2
PING 10.200.0.2 (10.200.0.2) 56(84) bytes of data.
64 bytes from 10.200.0.2: icmp_seq=1 ttl=64 time=25.0 ms
64 bytes from 10.200.0.2: icmp_seq=2 ttl=64 time=24.6 ms
[server]$ ping -c 2 192.168.4.64
PING 192.168.4.64 (192.168.4.64) 56(84) bytes of data.
64 bytes from 192.168.4.64: icmp_seq=1 ttl=64 time=25.2 ms
64 bytes from 192.168.4.64: icmp_seq=2 ttl=64 time=24.3 ms
```

4. The routing table on the server shows that the remote network is routed correctly:

```
[server]$ netstat -rn | grep tun0
192.168.4.0    10.200.0.1 255.255.255.0 UG 0 0 0 tun0
10.200.0.0 0.0.0.0        255.255.255.0 U  0 0 0 tun0
```

5. When we try to ping a remote host on the server-side LAN it fails, as was the case in the previous recipe. Vice versa, when we try to ping a client-side LAN host from a host on the server-side LAN, we see:

```
[siteB-host]$ ping -c 2 192.168.4.66
PING 192.168.4.66 (192.168.4.66) 56(84) bytes of data.
--- 192.168.4.66 ping statistics ---
2 packets transmitted, 0 received, 100% packet loss, time 999ms
```

6. By adding the appropriate routes on the gateways at both the sides, the routing is restored. First, the gateway on the server-side LAN:

```
[gateway1]> ip route add 192.168.4.0/24 via 10.198.0.10
```

Here, `10.198.0.10` is the LAN IP address of the VPN server.

Next, the gateway/router on the client-side LAN:

```
[gateway2]> ip route add 10.198.0.0/16 via 192.168.4.64
```

Here, `192.168.4.64` is the LAN IP address of the VPN client.

After this, the hosts on the LANs can reach each other.

# How it works...

Similar to the previous recipe, when a host on the Site A's LAN attempts to make a connection to a host on the Site B's LAN packets that are sent with a source and destination IP address:

- **Source IP** = `192.168.4.64`: Site A's LAN address
- **Destination IP** = `10.198.1.12`: Site B's LAN address

The remote host will want to reply with a packet with the source and destination IP addresses swapped. When the remote host wants to send the packet, it forwards the packet to the LAN gateway. However, the LAN gateway also does not know where to return the packets to, and will forward them out to its default gateway. When the packets reach a router that is connected directly to the Internet, then the router usually will decide to drop (throw away) the packets, causing the host to become unreachable.

A similar problem occurred in the previous recipe, but now the IP addresses of the packets are the actual Site A's and Site B's LAN IP addresses.

By adding the appropriate routes on both the sides, the problem is alleviated.

When troubleshooting this sort of routing issue, it is very important to start at the innermost network (the actual VPN, in this case) and then work your way outwards:

1. First, make sure the VPN endpoints can see each other.
2. Make sure the VPN client can reach the server LAN IP and vice versa.
3. Make sure the VPN client can reach a host on the server-side LAN.
4. Make sure a host on the server-side LAN can see the VPN client.
5. Make sure a host on the client-side LAN can see the VPN server.
6. Finally, make sure a host on the client-side LAN can see a host on the server-side LAN and vice versa.

# There's more...

Again, a quick and a dirty solution to the above issue is outlined in the *Server-side routing* recipe from `Chapter 2`, *Client-server IP-only Networks*. In that recipe, masquerading is used to make it appear as if all the traffic is coming from the OpenVPN server itself. In particular when connecting subnets over a VPN, this is not advisable, as masquerading makes it impossible to tell which client is connecting to which server and vice versa. Therefore, a fully-routed setup is preferred in this case.

## See also

- The *Routing: subnets on both sides* recipe from `Chapter 2`, *Client-server IP-only Networks*, which explains in detail how to set up routing on both the client and the server side

# All clients function except the OpenVPN endpoints

This recipe is again a continuation of the previous one. The previous recipe explained how to troubleshoot routing issues when connecting a client-side LAN (or subnet) to a server-side LAN. However, in the previous recipe, an omission in the routing configuration was made on purpose. In this recipe, we will focus on troubleshooting this quite common omission.

## Getting ready

We use the following network layout:

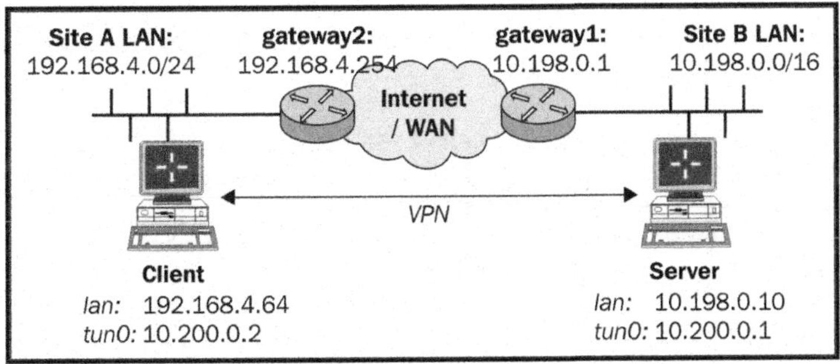


Set up the client and server certificates using the first recipe from `Chapter 2`, *Client-server IP-only Networks*. For this recipe, the server computer was running CentOS 6 Linux and OpenVPN 2.3.11. The client was running Fedora 22 Linux and OpenVPN 2.3.11. Keep the configuration file `example2-5-server.conf` from the *Routing: subnets on both sides* from `Chapter 2`, *Client-server IP-only Networks*, at hand, as well as the client configuration, `basic-udp-client.conf`, from the *Server-side routing* recipe from `Chapter 2`, *Client-server IP-only Networks*.

# How to do it...

1. Start the server:

```
[root@server]# openvpn --config example2-5-server.conf
```

2. Next, start the client:

```
[root@client]# openvpn --config basic-udp-client.conf
...
... Initialization Sequence Completed
```

3. Add the appropriate routes on the gateways at both the sides:

```
[gateway1]> ip route add 192.168.4.0/24 via 10.198.0.10
[gateway2]> ip route add 10.198.0.0/16 via 192.168.4.64
```

   After this, all the hosts on the LANs can reach each other.

4. We verify this by pinging various machines on the LANs on either of the sides:

```
[client]$ ping -c 2 10.198.0.10
[server]$ ping -c 2 192.168.4.64
[siteA-host]$ ping -c 2 10.198.0.1
[siteB-host]$ ping -c 2 192.168.4.66
```

   All of them work. However, when the VPN server tries to ping a host on the client-side LAN, it fails:

```
[server]$ ping -c 2 192.168.4.66
PING 192.168.4.66 (192.168.4.66) 56(84) bytes of data.
--- 192.168.4.66 ping statistics ---
2 packets transmitted, 0 received, 100% packet loss, time
1009ms
```

   Similarly, the client can only reach the LAN IP of the server and none of the other hosts.

5. On Linux and UNIX hosts, it is possible to explicitly specify the source IP address:

```
[server]$ ping -I 10.198.0.10 -c 2 192.168.4.66
PING 192.168.4.66 (192.168.4.66) 56(84) bytes of data.
64 bytes from 192.168.4.66: icmp_seq=1 ttl=63 time=25.5 ms
64 bytes from 192.168.4.66: icmp_seq=2 ttl=63 time=24.3 ms
```

That works! So, there is a problem with the source address of the packets.

6. By adding an extra route for the VPN subnet itself, to the gateways on both the ends, this issue is resolved:

```
[gateway1]> ip route add 10.200.0.0/24 via 10.198.0.10
[gateway2]> ip route add 10.200.0.0/24 via 192.168.4.64
```

7. Now, the VPN server can reach all the hosts on the client's subnet and vice versa:

```
[server]$ ping -c 2 192.168.4.66
PING 192.168.4.66 (192.168.4.66) 56(84) bytes of data.
64 bytes from 192.168.4.66: icmp_seq=1 ttl=63 time=25.3 ms
64 bytes from 192.168.4.66: icmp_seq=2 ttl=63 time=24.9 ms
```

# How it works...

To troubleshoot issues like these, it is very handy to write out all the source addresses and the destination addresses of the LANs involved. In this case, the problem occurs when the VPN server wants to connect to a host on the client-side LAN. On the VPN server, the packet that is sent to the client-side host is sent out of the VPN interface directly. Therefore, the source address of this packet is set to the IP address of the VPN interface itself. Thus, the packet has the following IP addresses:

- **Source IP** = `10.200.0.1`: VPN server's IP address
- **Destination IP** = `192.168.4.66`: Site A's LAN address

The remote host will want to reply with a packet with the source and destination IP addresses swapped. When the remote host wants to send the packet, it forwards the packet to the LAN gateway. However, the LAN gateway also does not know where to return the packets to, and will forward them out to its default gateway. When the packets reach a router that is connected directly to the Internet, that router usually will decide to drop (throw away) the packets, causing the host to become unreachable.

This problem occurs only on the VPN server and VPN client. On all other hosts on the client-side and server-side LAN, the LAN IP address is used and routing works as configured in the previous recipe.

By adding the appropriate routes on both the sides the problem is resolved.

# There's more...

A good use of NAT'ing in this recipe would be to remove any references to the VPN IP range from the routing tables. This can be done by just masquerading the VPN endpoint addresses. If this is done, the extra routes are no longer needed on the gateways on both the LANs. For example, by adding a NAT'ing rule on the server and a similar one on the client, the extra routes on the gateways are no longer needed.

```
[root@server]# iptables -t nat -I POSTROUTING -i tun0 -o eth0 \
    -s 10.200.0.0/24 -j MASQUERADE
[root@client]# iptables -t nat -I POSTROUTING -i tun0 -o eth0 \
    -s 10.200.0.0/24 -j MASQUERADE
```

Note that this is easily done on Linux and UNIX-based operating systems but it requires more effort on Windows.

# See also

- The *Routing: subnets on both sides* recipe from `Chapter 2`, *Client-server IP-only Networks*, which explains in detail how to set up routing on both the client and the server side

# Source routing

As the network configurations grow more complex, the requirement for more advanced features, such as the source routing features, increases. Source routing is typically used whenever a server is connected to a network (or the Internet) using two network interfaces (see the following image). In this case, it is important to ensure that the connections that are started on one of the interfaces are kept to that interface. If the incoming traffic for a (VPN) connection is made on the first interface but the return traffic is sent back over the second interface, then VPN connections, amongst others, will fail, as we shall see in this recipe. Source routing is an advanced feature of most of the modern operating systems. In this recipe, we will show how to set up source routing using the Linux `iproute2` tools, but the same can be achieved on other operating systems using similar tools.

# Getting ready

We use the following network layout:

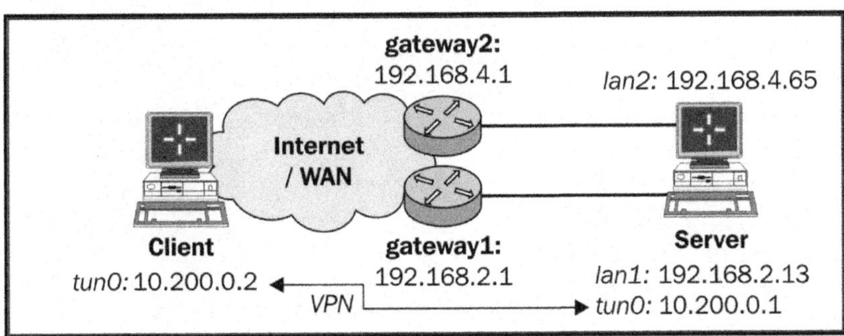


Set up the client and server certificates using the first recipe from `Chapter 2`, *Client-server IP-only Networks*. For this recipe, the server computer was running CentOS 6 Linux and OpenVPN 2.3.11 and was connected to a router with two IP addresses: `192.168.4.65` and `192.168.2.13`; the default gateway for the system was `192.168.2.1`, which means that the traffic will leave the interface with the IP address `192.168.2.13` by default. The secondary gateway had the IP address `192.168.4.1`. The client was running Windows 7 64bit and OpenVPN 2.3.11. The client IP address was `192.168.2.10` with default route `192.168.2.1`. Keep the configuration file `basic-udp-server.conf` from the *Server-side routing* recipe from `Chapter 2`, *Client-server IP-only Networks*, as well as the client configuration file `basic-udp-client.ovpn` from the *Using an ifconfig-pool block* recipe from `Chapter 2`, *Client-server IP-only Networks*.

# How to do it...

1. Start the server using the configuration file `basic-udp-server.conf`:

```
[root@server]# openvpn --config basic-udp-server.conf
```

2. Next, start the client:

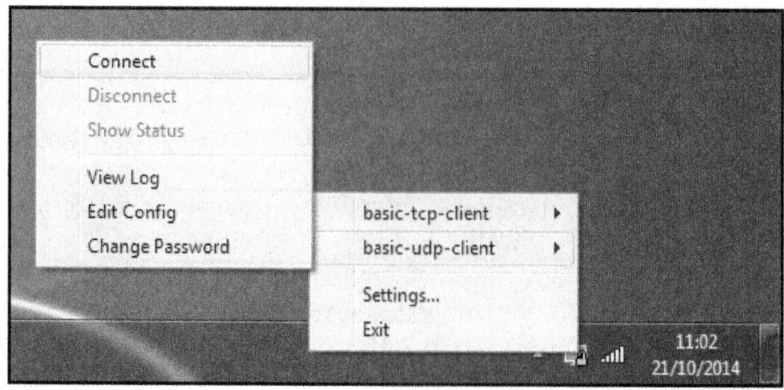


3. In this configuration, the remote server address `openvpnserver.example.com` resolves to `192.168.4.65`.

   The connection will fail to start and the client OpenVPN log file will show the following message repeated a few times:

```
Wed Aug 25 16:24:28 2010 TCP/UDP: Incoming packet rejected from
192.168.2.13:1194[2], expected peer address: 192.168.4.65:1194
(allow this incoming source address/port by removing --remote
or adding --float)
```

4. By adding a source routing rule to return all the traffic, which comes in on one interface (`192.168.4.65`) from a host on the other interface (the subnet `192.168.2.0/24`), wants to leave the interface (`192.168.2.0/24`) to the router associated with the incoming subnet (`192.168.4.1`), the connection is restored:

```
[root@server]# ip route add to default table 100 dev eth0 \
                via 192.168.4.1
[root@server]# ip rule add from 192.168.2.10 priority 50 \
                table 100
[root@server]# ip rule add to 192.168.2.10 priority 50 \
                 table 100
```

   Now, the client can successfully connect to the VPN server.

## How it works...

When a connection is made from the client `192.168.2.10` to the VPN server `192.168.4.65`, the return route is chosen to be the shortest one possible, which in the setup described here is `192.168.2.1`. The server operating system will set the return IP address of the packets to `192.168.2.13`, as that is the IP address of the interface associated with that network. This confuses the OpenVPN client, as it connects to host `192.168.4.65` but gets return traffic from `192.168.2.13`. By explicitly forcing traffic to go out the other interface ( `192.168.4.65`), this asymmetric routing issue is resolved.

The exact syntax of the source routing rules is highly dependent on the exact network configuration, but the general idea of the three commands outlined in the section *How to do it* is to:

- Create a routing table with ID `100` and set the default gateway device for this table to `eth0`, which has the IP address `192.168.4.65`
- Create a routing rule that any traffic which comes from client `192.168.2.10` is redirected to the routing table
- Create a routing rule that any traffic which wants to leave client `192.168.2.10` is redirected to the routing table

The routing rules would need to be tweaked for a live situation, as these rules block out certain other types of network traffic, but the principle is correct.

## There's more...

More advanced routing control can be done using **LARTC** (**Linux Advanced Routing and Traffic Control**). A better approach would be to mark packets coming on the interface and only redirect the marked packets to the correct outgoing interface.

# Routing and permissions on Windows

In this recipe, we will focus on the common error experienced by the users when the VPN client machine is running Windows without full or elevated privileges. Under certain circumstances, the OpenVPN client can connect successfully but the routes that are pushed out by the remote server are not correctly set up. This recipe will focus on how to troubleshoot and correct this error.

## Getting ready

Set up the client and server certificates using the first recipe from `Chapter 2`, *Client-server IP-only Networks*. For this recipe, the server computer was running CentOS 6 Linux and OpenVPN 2.3.11. The client was running Windows 7 64bit and OpenVPN 2.3.11. Keep the configuration file `basic-udp-server.conf` from the *Server-side routing* recipe from `Chapter 2`, *Client-server IP-only Networks*, as well as the client configuration file `basic-udp-client.ovpn` from the *Using an ifconfig-pool block* recipe from `Chapter 2`, *Client-server IP-only Networks*.

## How to do it...

1. Log in on Windows as a non-privileged user, being a user without `Power User` or `Administrator` privileges. Also, make sure to temporarily remove the **Run as Administrator** flag from OpenVPN to launch OpenVPN without elevated privileges. This can be done by unchecking the **Run this program as an administrator** flag in the OpenVPN GUI properties:

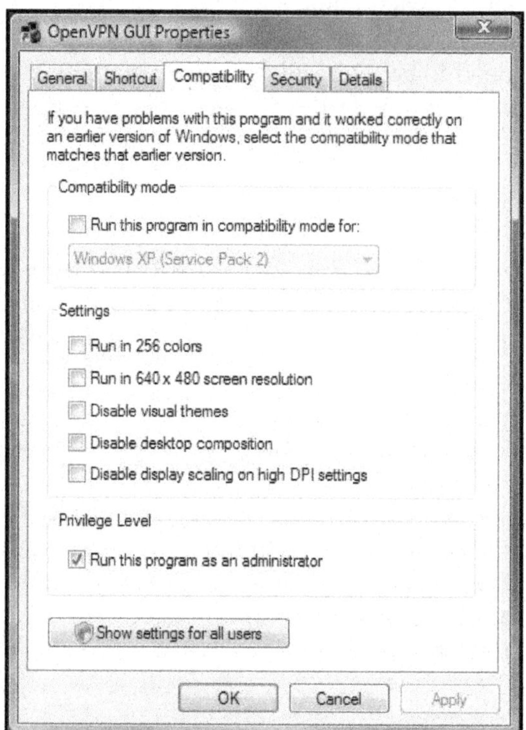

2. Start the server using the configuration file `basic-udp-server.conf`:

```
[root@server]# openvpn --config basic-udp-server.conf
```

3. Finally, start the client.

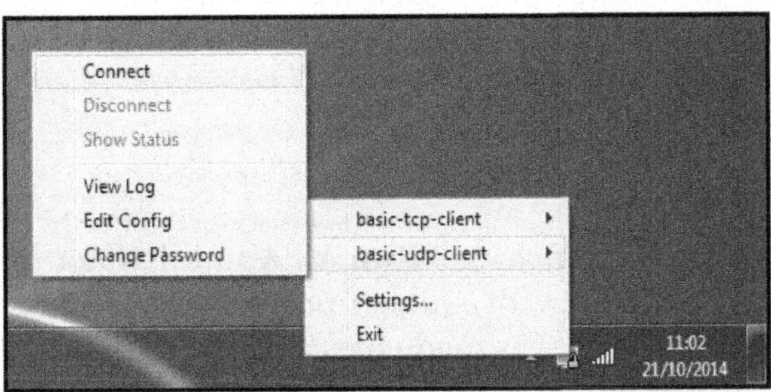


The connection will start and the OpenVPN GUI light will turn green. However, the client OpenVPN log file will show the following messages:

```
... C:\WINDOWS\system32\route.exe ADD 10.198.0.0 MASK 255.255.0.0
10.200.0.1
... ROUTE: route addition failed using CreateIpForwardEntry: Network
access is denied.   [status=65 if_index=2]
... Route addition via IPAPI failed [adaptive]
Thu Aug 26 16:47:53 2010 us=187000 Route addition fallback to route.exe
```

If you attempt to reach a host on the server-side LAN, it will fail:

```
[WinClient]C:\>ping 10.198.0.1
Pinging 10.198.0.1 with 32 bytes of data:
Request timed out.
Ping statistics for 10.198.0.1:
Packets: Sent = 1, Received = 0, Lost = 1 (100% loss)
```

The solution to this issue is to give the proper networking rights to the user, or to restore elevated privileges for OpenVPN again.

# How it works...

The OpenVPN client tries to open the TAP-Win32 adapter, which is allowed in a default installation. However, when the server pushes out a route to the client using:

```
push "route 10.198.0.0 255.255.0.0"
```

Then, the OpenVPN client will not be able to actually add this route to the system routing tables, due to missing administrator privileges. However, the VPN connection is successfully established and the GUI client shows a successful connection.

Note that even without the `push "route"` statement, the Windows OpenVPN GUI showed a green icon, suggesting the connection had started. Technically speaking, it is true that the connection has been established, but this should still be considered as a bug.

## There's more...

Windows XP and higher versions include a **Run As Administrator** service that allows a user to temporarily run a program with a higher privilege level. This mechanism was expanded in Windows Vista/7 and was made the default when launching applications. This has actually been the cause of numerous questions on the `openvpn-users` mailing list when running OpenVPN on these platforms.

# Unable to change Windows network location

The title of this recipe may not seem related to routing issues, but the Windows network location depends on routing to work. Starting with Windows Vista, Microsoft introduced the concept of network locations. By default, there are multiple network locations: **Home**, **Work** and **Public** for Windows 7 and **Private** and **Public** for Windows 8 and above. These network locations apply to all network adapters, including OpenVPN's virtual TAP-Win network adapter.

The **Home** network location is intended for a home network. Similarly, the **Work** network location also provides a high level of trust at work, allowing the computer to share files, connect to printers and so on. In Windows 8 and above, the **Home** and **Work** network locations are merged together to become the trusted **Private** network location. The **Public** network location is not trusted and access to network resources is restricted by Windows, even when the Windows firewall is disabled.

The routing properties of an OpenVPN setup determine whether the TAP-Win adapter is trusted or not, and thus whether file sharing is allowed. In this recipe, we will show how to change an OpenVPN setup so that the network location can be altered.

# Getting ready

Set up the client and server certificates using the first recipe from `Chapter 2`, *Client-server IP-only Networks*. For this recipe, the server computer was running CentOS 6 Linux and OpenVPN 2.3.11. The client was running Windows 7 64bit and OpenVPN 2.3.11. Keep the configuration file `example2-7-server.conf` from the *Redirecting the default gateway* recipe from `Chapter 2`, *Client-server IP-only Networks* at hand, as well as the client configuration file `basic-udp-client.ovpn` from the *Using an ifconfig-pool block* recipe from `Chapter 2`, *Client-server IP-only Networks*.

# How to do it...

1. Start the server using the configuration file `example-2-7-server.conf`:

```
[root@server]# openvpn --config example2-7-server.conf
```

2. Next, start the client.

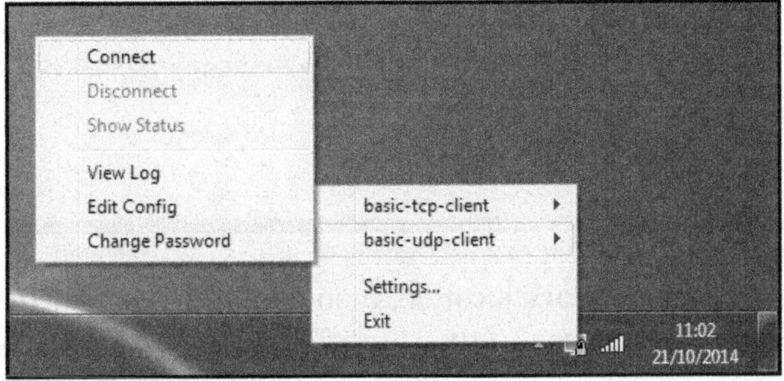


3. Go to the **Network and Sharing Center** and observe that the TAP adapter is in the section **Public Network** and that it is not possible to change this. Also, try to access a file share via the VPN tunnel. This should not be possible.
4. Change the server configuration by removing `def1` from the `push redirect-gateway def1` line:

```
push "redirect-gateway"
```

5. Restart the VPN connection on both sides.

6. As the VPN connection comes up, Windows will ask you for the location of the new network **Network**:

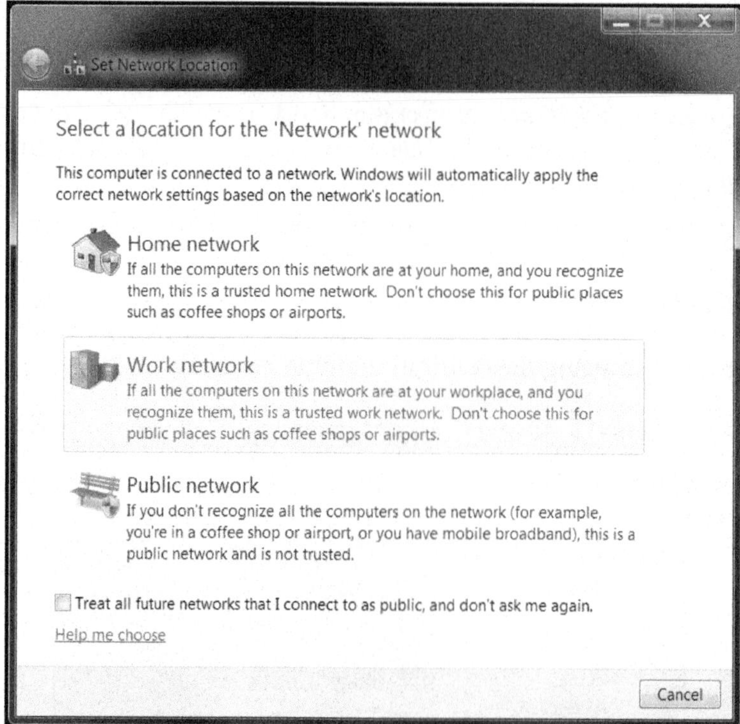


7. Choose the **Work network** location, then give the new network the name `VPN`.
8. Now, go to the **Network and Sharing Center** once more and observe that the TAP adapter (named **vpn0**) is in the work network location **VPN**:

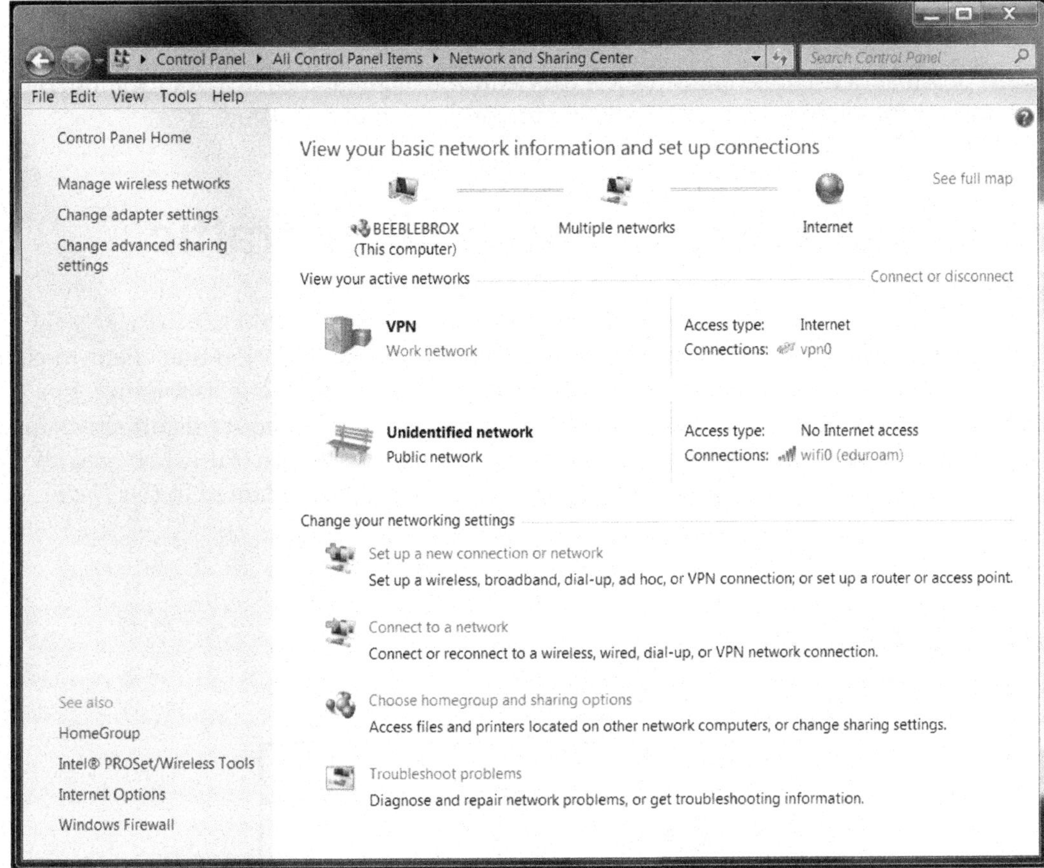


# How it works...

Even though all network traffic is routed over the VPN (using `redirect-gateway def1`) Windows does not trust the VPN adapter and hence will refuse full access over the VPN tunnel. Windows will only trust a network adapter if it advertises a default gateway (0.0.0.0/0), or the network adapter must be part of a Windows domain. This can be fixed by changing the server configuration to use:

```
push "redirect-gateway"
```

# There's more...

It is also possible to use the Windows Registry editor to change the network location, but this is not recommended, as it will mark all network adapters as trusted.

# Troubleshooting client-to-client traffic routing

In this recipe, we will troubleshoot a VPN setup where it is the intention that client-to-client traffic is enabled, but the server configuration directive "client-to-client" is missing. In a TUN-style network, it is possible to allow client-to-client traffic without this directive and it even allows the server administrator to apply firewalling rules to the traffic between clients. In a TAP-style network, this is generally not possible, as will be explained in the *There's more...* section.

# Getting ready

We use the following network layout:

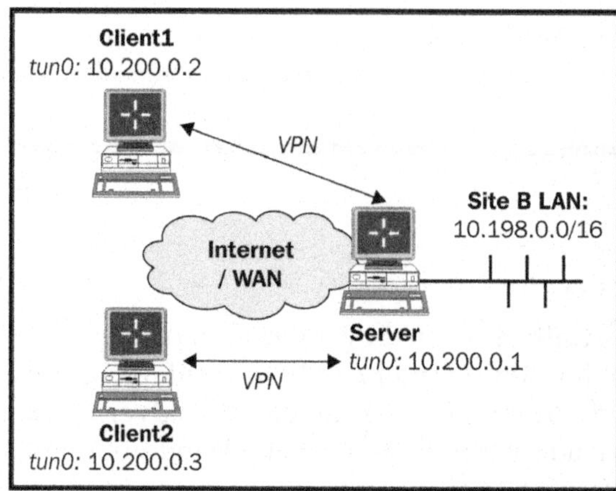

Set up the client and server certificates using the first recipe from `Chapter 2`, *Client-server IP-only Networks*. For this recipe, the server computer was running CentOS 6 Linux and OpenVPN 2.3.11. The first client was running Fedora 22 Linux and OpenVPN 2.3.11. The second client was running Windows 7 64bit and OpenVPN 2.3.11. Keep the configuration file `basic-udp-server.conf` from the *Server-side routing* recipe from `Chapter 2`, *Client-server IP-only Networks*, as well as the client configuration file `basic-udp-client.ovpn` from the *Using an ifconfig-pool block* recipe from `Chapter 2`, *Client-server IP-only Networks*.

# How to do it...

1. Start the server using the configuration file, `basic-udp-server.conf`:

```
[root@server]# openvpn --config basic-udp-server.conf
```

2. Next, start the Linux client.

```
[root@client]# openvpn --config basic-udp-client.conf
```

3. And finally, start the Windows client:

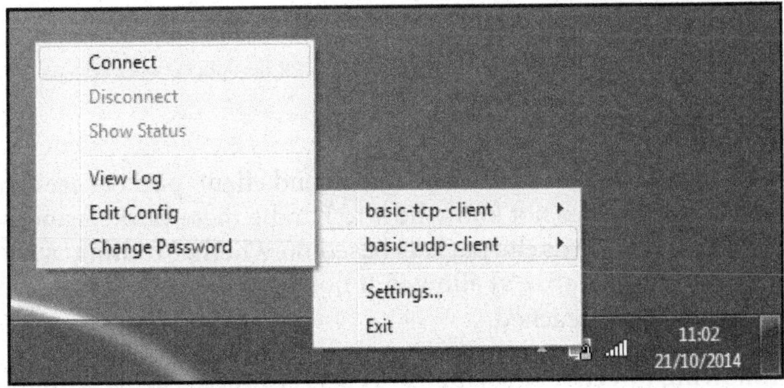


4. Next, try to ping the Windows client from the Linux client (make sure no firewalls are blocking the traffic):

```
[client]$ ping -c 2 10.200.0.3
PING 10.200.0.3 (10.200.0.3) 56(84) bytes of data.
--- 10.200.0.3 ping statistics ---
2 packets transmitted, 0 received, 100% packet loss, time
10999ms
```

It is possible that the host is already reachable, but in that case the firewall on the server is very permissive.

5. At this point, it is instructive to set up `iptables` logging on the VPN server:

```
[root@server]# iptables -I FORWARD -i tun+ -j LOG
```

Then try the ping again. This will result in the following messages in `/var/log/messages`:

```
... openvpnserver kernel: IN=tun0 OUT=tun0 SRC=10.200.0.2
DST=10.200.0.3 LEN=84 TOS=0x00 PREC=0x00 TTL=63 ID=0 DF
PROTO=ICMP TYPE=8 CODE=0 ID=40808 SEQ=1
... openvpnserver kernel: IN=tun0 OUT=tun0 SRC=10.200.0.2
DST=10.200.0.3 LEN=84 TOS=0x00 PREC=0x00 TTL=63 ID=0 DF
PROTO=ICMP TYPE=8 CODE=0 ID=40808 SEQ=2
```

The first client `10.200.0.2` is trying to reach the second client `10.200.0.3`. This issue can be resolved by adding the `client-to-client` configuration directive to the server configuration file and restarting the OpenVPN server, or it can be resolved by allowing tunnel traffic to be forwarded:

```
[server]# iptables -I FORWARD -i tun+ -o tun+ -j ACCEPT
[server]# echo 1 > /proc/sys/net/ipv4/ip_forward
```

# How it works...

When the first OpenVPN client tries to reach the second client, packets are sent to the server itself. The OpenVPN server does not know how to handle these packets and hands them off to the kernel. The kernel forwards the packets based on whether routing is enabled and whether the firewall rules (`iptables`) allow it. If not, then the packet is simply dropped and the second client is never reached.

By adding the following directive, the OpenVPN server process deals with the client-to-client traffic internally, bypassing the kernel forwarding, and the firewalling rules:

```
client-to-client
```

The alternative solution, which is slightly more secure but also less scalable, is to properly set up routing in the Linux kernel.

## There's more...

In a TAP-style network, the above `iptables` rule does not work. In a TAP-style network, all the clients are a part of the same broadcast domain. When the `client-to-client` directive is omitted and a client tries to reach another client, it first sends out `arp` who has messages to find out the MAC address of the other client. The OpenVPN server will ignore these requests and will also not forward them to other clients, regardless of whether an `iptables` rule is set or not. Hence, the clients cannot easily reach each other without the `client-to-client` directive, unless tricks like proxy-ARP are used.

## See also

- The *Enabling client-to-client traffic* recipe, from `Chapter 3`, *Client-server Ethernet-style Networks*, which explains how client-to-client traffic is set up in a TAP-style environment

# Understanding the MULTI: bad source warnings

In this recipe, we focus again on a VPN configuration where we try to connect a client-side LAN to a server-side LAN. Normally, this is done by adding a `client-config-dir` directive to the OpenVPN server configuration, and then by adding the appropriate CCD file. However, if the CCD file is not found or is not readable, then the VPN connection will function properly, but the hosts on the client-side LAN will not be able to reach the hosts on the server-side LAN and vice versa. In this case, the OpenVPN server log file will show messages of the form `MULTI: bad source`, if the verbosity is set high enough. In this recipe, we will first set up a VPN as is done in the *Routing: subnets on both sides* recipe from `Chapter 2`, *Client-server IP-only Networks*, but with a missing CCD file for the client. Then, we will show how to trigger the `MULTI: bad source` warnings and what can be done to resolve the issue.

# Getting ready

We use the following network layout:

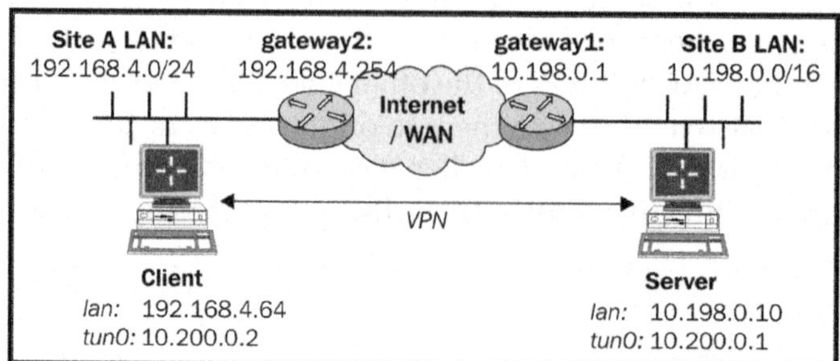


Set up the client and server certificates using the first recipe from the `Chapter 2`, *Client-server IP-only Networks*. For this recipe, the server computer was running CentOS 6 Linux and OpenVPN 2.3.11. The client was running Fedora 22 Linux and OpenVPN 2.3.11. Keep the configuration file `example2-5-server.conf` from the *Using client-config-dir files* recipe from `Chapter 2`, *Client-server IP-only Networks*. For the client, keep the configuration file `basic-udp-client.conf` from the *Server-side routing* recipe from `Chapter 2`, *Client-server IP-only Networks*.

# How to do it...

1. First, make sure the client CCD file is not accessible:

   ```
   [root@server]# chmod 700 /etc/openvpn/cookbook/clients
   ```

2. Start the server using the configuration file `example2-5-server.conf` and with increased verbosity:

   ```
   [root@server]# openvpn --config example2-5-server.conf --verb 5
   ```

3. Next, start the client to connect successfully:

   ```
   [root@client]# openvpn --config basic-udp-client.conf
   ...
   ... Initialization Sequence Completed
   ```

   However, when a host on the client-side LAN tries to reach a machine on the server-side LAN, the following message appears in the OpenVPN server log file:

```
... openvpnclient1/client-ip:58370 MULTI: bad source address
from client [192.168.4.66], packet dropped
```

In this recipe, the root cause of the problem can be resolved as done in the *Troubleshooting client-config-dir issues* recipe from `Chapter 6`, *Troubleshooting OpenVPN – Configurations*, fix the permissions of the directory `/etc/openvpn/cookbook/clients` and reconnect the OpenVPN client.

# How it works...

In order to connect a remote LAN to an OpenVPN server, two server-configuration directives are needed:

```
route remote-lan remote-mask
client-config-dir /etc/openvpn/cookbook/clients
```

And also a CCD file containing the name of the client certificate. The CCD file contains:

```
iroute remote-lan remote-mask
```

Without this, the OpenVPN server does not know which VPN client the remote network is connected to. If a packet comes in from a client that the OpenVPN server does not know about, then the packet is dropped and, with "verb 5" or higher, the warning `MULTI: bad source` is printed.

# There's more...

Apart from the warnings explained above, there is one other major reason for the `MULTI: bad source` messages to occur.

## Other occurrences of the MULTI: bad source message

Sometimes the `MULTI: bad source` message is printed in the OpenVPN server log file even when no client-side LAN is connected to the VPN client. This happens most often with VPN clients running Windows. When a file share is accessed over the VPN connection, Windows sometimes sends packets with a different source IP address to that of the VPN interface. These packets are not recognized by the OpenVPN server and the warning is printed. The solution to this issue is not known.

## See also

- The *Routing: subnets on both sides* recipe from `Chapter 2`, *Client-server IP-only Networks*, which explains the basics of setting up a `client-config-dir` setup
- The *Troubleshooting client-config-dir issues* recipe from `Chapter 6`, *Troubleshooting OpenVPN – Configurations*, which goes deeper into some of the frequently made mistakes when using the `client-config-dir` directive

# Failure when redirecting the default gateway

In this recipe, we will troubleshoot an infrequent yet very persistent issue that can occur when setting up a VPN connection. When the `redirect-gateway` directive is used to redirect the default gateway on an OpenVPN client, it sometimes causes the client to lose all the Internet connections. This particularly occurs when the client machine on which OpenVPN is running is connected to the rest of the network or with the Internet using a PPP-based connection, such as PPPoE or PPPoA, especially, when using a GPRS/UMTS connections via a mobile phone.

When this occurs, OpenVPN sometimes is not capable of determining the default gateway before it is redirected. After the default gateway is redirected to the OpenVPN tunnel, the whole tunnel collapses on itself, as all the traffic, including the encrypted tunnel traffic itself, is redirected into the tunnel, causing the VPN to lock up.

This recipe will show how to detect this situation and what can be done about it. In this recipe, we will not use a GPRS/UMTS connection but we will use a PPP-over-SSH connection, which behaves in a similar fashion and is more readily available.

## Getting ready

We use the following network layout:

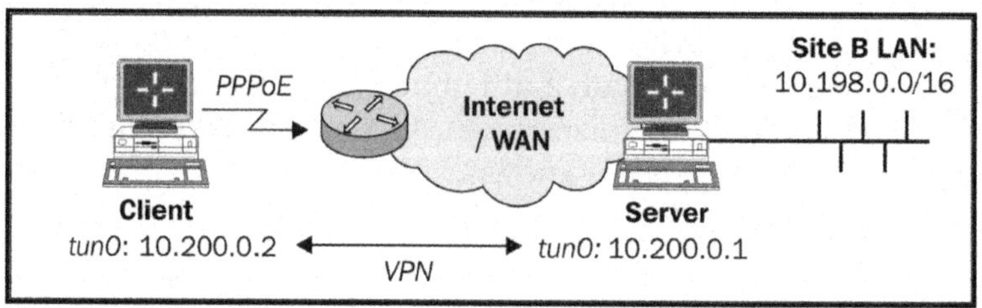

Set up the client and server certificates using the first recipe from `Chapter 2`, *Client-server IP-only Networks*. For this recipe, the server computer was running CentOS 6 Linux and OpenVPN 2.3.11. The client was running Fedora 22 Linux and OpenVPN 2.3.11. Keep the configuration file `basic-udp-server.conf` from the *Server-side routing* recipe from `Chapter 2`, *Client-server IP-only Networks*.

Make sure the client is connected to the network using a PPP connection, as otherwise the issue described in the title of this recipe will not occur. For this recipe, a PPP-over-SSH connection and the default route was altered to point to the `ppp0` device.

# How to do it...

1. Start the server and add an extra parameter to direct the default gateway:

```
[root@server]# openvpn --config basic-udp-server.conf \
  --push "redirect-gateway"
```

2. Create the client configuration file:

```
client
proto udp
# next is the IP address of the VPN server via the
# PPP-over-SSH link
remote 192.168.222.1
port 1194

dev tun
nobind

ca       /etc/openvpn/cookbook/ca.crt
cert     /etc/openvpn/cookbook/client1.crt
key      /etc/openvpn/cookbook/client1.key
tls-auth /etc/openvpn/cookbook/ta.key 1

user nobody
verb 5
```

Save it as `example7-9-client.conf`.

3. Check the system routes before starting the client:

```
[root@client]# netstat -rn
172.30.0.10     172.30.0.1      255.255.255.255 UGH 0 0 0 eth0
192.168.222.1   0.0.0.0         255.255.255.255 UH  0 0 0 ppp0
0.0.0.0         192.168.222.1   0.0.0.0         UG  0 0 0 ppp0
```

4. Now, start the client:

```
[root@client]# openvpn --config example7-9-client.conf
```

The connection will start but after a few seconds will stop and the log file will contain a warning message:

```
... OpenVPN ROUTE: omitted no-op route:
192.168.222.1/255.255.255.255 -> 192.168.222.1
```

5. Check the system routes again:

```
[client]$ netstat -rn
172.30.0.19     172.30.0.1      255.255.255.255 UGH 0 0 0 eth0
192.168.222.1   0.0.0.0         255.255.255.255 UH  0 0 0 ppp0
192.16.186.192 0.0.0.0          255.255.255.192 U   0 0 0 eth0
10.200.0.0   0.0.0.0         255.255.248.0   U   0 0 0 tun0
10.198.0.0      10.200.0.1   255.255.0.0     UG  0 0 0 tun0
0.0.0.0         10.200.0.1   0.0.0.0         UG  0 0 0 tun0
```

The default gateway is now the VPN tunnel but the original route to the gateway is now gone.

All the connections on the client have stopped. What's worse, when the OpenVPN client is aborted (by pressing Ctrl +C in the terminal window) the default route is not restored, as the OpenVPN process does not have the proper rights to do so:

```
TCP/UDP: Closing socket
/sbin/ip route del 10.198.0.0/16
RTNETLINK answers: Operation not permitted
ERROR: Linux route delete command failed: external program exited with
error status: 2
/sbin/ip route del 192.168.222.1/32
RTNETLINK answers: Operation not permitted
ERROR: Linux route delete command failed: external program exited with
error status: 2
/sbin/ip route del 0.0.0.0/0
RTNETLINK answers: Operation not permitted
ERROR: Linux route delete command failed: external program exited with
error status: 2
```

```
/sbin/ip route add 0.0.0.0/0 via 192.168.222.1
RTNETLINK answers: Operation not permitted
ERROR: Linux route add command failed: external program exited with error
status: 2
Closing TUN/TAP interface
```

The result is that the default gateway on the client machine is gone. The only solution is to reload the network adapter so that all the system defaults are restored.

The solution to the above problem is to use the following as is done in the *Redirecting the default gateway* recipe from `Chapter 2`, *Client-server IP-only Networks*:

```
push "redirect-gateway def1"
```

# How it works...

When the OpenVPN client initializes, it always tries to create a direct route to the OpenVPN server via the existing system gateway. Under certain circumstances this fails, mostly due to an odd network configuration. It is seen most often when the default gateway is a dial-up or PPPoE connection, which is used in certain ADSL/VDSL setups and especially when using GPRS/UMTS connections.

When the OpenVPN client is instructed to redirect all the traffic over the VPN tunnel, it normally sends the encrypted VPN traffic itself over a direct link to the OpenVPN server. You can think of the encrypted VPN traffic as outside of the tunnel. However, when this direct route is missing, then this outside traffic is also sent into the tunnel, creating a tunneling loop from which the VPN can never recover.

In the example used in this recipe, the situation is made worse by using the client configuration directive:

```
user nobody
```

This tells the OpenVPN process to drop all the privileges after starting. When the client is aborted because the tunnel is not functioning properly, the client is not capable of restoring the original gateway and the system is left in a non-functioning state:

```
[client]$ netstat -rn
194.171.96.27   192.16.186.254 255.255.255.255 UGH 0 0 0 eth0
192.168.222.1   0.0.0.0        255.255.255.255 UH  0 0 0 ppp0
192.16.186.192 0.0.0.0         255.255.255.192 U   0 0 0 eth0
```

Only by adding a new default gateway can the network be restored.

The proper fix is to use:

```
push "redirect-gateway def1"
```

This will not overwrite the existing default gateway but will add two extra routes:

```
0.0.0.0    10.200.0.1 128.0.0.0  UGH 0 0 0 tun0
128.0.0.0 10.200.0.1 128.0.0.0  UGH 0 0 0 tun0
```

Both of which cover half the available network space. These two routes effectively replace the existing default route whilst not overwriting it.

## There's more...

This "biting your own tail" problem was much more common with older versions of OpenVPN. In current versions of OpenVPN, the detection of the default gateway was much improved and this problem now rarely occurs anymore. However, it is useful to see what happens when the problem does occur.

## See also

- The *Redirecting the default gateway* recipe from `Chapter 2`, *Client-server IP-only Networks*, which explains how to properly redirect all traffic via the VPN tunnel

# 8
# Performance Tuning

In this chapter, we will cover the following troubleshooting topics:

- Optimizing performance using `ping`
- Optimizing performance using `iperf`
- Comparing IPv4 and IPv6 speed
- OpenSSL cipher speed
- OpenVPN in Gigabit networks
- Compression tests
- Traffic shaping
- Tuning UDP-based connections
- Tuning TCP-based connections
- Analyzing performance using `tcpdump`

## Introduction

This chapter focuses on getting the best performance out of an OpenVPN setup. There are several parameters that can be tuned on both the server side and the client side for getting the highest throughput and the lowest latency. However, the optimal settings of these parameters largely depend on the network layout. The recipes in this chapter will therefore provide guidelines on how to tune these parameters and how to measure the increase or decrease in performance. These guidelines can then be applied to other network layouts to find the optimal performance.

# Optimizing performance using ping

In this recipe, we will use the low-level `ping` command to determine the optimal **Maximum Transfer Unit** (**MTU**) size for our OpenVPN setup. Finding the right MTU size can have a tremendous impact on performance, especially, when using satellite links, or even some cable/ADSL providers. Especially, broadband connections using the **PPPoE** (**PPP over Ethernet**) protocol often have a non-standard MTU size. In a regular LAN setup, it is hardly ever required to optimize the MTU size, as OpenVPN's' default settings are close to optimal.

## Getting ready

Make sure the client and the server computers are connected over a network. For this recipe, the server computer was running CentOS 6 Linux. The client was running Fedora 22 Linux, but instructions for a Windows client are given as well.

## How to do it...

1. We first verify that we can reach the server from the client:

   ```
   [client]$ ping -c 2 <openvpn-server-ip>
   ```

   This will send two ICMP ping packets to the server and two replies should be returned. If not, then a firewall or `iptables` rule is blocking ICMP traffic. Ensure that the server can be reached using `ping` before proceeding.

2. Next, try sending a large ping packet from the client to the server, with the `Don't Fragment` (**DF**) bit set. Strangely enough, on Linux, this is done using the parameter `-M do`.

   ```
   [client]$ ping -c 2 -M do -s 1600 <openvpn-server-ip>
   ```

   Normally, this command is not successful:

   ```
   From 172.30.0.128 icmp_seq=1 Frag needed and DF set (mtu =
   1500)
   ```

   The maximum size of a packet that can be sent from this interface is 1500 bytes. From this, the Ethernet headers (normally 28 bytes) need to be subtracted, which means that the maximum size of an ICMP packet is 1472 bytes:

```
[client]$ ping -c 2 -M do -s 1472 <openvpn-server-ip>
PING 172.30.0.128 (172.30.0.128) 1472(1500) bytes of data.
1480 bytes from 172.30.0.128: icmp_seq=1 ttl=128 time=0.630 ms
1480 bytes from 172.30.0.128: icmp_seq=2 ttl=128 time=0.398 ms
```

3. For Windows clients, the syntax of the `ping` command is slightly different:

   ```
   [winclient]C:> ping -f -l 1600 <openvpn-server-ip>
   Packet needs to be fragmented but DF set.
   ```

   And:

   ```
   [winclient]C:> ping -f -l 1472 <openvpn-server-ip>
   Pinging 172.30.0.1 with 1472 bytes of data:
   Reply from 172.30.0.1: bytes=1472 time<1ms TTL=64
   ```

   The payload size of 1472 bytes is actually the regular size for an Ethernet-based network, even though this recipe was performed over a cable connection.

A good initial value for OpenVPN's' `tun-mtu` setting is the maximum payload size plus the 28 bytes that were subtracted earlier. However, it does not mean this is the optimal value, as we will see in the later recipes.

## How it works...

The ICMP protocol which the `ping` command uses has the option to set a flag `Don't Fragment` (DF). With this bit set, an ICMP packet may not be broken up into separate pieces before it reaches its destination. If the packet were needed to be broken up by a router before it could be transmitted, it is dropped and an ICMP error code is returned. This provides a very easy method to determine the largest packet that can be transmitted to the server and vice versa. In particular, in high-latency networks, for example, when a satellite link is used, it is very important to limit the number of packets and to maximize the size of each packet.

By smartly using the `ping` command, the maximum packet size can be determined. This size can then be used to further optimize the OpenVPN performance.

## There's more... Ping tunnel method

In some network setups, ICMP traffic is filtered, rendering this recipe useless. If it is possible to reach the OpenVPN server, then the tunnel can also be used to find the maximum payload size.

Start the OpenVPN server with the extra flags:

```
cipher none
auth none
```

Do the same for the OpenVPN client. Make sure compression is turned off (or simply not specified) and that the `fragment` option is not used. This will start a clear-text tunnel over which we can send ICMP packets of various sizes.

Ping the remote end's VPN IP address, for example:

```
[client]$ ping -c 2 -M do -s 1472 10.200.0.1
```

When the ICMP packet becomes too large, the traffic will be dropped by an intermittent router. Lower the ICMP packet size until the ping returns successfully. From that value, the MTU size can be derived.

## See also

- The *Tuning UDP-based connections* recipe, which will explain in more detail how to tune the performance of UDP-based setups
- The *Tuning TCP-based connections* recipe, which goes deeper into the details of tuning TCP-based setups and also explains some of the intricacies of the MTU setting of the network adapter

# Optimizing performance using iperf

This recipe is not really about OpenVPN but more about how to use the network performance measurement tool `iperf` in an OpenVPN setup. The `iperf` utility can be downloaded from `http://sourceforge.net/projects/iperf/` for Linux, Windows, and MacOS.

In this recipe, we will run `iperf` outside of OpenVPN and over the VPN tunnel itself, after which the differences in performance will be explained.

## Getting ready

We use the following network layout:

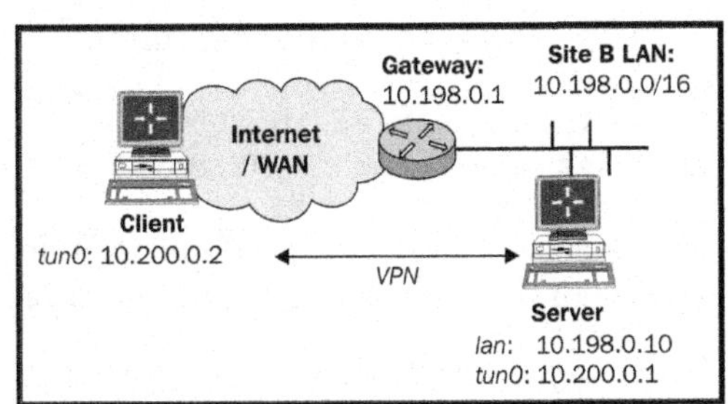


Set up the client and server certificates using the *Setting up the public and private keys* recipe from `Chapter 2`, *Client-server IP-only Networks*. For this recipe, the server computer was running CentOS 6 Linux and OpenVPN 2.3.11. The client was running Fedora 22 Linux and OpenVPN 2.3.11. Keep the configuration file `basic-udp-server.conf` from the *Server-side routing* recipe from `Chapter 2`, *Client-server IP-only Networks*, as well as the client configuration file `basic-udp-client.conf`.

## How to do it...

1. Start the server:

```
[root@server]# openvpn --config basic-udp-server.conf
```

2. Next, start the client:

```
[root@client]# openvpn --config basic-udp-client.conf
...
... Initialization Sequence Completed
```

3. Next, we start `iperf` on the server:

```
[server]$ iperf -s
```

4. First, we measure the performance outside the tunnel:

```
[client]$ iperf -l 1M -n 8M -c <openvpn-server-ip>
[  3]  0.0-15.2 sec  8 MBytes  4.1 Mbits/sec
```

This actually measures the performance of data being sent to the server. The cable network used in this recipe has a theoretical upload limit of 4 Megabits per second (Mbps), which we are achieving in this test.

5. Next, we measure the performance inside the tunnel:

```
[client]$ iperf -l 1M -n 8M -c 10.200.0.1
[  3]  0.0-17.0 sec  8 MBytes  3.95 Mbits/sec
```

With this network setup, there is a small performance difference between traffic sent outside of the tunnel and traffic sent via the tunnel.

6. A second test is done over a 802.11n wireless network:

```
[client]$ iperf -c <openvpn-server-ip>
[  4]  0.0-10.8 sec  7.88 MBytes  6.10 Mbits/sec
```

Versus:

```
[client]$ iperf -c 10.200.0.1
[  5]  0.0-11.3 sec  5.25 MBytes  3.91 Mbits/sec
```

Here, there is a noticeable drop in performance, suggesting that the OpenVPN is not configured optimally. There was a lot of noise on this wireless network, which makes it difficult to optimize.

# How it works...

The `iperf` tool is very straightforward: it sets up a TCP connection (or UDP, if desired) and measures how fast it can send or receive data over this connection. Normally, traffic is tested in only one direction, although a dual test can be triggered using the `-r` flag.

# There's more...

Tuning network performance depends heavily on both the network latency and the available bandwidth, as is outlined in more detail here.

## Client versus server iperf results

Both the client and the server `iperf` processes report the network throughput after a `iperf -c` session has ended. Practice shows that the numbers reported by the server used in this recipe were more accurate than the numbers reported by the client. On the cable network used when writing this recipe, the maximum upload speed is about 4 Mbps. The client sometimes reported speeds larger than 4.4 Mbps, whereas the server reported a more accurate 4.1 Mbps.

## Network latency

One of the main reasons for the lack of performance drop over the cable network versus the performance drop over the wireless network is due to network latency. On the cable network, the latency was very stable at about 11 ms. On the wireless network, the latency varied between 2 ms and 90 ms. Especially, this variation in latency can skew the `iperf` performance measurements, making it very hard to optimize the OpenVPN parameters.

## Gigabit networks

Performance tests on Gigabit networks show that the VPN itself is becoming the bottleneck. A normal TCP connection would show a transfer rate of 900 Mbps, whereas a TCP connection via an untuned OpenVPN tunnel would not perform faster than about 320 Mbps. We will come back to this later in this chapter.

## See also

- The recipe *OpenVPN in Gigabit networks*, which will explain in more detail how to tune OpenVPN for better performance over high-speed networks

# Comparing IPv4 and IPv6 speed

This recipe is a continuation of the previous recipe, but here we will focus on the performance difference between tunneling Pv4 traffic and IPv6 traffic. In this recipe, we will run `iperf` over the VPN tunnel using IPv4 addresses and IPv6 addresses inside the tunnel, after which the differences in performance will be explained.

# Getting ready

We use the following network layout:

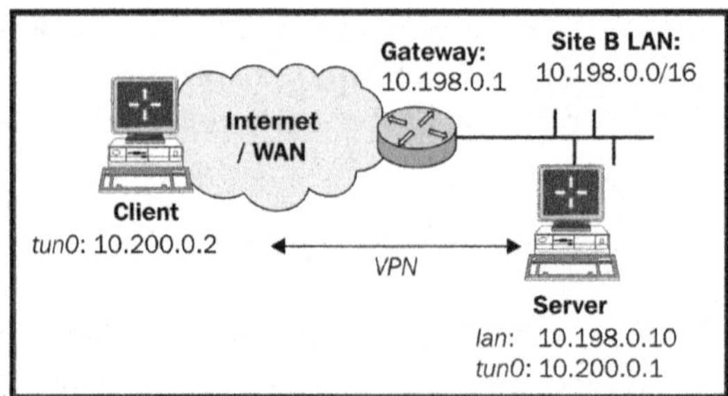


Set up the client and server certificates using the *Setting up the public and private keys* recipe from `Chapter 2`, *Client-server IP-only Networks*. For this recipe, the server computer was running CentOS 6 Linux and OpenVPN 2.3.11. The client was running Fedora 22 Linux and OpenVPN 2.3.11. Keep the configuration file `example-2-4-server.conf` from the *Adding IPv6 support* recipe from `Chapter 2`, *Client-server IP-only Networks*, as well as the client configuration file `basic-udp-client.conf`.

# How to do it...

1. Start the server:

```
[root@server]# openvpn --config example-2-4-server.conf
```

2. Next, start the client:

```
[root@client]# openvpn --config basic-udp-client.conf
...
... Initialization Sequence Completed
```

3. Next, we start `iperf` on the server:

```
[server]$ iperf -s
```

4. First, we measure the performance when tunneling IPv4 traffic:

```
[client]$ iperf -l 1M -n 8M -c 10.200.0.1
[  3]  0.0-17.0 sec  8 MBytes  3.95 Mbits/sec
```

5. Next, we measure the performance using IPv6 packets:

```
[client]$ iperf -l 1M -n 8M -c  2001:db8:100::1
[  3]  0.0-17.7 sec  8 MBytes  3.78 Mbits/sec
```

This shows a performance difference of roughly 5%. This difference is measured consistently over all types of networks.

## How it works...

An IPv6 address is longer than an IPv4 address. The source and destination addresses for all packets are stored inside the encrypted packets that go over the OpenVPN tunnel. Thus, the larger the addressing scheme used, the less bytes are left for the actual "payload". An IPv6 packet can actually carry 20 bytes less "payload" than an IPv4 packet. These 20 bytes account for the 5% performance difference. There is very little that can be done about this.

## There's more...

Tuning network performance depends heavily on the network characteristics, as well as the tuning tools used, as is outlined in more detail here.

### Client versus server iperf results

Both the client and the server `iperf` processes report the network throughput after an `iperf -c` session has ended. Practice shows that the numbers reported by the server used in this recipe were more accurate than the numbers reported by the client. Also, more accurate results are achieved by running `iperf` with a fixed data size instead of the default fixed time interval of 10 seconds. We specify a fixed block size (1 Megabyte) and a fixed total size (8 Megabyte) using `iperf -l 1M -n 8M -c <IP-address>`.

This increases accuracy and improves the consistency of the numbers reported on the client and server side.

# OpenSSL cipher speed

OpenVPN uses OpenSSL to perform all cryptographic operations. This means that the performance of an OpenVPN client or server depends on how fast the incoming traffic can be decrypted and how fast the outgoing traffic can be encrypted. For a client with a single connection to the OpenVPN server, this is almost never an issue, but with an OpenVPN server with hundreds of clients, the cryptographic performance becomes very important. Also, when running OpenVPN over a high-speed network link (Gigabit or higher), the cryptographic performance also plays an important role.

In this recipe, we will show how to measure the performance of the OpenSSL cryptographic routines and how this measurement can be used to improve the performance of an OpenVPN server.

## Getting ready

This recipe is performed on a variety of computers:

- An old laptop with an Intel Core2 Duo T9300 processor running at 2.5 GHz, running Fedora Linux 22 64bit
- An older server with an Intel Xeon X5660 processor running at 2.8 GHz and with support for the AESNI instructions, running CentOS 6 64bit
- A high-end server with an Intel Xeon E5-2697A v4 processor running at 2.6 GHz and with support for the AESNI instructions, running CentOS 6 64bit

The recipe can easily be performed on MacOS as well. Each computer had OpenVPN 2.3 installed, with the accompanying OpenSSL libraries.

## How to do it...

On each system, the following OpenSSL commands are run:

```
$ openssl speed -evp bf-cbc
$ openssl speed -evp aes-128-cbc
$ openssl speed -evp aes-256-cbc
```

The first command tests the speed of the OpenVPN default BlowFish cryptographic cipher. The second and third test the performance of the 128 and 256-bit AES ciphers, which are very commonly used to secure websites. All commands were run twice on the new high-end server: once with support for the AES-NI instruction set turned on and once with AES-NI support off using the `$ OPENSSL_ia32=0 openssl speed -evp <cipher>`.

The results are displayed in the following table. All numbers in the tables are the bytes per second processed when encrypting a block of data. The size of the block of data is listed in the columns.

For the `BlowFish` cipher, the following results were recorded:

| **Type** | **256 bytes** | **1024 bytes** | **8192 bytes** |
|---|---|---|---|
| Laptop | 95851.54k | 95426.22k | 95862.84k |
| Old Server | 111466.67k | 111849.47k | 112162.13k |
| New Server | 151329.96k | 152054.10k | 152428.54k |
| New Server, no AES-NI | 151128.49k | 151951.02k | 152048.98k |

For the `AES128` cipher, the following results were recorded:

| **Type** | **256 bytes** | **1024 bytes** | **8192 bytes** |
|---|---|---|---|
| Laptop | 85588.05k | 179870.91k | 183104.85k |
| Old Server | 758884.44k | 762378.58k | 755960.49k |
| New Server | 802229.85k | 806787.75k | 807682.05k |
| New Server, no AES-NI | 160414.98k | 361608.53k | 368836.61k |

And for `AES256`:

| **Type** | **256 bytes** | **1024 bytes** | **8192 bytes** |
|---|---|---|---|
| Laptop | 60698.20k | 130553.15k | 132085.73k |
| Old Server | 560398.93k | 562632.92k | 564687.49k |
| New Server | 577053.35k | 578981.21k | 579532.12k |
| New Server, no AES-NI | 114444.29k | 266473.47k | 270030.17k |

# How it works...

The output of the `openssl speed` command shows that the encryption and decryption performance is dependent on both the encryption key and the hardware used. Most OpenVPN packets are about 1500 bytes, so the column 1024 bytes is the most interesting column to look at.

The `BlowFish` cipher results are quite interesting if you take the processor speed into account: if you divide the `BlowFish` performance by the processor clock speed the numbers are very similar. This means that the `BlowFish` performance is bound purely by the processor clock speed. An older type processor running at a higher clock speed might actually outperform a newer processor with a slightly lower clock speed.

For the `AES128` and `AES256` ciphers, this is no longer true. Here the modern i5/i7 and Xeon architectures are much faster than the older Pentium 4 and Athlon architectures. With the AES-NI extensions, the performance jumps by a factor of 4. If an OpenVPN server is set up that must support many clients, then this cryptographic cipher is an excellent choice, provided that the server CPU supports these extensions.

This recipe also provides a simple test of whether the AES-NI instructions are available and whether they are actually picked up by the underlying OpenSSL library. If the speed results between `openssl` and `OPENSSL_ia32cap=0 openssl` do not differ, then the AES-NI instructions are not being used for encryption or decryption.

# There's more...

The choice of the cryptographic cipher on the performance of OpenVPN is minimal for a single client. Measurements done for this recipe indicate that the client CPU has a load of less than 8% when downloading a file at the highest speed over the VPN tunnel on a modern system. However, on the older desktop, the choice of cryptographic cipher does become important: upload speed drops from 760 kbps to 720 kbps when the `BlowFish` cipher changes to the `AES256` cipher. In particular, when older hardware or certain home router equipment is used, this can quickly become a bottleneck. Most home wireless routers capable of running OpenVPN, for example, the wireless routers that support the DD-WRT or OpenWRT distributions, have a processor speed of about 250 MHz. This processor speed can quickly become the bottleneck if this router is also used as an OpenVPN server, especially when multiple clients connect simultaneously.

## See also

- The *Cipher mismatches* recipe from `Chapter 6`, *Troubleshooting OpenVPN – Configurations,* which explains in more detail how to troubleshoot cipher mismatches in the client and server configuration files.

# OpenVPN in Gigabit networks

With the advent of high-speed networks, the need for a high-speed VPN has also increased. OpenVPN is not particularly built for high speeds, but with modern hardware and the right encryption ciphers it is possible to achieve near-gigabit speeds with OpenVPN 2.4. This recipe will show you how to achieve these speeds.

## Getting ready

We use the following network layout:

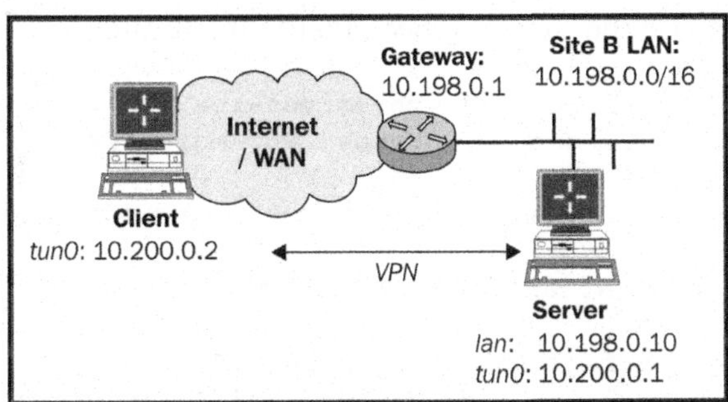


The client used in this recipe was a laptop with a Core i7-4810 processor with a maximum Turboboost speed of 3.8 GHz. The server was a server with an Xeon E5-2697A v4 processor with a maximum Turboboost speed of 3.6 GHz. Connect the client and the server both to a Gigabit Ethernet switch. Set up the client and server certificates using the *Setting up the public and private keys* recipe from `Chapter 2`, *Client-server IP-only Networks*. For this recipe, the server computer was running CentOS 6 Linux and OpenVPN 2.4.0.

The client was running Fedora 22 Linux and OpenVPN 2.4.0. Keep the configuration file `basic-udp-server.conf` from the *Server-side routing* recipe from `Chapter 2`, *Client-server IP-only Networks*, as well as the client configuration file `basic-udp-client.conf`.

# How to do it...

1. Start the server:

```
[root@server]# openvpn --config basic-udp-server.conf
```

2. Next, start the client:

```
[root@client]# openvpn --config basic-udp-client.conf
...
... Initialization Sequence Completed
```

3. Next, we start `iperf` on the server:

```
[server]$ iperf -s
```

4. First, we measure the performance outside the tunnel:

```
[client]$ iperf -c <openvpn-server-ip>
[  3]  0.0-10.0 sec  11 GBytes  900 Mbits/sec
```

   For a Gigabit Ethernet network, this is close to the theoretical limit.

5. Next, we measure the performance inside the tunnel:

```
[client]$ iperf -l 1M -n 8M -c 10.200.0.1
[  4]  0.0-10.2 sec  292 MBytes  233 Mbits/sec
```

   This is the performance of a default OpenVPN tunnel.

6. Stop both the client and server OpenVPN processes.
7. Now, we switch to an AES-256 cipher to make use of the AES-NI instructions that both processors support:

```
[server]# openvpn --config basic-udp-server.conf --cipher aes-
256-cbc
```

And the client:

```
[client]# openvpn --config basic-udp-client.conf --cipher aes-
256-cbc
...
... Initialization Sequence Completed
```

8. Again, we measure the performance inside the tunnel, testing both directions:

```
[client]$ iperf -l 1M -n 8M -c 10.200.0.1 -r
[  4]  0.0-10.2 sec  762 MBytes  610 Mbits/sec
[  5]  0.0-10.2 sec  807 MBytes  646 Mbits/sec
```

This clearly shows that the AES-NI instructions make a difference.

9. Stop both the client and server OpenVPN processes again.
10. Now, we switch to AES-256-GCM, a new cipher algorithm supported by OpenVPN 2.4, which is more efficient compared to an AES-256 cipher and SHA2 HMAC function:

```
[server]# openvpn --config basic-udp-server.conf --cipher aes-
256-gcm
```

And the client:

```
[client]# openvpn --config basic-udp-client.conf --cipher aes-
256-gcm
...
... Initialization Sequence Completed
```

11. Again, we measure the performance inside the tunnel, testing both directions:

```
[client]$ iperf -l 1M -n 8M -c 10.200.0.1 -r
[  4]  0.0-10.2 sec  1.07 GBytes  859 Mbits/sec
[  5]  0.0-10.2 sec  1.08 GBytes  865 Mbits/sec
```

The last performance numbers are actually quite close to the maximum speed that can be achieved over an OpenVPN tunnel on a Gigabit Ethernet network.

## How it works...

When processors are used that have a high clock speed and have support for the AES-NI instructions, OpenVPN and the operating system are capable of keeping up with the flood of packets that is coming in and needs to be sent out at Gigabit Ethernet speeds.

The new AES-256-GCM encryption cipher especially helps here, as the encryption and authentication (HMAC) are done in one step. This greatly improves performance, in part due to shorter computing time and in part due to the fact that this cipher has a smaller encryption overhead for each packet, leaving more bytes for the actual "payload".

# There's more...

Tuning network performance on Gigabit Ethernet depends heavily on the hardware and operating system used.

## Plain-text tunnel

Another interesting test to run is to turn off all encryption and authentication (`--cipher none --auth none`) and then run the `iperf` tests once more. With the hardware used in this recipe the following numbers were achieved:

```
[  4]  0.0-10.2 sec  1.09 GBytes  874 Mbits/sec
[  5]  0.0-10.2 sec  1.10 GBytes  879 Mbits/sec
```

These numbers are even closer to the actual line speed, mostly due to the fact that there is no encryption overhead, leaving optimal space for the "payload".

## Windows performance

The `iperf` tool is also available on Windows, so the above recipe can also be done using a Windows client and/or server. The results are very different compared to the Linux client or server. We can achieve similar "raw" Ethernet speeds by using `[WinClient]> iperf -w 128K -c <openvpn-server-ip>`.

However, performance over the OpenVPN tunnel, with or without encryption, is well below 200 Mbps, even with the fastest processors used. Most likely, this is due to a design issue in the Windows TAP driver. This issue is currently under investigation.

# Compression tests

OpenVPN has built-in support for LZO compression if compiled properly. All Windows binaries have LZO compression available by default. In this recipe, we will show what is the performance of using LZO compression when transferring both easily compressible data (such as web pages) and non-compressible data (such as photographs or binaries).

# Getting ready

We use the following network layout:

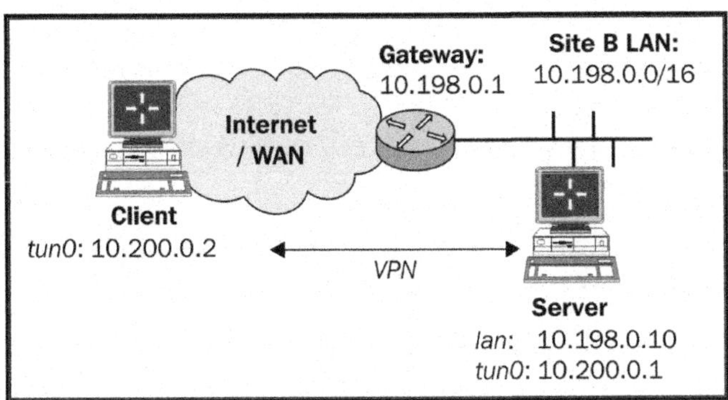


Set up the client and server certificates using the *Setting up the public and private keys* recipe from `Chapter 2`, *Client-server IP-only Networks*. For this recipe, the server computer was running CentOS 6 Linux and OpenVPN 2.3.11. The first client was running Fedora 22 Linux and OpenVPN 2.3.11. Keep the configuration file `basic-udp-server.conf` from the *Server-side routing* recipe from `Chapter 2`, *Client-server IP-only Networks,* as well as the client configuration file `basic-udp-client.conf`. The recipe was repeated with a second client running Windows 7 64bit and OpenVPN 2.3.11. Keep the configuration file `basic-udp-server.conf` from the *Server-side routing* recipe from `Chapter 2`, *Client-server IP-only Networks,* as well as the client configuration file `basic-udp-client.ovpn` from the *Using an ifconfig-pool block* .

# How to do it...

1. Append the following line to the `basic-udp-server.conf` file:

```
comp-lzo
```

   Save it as `example8-6-server.conf`.

2. Start the server:

```
[root@server]# openvpn --config example8-6-server.conf
```

3. Similarly, for the client, add a line to the `basic-udp-client.conf` file:

   ```
   comp-lzo
   ```

   Save it as `example8-6-client.conf`.

4. Start the client:

   ```
   [root@client]# openvpn --config example8-6-client.conf
   ```

5. Next, we start `iperf` on the server:

   ```
   [server]$ iperf -s
   ```

6. First, we measure the performance when transferring data outside of the tunnel:

   ```
   [client]$ iperf -c <openvpn-server-ip>
   ```

   This results in a throughput of about 50 Mbps over an 802.11n wireless network.

7. Next, non-compressible data:

   ```
   [client]$ dd if=/dev/urandom bs=1024k count=60 of=random
   [client]$ iperf -c 10.200.0.1 -F random
   [  4]  0.0-10.0 sec  35.0 MBytes  29.3 Mbits/sec
   ```

   In the first step, we create a 60MB file with random data. Then, we measure the `iperf` performance when transferring this file.

8. And finally, compressible data (a file filled with zeroes):

   ```
   [client]$ dd if=/dev/zeroes bs=1024k count=60 of=zeroes
   [client]$ iperf -c 10.200.0.1 -F zeroes
   [  5]  0.0- 5.9 sec  58.6 MBytes  83.3 Mbits/sec
   ```

   The performance of the VPN tunnel when transferring compressible data such as text files and web pages is shown.

9. The same measurement can be made using a Windows PC. Add the following line to the `basic-udp-client.ovpn` file:

   ```
   comp-lzo
   ```

   Save it as `example8-6.ovpn`.

10. Start the client.

The results of the `iperf` measurement are slightly different:

- Outside the tunnel: 50 Mbps
- Non-compressible data: 16 Mbps
- Compressible data: 22 Mbps

Clearly, the OpenVPN configuration needs to be optimized, but that is outside the scope of this recipe. These results do show that for both Windows and Linux clients, there is a significant performance boost when the data that is sent over the tunnel is easily compressible.

# How it works...

When compression is enabled, all packets that are sent over the tunnel are compressed before they are encrypted and transferred to the other side. Compression is done using the LZO library, which is integrated into OpenVPN. This compression is done on-the-fly, which means that the compression ratios achieved are not as good as when compressing the data in advance. When transferring text pages, the performance gain is nevertheless significant.

# There's more...

When the following configuration directive is used, adaptive compression is enabled by default:

```
comp-lzo
```

When OpenVPN detects that a particular piece of data is not compressible, it sends the data to the remote VPN endpoint without compressing it first. By specifying the following on both ends each packet is always compressed:

```
comp-lzo yes
```

Depending on the type of data that is transferred, the performance is slightly better.

# Traffic shaping

In this recipe, we will use traffic shaping to limit the upload speed of an OpenVPN client. This can be used to throttle the bandwidth of a client to the server, or from client to client. Note that OpenVPN traffic shaping cannot be used to throttle the download speed of OpenVPN clients. Throttling download speeds can best be achieved using external traffic control tools, such as the `tc` utility on Linux, which is part of the LARTC package.

## Getting ready

We use the following network layout:

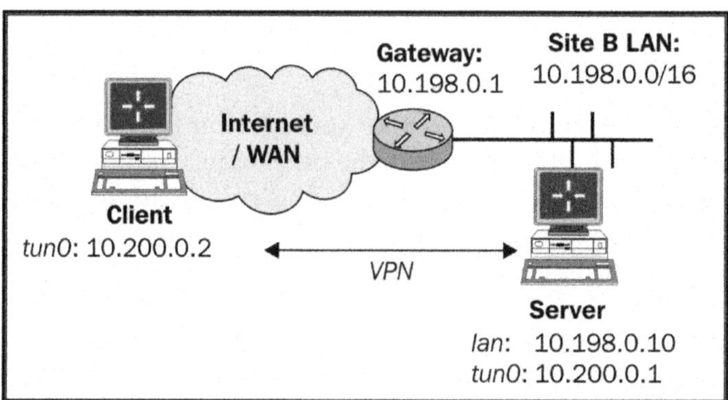


Set up the client and server certificates using the *Setting up the public and private keys* recipe from `Chapter 2`, *Client-server IP-only Networks*. For this recipe, the server computer was running CentOS 6 Linux and OpenVPN 2.3.11. The client was running Windows 7 64 bit and OpenVPN 2.3.11. Keep the configuration file `basic-udp-server.conf` from the *Server-side routing* recipe from `Chapter 2`, *Client-server IP-only Networks,* as well as the client configuration file `basic-udp-client.ovpn` from the *Using an ifconfig-pool block* recipe.

## How to do it...

1. Append the following line to the `basic-udp-server.conf` file:

```
push "shaper 100000"
```

This will throttle the upload speed of the VPN clients to 100,000 bytes per second (100 kbps). Save it as `example8-7-server.conf`.

2. Start the server:

```
[root@server]# openvpn --config example8-7-server.conf
```

3. Start the client:

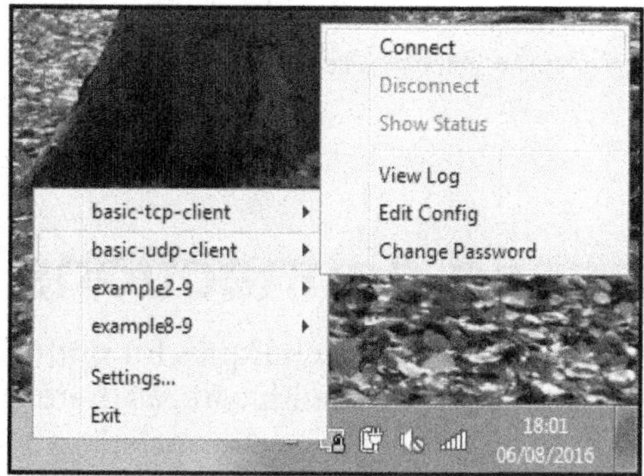


4. Next, we start `iperf` on the server:

```
[server]$ iperf -s
```

5. When we run `iperf` on the Windows PC, the performance is close to 100 KB/s:

```
Console

c:\>iperf -c 10.200.0.1 -f K
------------------------------------------------------------
Client connecting to 10.200.0.1, TCP port 5001
TCP window size: 8.00 KByte (default)
------------------------------------------------------------
[164] local 10.200.0.2 port 49258 connected with 10.200.0.1 port 5001
[ ID] Interval       Transfer     Bandwidth
[164]  0.0-10.2 sec   864 KBytes  84.4 KBytes/sec

c:\>_
```

6. The PNG number of bytes being sent over the tunnel, including encryption overhead, is actually very close to 100,000 bytes per second.

## How it works...

When the OpenVPN client connects to the server, the server pushes out an option to shape outgoing traffic over the VPN tunnel to 100 KB/s. Whenever traffic is sent over the tunnel, the OpenVPN client itself limits the outgoing traffic to a maximum of 100 KB/s. The download speed is not affected by this, and note that the following directive cannot be used on the OpenVPN server itself:

```
shaper 100000
```

To throttle traffic leaving the server, more advanced traffic control tools such as `tc` for Linux should be used.

# Tuning UDP-based connections

In this recipe, we focus on some of the basic techniques for optimizing UDP-based VPN tunnels. These techniques need to be applied with care, as there is no fool-proof method for optimizing OpenVPN performance. The actual performance gain varies with each network setup. Therefore, this recipe only shows some of the configuration directives that can be used for this optimization.

## Getting ready

We use the following network layout:

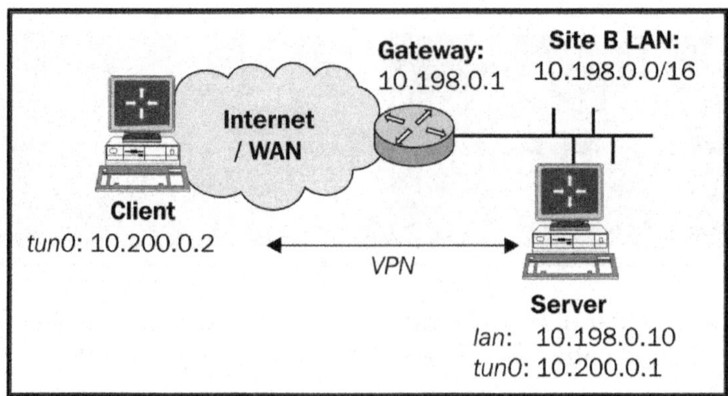

Set up the client and server certificates using the *Setting up the public and private keys* recipe from `Chapter 2`, *Client-server IP-only Networks*. For this recipe, the server computer was running CentOS 6 Linux and OpenVPN 2.3.11. The client was running Fedora 22 Linux and OpenVPN 2.3.11. Keep the configuration file `basic-udp-server.conf` from the *Server-side routing* recipe from `Chapter 2`, *Client-server IP-only Networks*, as well as the client configuration file `basic-udp-client.conf`.

# How to do it...

1. Append the following line to the `basic-udp-server.conf` file:

```
fragment 1400
```

2. Save it as `example8-8-server.conf`.
3. Start the server:

```
[root@server]# openvpn --config example8-8-server.conf
```

4. Similarly, for the client, add a line to the `basic-udp- client.conf` file:

```
fragment 1400
```

5. Save it as `example8-8-client.conf`.
6. Start the client:

```
[root@client]# openvpn --config example9-6-client.conf
```

7. Next, we start `iperf` on the server:

```
[server]$ iperf -s
```

8. First, we measure the performance outside the tunnel:

```
[client]$ iperf -c <openvpn-server-ip>
[  4]  0.0-16.7 sec  8.00 MBytes  4.03 Mbits/sec
```

This actually measures the performance of data being sent to the server. The cable network used in this recipe has a theoretical upload limit of 4 Mbps. Note that this result is nearly the same as found in the recipe *Optimizing performance using iperf*.

9. Next, we measure the performance inside the tunnel:

```
[client]$ iperf -c 10.200.0.1
[  4]  0.0-18.3 sec  8.00 MBytes  3.66 Mbits/sec
```

   A slight penalty is incurred due to the OpenVPN tunnel, but the results are nearly identical to the results found in the recipe *Optimizing performance using iperf*.

   Fragmentation does have an effect on the `ping` round-trip times, however.

10. For various values of the `fragment` option, run the `ping` command from the client to server:

```
[client]$ ping -c 10 10.200.0.1
```

The results are listed in the following table:

| Fragmentation size | Ping result |
|---|---|
| Default (1500) | 9.4 +/- 1.0 ms |
| 1400 | 9.9 +/- 1.5 ms |
| 400 | 19.2 +/- 8 ms |

Thus, adding the `fragment` option to the server configuration is not a viable option for this network setup. However, in other network setups, this might improve performance.

## How it works...

The OpenVPN configuration directive `fragment 1400` causes all encrypted packets that are larger than 1400 bytes to be fragmented. If the network latency is low enough, this does not have a noticeable effect on performance, as the `iperf` results. By lowering the fragmentation size, packets are split into more and more packets. This causes the round-trip time for larger packets to increase. If the network latency is already high, this will cause even more latency issues. Hence, the `fragment` option and associated `mssfix` option must be used with care.

## There's more...

The `fragment` directive is often used in conjunction with the `mssfix` directive:

```
mssfix [maximum-segment-size]
```

This directive announces to TCP sessions running over the tunnel that they should limit their send packet sizes so that after OpenVPN has encapsulated them; the resulting UDP packet size that OpenVPN sends to its peer will not exceed the maximum segment size. It is also used internally by OpenVPN to set the maximum segment size of outbound packets. If no maximum segment size is specified, the value from the `fragment` directive is used.

Ideally, the `mssfix` and `fragment` directives are used together, where `mssfix` will try to keep TCP from needing packet fragmentation in the first place, and if big packets come through anyhow (for example, from protocols other than TCP), the `fragment` directive will internally fragment them.

## See also

- The next recipe in this chapter, which explains how to tune TCP-based connections in a very similar manner

# Tuning TCP-based connections

In this recipe, we focus on some of the basic techniques for optimizing TCP-based VPN tunnels. In a TCP-based VPN setup, the connection between the VPN endpoints is a regular TCP connection. This has advantages and drawbacks. The main advantage is that it is often easier to set up a TCP connection than a UDP connection, mostly due to firewall restrictions. The main drawback of tunneling TCP traffic over a TCP-based tunnel is that there is chance of severe performance penalties, especially when the network connection is poor. This performance penalty is caused by the *tcp-over-tcp* syndrome. The TCP protocol guarantees the ordered delivery of packets, thus if a packet is dropped along the way, the packet will be resent. Once the new packet is received, the packet order is restored. Until that time, all packets after the `lost` packet are on hold. The problem with tunneling TCP traffic over a TCP connection is that both layers want to guarantee ordered packet delivery. This can lead to a large amount of retransmits and hence to a large performance penalty.

When tuned correctly, however, an OpenVPN tunnel over a TCP connection can achieve the same performance as an OpenVPN tunnel over a UDP connection. In this recipe, we will show some techniques for tuning such a TCP-based OpenVPN connection.

# Getting ready

We use the following network layout:

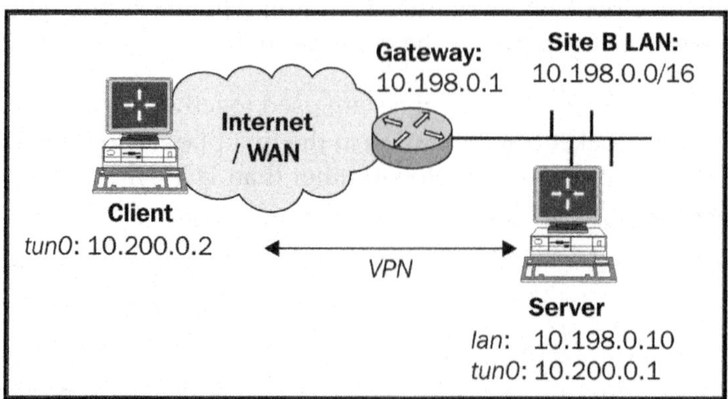


Set up the client and server certificates using the *Setting up the public and private keys* recipe from `Chapter 2`, *Client-server IP-only Networks*. For this recipe, the server computer was running CentOS 6 Linux and OpenVPN 2.3.11. The client was running Windows 7 64bit and OpenVPN 2.3.11. Keep the configuration file `basic-udp-server.conf` from the *Server-side routing* recipe from `Chapter 2`, *Client-server IP-only Networks*, as well as the client configuration file `basic-udp-client.ovpn` from the *Using an ifconfig-pool block* recipe.

# How to do it...

1. Create the server configuration file:

```
proto tcp
port 1194
dev tun
server 10.200.0.0 255.255.255.0

ca      /etc/openvpn/cookbook/ca.crt
cert    /etc/openvpn/cookbook/server.crt
key     /etc/openvpn/cookbook/server.key
dh      /etc/openvpn/cookbook/dh2048.pem
```

```
tls-auth /etc/openvpn/cookbook/ta.key 0

persist-key
persist-tun
keepalive 10 60

topology subnet

user  nobody
group nobody

daemon
log-append /var/log/openvpn.log

tcp-nodelay
```

2. Save it as `example8-9-server.conf`.
3. Start the server:

```
[root@server]# openvpn --config example8-9-server.conf
```

4. Next, create the client configuration file:

```
client
proto tcp
remote openvpnserver.example.com
port 1194

dev tun
nobind

remote-cert-tls server
ca       "c:/program files/openvpn/config/ca.crt"
cert     "c:/program files/openvpn/config/client2.crt"
key      "c:/program files/openvpn/config/client2.key"
tls-auth "c:/program files/openvpn/config/ta.key" 1
```

5. Save it as `example8-9.ovpn`.

6. Start the client:

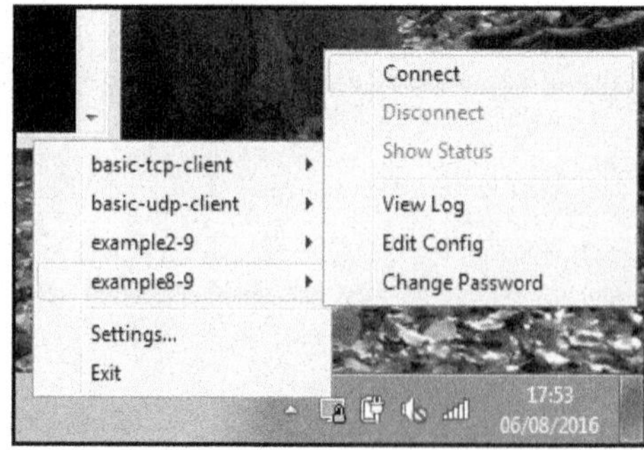


7. Next, start `iperf` on the server:

```
[server]$ iperf -s
```

8. Then, measure the performance of the tunnel:

```
[WinClient]> iperf -c 10.200.0.1 -w 128k
```

On this particular network, the following settings were tested:

| Protocol | Result |
|---|---|
| UDP | 147 Mbits/sec |
| TCP | 115 Mbits/sec |
| TCP with tcp-nodelay | 146 Mbits/sec |

As can be seen, the performance of running OpenVPN over TCP is almost identical to the performance of OpenVPN over UDP, when the `--tcp-nodelay` directive is used.

## How it works...

When OpenVPN uses TCP as its underlying protocol, all packets are transferred over a regular TCP connection. By default, TCP connections make use of the Nagle algorithm, where smaller packets are held back and collected before they are sent. For an OpenVPN tunnel, this has an adverse effect on performance in most cases, hence it makes sense to disable the Nagle algorithm. By adding the `--tcp-nodelay` directive, we disable the Nagle algorithm and we see an immediate increase in performance.

## There's more...

The two important parameters that can be tweaked for TCP-based connections are:

- The `--tcp-nodelay` directive
- The MTU size of the TUN/TAP-Win32 adapter via either the `--tun-mtu` or `--link-mtu` directives

On Linux, the MTU size of the TUN (or TAP) adapter can be adjusted on-the-fly, but on Windows, this is not as easy. OpenVPN must be configured to match the MTU size as specified on the server. Before the new MTU size is used, however, the MTU of the TAP adapter must be adjusted. Starting with Windows Vista, it is now also possible to do this on-the-fly, using the `netsh` command:

- First, find the right sub-interface number:

```
[winclient]C:> netsh interface ipv4 show subinterfaces
```

- Next, in order to change the MTU size of a sub-interface, use:

```
[winclient]C:> netsh interface ipv4 set subinterface "1"
mtu=1400
```

Note that these commands must be run with elevated privileges.

If the MTU setting of the Windows TAP-Win32 adapter is larger than the MTU size configured by OpenVPN, the following message can appear in the OpenVPN log file:

```
... read from TUN/TAP  [State=AT?c Err=[c:\src\21\tap-win32\tapdrvr.c/2447]
#O=4 Tx=[29510,0] Rx=[15309,0] IrpQ=[0,1,16] PktQ=[0,22,64] InjQ=[0,1,16]]:
More data is available.  (code=234)
```

For this particular network, all changes made to the MTU size (with the appropriate Windows reboot) did not have a positive effect on performance.

# Analyzing performance using tcpdump

In this recipe, we will analyze the performance of an OpenVPN setup using the `tcpdump` utility. It is also possible to use the Wireshark utility, which is available for Linux, Windows, and Mac OS X. While this recipe does not cover any new OpenVPN functionality, it is useful to show how such an analysis can be made.

# Getting ready

We use the following network layout:

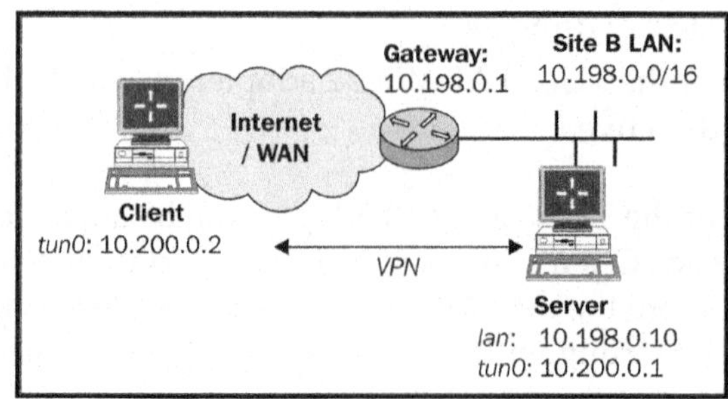


Set up the client and server certificates using the *Setting up the public and private keys* recipe from `Chapter 2`, *Client-server IP-only Networks*. For this recipe, the server computer was running CentOS 6 Linux and OpenVPN 2.3.11. The client was running Fedora 22 Linux and OpenVPN 2.3.11. Keep the configuration file `example8-8-server.conf` from the *Tuning UDP-based connections* recipe from `Chapter 2`, *Client-server IP-only Networks*, as well as the client configuration, `example8-8-client.conf`, from the same recipe.

# How to do it...

1. Start the server:

```
[root@server]# openvpn --config example8-8-server.conf
```

2. Next, start the client:

```
[root@client]# openvpn --config example8-8-client.conf
```

3. On the server, run `tcpdump` to watch for the incoming packets on the network interface (not the tunnel interface itself):

```
[root@server]# tcpdump -nnl -i eth0 udp port 1194
```

   This instructs `tcpdump` to listen on the local network interface for all UDP traffic on port `1194`, which is the OpenVPN default.

4. From the client, ping the server's VPN IP address with two different sizes:

```
[client]$ ping -c 2 -s 1300 10.200.0.1
[client]$ ping -c 2 -s 1400 10.200.0.1
```

The following packets are seen in the `tcpdump` screen:

```
Example 9-6
File  Edit  View  Terminal  Help
$ tcpdump -nnl -i eth0 udp port 1194
### ping -s 1300
17:32:06.906635 IP 172.30.0.130.43817 > 172.30.0.1.1194: UDP, length 1373
17:32:06.908359 IP 172.30.0.1.1194 > 172.30.0.130.43817: UDP, length 1373
17:32:07.908039 IP 172.30.0.130.43817 > 172.30.0.1.1194: UDP, length 1373
17:32:07.909785 IP 172.30.0.1.1194 > 172.30.0.130.43817: UDP, length 1373
### ping -s 1400
17:32:11.129258 IP 172.30.0.130.43817 > 172.30.0.1.1194: UDP, length 757
17:32:11.129380 IP 172.30.0.130.43817 > 172.30.0.1.1194: UDP, length 757
17:32:11.131245 IP 172.30.0.1.1194 > 172.30.0.130.43817: UDP, length 757
17:32:11.131368 IP 172.30.0.1.1194 > 172.30.0.130.43817: UDP, length 757
17:32:12.130396 IP 172.30.0.130.43817 > 172.30.0.1.1194: UDP, length 757
17:32:12.130523 IP 172.30.0.130.43817 > 172.30.0.1.1194: UDP, length 757
17:32:12.132641 IP 172.30.0.1.1194 > 172.30.0.130.43817: UDP, length 757
17:32:12.133167 IP 172.30.0.1.1194 > 172.30.0.130.43817: UDP, length 757
```

The first ICMP packets are sent unfragmented, as they are smaller than 1400 bytes. The second set of encrypted ICMP packets is larger than the fragment size (1400) and hence are split into two parts.

## How it works...

The OpenVPN configuration directive `fragment 1400` causes all the encrypted packets that are larger than 1400 bytes to be fragmented. When watching the encrypted traffic, this can be verified by pinging the OpenVPN server. Note that packets which need to be fragmented are fragmented evenly: all packets have the same size.

Also, note that the following command causes the encrypted packet to be larger than 1400 bytes:

```
[client]$ ping -c 2 -s 1400 10.200.0.1
```

The encryption needed for the secure tunnel adds extra overhead to the packets that are transmitted. This is one of the root causes for a performance penalty when using VPN tunnels (not just OpenVPN) compared to non-encrypted traffic. In most networks, this overhead is not noticed, but it always exists.

# See also

- The *Tuning UDP-based connections* recipe in this chapter, which explains how to use the `fragment` directive

# 9

# OS Integration

In this chapter, we will cover the following recipes:

- Linux – using `NetworkManager`
- Linux – using `pull-resolv-conf`
- Windows – elevated privileges
- Windows – using the CryptoAPI store
- Windows – updating the DNS cache
- Windows – running OpenVPN as a service
- Windows – public versus private network adapters
- Windows – routing methods
- Windows 8+- ensuring DNS lookups are secure
- Android- using the OpenVPN for Android clients
- Push-peer-info – pushing options to Android clients

## Introduction

In this chapter, we will focus on how to use OpenVPN on Linux, Windows, and Android. For each operating system, an entire chapter could be written to describe the intricacies of running OpenVPN in both the client and server mode, but as space is limited, we will focus only on the interaction of the OpenVPN client with the OS. The purpose of the recipes in this chapter is to outline some of the common pitfalls when running OpenVPN on a particular platform. The recipes focus mainly on the configuration of OpenVPN itself, not on how to integrate a working VPN setup into the rest of the network infrastructure.

# Linux – using NetworkManager

When Linux is used as a desktop operating system, the network configuration is configured using the Linux NetworkManager in most of the cases. This package allows a non-root user to start and stop the network connections, connect and disconnect from wireless networks, and also to set up several types of VPN connections, including OpenVPN. In this recipe, we will show how to configure an OpenVPN connection using the GNOME variant of the NetworkManager.

## Getting ready

Set up the client and server certificates using the first recipe from `Chapter 2`, *Client-server IP-only Networks*. For this recipe, the server computer was running CentOS 6 Linux and OpenVPN 2.3.11. The client was running Fedora 22 Linux and OpenVPN 2.3.11. This version of Linux comes with NetworkManager 1.0.8, including the `NetworkManager-openvpn` plugin. The `NetworkManager-openvpn` plugin is not installed by default and needs to be explicitly added to the system. Keep the configuration file, `basic-udp-server.conf`, in the *Server-side routing* recipe from `Chapter 2`, *Client-server IP-only Networks*, at hand.

## How to do it...

1. Start the NetworkManager configuration screen by right-clicking on the NetworkManager icon in the taskbar and selecting **Edit Connections**. A window will pop up.
2. Choose the **VPN** tab to set up a new VPN connection:

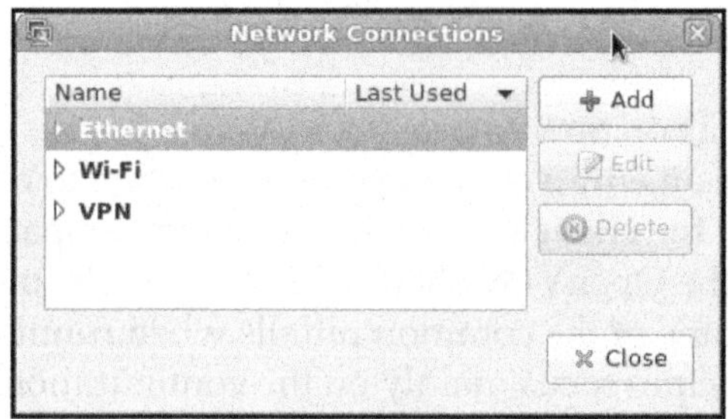

3. Click on the **Add** button to bring up the next screen:

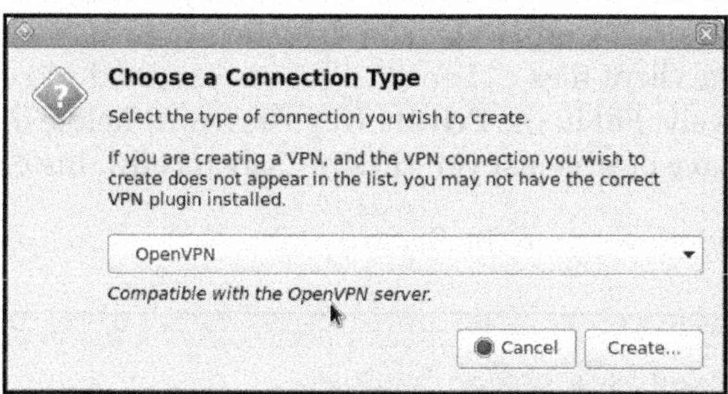


4. Select the **OpenVPN** as the VPN type and click on the **Create...** button. If the VPN connection type **OpenVPN** is not available, then the `NetworkManager-openvpn` plugin is not installed.
5. Fill in the details of the **VPN** tab of the next window:

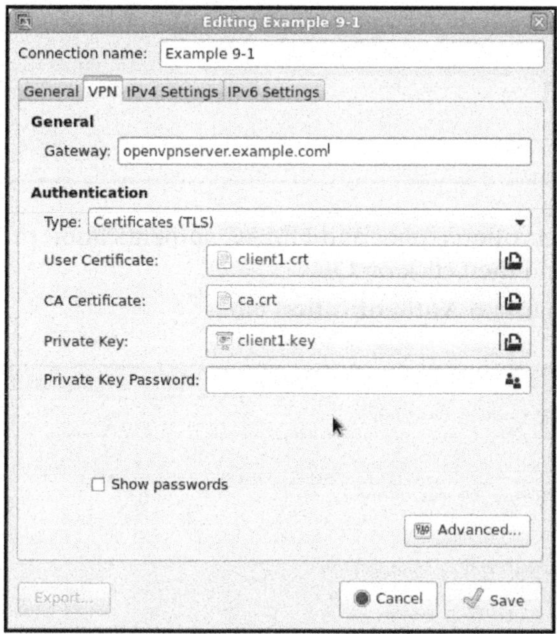

The **Gateway** is the hostname or IP address of the OpenVPN server. The **Type** of authentication is **Certificates (TLS)**. Then, for the **User Certificate**, **CA Certificate**, and **Private Key** fields, browse to the directory where the client files `client1.crt`, `ca.crt`, and `client1.key` are located, respectively. Fill in the **Private Key Password** fields, if required. Do not click on the **Save** button just yet, click on **Advanced...** instead.

6. In the next window, go to the **Security** tab:

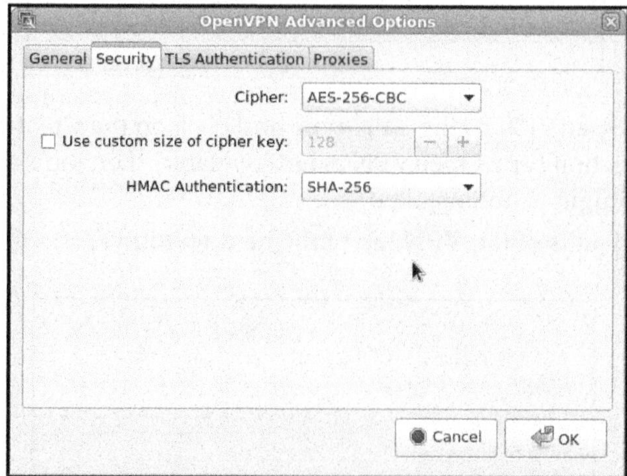


7. Select the encryption cipher and HMAC authentication protocol to use for the connection and then click on **OK**.
8. Then, go to the **TLS Authentication** tab.

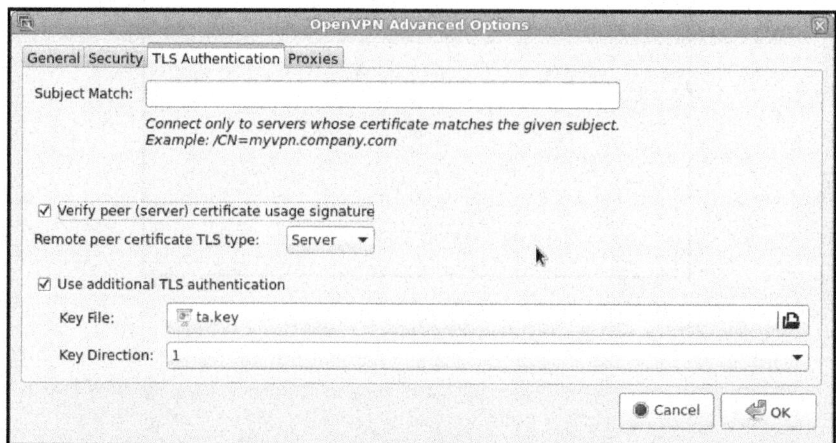

9. Enable **Verify peer (server) certificate usage signature**, then select **Use additional TLS authentication**, and browse to the location of the `ta.key` file. Choose **1** for the key direction.
10. Click on **OK** when done and then click on **Apply** to save the new VPN connection.
11. Next, start the server:

```
[root@server]# openvpn --config basic-udp-server.conf
```

12. And finally, on the client, start the VPN connection by clicking on the NetworkManager icon, choosing**VPN Connections** and selecting **Example 9-1**:

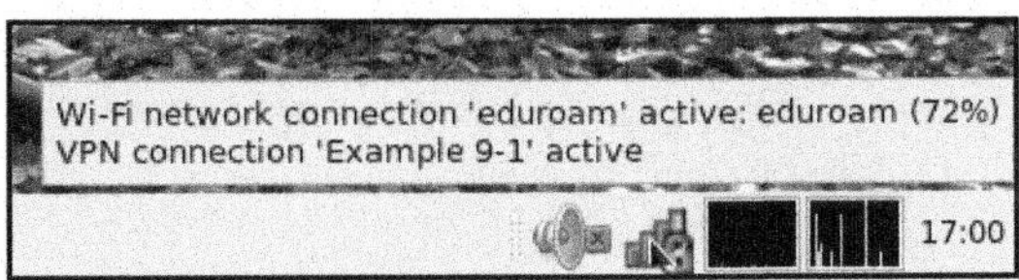


You can verify whether the VPN connection is established correctly by pinging the VPN server IP.

## How it works...

The `NetworkManager-openvpn` plugin is a GUI for setting up an OpenVPN client configuration file. All the settings made are the equivalent of setting up the client configuration file as done in the *Server-side routing* recipe from `Chapter 2`, *Client-server IP-only Networks*.

## There's more...

The `NetworkManager-openvpn` plugin supports some advanced configuration settings:

## Setting up routes using NetworkManager

The `NetworkManager-openvpn` plugin can also be used to set up VPN-specific routes. Open the main VPN configuration screen again and go to the **IPv4 Settings** tab. Click on the **Routes...** button on this screen:

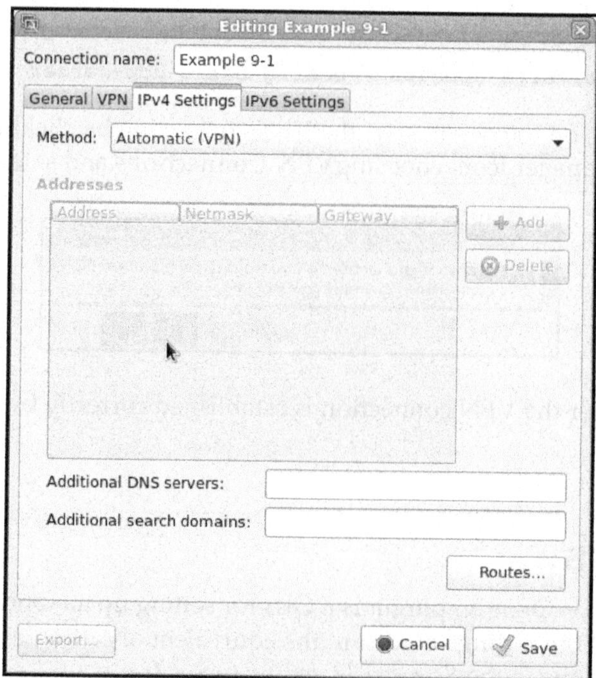


A new window will appear:

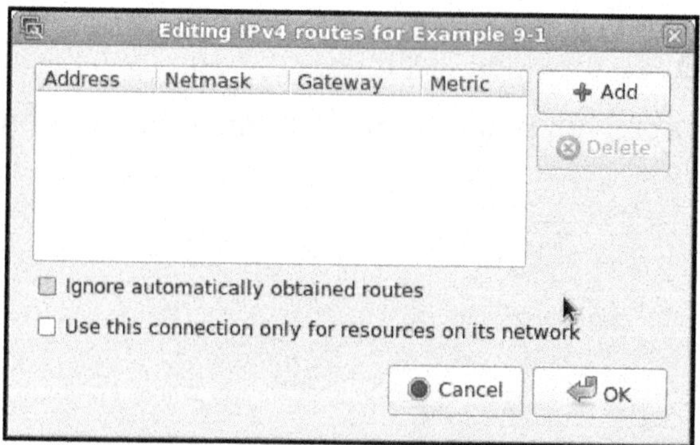

Routes pushed by the server can be overruled using the **Ignore automatically obtained routes** option. By default, the `NetworkManager-openvpn` plugin will enable `redirect-gateway`, even if it is not pushed by the server. This behavior can be overruled by checking the **Use this connection only for resources on its network** checkbox.

## DNS settings

The `NetworkManager-openvpn` plugin also updates the `/etc/resolv.conf` file if the OpenVPN server pushes out DNS servers using the following directive:

```
push "dhcp-option DNS a.b.c.d"
```

## Scripting

Note that NetworkManager does not allow scripting or plugins on the client side, as they are a security risk when configured by a non-root user.

Doesn't Work :( - I have resolvconf pkg installed too

# Linux – using pull-resolv-conf

One of the most common pitfalls when setting up a VPN connection on Linux is when the OpenVPN server pushes out new DNS settings. In the previous recipe, we saw that the `NetworkManager-openvpn` plugin also updated the system configuration file that contained the DNS setting, `/etc/resolv.conf`. If the command line is used, this is not done automatically. By default, OpenVPN comes with two scripts to add and remove DNS servers from the `/etc/resolv.conf` file. This recipe will show how to use these scripts.

- I used the down-root plugin w/ client.up/down scripts that
- I copy-pasted into /etc/openvpn from openvpn wiki.
- I couldn't find a /contrib/pull-resolv-conf dir w/ those two up/down scripts either on my machine

## Getting ready

We will use the following network layout:

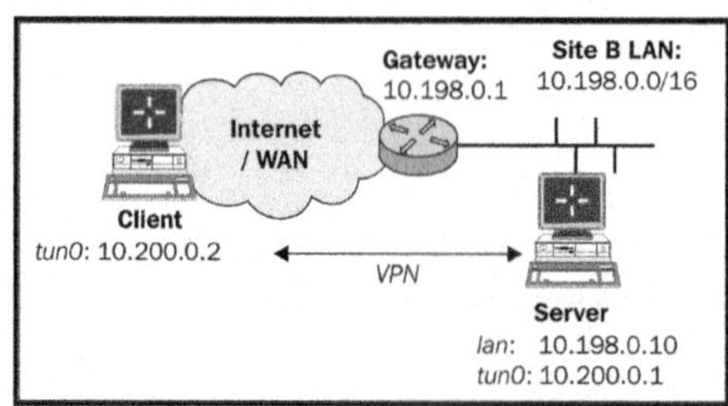


Set up the client and server certificates using the first recipe from `Chapter 2`, *Client-server IP-only Networks*. For this recipe, the server computer was running CentOS 6 Linux and OpenVPN 2.3.11. The client was running Fedora 22 Linux and OpenVPN 2.3.11. Keep the `basic-udp-server.conf` configuration file from the *Server-side routing* recipe from `Chapter 2`, *Client-server IP-only Networks*, as well as the `basic-udp-client.conf` client configuration file at hand.

## How to do it...

1. Append the following line to the `basic-udp-server.conf` file:

   ```
   push "dhcp-option DNS 10.198.0.1"
   ```

   Here, `10.198.0.1` is the address of a DNS server on the VPN server LAN. Save it as `example9-2-server.conf`.

2. Start the server:

   ```
   [root@server]# openvpn --config example9-2-server.conf
   ```

3. Similarly, for the client, add the following lines to the `basic-udp-client.conf` file:

   ```
   script-security 2
   up   "/etc/openvpn/cookbook/client.up"
   down "/etc/openvpn/cookbook/client.down"
   ```

4. Save it as `example9-2-client.conf`. Copy over the `client.up` and `client.down` files from the OpenVPN `contrib` directory and make them executable. On CentOS 6 and Fedora 22, these files are located in the `/usr/share/doc/openvpn-2.3.11/contrib/pull-resolv-conf` directory:

```
[root@client]# cd /etc/openvpn/cookbook
[root@client]# cp /usr/share/doc/openvpn-2.3.11/contrib/pull-
resolv-conf/client.* .
[root@client]# chmod 755 client.*
```

5. And finally, start the client:

```
[root@client]# openvpn --config example9-2-client.conf
```

After the VPN connection comes up, check the contents of the `/etc/resolv.conf` file. The first line should contain the DNS server as specified by the OpenVPN server:

```
nameserver 10.198.0.1
```

When the VPN connection is terminated, the entry is removed again.

# How it works...

The scripts supplied with OpenVPN parse the environment variable, `foreign_option_*`, and look for DOMAIN and DNS settings. These settings are then written out to the beginning of the `/etc/resolv.conf` file. This causes the DNS server and the DOMAIN pushed by the OpenVPN server to take precedence over the system's DNS and DOMAIN settings.

When the VPN connection is dropped, the same settings are removed from the `/etc/resolv.conf` file.

# There's more...

Note that when the `NetworkManager-openvpn` plugin is used, these scripts are not necessary, as the NetworkManager itself updates the `/etc/resolv.conf` file.

# Windows – elevated privileges

With the introduction of Windows Vista, Microsoft introduced **User Access Control** (**UAC**). UAC is meant to safeguard users from running programs that can modify the operating system itself. Before such a program is run, a privilege elevation is required even if the user has full administrator rights. A dialog box appears that the user must click on before the execution begins. In order to run OpenVPN, elevated privileges are needed, as OpenVPN wants to open a system device and start a VPN connection. Especially if routes need to be added to the system, elevated privileges are essential.

With OpenVPN 2.3+, privilege elevation is built into the OpenVPN GUI application. That is, even if the **Run as Administrator** flag is turned off, the OpenVPN GUI application will still request elevated privileges when it is launched. This recipe will demonstrate this behavior, which was not present in older versions of OpenVPN.

## Getting ready

Set up the client and server certificates using the first recipe from `Chapter 2`, *Client-server IP-only Networks*. For this recipe, the server computer was running CentOS 6 Linux and OpenVPN 2.3.11. The client computer was running Windows 7 SP1 and OpenVPN 2.3.11. Keep the configuration file, `basic-udp-server.conf`, from the *Server-side routing* recipe from `Chapter 2`, *Client-server IP-only Networks*. For the client, keep the configuration file, `basic-udp-client.ovpn`, from the *Using an ifconfig-pool block* recipe from `Chapter 2`, *Client-server IP-only Networks* at hand.

## How to do it...

1. First, start the server:

```
[root@server]# openvpn --config basic-udp-server.conf
```

2. Make sure that the OpenVPN is not running and that the tray icon is not present.
3. Before starting the OpenVPN GUI, right-click on the OpenVPN GUI icon that was placed on your desktop after installing the OpenVPN 2.3.11 installer for Windows.
4. In the **Properties** screen that comes up, click on the **Compatibility** tab and disable **Run this program as an administrator**:

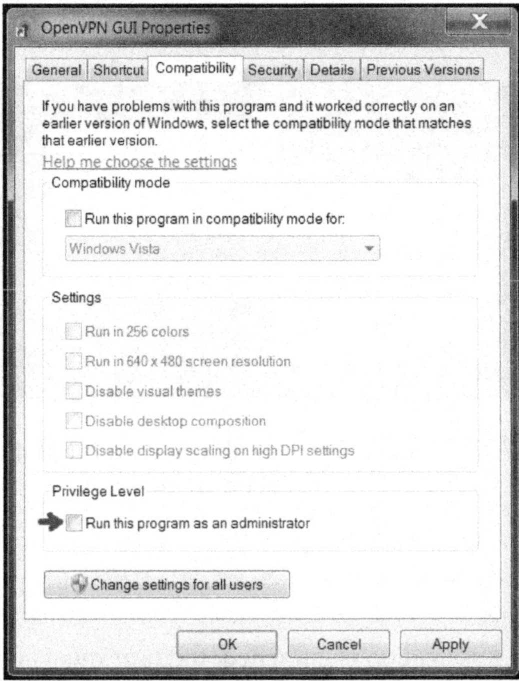


5. Click on **OK**.
6. Start the OpenVPN GUI. Note that it will still prompt for permissions (the following screenshot is for Windows Vista, but a similar window will pop up for Windows 7+):

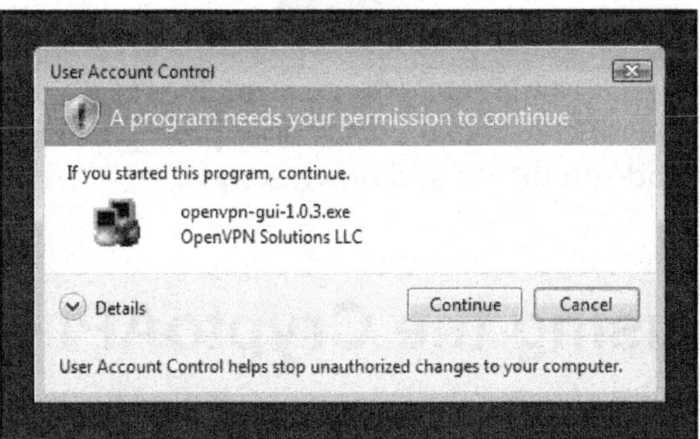


7. Click on **Continue** to start the OpenVPN GUI as usual.

8. Start the OpenVPN client by launching the `example5-1` configuration file:

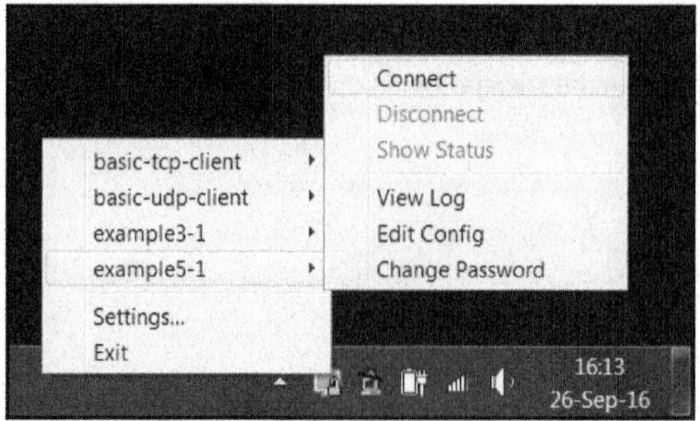


9. Verify that the VPN connection is established and that the log file, `c:\temp\openvpn.log`, has been created.

## How it works...

When the OpenVPN GUI application is launched, the user must always confirm that it can run with elevated privileges. This is now built into the OpenVPN GUI application itself, and is visible by noticing the shield at the right bottom of the application's icon:

After that, the OpenVPN GUI can launch other executables that will also inherit these privileges. When the GUI launches the `openvpn.exe` process, it can open the VPN adapter, alter the routing tables, and run the up and down scripts.

# Windows – using the CryptoAPI store

OpenVPN has the capability of using the Windows CryptoAPI store to retrieve the public and private key needed for setting up a connection. This improves security somewhat, as the CryptoAPI store is more secure than the plaintext `.crt` and `.key` files that are normally used to set up an OpenVPN connection.

In this recipe, we will configure an OpenVPN client to retrieve the required information from the CryptoAPI store when connecting to the server. This recipe was tested on Windows 7, but it will also work on other versions of Windows.

## Getting ready

Set up the client and server certificates using the first recipe from `Chapter 2`, *Client-server IP-only Networks*. For this recipe, the server computer was running CentOS 6 Linux and OpenVPN 2.3.11. The client computer was running Windows 7 SP1 and OpenVPN 2.3.11. Keep the configuration file, `basic-udp-server.conf`, from the *Server-side routing* recipe in `Chapter 2`, *Client-server IP-only Networks* at hand.

## How to do it...

1. First, we need to import the client certificate into the CryptoAPI store. In order to do that we must convert the existing `client2.crt` and `client2.key` files to PKCS12 format. Open a Windows command shell and change the directory to the location where these files are located:

   ```
   [winclient]C:> cd C:\Program Files\OpenVPN\config
   [winclient]C:\Program Files\OpenVPN\config>..\bin\openssl
   pkcs12
   -export -in client2.crt -inkey client2.key -out client2.p12
   Enter pass phrase for client2.key: [existing password]
   Enter Export Password: [new export password]
   Verifying - Enter Export Password: [repeat export password]
   ```

2. Next, import the PKCS12 file into the Windows CryptoAPI store:

   ```
   [winclient]C:\Program Files\OpenVPN\config>start client2.p12
   ```

   The certificate import wizard will start.

3. Click on **Next** on the first screen and again click on **Next** on the second screen. Then, you must supply the export password from the previous step:

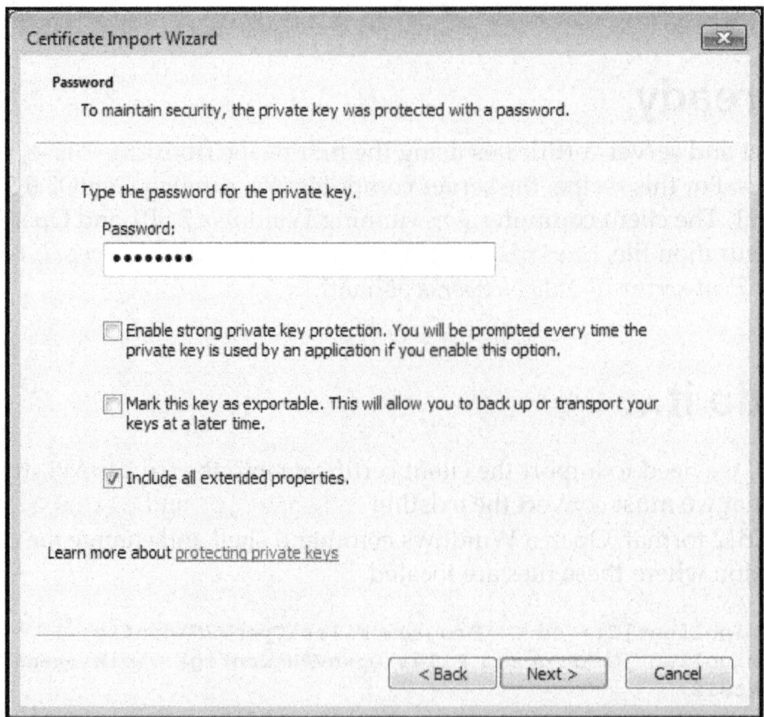


If you select the **Enable strong private key protection. You will be prompted every time the private key is used by an application if you enable this option** checkbox, the certificate and private key are even better protected, but you will be required to retype the password every time OpenVPN starts.

4. Click on **Next**. In the next screen, select the default option, **Automatically select the certificate store**, and click on **Next** once more. By clicking on **Finish** in the next screen, the certificate import is completed.

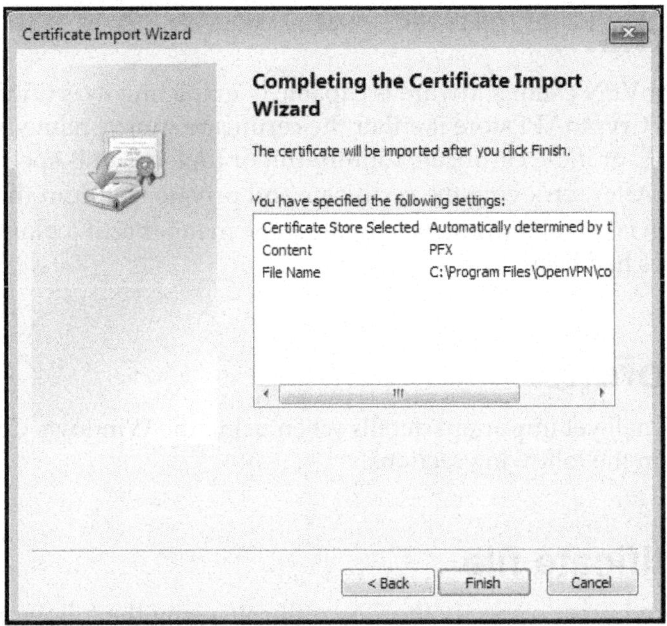


5. Create the client configuration file:

```
client
proto udp
remote openvpnserver.example.com
port 1194

dev tun
nobind

remote-cert-tls server
tls-auth "c:/program files/openvpn/config/ta.key" 1
ca          "c:/program files/openvpn/config/ca.crt"
cryptoapicert  "SUBJ:Client2"
```

6. Save the configuration file as `example9-4.ovpn`. Start the server:

```
[root@server]# openvpn --config basic-udp-server.conf
```

7. Start the VPN connection using the OpenVPN GUI.

The VPN connection should be established without asking for a private key password. If the CryptoAPI option, **Enable strong private key protection**, was enabled, a separate dialog will pop up to ask for the CryptoAPI password.

# How it works...

The Windows OpenVPN client software is capable of extracting a certificate and public key from the Windows CryptoAPI store if either the certificate subject name is specified using the keyword, `SUBJ:`, or if the certificate thumbprint or fingerprint is specified using the keyword, `THUMB:`. After retrieving the certificate and private key from the CryptoAPI store, the VPN connection is established in exactly the same manner as if a plaintext certificate and private key files had been used.

# There's more...

There are several small yet important details when using the Windows CryptoAPI store. We will cover this in the following sections.

## The CA certificate file

Note that it is still required to specify the CA certificate using the following line:

```
ca c:/program files/openvpn/config/ca.crt
```

In theory, it would be possible to also retrieve the CA certificate from the CryptoAPI store, but this is currently not implemented in OpenVPN. Also, note that the CA certificate file needs to contain the certificate authority that was used to sign the server-side certificate, not the client-side certificate.

## Certificate fingerprint

Instead of supplying `cryptoapicert SUBJ:<subject name>`, it is also possible to specify `cryptoapicert THUMB:<fingerprint>`.

The fingerprint or thumbprint of an X509 certificate can be retrieved both by either looking up the `Thumb` property for the imported certificate in the Windows Certificate store or by typing the OpenSSL command:

```
C:\Program Files\OpenVPN\config>..\bin\openssl x509 \
    -fingerprint -noout -in client2.crt
SHA1
Fingerprint=91:93:72:7D:0D:D7:33:58:81:DA:DE:2C:17:1E:36:43:58:40:BF:50
```

# Windows – updating the DNS cache

A frequently recurring question on the OpenVPN users mailing lists is related to the DNS name resolution on Windows after the VPN connection is established. If the OpenVPN server pushes out a new DNS server, then this is automatically picked up by the OpenVPN client, yet the name resolution does not always work right after establishing the connection. This has little to do with OpenVPN and more to do with the way the Windows DNS caching service works. As this question comes up quite regularly, a new directive, `register-dns`, was added in OpenVPN 2.1.3. When this directive is specified, OpenVPN updates the Windows DNS cache and registers the VPN IP address in the Windows DNS tables. As this feature was introduced only recently, this recipe will also show how the Windows DNS cache can be updated using a script when the VPN connection is established. Some users disable the DNS caching service altogether, which seems to have little impact on the operating system, except for a small performance penalty when using a slow network.

## Getting ready

Set up the client and server certificates using the first recipe from `Chapter 2`, *Client-server IP-only Networks*. For this recipe, the server computer was running CentOS 6 Linux and OpenVPN 2.3.11. The client computer was running Windows 7 SP1 and OpenVPN 2.3.11. Keep the server configuration file, `example9-2-server.conf`, from the *Linux: using pull-resolv-conf* recipe at hand, as well as the client configuration file, `basic-udp-client.ovpn`, from the *Using an ifconfig-pool block* recipe in `Chapter 2`, *Client-server IP-only Networks*.

## How to do it...

1. Start the server:

```
[root@server]# openvpn --config example9-2-server.conf
```

2. Add a line to the `basic-udp-client.ovpn` configuration file:

```
register-dns
```

3. Save this configuration file as `example9-5.ovpn`. Start the OpenVPN client.

   The OpenVPN GUI status window will show that the Windows service `dnscache` has restarted:

```
example9-5.log - Notepad
File Edit Format View Help
Mon Sep 26 16:39:16 2016 us=348843 TAP-WIN32 device [vpn0] opened: \\.\Global
\{0A98E2CD-E31A-4D47-B5EF-03F98D3A49FB}.tap
Mon Sep 26 16:39:16 2016 us=348843 TAP-Windows Driver Version 9.21
Mon Sep 26 16:39:16 2016 us=348843 TAP-Windows MTU=1500
Mon Sep 26 16:39:16 2016 us=348843 Set TAP-Windows TUN subnet mode
network/local/netmask = 10.200.0.0/10.200.0.2/255.255.255.0 [SUCCEEDED]
Mon Sep 26 16:39:16 2016 us=348843 Notified TAP-Windows driver to set a DHCP
IP/netmask of 10.200.0.2/255.255.255.0 on interface {0A98E2CD-E31A-4D47-B5EF-
03F98D3A49FB} [DHCP-serv: 10.200.0.254, lease-time: 31536000]
Mon Sep 26 16:39:16 2016 us=348843 DHCP option string: 0604c010 b90c
Mon Sep 26 16:39:16 2016 us=348843 Successful ARP Flush on interface [18]
{0A98E2CD-E31A-4D47-B5EF-03F98D3A49FB}
Mon Sep 26 16:39:21 2016 us=606052 TEST ROUTES: 0/0 succeeded len=0 ret=1 a=0 u/d=up
Mon Sep 26 16:39:21 2016 us=606052 Initialization Sequence Completed
Mon Sep 26 16:39:21 2016 us=606052 MANAGEMENT:
>STATE:1474900761,CONNECTED,SUCCESS,10.200.0.2,192.168.96.101
Mon Sep 26 16:39:21 2016 Start net commands...
Mon Sep 26 16:39:21 2016 C:\Windows\system32\net.exe stop dnscache
Mon Sep 26 16:39:24 2016 C:\Windows\system32\net.exe start dnscache
```

   After the VPN connection is established, verify that the name resolution is using the VPN-supplied DNS server, for example, by using the `nslookup` command.

## How it works...

When the VPN connection is established, the OpenVPN client software sends a DHCP packet to the TAP-Win32 adapter with the IP address, default gateway, and the other network-related information, such as a new DNS server. This information is picked up by the operating system but the local DNS caching service is not notified immediately. The `register-dns` directive executes the following commands:

```
net stop dnscache
net start dnscache
ipconfig /flushdns
ipconfig /registerdns
```

By forcing a restart of the DNS caching service, the DNS server supplied by the VPN connection is used immediately.

## See also

- The *Windows 8+ – ensuring DNS lookups are secure* recipe later in this chapter, which goes into detail of how to ensure that DNS lookups are passed over the VPN tunnel only

# Windows – running OpenVPN as a service

One of the lesser known features of the Windows version of OpenVPN is its ability to run it as a service. This allows OpenVPN to start and establish a VPN connection without a user logging in on the system. The OpenVPN service is installed by default, but is not started automatically.

In this recipe, we will show how the OpenVPN service can be controlled using the OpenVPN GUI application and how to perform troubleshooting on the service.

## Getting ready

Set up the client and server certificates using the first recipe from `Chapter 2`, *Client-server IP-only Networks*. For this recipe, the server computer was running CentOS 6 Linux and OpenVPN 2.3.11. The client computer was running Windows 7 SP1 and OpenVPN 2.3.11. Keep the configuration file, `basic-udp-server.conf`, from the *Server-side routing* recipe in `Chapter 2`, *Client-server IP-only Networks* at hand. For the client, keep the configuration file, `basic-udp-client.ovpn`, from the *Using an ifconfig-pool block* recipe in `Chapter 2`, *Client-server IP-only Networks* at hand.

## How to do it...

1. Start the server:

```
[root@server]# openvpn --config basic-udp-server.conf
```

2. Before starting the OpenVPN GUI application on the client side, we first launch the Windows registry editor, `regedit` (using elevated privileges). Find the `HKEY_LOCAL_MACHINE\SOFTWARE\OpenVPN-GUI` key.

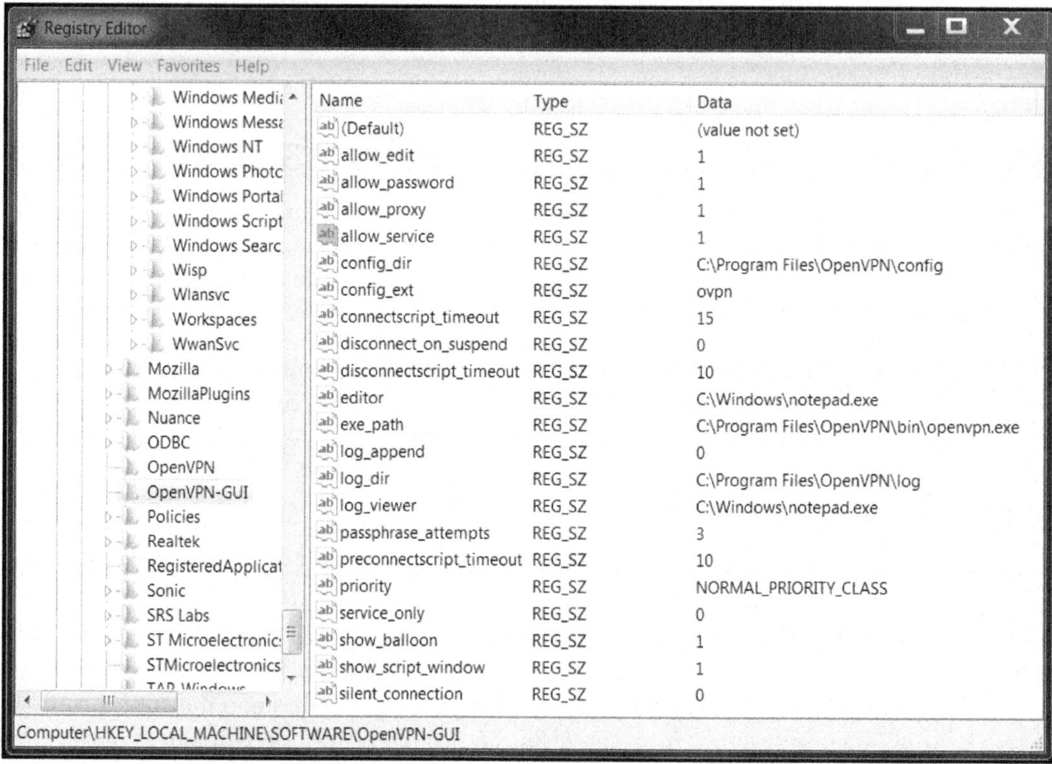


3. Take a note of the `config_dir` registry key, which is normally set to `C:\Program Files\OpenVPN\config`.
4. Set the registry key **allow_service** to **1**. Also, take note of the registry key, `log_dir`, which is normally set to `C:\Program Files\OpenVPN\log`.
5. Now, browse to the registry key, `HKEY_LOCAL_MACHINE\SOFTWARE\OpenVPN`, and check the `config_dir` and `log_dir` keys again. They should be pointing to the same directories as for the OpenVPN GUI application.

6. Close the registry editor.
7. Launch the OpenVPN GUI. Right-click on the icon in the taskbar. A new menu option will have appeared.

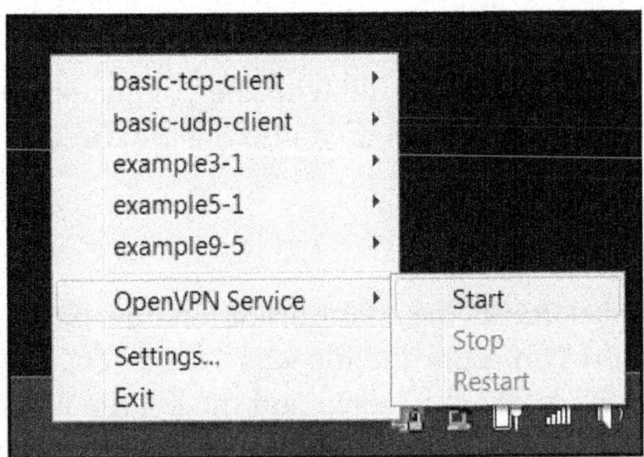


   But do not start the service yet.

8. First, modify the client configuration file, `basic-udp-client.ovpn`, by changing the following lines:

```
cert     "c:/program files/openvpn/config/client2.crt"
key      "c:/program files/openvpn/config/client2.key"
```

   Change these to the following:

```
cert     "c:/program files/openvpn/config/client1.crt"
key      "c:/program files/openvpn/config/client1.key"
```

   The `client2.key` client certificate from `Chapter 2`, *Client-server IP-only Networks*, is protected by a password, whereas the `client1.key` file is not. Save the configuration file as `example9-6.ovpn`.

9. Move all other `.ovpn` files to another directory to make sure that this is the only `.ovpn` file in the `config` directory.
10. Now, start the OpenVPN service. After a while, the VPN connection will be established, as can be seen on both the client and the server in the log files.

## How it works...

A Windows service is launched at system startup before a user is logged in. The OpenVPN service scans the directory pointed to by the registry key, `HKEY_LOCAL_MACHINE\SOFTWARE\OpenVPN\config_dir`.

This starts an OpenVPN process for each file with the `.ovpn` extension in that directory. The output of each of these processes is logged into the log directory pointed to by the registry key:

```
HKEY_LOCAL_MACHINE\SOFTWARE\OpenVPN\log_dir
```

Here, the log filename is the same as the configuration name, but now with the `.log` extension. For this recipe, the configuration file was `C:\Program Files\OpenVPN\config\example9-6.ovpn` and the log file was `C:\Program Files\OpenVPN\log\example9-6.log`.

There is no need to launch the OpenVPN GUI to start these connections, but the GUI application does offer a convenient method of managing the OpenVPN service, if the right registry key is added.

## There's more...

There are a few important notes when using the OpenVPN service, which are outlined here.

## Automatic service startup

To make the OpenVPN service start at system startup, open the **Services** administrative control panel by navigating to **Control Panel** | **Administrative Tools** | **Services**. Double-click on the **OpenVPN Service** to open the properties and set the **Startup type** field to **Automatic**:

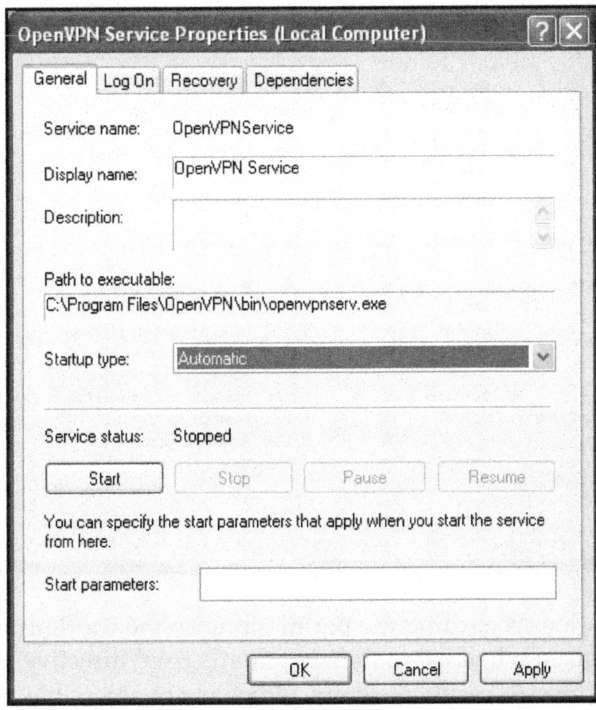


Click on **OK** and close the **Services** administrative control panel. Reboot Windows and verify on the server side that the client is connecting at system startup.

## OpenVPN user name

When the OpenVPN service is used, the corresponding OpenVPN processes are normally run under the account **SYSTEM**, as can be seen in the following screenshot:

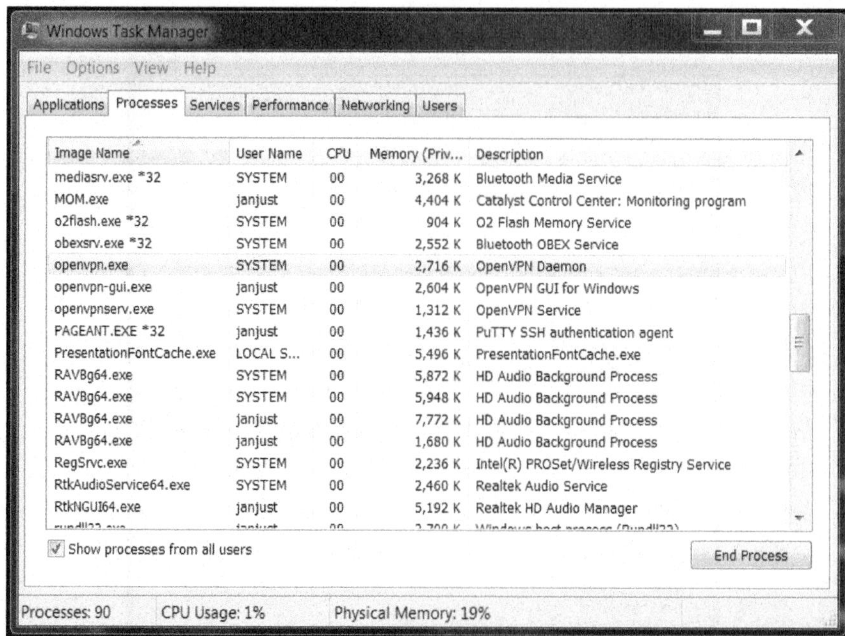


This has some implications regarding the permissions on the configuration files. Special care also needs to be taken when using the `cryptoapicert` directive, as by default, those certificates end up in the user certificate store, which is not accessible to the **SYSTEM** account. It is possible to use the `cryptoapicert` directive, but the imported certificate must be installed as a (local) system certificate and not as a user certificate.

## See also

- The *Windows – using the CryptoAPI store* recipe earlier in this chapter, which explains how to use the Windows CryptoAPI store to store the user certificate and private key

# Windows – public versus private network adapters

With Windows Vista and 7, Microsoft introduced the concept of network classes. Network interfaces can be part of a **Private** or **Public** network. When using OpenVPN, one must be careful in which type of network the adapter is placed. By default, OpenVPN's TAP-Win32 adapter is placed in a **Public** network, which has a side-effect that it is not possible to mount file shares. In this recipe, we will show how to change the network type so that the trusted services such as file sharing are possible over a VPN connection. While this has little to do with configuring the OpenVPN per se, this issue comes up often enough to warrant a recipe.

## Getting ready

Set up the client and server certificates using the first recipe from `Chapter 2`, *Client-server IP-only Networks*. For this recipe, the server computer was running CentOS 6 Linux and OpenVPN 2.3.11. The client computer was running Windows 7 SP1 and OpenVPN 2.3.11. Keep the configuration file, `basic-udp-server.conf`, from the *Server-side routing* recipe in `Chapter 2`, *Client-server IP-only Networks* at hand. For the client, keep the configuration file, `basic-udp-client.ovpn`, from the *Using an ifconfig-pool block* recipe in `Chapter 2`, *Client-server IP-only Networks* at hand.

## How to do it...

1. Append the following line to the `basic-udp-server.conf` file:

   ```
   push "route 0.0.0.0 0.0.0.0 vpn_gateway 300"
   ```

2. Save it as `example9-7-server.conf`. Start the server:

   ```
   [root@server]# openvpn --config example9-7-server.conf
   ```

3. On the Windows client, launch the OpenVPN GUI.
4. After the VPN connection is established, a window will pop up asking you what type of network this is. For Windows 7, you can choose **Home**, **Work**, or **Public**; for Windows 8+, the choice is either **Private** or **Public**.

5. Select the **Work** network, and then open the **Network and Sharing Center**:

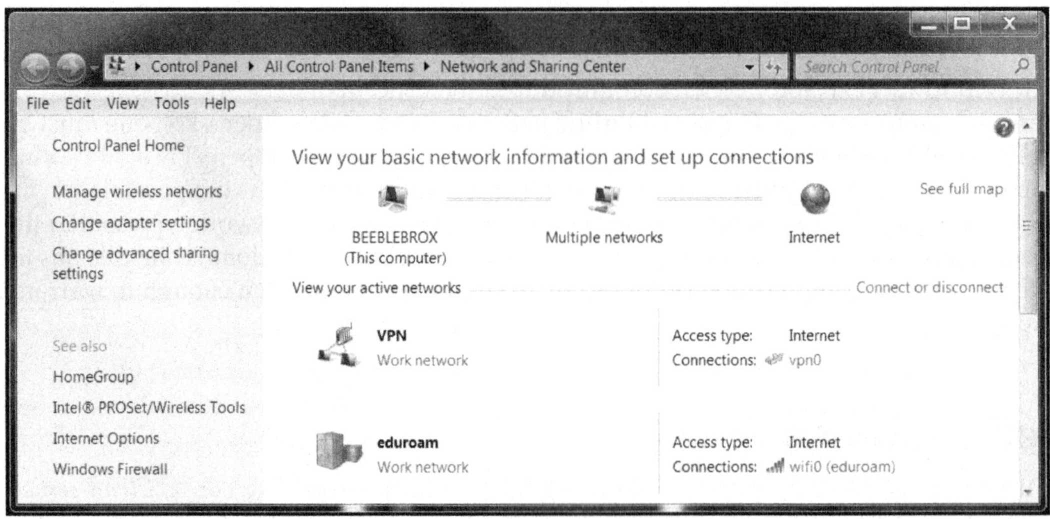


# How it works...

With Windows 7+, each network type has different access rights. The network type with the fewest rights is **Public**, which means that the applications can set up TCP/IP connections, but they cannot access any of the resources available in the **Work** or **Private** networks, such as local printers and the local disks. When sharing resources that are on the same network as the OpenVPN client, this can become an issue.

Windows determines the type of network by looking at whether a default gateway is present for that network. If no default gateway is specified, the network is considered to be untrustworthy and hence it is made public. There is no option to easily change this afterward.

To overcome this peculiarity, we supply a default gateway with a very high metric:

```
push "route 0.0.0.0 0.0.0.0 vpn_gateway 300"
```

Using a very high metric, we avoid the problem that all network traffic is routed over the VPN, which can lead to *biting-your-own-tail* problems.

## See also

- The *Windows – elevated privileges* recipe earlier in this chapter, which explains in more detail about how to run the OpenVPN GUI application with elevated privileges

# Windows – routing methods

When routes are pushed to a Windows client, there are two methods for adding these routes to the system routing tables:

- Using the IPAPI helper functions (the default)
- Using the `ROUTE.EXE` program

In most cases, the IPAPI method works fine, but sometimes, it is necessary to overrule this behavior. In this recipe, we will show how this is done and what to look for in the client log file to verify that the right method has been chosen.

## Getting ready

Set up the client and server certificates using the first recipe from `Chapter 2`, *Client-server IP-only Networks*. For this recipe, the server computer was running CentOS 6 Linux and OpenVPN 2.3.11. The client computer was running Windows 7 SP1 and OpenVPN 2.3.11. Keep the configuration file, `basic-udp-server.conf`, from the *Server-side routing* recipe in `Chapter 2`, *Client-server IP-only Networks* at hand. For the client, keep the configuration file, `basic-udp-client.ovpn`, from the *Using an ifconfig-pool block* recipe in `Chapter 2`, *Client-server IP-only Networks* at hand.

## How to do it...

1. Start the server:

```
[root@server]# openvpn --config basic-udp-server.conf
```

2. Add the following lines to the `basic-udp-client.ovpn` configuration file:

```
verb 5
route-method ipapi
```

3. Save this configuration file as `example9-8.ovpn`. Start the OpenVPN client with this configuration.
4. After the connection has been established, bring up the **Show Status** window again and look at the last lines of the connection log. The log will show lines similar to the following:

```
...  C:\WINDOWS\system32\route.exe ADD 10.198.0.0 MASK
255.255.0.0 10.200.0.1
... Route addition via IPAPI succeeded
... Initialization Sequence Completed
```

   Even though the `route-method` directive was set to `ipapi`, the log file prints out the path of the Windows `route.exe` command. The second line shows that the route was actually added using the IPAPI helper functions.

5. Now, modify the configuration file, `example9-8.ovpn`, to the following:

```
verb 5
route-method exe
```

6. Restart the OpenVPN client.
7. Look at the last lines of the connection log again. This time the message, **Route addition via IPAPI succeeded**, will not be present in the log file, which means that the `route.exe` command was used. Instead, you will see something similar to this:

```
...  C:\WINDOWS\system32\route.exe ADD 10.198.0.0 MASK
255.255.0.0 10.200.0.1
... env_block: add PATH=C:\Windows\System32;C:\Windows;...
... Initialization Sequence Completed
```

   The line starting with `env_block` indicates that a set of environment variables were set up prior to launching the external `route.exe` command.

## How it works...

The `route-method` directive has three options:

- `adaptive`: First, try the IPAPI method, and fallback to the `route.exe` method if IPAPI fails. This is the default.
- `ipapi`: Always use the IPAPI helper functions to add routes.
- `exe`: Always use the external program, `route.exe`.

Based on this directive, the OpenVPN client will choose how to add routes to the Windows routing tables. Note that if OpenVPN cannot add a route, it will not abort the connection. The current OpenVPN GUI does not detect this and will show a green icon in the taskbar, suggesting a fully successful connection.

## There's more...

OpenVPN is preconfigured to look for the `route.exe` program in the directory where Windows is installed, usually `C:\WINDOWS\system32`. If Windows is installed in a different directory, the `win-sys` directive can be used. The `win-sys` directive has two options:

- The default option, `env`, which means that the OpenVPN client will use the contents of the environment variable, `windir`, to locate the Windows operating system. This environment variable is always set in a normal Windows setup. Starting with OpenVPN 2.3, this is the default setting and a warning message is printed if `win-sys env` is specified.
- The directory name where the Windows operating system can be found, for example, `D:\WINDOWS`. This should be used only if the `route.exe` program is in a non-standard location.

# Windows 8+ – ensuring DNS lookups are secure

Starting with Windows 8.1, Microsoft introduced a new feature for resolving hostnames to IP addresses. Whenever an application wants to resolve a hostname, a DNS query is sent out over all network adapters found in the system. The answer from the first adapter that responds to the query is used.

If a user wants to tunnel all traffic over a VPN in a secure manner, then this feature is not desirable. In a hostile network environment, a bogus IP address could be returned or even the fact that a DNS lookup for a particular host is made could be considered dangerous.

Starting with OpenVPN 2.3.10, a new option, `block-outside-dns`, was added to suppress this feature. In this recipe, we will show how to use this option.

## Getting ready

Set up the client and server certificates using the first recipe from `Chapter 2`, *Client-server IP-only Networks*. For this recipe, the server computer was running CentOS 6 Linux and OpenVPN 2.3.11. The client computer was running Windows 8.1 and OpenVPN 2.3.11. Keep the configuration file, `basic-udp-server.conf`, from the *Server-side routing* recipe in `Chapter 2`, *Client-server IP-only Networks* at hand. For the client, keep the configuration file, `basic-udp-client.ovpn`, from the *Using an ifconfig-pool block* recipe in `Chapter 2`, *Client-server IP-only Networks* at hand.

## How to do it...

1. Start the server:

```
[root@server]# openvpn --config basic-udp-server.conf
```

2. Add the following lines to the `basic-udp-client.ovpn` configuration file:

```
verb 5
block-outside-dns
```

3. Save this configuration file as `example9-9.ovpn`. Start the OpenVPN client with this configuration.
4. After the connection has been established, bring up the **Show Status** window again and look at the last lines of the connection log. The output should be similar to the following:

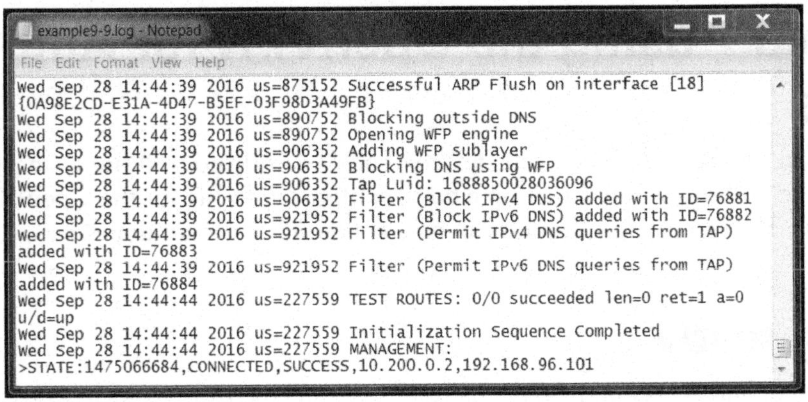

```
example9-9.log - Notepad
File Edit Format View Help
Wed Sep 28 14:44:39 2016 us=875152 Successful ARP Flush on interface [18]
{0A98E2CD-E31A-4D47-B5EF-03F98D3A49FB}
Wed Sep 28 14:44:39 2016 us=890752 Blocking outside DNS
Wed Sep 28 14:44:39 2016 us=890752 Opening WFP engine
Wed Sep 28 14:44:39 2016 us=906352 Adding WFP sublayer
Wed Sep 28 14:44:39 2016 us=906352 Blocking DNS using WFP
Wed Sep 28 14:44:39 2016 us=906352 Tap Luid: 1688850028036096
Wed Sep 28 14:44:39 2016 us=906352 Filter (Block IPv4 DNS) added with ID=76881
Wed Sep 28 14:44:39 2016 us=921952 Filter (Block IPv6 DNS) added with ID=76882
Wed Sep 28 14:44:39 2016 us=921952 Filter (Permit IPv4 DNS queries from TAP)
added with ID=76883
Wed Sep 28 14:44:39 2016 us=921952 Filter (Permit IPv6 DNS queries from TAP)
added with ID=76884
Wed Sep 28 14:44:44 2016 us=227559 TEST ROUTES: 0/0 succeeded len=0 ret=1 a=0
u/d=up
Wed Sep 28 14:44:44 2016 us=227559 Initialization Sequence Completed
Wed Sep 28 14:44:44 2016 us=227559 MANAGEMENT:
>STATE:1475066684,CONNECTED,SUCCESS,10.200.0.2,192.168.96.101
```

In this log file, the **Windows Filtering Platform** (**WFP**) is initialized and special rules are added to block DNS traffic.

5. Stop the OpenVPN client and check the log file again. You should see a line indicating that the WFP engine is shut down, thereby removing the filtering rules added by OpenVPN:

```
... Closing TUN/TAP interface
... Uninitializing WFP
```

## How it works...

With the `block-outside-dns` directive, a set of Windows filtering rules are created after the VPN connection has been established. These filter (or firewalling) rules prevent DNS lookups from being sent over all network adapters found on the Windows client, except for queries made over the TAP adapter. When the OpenVPN connection is terminated, the WFP rules are removed.

## There's more...

Be careful when using this option with OpenVPN 2.3 when you have multiple simultaneous tunnels open. In some cases, the WFP rules that are added by the first tunnel are not restored properly when the second tunnel is shut down, thereby blocking all DNS traffic.

# Android – using the OpenVPN for Android clients

OpenVPN can also be used on mobile devices, such as Android or iPhone smartphones. In this recipe, we will show how to set up a basic configuration file for the OpenVPN for the Android app. The same configuration can be used on iPhones and iPads.

## Getting ready

Set up the client and server certificates using the first recipe from `Chapter 2`, *Client-server IP-only Networks*. For this recipe, the server computer was running CentOS 6 Linux and OpenVPN 2.3.11. The client device was running Android 4.2 and OpenVPN for Android version 0.6.57. Keep the configuration file, `basic-udp-server.conf`, from the *Server-side routing* recipe in `Chapter 2`, *Client-server IP-only Networks* at hand. For the client, keep the configuration file, `basic-udp-client.ovpn`, from the *Using an ifconfig-pool block* recipe in `Chapter 2`, *Client-server IP-only Networks* at hand.

## How to do it...

1. Start the server:

   ```
   [root@server]# openvpn --config basic-udp-server.conf
   ```

2. Create the OpenVPN app profile by converting the `basic-udp-client.ovpn` file to an inline configuration file. This is done by replacing all references to external files with the inline blobs. We then add these inline blobs by copying the contents from the external files. The resulting configuration file will look similar to this:

   ```
   client
   proto udp
   remote openvpnserver.example.com
   port 1194
   dev tun
   nobind
   remote-cert-tls server
   key-direction 1
   push-peer-info

   <ca>
   ```

```
-----BEGIN CERTIFICATE-----
MIIGDzCCA/egAwIBAgIJAJOj7Wg...
...
-----END CERTIFICATE-----
</ca>

<cert>
-----BEGIN CERTIFICATE-----
MIIFKzCCAxOgAwIBAgIBAjANBgi...
...
-----END CERTIFICATE-----
</cert>

<key>
-----BEGIN RSA PRIVATE KEY-----
MIIEvgIBADANBgkqhkiG9w0BAQEF...
...
-----END RSA PRIVATE KEY-----
</key>

<tls-auth>
-----BEGIN OpenVPN Static key V1-----
5f5b2bfff373961654089871b40a39eb
...
-----END OpenVPN Static key V1-----
</tls-auth>
```

3. Save this configuration file as `example9-10.ovpn`.
4. Transfer the app configuration file to the Android smartphone.
5. Start the OpenVPN for Android app and import the `example9-10.ovpn` profile. If all goes well, you should see an output similar to this:

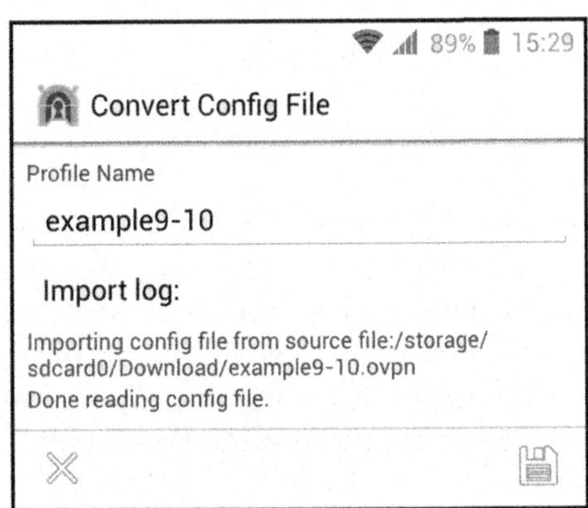

6. Launch the OpenVPN profile. After the connection has been established, the app will show the current status and log with the top line showing **Connected: SUCCESS, 10.200.0.2, 192.168.96.101, 1194:**

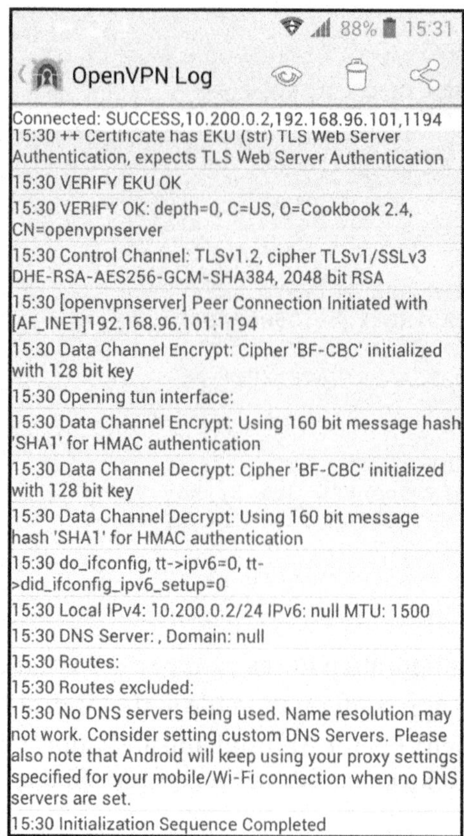


# How it works...

The OpenVPN for Android app is based on the same source code as the open source OpenVPN software. Hence, almost all options that can be specified in a normal configuration file can also be specified in an OpenVPN app profile. However, it is recommended to include all certificate and keying information inside the profile, as it makes it much easier to transfer the configuration to the device.

## There's more...

If you want to transfer the app profile by uploading it to a web server first, then make sure that the file type and extensions remain intact. The mobile device will treat the configuration file as a plain text file if it does not recognize it as an OpenVPN profile and you will not be able to import it into the OpenVPN for Android app. In such cases, it may be desirable to transfer the `.ovpn` file inside a ZIP (`.zip`) file.

## See also

- The *Inline certificates* recipe in the next chapter, which goes into detail on using inline certificates

# Push-peer-info – pushing options to Android clients

This recipe is a continuation of the previous recipe. When integrating mobile clients into an existing OpenVPN setup, it is often necessary to treat these mobile clients differently from the regular OpenVPN clients. In some cases, it will be necessary to redirect all traffic for mobile clients over the VPN tunnel or a different encryption scheme needs to be used to optimize the OpenVPN app on the Android device. In this recipe, we will demonstrate how to push an option to an Android client, while leaving the options for all other clients unchanged.

## Getting ready

Set up the client and server certificates using the first recipe from `Chapter 2`, *Client-server IP-only Networks*. For this recipe, the server computer was running CentOS 6 Linux and OpenVPN 2.4. The client device was running Android 4.2 and OpenVPN for Android version 0.6.57. Keep the configuration file, `basic-udp-server.conf`, from the *Server-side routing* recipe in `Chapter 2`, *Client-server IP-only Networks* at hand. For the client, keep the configuration file, `example9-10.ovpn`, from previous recipe at hand.

# How to do it...

1. Append the following lines to the `basic-udp-server.conf` server configuration file:

```
script-security 2
client-connect    /etc/openvpn/cookbook/example9-11.sh
```

2. Save it as `example9-11-server.conf`. Next, create the connect script:

```
#!/bin/bash

# Redirect the default gateway for all Android clients
if [ "x_${IV_PLAT}" = "x_android" ]
then
    echo "push "redirect-gateway def1"" >> $1
fi
```

3. Save this file as `example9-11.sh`. Make sure that the script is executable and start the server:

```
[root@server]# chmod 755 example9-11.sh
[root@server]# openvpn --config example9-11-server.conf
```

4. Start the OpenVPN for Android app and establish the VPN connection.
5. After the connection has been established, use another app, such as Fing, to ensure that all traffic is redirected via the OpenVPN tunnel:

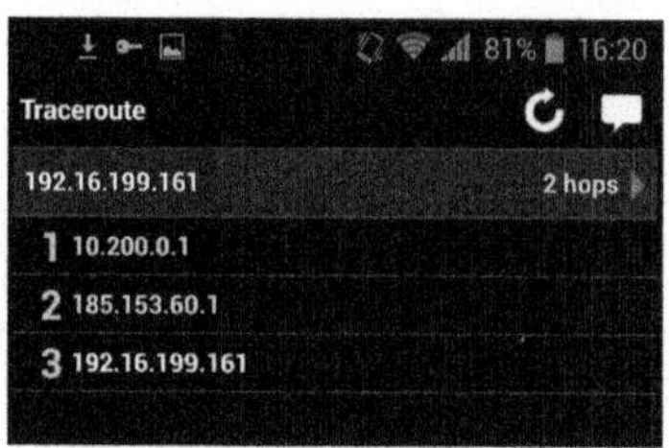


6. The first address in the traceroute output is `10.200.0.1`, demonstrating that the traffic is redirected via the OpenVPN server.

## How it works...

In the OpenVPN for Android configuration, we added the `push-peer-info` option. This causes the OpenVPN client to send configuration details to the server. Starting with OpenVPN 2.4, these configuration details are available both inside plugins and scripts. The `client-connect` script examines the environment variable, `IV_PLAT`, and pushes a `redirect-gateway` if an Android client is connecting.

## There's more...

The `push-peer-info` option is available in all OpenVPN 2.3 clients. However, support on the server side to actually process this information was added in version 2.4. The following peer information is sent to the server:

- `IV_COMP_STUB=1, IV_COMP_STUBv2=1`: This indicates that the client supports compression stubs. It also means that the server can push compression options to the client.
- `IV_GUI_VER=de.blinkt.openvpn_0.6.57`: This indicates the client GUI version. In this case, the OpenVPN for Android client version 0.6.57 was used.
- `IV_HWADDR=00:00:00:00:00:00`: This indicates the client's Ethernet hardware address. On Android clients, this option is always `00:00:00`, but on other platforms the MAC address of the TUN/TAP adapter is transmitted.
- `IV_LZ4=1, IV_LZ4v2=1, IV_LZO=1`: This indicates that the client supports LZ4, LZ4v2, and LZO compression.
- `IV_NCP=2`: This indicates that the client supports encryption cipher negotiation. This allows the client and server to negotiate the most optimal compression and HMAC algorithms.
- `IV_PLAT=android`: This indicates the client platform.
- `IV_PROTO=2`: This indicates the version of the push-peer-info format. In the future, the format or set of variables sent to the server might change, which would warrant an increase in the version number.
- `IV_RGI6=1`: This indicates that the client supports redirection of the IPv6 gateway address.
- `IV_SSL=OpenSSL_1.0.2h__3_May_2016`: This indicates the SSL library and version that is used by the OpenVPN client. This could be important to determine whether a particular client is susceptible to a crypto library vulnerability.
- `IV_VER=2.4_master`: This indicates the version of the OpenVPN software on the client.

# 10

# Advanced Configuration

In this chapter, we will cover:

- Including configuration files in config files
- Multiple remotes and remote-random
- Inline certificates
- Connection blocks
- Details of `ifconfig-pool-persist`
- Connecting using a SOCKS proxy
- Connecting via an HTTP proxy
- Connecting via an HTTP proxy with authentication
- IP-less setups – `ifconfig-noexec`
- Port sharing with an HTTPS server
- Routing features – `redirect-private`, `allow-pull-fqdn`
- Filtering out pushed options
- Handing out public IP addresses

## Introduction

The recipes in this last chapter will cover the advanced configuration of OpenVPN. This chapter will focus on some of the less well-known configuration options that OpenVPN offers, as well as some advanced recipes for real-life deployments. The recipes will cover both advanced server configuration, such as the use of connection blocks and inline certificates, as well as advanced client configuration, such as using a proxy server to connect to an OpenVPN server.

# Including configuration files in config files

One of the lesser-known possibilities when using configuration files is the ability to include other configuration files. This can be especially handy when setting up a complex OpenVPN server, where multiple OpenVPN instances are offered simultaneously. The common configuration directives can be stored in a single file, whereas the connection-specific parts can be stored in a file for each instance. In this recipe, we will set up two OpenVPN instances, one using UDP and the other using TCP as the transport protocol.

Note that this option does not allow for the sharing of VPN IP address ranges between instances.

## Getting ready

Set up the client and server certificates using the first recipe from `Chapter 2`, *Client-server IP-only Networks*. For this recipe, the server computer was running CentOS 6 Linux and OpenVPN 2.3.11.

## How to do it...

1. First, create the common configuration file:

```
dev tun

ca       /etc/openvpn/cookbook/ca.crt
cert     /etc/openvpn/cookbook/server.crt
key      /etc/openvpn/cookbook/server.key
dh       /etc/openvpn/cookbook/dh2048.pem
tls-auth /etc/openvpn/cookbook/ta.key 0

persist-key
persist-tun
keepalive 10 60

push "route 10.198.0.0 255.255.0.0"
topology subnet

user  nobody
group nobody

daemon
```

Save it as `example10-1-common.conf`. Note that this configuration file does not include a protocol specification or server line. Also, note that we will be using the same server certificate for both OpenVPN instances.

2. Next, create the following server configuration file for UDP-based connections:

```
config example10-1-common.conf

proto udp
port 1194
server 10.200.0.0 255.255.255.0

log-append /var/log/openvpn-udp.log
```

   Save it as `example10-1-server1.conf`.

3. And createa server configuration file for TCP-based connections:

```
config example10-1-common.conf

proto tcp
port 443
server 10.201.0.0 255.255.255.0

log-append /var/log/openvpn-tcp.log
```

   Save it as `example10-1-server2.conf`. This instance is listening on the HTTPS port`443`, which is an often-used trick to circumvent very strict firewalls, or to work around a badly configured firewall.

4. Start both servers:

```
[root@server]# openvpn --config example10-1-server1.conf
[root@server]# openvpn --config example10-1-server2.conf
```

   Check the log files to see if both the servers have successfully started.

## How it works...

OpenVPN configuration files are treated very similarly to command line options. As the `--config` command line option is used almost always, it is also possible to use it inside a configuration file again. This allows for a split in the configuration options, where directives that are common to all OpenVPN instances can be stored in a single file for easy maintenance. The instance-specific directives (such as the `server` directive) can then be stored in much smaller configuration files, which are also less likely to change over time. This again eases maintenance of a large-scale OpenVPN server setup.

OpenVPN has a built-in protection mechanism to avoid including the same configuration file recursively.

# Multiple remotes and remote-random

OpenVPN has (limited) built-in support for automatic failover and load-balancing: if the connection to one OpenVPN server cannot be established, then the next configured server is chosen. The `remote-random` directive can be used to load-balance many OpenVPN clients across multiple OpenVPN servers. In this recipe, we will set up two OpenVPN servers and then use the `remote-random` directive to have a client choose either one of the two servers.

Note that OpenVPN does not offer transparent failover, in which case the existing connections are transparently migrated to another server. Transparent failover is much harder to achieve with a VPN setup (not just OpenVPN), as the secure session keys need to be migrated from one server to the other as well. This is currently not possible with OpenVPN.

## Getting ready

We will use the following network layout:

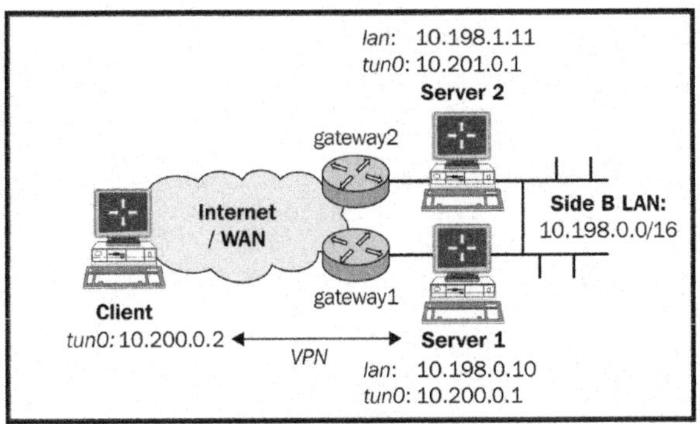


Set up the client and server certificates using the first recipe from `Chapter 2`, *Client-server IP-only Networks*. For this recipe, the server computer was running CentOS 6 Linux and OpenVPN 2.3.11. The client was running Fedora 22 Linux and OpenVPN 2.3.11. Keep the configuration file, `basic-udp-server.conf`, from the *Server-side routing* recipe from `Chapter 2`, *Client-server IP-only Networks,* as well as the client configuration file, `basic-udp-client.conf` at hand.

# How to do it...

1. Start both servers:

```
[root@server1]# openvpn --config basic-udp-server.conf
[root@server2]# openvpn --config basic-udp-server.conf
```

   Check the log files to see that both the servers have successfully started.

   Note that we can use the exact same configuration file on both servers. By using masquerading, the VPN clients will appear to come from either `server1` or `server2`.

2. Set up masquerading on both servers:

```
[root@server1]# iptables -t nat -I POSTROUTING -o eth0 \
    -j MASQUERADE
[root@server2]# iptables -t nat -I POSTROUTING -o eth0 \
    -j MASQUERADE
```

3. Create the client configuration file:

```
client
proto udp
remote openvpnserver1.example.com 1194
remote openvpnserver2.example.com 1194
remote-random
dev tun
nobind

remote-cert-tls server
tls-auth /etc/openvpn/cookbook/ta.key 1
ca       /etc/openvpn/cookbook/ca.crt
cert     /etc/openvpn/cookbook/client1.crt
key     /etc/openvpn/cookbook/client1.key
```

4. Save it as `example10-2-client.conf`.
5. Start the client:

```
[root@client]# openvpn --config example10-2-client.conf
```

The OpenVPN client will randomly choose which server to connect to.

After the connection has been established, stop the first OpenVPN process on the server that the client connected to:

```
[root@server1]# killall openvpn
```

And wait for the client to reconnect. After the default timeout period, the client will reconnect to an alternate server.

# How it works...

When the OpenVPN client starts up and `remote-random` is specified, it randomly picks a server from the list of available remote servers. If the VPN connection to this server cannot be established, it will pick the next server from the list, and so on. When the VPN connection is dropped, for example, due to a failing server, the OpenVPN client will try to reconnect after a default timeout period. In the server configuration file used in the *Server-side routing* recipe from `Chapter 2`, *Client-server IP-only Networks*, the timeout period is configured using the `keepalive` option.

# There's more...

When setting up a failover OpenVPN solution there are many things to consider, some of which are outlined here.

## Mixing TCP and UDP-based setups

It is also possible to mix TCP and UDP-based setups by specifying the protocol type with the `remote` directive:

```
remote openvpnserver1.example.com 1194 udp
remote openvpnserver2.example.com 1194 tcp
```

It is much handier to use connection blocks in this case. The use of connection blocks is explained later in this chapter.

## Advantage of using TCP-based connections

There is one major advantage when using a TCP-based setup in combination with a failover solution. If the OpenVPN server to which a client is connected is unavailable, the TCP connection will fail almost immediately. This leads to a very short timeout period after which the OpenVPN client will try to reconnect. With a UDP-based setup, the client cannot so easily detect whether the server is unavailable and must first wait for the `keepalive` timeout to pass.

## Automatically reverting to the first OpenVPN server

A question that is asked from time to time is whether it is possible to configure OpenVPN to also support automatic reverting: a second OpenVPN instance is set up to provide a failover solution. When the main OpenVPN server is unavailable, the backup instance takes over. However, when the main OpenVPN server comes back online, the clients are not automatically reconnected to the main server. For this, a client reset (or server reset of the second OpenVPN instance) is required. It is possible to achieve this using scripting but it depends largely on what type of connectivity is considered acceptable: it takes some time for an OpenVPN client to detect when the remote server is not responding and to reconnect. The VPN connectivity will be intermittent in such a setup. Especially when the network connection to the main OpenVPN server is not stable, this can lead to very low availability.

A quick and dirty method to have all clients revert back to the first server is to use the management interface on the second server and disconnect all clients.

## See also

- The *Server-side routing* recipe from `Chapter 2`, *Client-server IP-only Networks*, which explains the basic setup of OpenVPN
- The *Connection blocks* recipe, which shows an alternate and more flexible method for supporting multiple servers in a single client configuration file

# Inline certificates

To ease the deployment of OpenVPN configuration, and public and private key files, a new feature is available to include all of them in a single file. This is done by integrating the contents of the `ca`, `cert`, `key`, and optionally the `tls-auth` file into the client configuration file itself. In this recipe, we will set up such a configuration file and use it to connect to our standard OpenVPN server.

## Getting ready

We will use the following network layout:

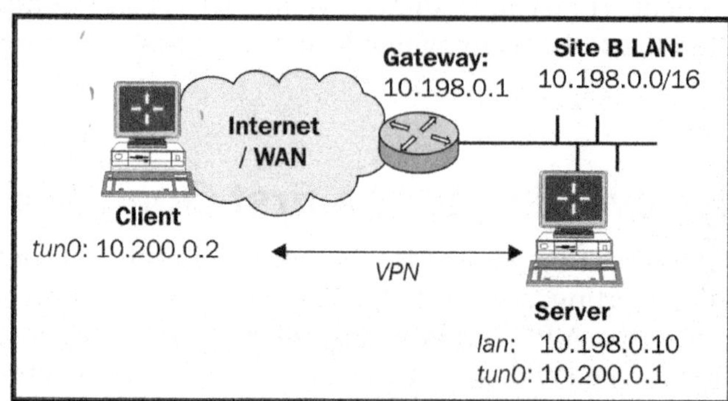


Set up the client and server certificates using the first recipe from `Chapter 2`, *Client-server IP-only Networks*. For this recipe, the server computer was running CentOS 6 Linux and OpenVPN 2.3.11. The client was running Fedora 22 Linux and OpenVPN 2.3.11. Keep the configuration file, `basic-udp-server.conf`, from the *Server-side routing* recipe from `Chapter 2`, *Client-server IP-only Networks* at hand, as well as the client configuration file, `basic-udp-client.conf`.

# How to do it...

1. First, start the server:

```
[root@server]# openvpn --config basic-udp-server.conf
```

2. Create the client configuration file:

```
client
proto udp
remote openvpnserver.example.com
port 1194
dev tun
nobind

remote-cert-tls server
key-direction 1

<ca>
-----BEGIN CERTIFICATE-----
# insert base64 blob from ca.crt
-----END CERTIFICATE-----
</ca>

<cert>
-----BEGIN CERTIFICATE-----
# insert base64 blob from client1.crt
-----END CERTIFICATE-----
</cert>

<key>
-----BEGIN PRIVATE KEY-----
# insert base64 blob from client1.key
-----END PRIVATE KEY-----
</key>

<tls-auth>
-----BEGIN OpenVPN Static key V1-----
# insert ta.key
-----END OpenVPN Static key V1-----
</tls-auth>
```

Insert the contents of the `ca.crt`, `client1.crt`, `client1.key` and `ta.key` files in the configuration. Save it as `example10-3-client.conf`.

3. Then, connect the client:

```
[root@client]# openvpn --config example10-3-client.conf
```

## How it works...

When OpenVPN parses the configuration file, it scans for the directives `ca`, `cert`, `key`, and `tls-auth`, (and `dh` for server configuration files), but also for XML-like blobs starting with <ca>, <cert>, <key>, <tls-auth> and <dh> respectively. If an XML-like block is found, then the contents of this XML-like block are then read and treated in the same manner as when a file is specified. When all the required configuration files or blocks are present, the connection is established.

Note that it is not required to treat all of the aforementioned configuration directives in the same manner. It is also possible to only specify an inline-block for the CA certificate and `tls-auth` files, as these files tend to be static for all the clients.

## There's more...

As stated in the first version of the OpenVPN 2 Cookbook, it was also possible to specify an inline file using the `[[inline]]` tag. However, this tag was never properly documented and starting with OpenVPN 2.3 it is no longer functional.

# Connection blocks

Similar to the inline certificates used in the previous recipe, it is also possible to specify connection blocks. These connection blocks are treated as multiple definitions for remote servers and they are tried in order until a VPN connection is established. The advantage of using a connection block is that for each remote server, server-specific parameters can be specified, such as the protocol (UDP or TCP), the remote port, whether a proxy server should be used, and so on.

In this recipe, we will set up two servers, one listening on a UDP port and the other on a TCP port. We will then configure the OpenVPN client to try the first server using a UDP connection. If the connection cannot be established, the client will attempt to connect to the second server using a TCP connection.

# Getting ready

We will use the following network layout:

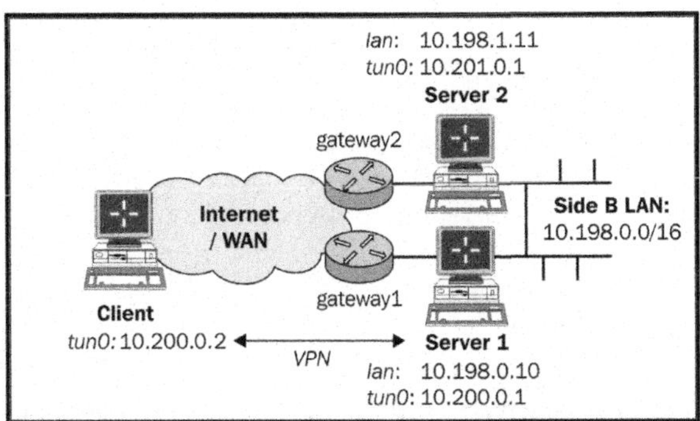


Set up the client and server certificates using the first recipe from `Chapter 2`, *Client-server IP-only Networks*. For this recipe, the server computer was running CentOS 6 Linux and OpenVPN 2.3.11. The client was running Fedora 22 Linux and OpenVPN 2.3.11. Keep the configuration file, `basic-udp-server.conf`, from the *Server-side routing* recipe from `Chapter 2`, *Client-server IP-only Networks,* as well as the server configuration file, `example8-9-server.conf`, from the *Tuning TCP-based connections* recipe from `Chapter 8`, *Performance Tuning*.

# How to do it...

1. Start both the servers:

```
[root@server1]# openvpn --config basic-udp-server.conf
[root@server2]# openvpn --config example8-9-server.conf
```

2. Check the log files to check that both the servers have successfully started.
3. Create the client configuration file:

```
client
dev tun

<connection>
remote openvpnserver1.example.com
proto udp
port 1194
</connection>
```

```
<connection>
remote openvpnserver2.example.com
proto tcp
port 1194
</connection>

remote-cert-tls server
ca       /etc/openvpn/cookbook/ca.crt
cert     /etc/openvpn/cookbook/client1.crt
key      /etc/openvpn/cookbook/client1.key
tls-auth /etc/openvpn/cookbook/ta.key 1
```

4. Save it as `example10-4-client.conf`.
5. Start the client:

```
[root@client]# openvpn --config example10-4-client.conf
```

6. After the connection has been established, stop the first OpenVPN process on the server that the client connected to:

```
[root@server1]# killall openvpn
```

   And wait for the client to reconnect. After the default timeout period, the client will reconnect to the alternate server using the TCP protocol.

# How it works...

When the OpenVPN client starts up, it attempts to connect to the server specified in the first `<connection>` block. If that connection fails, it will try the next `<connection>` block entry and so forth. When an OpenVPN server becomes unavailable or is stopped, the client will automatically restart and try to connect to the first available OpenVPN server again.

The OpenVPN client first parses the global directives, which are specified outside the `<connection>` blocks. For each block, the global directives are then overruled using block-specific directives. This makes it easier to specify in the `<connection>` blocks only those parameters that are different for each connection.

# There's more...

Connection blocks, as well as inline certificates, are very handy features to easily distribute OpenVPN configurations using a single file. However, a consequence of these features is that the use of the command line to overrule the directives specified in the configuration file becomes harder, if not impossible. There are a few other things to keep in mind when using connection blocks.

## Allowed directives inside connection blocks

There are only a few directives allowed inside a connection block:

- `bind` and `bind-ipv6`
- `connect-retry`, `connect-retry-max`, and `connect-timeout`
- `explicit-exit-notify`
- `float`
- `http-proxy`, `http-proxy-option`, `http-proxy-retry`, and `http-proxy-timeout`
- `link-mtu` and `link-mtu-extra`
- `local lport`
- `mssfix`
- `nobind`
- `port`
- `proto`
- `remote` and `rport`
- `socks-proxy` and `socks-proxy-retry`
- `tun-mtu` and `tun-mtu-extra`

All other directives are considered global and can only be specified once.

## Pitfalls when mixing TCP and UDP-based setups

Connection blocks make it very easy to mix TCP and UDP-based setups. The downside is that the global parameters specified in the configuration file must be valid for both the TCP and UDP-based setups.

## See also

- The *Multiple remotes and remote-random* recipe earlier in this chapter, which explains how to achieve the same setup without using connection blocks

# Details of ifconfig-pool-persist

One of the options available in OpenVPN that can lead to a lot of confusion is `ifconfig-pool-persist`. This directive tells the OpenVPN server to maintain a persistent list of IP addresses handed out to different clients. When a client reconnects at a later time, the previously-used address is reused. This is only one of three methods for assigning static addresses to an OpenVPN client. The other two methods are:

- Using an `ifconfig-push` statement in a client-connect script
- Using an `ifconfig-push` statement in a client-configuration file

Both of these take precedence over the entries found in the `ifconfig-pool-persist` file. Experience has shown that it is often a good idea to temporarily disable this option when an OpenVPN setup is not working properly.

In this recipe, we will demonstrate how to use `ifconfig-pool-persist` and what the pitfalls are.

## Getting ready

We will use the following network layout:

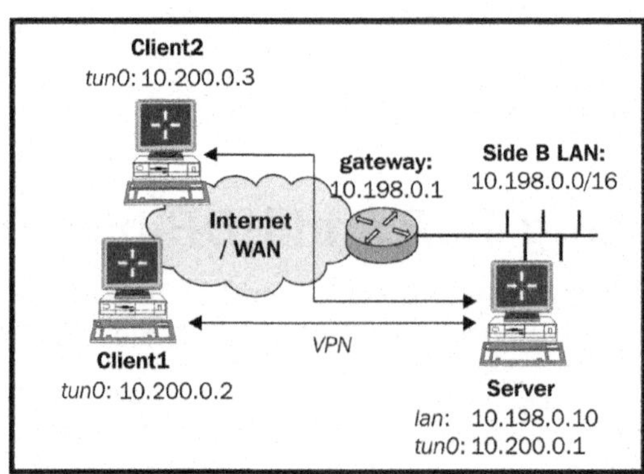

Set up the client and server certificates using the first recipe from `Chapter 2`, *Client-server IP-only Networks*. For this recipe, the server computer was running CentOS 6 Linux and OpenVPN 2.3.11. The client was running Fedora 22 Linux and OpenVPN 2.3.11. Keep the configuration file, `basic-udp-server.conf`, from the *Server-side routing* recipe from `Chapter 2`, *Client-server IP-only Networks* at hand, as well as the client configuration file, `basic-udp-client.conf`, from the same recipe. The second client was running Windows 7 64 bit and OpenVPN 2.3.11. For this client, keep the client configuration file, `basic-udp-client.ovpn`, from the *Using an ifconfig-pool block* recipe from `Chapter 2`, *Client-server IP-only Networks* at hand.

# How to do it...

1. Create the server configuration file by adding the following line to the `basic-udp-server.conf` file:

```
ifconfig-pool-persist /etc/openvpn/cookbook/ipp.txt
```

2. Save it as `example10-4-server.conf` file.
3. Start the server:

```
[root@server]# openvpn --config example10-4-server.conf
```

   An empty file, `/etc/openvpn/cookbook/ipp.txt`, will be created as the server starts up.

4. Connect the first client:

```
[root@client]# openvpn --config basic-udp-client.conf
```

   Normally, this client will be assigned `10.200.0.2`, which is the first available IP address in the `server` IP range.

5. Stop both the client and the server. List the contents of the `ipp.txt` file:

```
[root@server]# cat /etc/openvpn/cookbook/ipp.txt
client1,10.200.0.2
```

6. Start the server again. Now, connect the second client, which has a different certificate:

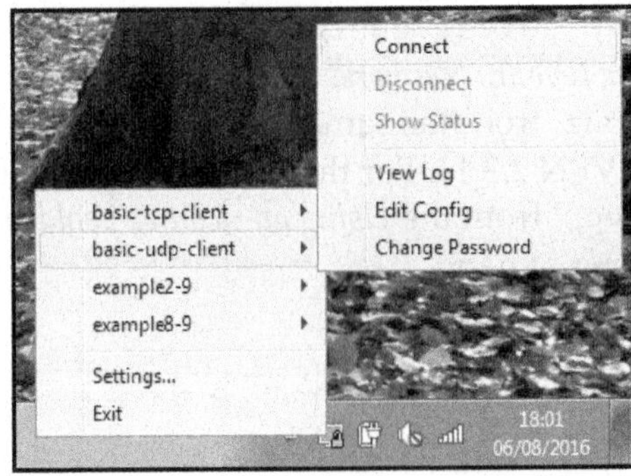


This client will now be assigned the address `10.200.0.3`. Without the `ifconfig-pool-persist` option, it would have been assigned the first available address, which is `10.200.0.2`.

# How it works...

When the OpenVPN server starts, it reads the `ipp.txt` file, if it exists, and it tries to re-assign the IP addresses to the client certificates found in the file. Whenever an OpenVPN client with one of the existing client certificates connects, it is assigned the address found in the `ipp.txt` file, unless the server VPN IP address space is too small for the number of already-connected clients. In that case, the client receives the first available address from the server VPN IP address space.

The first client that connected received the first available address, `10.200.0.2`, from the VPN IP server address range. When the OpenVPN server shuts down, this information is recorded in the `ipp.txt` file. The second time the OpenVPN server started, this information was reloaded and the address, `10.200.0.2`, was held in reserve for the client with certificate `client1`. When the second client connected with certificate `client2`, it received the next available address in the server VPN IP address range, which is `10.200.0.3`. When the server shuts down again, this information is also recorded in the `ipp.txt` file.

This means that from now on, the first client will always receive the `.2` address and the second client the `.3` address. However, it is not a guarantee that the listed IP addresses will be assigned to a particular client certificate. The exception occurs when many VPN clients connect to the server. If the VPN IP address range is exhausted and the first client is not connected at that time, its address is recycled for other VPN clients. If the client with certificate `client1` then tries to connect to the server, it will be assigned the first available address. For a guaranteed assignment, a `client-config-dir` file should be used.

# There's more...

When using the `ifconfig-pool-persist` directive, there are a few pitfalls to watch out for.

## Specifying the update interval

Because we did not explicitly specify an update interval, the `ipp.txt` file is updated every 600 seconds (10 minutes). This can also be seen by looking at the `ipp.txt` file right after a new client connects: the newly-found client certificate and VPN IP are not listed in the `ipp.txt` file until the first update interval passes or when the OpenVPN server process shuts down.

It is also possible to specify an update interval of `0` seconds, which means that the `ipp.txt` file is never updated. This causes the OpenVPN server to associate IP addresses with the client certificate names found in the `ipp.txt` file at the startup but these associations will never change afterwards.

## Caveat – the duplicate-cn option

The `duplicate-cn` option can be used to allow the same client certificate to connect to the same server a number of times. If this option is used, the `ifconfig-pool-persist` option becomes useless, as the same client certificate will be connected twice. This means that the OpenVPN server has to hand out two different IP addresses to each client and the entry in the `ipp.txt` file becomes meaningless.

## When topology net30 is used

When the server option `topology net30` is used, the format of the `ipp.txt` file is slightly different. In the `net30` topology mode, each client is assigned a `/30` network address consisting of four IP addresses: the network address, the VPN server endpoint address, the actual client VPN IP address, and the broadcast address for the `/30` network. In the `ipp.txt` file, the first of these is recorded:

```
client1,10.200.0.4
client2,10.200.0.8
```

# Connecting using a SOCKS proxy

Under certain circumstances, it is not possible to directly connect to an OpenVPN server. This happens most often when firewalls are restricting UDP-based traffic. In such cases, OpenVPN can connect to an OpenVPN server via an intermediary host known as a proxy. OpenVPN supports two types of proxies, SOCKS and HTTP-based, both of which work only using TCP-based configurations. This recipe will outline how to access an OpenVPN server via a SOCKS proxy, whereas the next two recipes will show how to use an HTTP proxy, both with and without authentication.

SOCKS proxies can very easily be set up using almost any SSH client. On Linux and Mac OS X, it can be done using the `ssh` or `slogin` commands, whereas, on Windows, the free SSH client PuTTY can be used. In this recipe, we will use SSH on a Linux client to set up a public SOCKS proxy. A Windows OpenVPN client will connect using this proxy.

## Getting ready

We will use the following network layout:

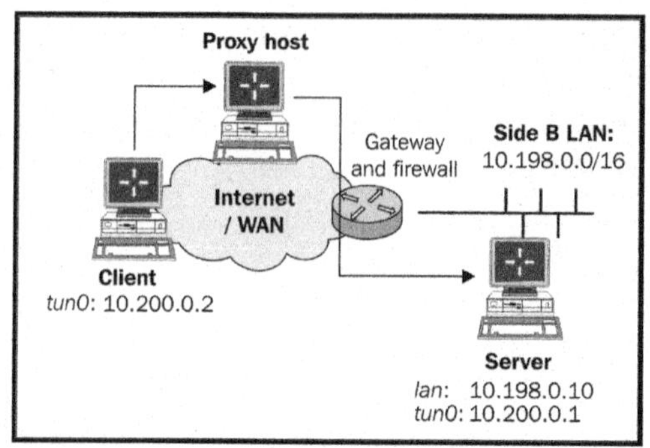

Set up the client and server certificates using the first recipe from `Chapter 2`, *Client-server IP-only Networks*. For this recipe, the server computer was running CentOS 6 Linux and OpenVPN 2.3.12. The client was running Windows 7 64 bit and OpenVPN 2.3.10. Keep the configuration file, `example8-9-server.conf`, from the *Tuning TCP-based connections* recipe from `Chapter 8`, *Performance Tuning* at hand. For the client, keep the configuration file, `basic-tcp-client.ovpn`, from *Using an ifconfig-pool block* recipe from the `Chapter 2`, *Client-server IP-only Networks* at hand.

# How to do it...

1. Start the server:

```
[root@server]# openvpn --config example8-9-server.conf
```

2. Right-click on the OpenVPN GUI tray icon and select **Settings**. Fill in the name or IP address of the **SOCKS proxy** host, and then click on **OK**:

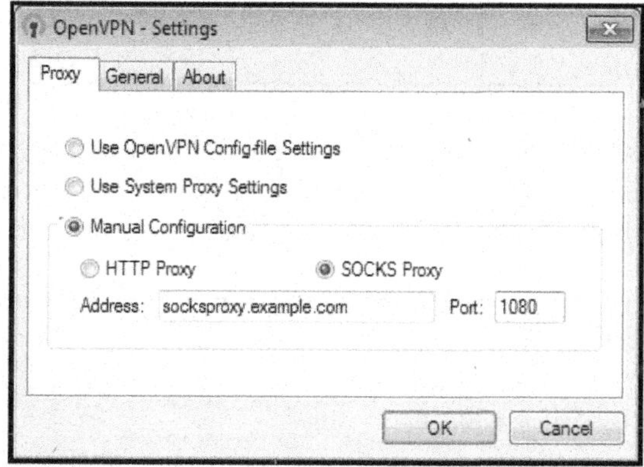


3. Set up a **SOCKS proxy** by setting up an SSH connection on the intermediary proxy host. The destination address for the SSH connection is a server which can reach the OpenVPN server:

```
[socks-proxy]$ ssh -g -D 1080 remote-host.example.com
```

4. Now start the OpenVPN client in another terminal window:

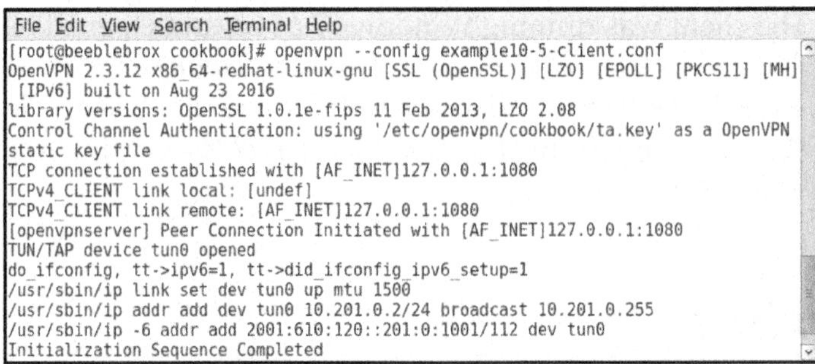


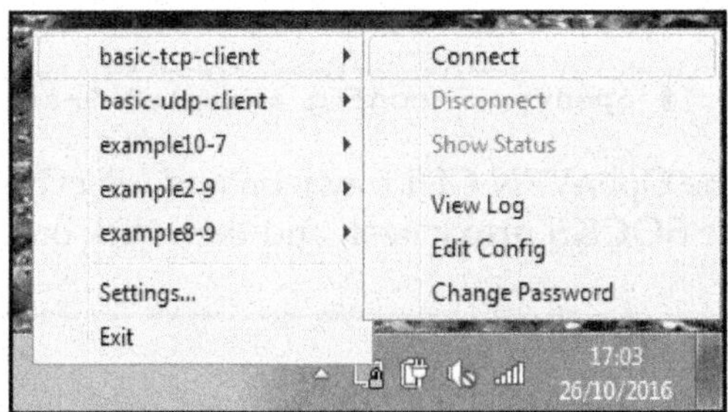


5. The connection log will show that OpenVPN first connects to the remote proxy host (in this screenshot, the IP address `192.168.3.17` was used). This connection is then forwarded to the OpenVPN server and the VPN is established:

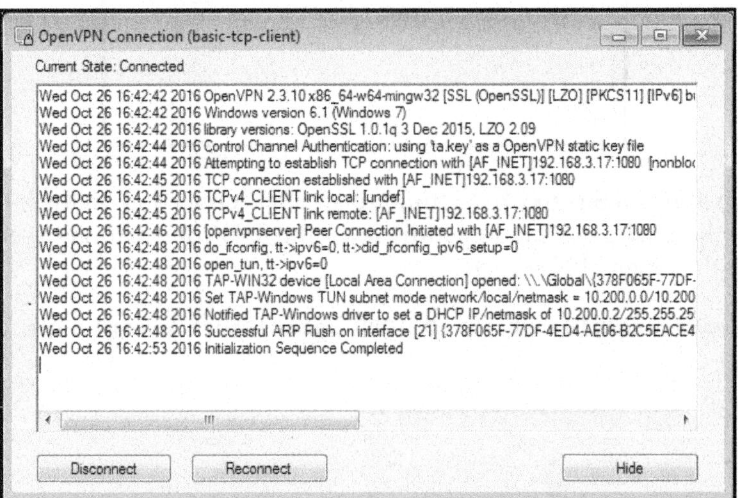

## How it works...

A **SOCKS proxy** host acts as an intermediary between the (OpenVPN) client and the server. SOCKS proxies can also be configured in most web browsers and are often used to gain access through a hotel or corporate firewall. The client first connects to the **SOCKS proxy** host and then requests a new connection to the actual endpoint, which is the OpenVPN server in this case. If the connection is allowed by the SOCKS host, the connection is established and the VPN connection can be set up.

## There's more...

Before using a proxy host to set up a VPN connection, there are a few things to consider:

### Performance

Proxy hosts tend to have a severe impact on the performance of a VPN setup. Both the bandwidth and the latency are usually affected when proxy hosts are used. This is mostly caused by having to connect to a separate host. There is little that can be done about this drop in performance.

### SOCKS proxies via SSH

SSH can be a very handy tool to set up a **SOCKS proxy** host, over which an OpenVPN connection can be set up. Apart from the drawback mentioned above, this introduces another penalty: both the SSH connection and the VPN connection will normally be encrypted. Thus, tunneling traffic over an encrypted VPN link, which in itself is tunneled over an encrypted SSH link, is double encrypted!

A question that you should ask yourself if you are tunneling VPN traffic over an SSH tunnel is: why? What type of traffic needs to be tunneled over a VPN link that cannot be tunneled via a SOCKS-over-SSH tunnel? Most modern web browsers and e-mail clients have built-in support for SOCKS hosts, eliminating the need for a full-blown VPN. File sharing protocols such as Windows file sharing (**Common Internet File System** (**CIFS**)) can also be tunneled over an SSH connection. In those cases, a VPN tunnel adds only extra complexity.

## SOCKS proxies using plain-text authentication

In OpenVPN 2.2 and higher, support is added to connect to a SOCKS proxy that required authentication. For OpenVPN 2.2, plain-text authentication support is added. Though the name "plain text" may suggest otherwise, the authentication mechanism is secure, as the connection to the **SOCKS proxy** host is encrypted first.

## See also

- The next two recipes in this chapter will deal with connecting an OpenVPN client to a server via an HTTP proxy

# Connecting via an HTTP proxy

As stated in the previous recipe, it is not possible to directly connect to an OpenVPN server under certain circumstances. In such cases, OpenVPN can connect to an OpenVPN server via an intermediary host known as a proxy. This recipe will outline how to access an OpenVPN server via an proxy.

The HTTP proxy used in this recipe is a Linux-based Apache `httpd` server with the `mod_proxy` module loaded. This module can be configured to allow `CONNECT` requests. This type of request is needed to connect to secure web servers (HTTPS) as well as to an OpenVPN server. If the `CONNECT` request is not allowed, then the HTTP proxy cannot be used to set up an OpenVPN connection.

## Getting ready

We will use the following network layout:

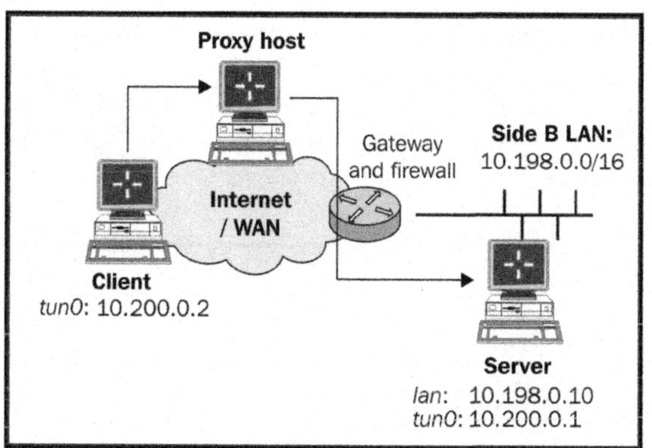


Set up the client and server certificates using the first recipe from `Chapter 2`, *Client-server IP-only Networks*. For this recipe, the server computer was running CentOS 6 Linux and OpenVPN 2.3.12. The client was running Windows 7 64 bit and OpenVPN 2.3.11. Keep the configuration file, `example8-9-server.conf`, from the *Tuning TCP-based connections* recipe from `Chapter 8`, *Performance Tuning*, as well as the client configuration file, `example8-9.ovpn`, from the same recipe.

# How to do it...

1. Start the server:

```
[root@server]# openvpn --config example8-9-server.conf
```

2. Modify the client configuration file, `example8-9.ovpn`, by adding the lines:

```
http-proxy http-proxy-host 80
verb 4
```

   Here, `http-proxy-host` is either the name or the IP address of the host running the HTTP proxy software. In this recipe, the HTTP proxy was running on the HTTP default port `80`. Save the configuration file as `example10-6.ovpn`.

3. Start the client, and then check the connection log.

   The connection log will show that the OpenVPN client first connects to the HTTP proxy host and then sends an `HTTP 'CONNECT'` request to connect to the OpenVPN server:

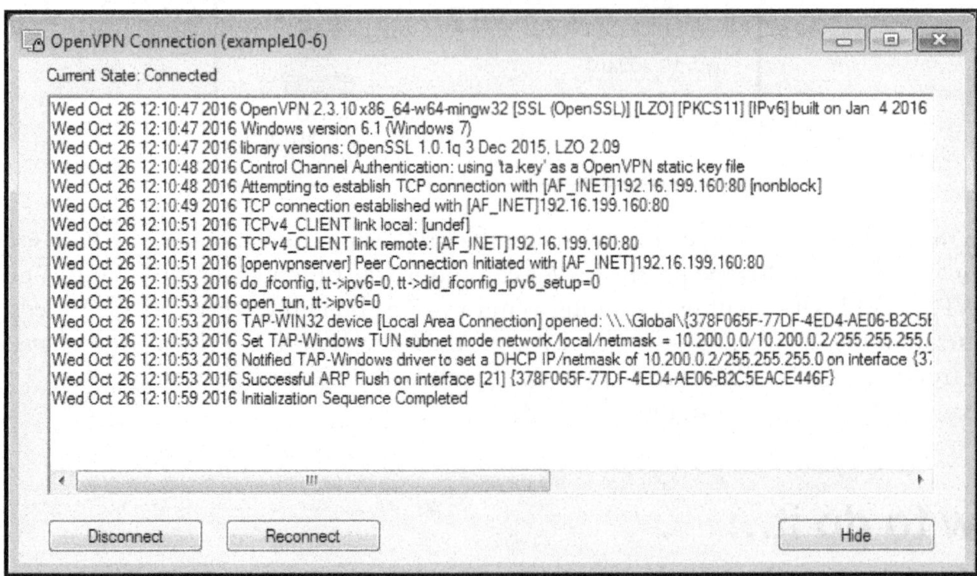


   The HTTP proxy host responds with the HTTP code `200` meaning `OK`, after which the VPN connection is established.

# How it works...

An HTTP proxy host acts as an intermediary between the (OpenVPN) client and the server. HTTP proxies can be configured in most web browsers and are often used to gain access through a hotel or a corporate firewall. The client first connects to the HTTP proxy host and then requests a new connection to the actual endpoint using the `HTTP 'CONNECT'` request. If the HTTP proxy host allows the `CONNECT` request, the HTTP code `200` is returned and the connection to the OpenVPN server is granted. From here on, the OpenVPN connection is set up in a similar fashion to a regular TCP-based setup.

# There's more...

When using an HTTP proxy host to connect to an OpenVPN server, there are a few caveats.

## http-proxy options

There are a few options available in OpenVPN to configure the way in which OpenVPN connects with the HTTP proxy host:

- `http-proxy-timeout` (`n`): This sets the timeout when connecting to the HTTP proxy host to (`n`) seconds. The default value is 5 seconds.
- `http-proxy-option AGENT` (`string`): This sets the HTTP agent to (`string`) when connecting to the HTTP proxy host. Some proxies allow connections from "well-known" web browsers only.
- `http-proxy-option VERSION 1.1`: This sets the HTTP protocol version to 1.1. The default is HTTP/1.0. OpenVPN 2.1 is not fully HTTP/1.1 compliant when connecting to an HTTP proxy host, causing some proxies to refuse access. This is fixed in OpenVPN 2.2.

## Dodging firewalls

Please note that OpenVPN makes no attempt to hide itself from a firewall. Modern firewalls that perform the so-called deep-packet inspection can easily detect the type of traffic that OpenVPN is using to connect to the OpenVPN server and can block access based on that.

## Performance

Similar to SOCKS proxies, HTTP proxy hosts tend to have an impact on the performance of a VPN setup. Both the bandwidth and the latency are usually affected when proxy hosts are used. This is mostly caused by having to connect to a separate host.

## Using the OpenVPN GUI

In Windows, you can also the use OpenVPN GUI application to set up an HTTP proxy server:

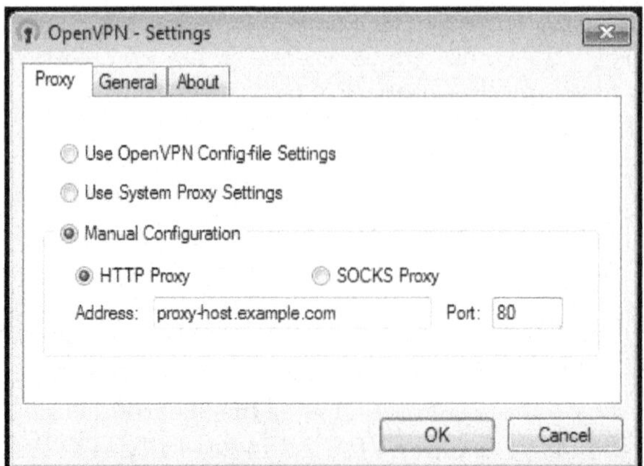


## See also

- The previous and next recipes in this chapter deal with connecting via a **SOCKS proxy** host and connecting via an HTTP proxy with authentication

# Connecting via an HTTP proxy with authentication

In the previous recipe, a plain HTTP proxy was used to connect to an OpenVPN server. As a follow-up, in this recipe we will show how an OpenVPN connection can be set up when the HTTP proxy server requires authentication.

The HTTP proxy used in this recipe is a Linux-based Apache `httpd` server with the `mod_proxy` module loaded and configured for basic authentication.

## Getting ready

We will use the following network layout:

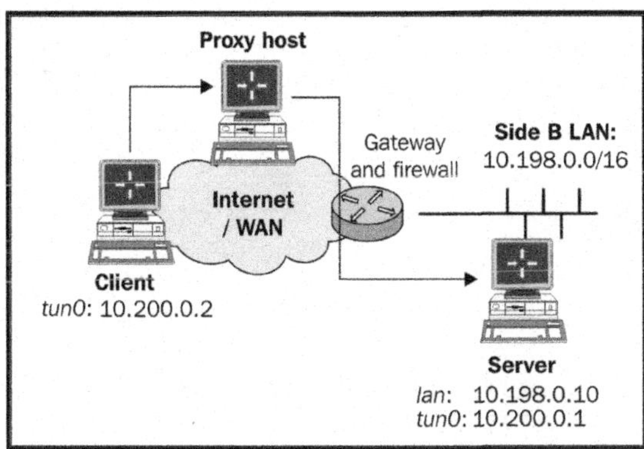


Set up the client and server certificates using the first recipe from `Chapter 2`, *Client-server IP-only Networks*. For this recipe, the server computer was running CentOS 6 Linux and OpenVPN 2.3.12. The client was running Fedora 22 Linux and OpenVPN 2.3.11. Keep the configuration file, `example8-9-server.conf`, from the *Tuning TCP-based connections* recipe from `Chapter 8`, *Performance Tuning*, as well as the client configuration file, `basic-tcp-client.conf`, from the *Server-side routing* recipe from `Chapter 2`, *Client-server IP-only Networks* at hand.

## How to do it...

1. Start the server:

```
[root@server]# openvpn --config example8-9-server.conf
```

2. Set up the HTTP proxy server to support basic authentication. For the Apache `httpd` server used in this recipe, the following `proxy.conf` file was used:

```
LoadModule proxy_module modules/mod_proxy.so
LoadModule proxy_balancer_module modules/mod_proxy_balancer.so
LoadModule proxy_ftp_module modules/mod_proxy_ftp.so
LoadModule proxy_http_module modules/mod_proxy_http.so
LoadModule proxy_connect_module modules/mod_proxy_connect.so

ProxyRequests On
```

```
ProxyVia On
AllowCONNECT 1194
KeepAlive on

<Proxy *>
    Order deny,allow
    Deny from all
    Require user cookbook
    AuthType Basic
    AuthName "Password Required"
    AuthUserFile /etc/httpd/conf/proxy-password
</Proxy>
```

3. Create the `proxy-password` file using Apache's `htpasswd` command:

```
[root@proxyhost]# cd /etc/httpd/conf
[root@proxyhost]# htpasswd -c proxy-password cookbook
```

4. Add the following lines to the client configuration file, `basic-tcp-client.conf`:

```
verb 5
http-proxy proxy.example.com 80 /etc/openvpn/cookbook/proxypass
```

5. Save the configuration file as `example10-7-client.conf`.
6. Create a plain-text file containing the username and password created in step 3; for example, by using:

```
[client]# echo -e "cookbook\ncookbook" > proxy-password
```

7. Start the client and wait for the connection to be established:

```
[client]# openvpn --config example10-7-client.conf
```

8. Next, we take a closer look at the client logfile. If the right username and password are entered, the HTTP proxy grants access to connect to the OpenVPN server and the VPN connection is established:

```
Attempting to establish TCP connection with
[AF_INET]proxy.example.com:80 [nonblock]
TCP connection established with [AF_INET]proxy.example.com:80
Send to HTTP proxy: 'CONNECT openvpnserver.example.com:1194
HTTP/1.0'
Attempting Basic Proxy-Authorization
HTTP proxy returned: 'HTTP/1.0 200 Connection Established'
TCPv4_CLIENT link local: [undef]
```

```
TCPv4_CLIENT link remote: [AF_INET]proxy.example.com:80
TLS: Initial packet from [AF_INET]proxy.example.com:80,
sid=3593eadc c87fb5d4
VERIFY OK: depth=1, C=US, O=Cookbook 2.4, CN=Cookbook 2.4 CA,
emailAddress=openvpn@example.com
Validating certificate key usage
++ Certificate has key usage  00a0, expects 00a0
VERIFY KU OK
Validating certificate extended key usage
++ Certificate has EKU (str) TLS Web Server Authentication,
expects TLS Web Server Authentication
VERIFY EKU OK
VERIFY OK: depth=0, C=US, O=Cookbook 2.4, CN=openvpnserver
Data Channel Encrypt: Cipher 'BF-CBC' initialized with 128 bit
key
```

As can be seen from the connection log, the OpenVPN client attempts basic proxy authorization when connecting to the HTTP proxy server. If the authentication is successful, the HTTP proxy grants access to the client to connect to the server.

## How it works...

Similar to the previous recipe, the OpenVPN client first connects to the HTTP proxy host. It attempts to authenticate to the HTTP proxy using basic authentication, using the username and password supplied in the proxy password file, `/etc/openvpn/cookbook/proxypass`. After successful authentication, the client then sends an `HTTP 'CONNECT'` request to connect to the OpenVPN server. From here on, the OpenVPN connection is set up in a similar fashion to a regular TCP-based setup.

## There's more...

OpenVPN supports multiple authentication mechanisms when connecting to an HTTP proxy.

## NTLM proxy authorization

OpenVPN also supports HTTP proxies that use NTLM proxy authorization, where **NTLM** stands for **NT Lan Manager**. Typically, this type of proxy is used in a Microsoft Windows environment. Unfortunately, OpenVPN's implementation of NTLM authorization is rather limited. It does not send out proper NTLMSSP messages and it works only with a very limited set of proxies. To enable support for this type of proxy add `http-proxy proxyhost proxyport stdin ntlm` or `http-proxy proxyhost proxyport stdin ntlm2`, where `stdin` instructs OpenVPN to query the username and password on the command prompt.

## Authentication methods

OpenVPN also supports HTTP `digest` authentication, which is more secure than the plain-text authentication outlined in this recipe. You can also use the option `auto-nct` with the `http-proxy` authentication directive to reject weak proxy authentication methods.

## OpenVPN GUI limitations

The current OpenVPN GUI does not allow you to specify a username or password in the GUI. This was supported in older versions of the Windows OpenVPN GUI application. As this feature is not widely used it was removed during the rewrite of the GUI.

## See also

- The previous recipe in this chapter, where a connection is established using an HTTP proxy without extra authentication

# IP-less setups – ifconfig-noexec

The goal of this recipe is to create an OpenVPN tunnel without assigning IP addresses to the endpoints of the tunnel. In a routed network setup, this ensures that the tunnel endpoints can never be reached through themselves, which adds some security and can also make the routing tables a bit shorter. In the OpenVPN configuration files, an IP address needs to be specified, but it is never assigned to the tunnel interface.

This recipe has only been tested on Linux systems, as it requires some network-interface configuration that is not available on other platforms.

## Getting ready

We will use the following network layout:

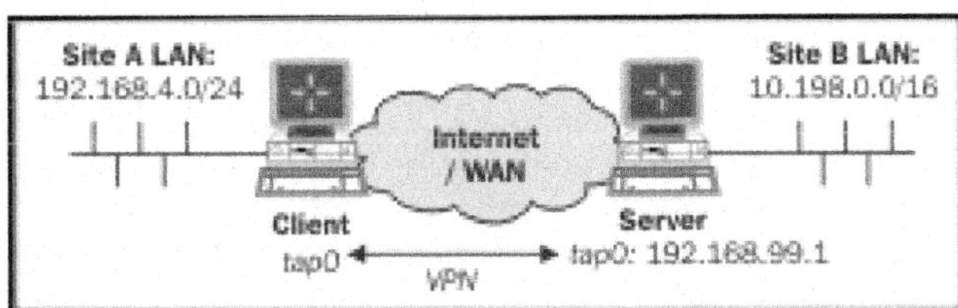


Make sure that the client and server are not on the same local network. If the client and server can contact each other directly then this recipe will fail. Set up the client and server certificates using the first recipe from `Chapter 2`, *Client-server IP-only Networks*. In this recipe, the server computer was running CentOS 6 Linux and OpenVPN 2.3.12. The client was running Fedora 22 Linux and OpenVPN 2.3.11. Keep the server config file, `example3-1-server.conf`, from the *Simple configuration – non-bridged* recipe from `Chapter 3`, *Client-server Ethernet-style Networks*.

## How to do it...

1. Create the server configuration file by adding a line to the `example3-1-server.conf` file:

```
route 192.168.4.0 255.255.255.0 192.168.99.1
```

2. Save it as `example10-8-server.conf`.
3. Start the server:

```
[root@server]# openvpn --config example10-8-server.conf
```

4. Create the client configuration file:

```
client
proto udp
remote openvpnserver.example.com
port 1194

dev tap
nobind

remote-cert-tls server
tls-auth /etc/openvpn/cookbook/ta.key 1
ca       /etc/openvpn/cookbook/ca.crt
cert     /etc/openvpn/cookbook/client1.crt
key      /etc/openvpn/cookbook/client1.key

script-security 2
ifconfig-noexec
up /etc/openvpn/cookbook/example10-8-up.sh

route-noexec
route-up /etc/openvpn/cookbook/example10-8-route-up.sh
```

5. Save it as `example-10-8-client.conf`.
6. Next, create the `example10-8-up.sh` script:

```
#!/bin/bash

/sbin/ifconfig $1 0.0.0.0 up
# needed for TAP interfaces !!!
echo 1 > /proc/sys/net/ipv4/conf/$1/proxy_arp
```

7. Save it as `/etc/openvpn/cookbook/example10-8-up.sh`.
8. Similarly, create the `example10-8-route-up.sh` script:

```
#!/bin/bash

# add an explicit route back to the VPN endpoint
/sbin/ip route add $route_vpn_gateway/32 dev $dev

n=1;
while [ $n -le 100 ]
do
  network=`env | sed -n \
     "/^"route_network_${n}=/s/^route_network_${n}=//p"`"
  netmask=`env | sed -n \
     "/^"route_netmask_${n}=/s/^route_netmask_${n}=//p"`"
```

```
    if [ -z "$"network" -o -z "$"netmask" ]
    then
      break
    fi

    /sbin/ip route add $network/$netmask dev $dev
    let n=n+1
  done
```

9. Save it as `/etc/openvpn/cookbook/example10-8-route-up.sh`.
10. Make sure both scripts are executable and both of them start the client:

```
[[root@client]# chmod 755 /etc/openvpn/cookbook/example10-8*.sh
[root@client]# openvpn --config example10-8-client.conf
```

11. After the client successfully connects to the OpenVPN server, check the `tap0` interface and the routing tables, and verify that you can ping the server:

```
[root@client]# ip addr show tap0
13: tap0: <BROADCAST,MULTICAST,UP,LOWER_UP> mtu 1500 qdisc
pfifo_fast state UNKNOWN group default qlen 100
link/ether b6:b3:0e:41:d5:4d brd ff:ff:ff:ff:ff:ff
inet6 fe80::b4b3:eff:fe41:d54d/64 scope link
   valid_lft forever preferred_lft forever
[root@client]# netstat-rn
Kernel IP routing table
Destination Gateway   Genmask         Flags[...]  Iface
192.168.4.0 0.0.0.0   255.255.255.0 U    0 0 0 eth0
10.198.0.0  0.0.0.0   255.255.0.0   U    0 0 0 tap0
[...]
[root@client]# ping -c 2 192.168.99.1
PING 192.168.99.1 (192.168.99.1) 56(84) bytes of data.
64 bytes from 192.168.99.1: icmp_seq=1 ttl=64 time=25.7 ms
64 bytes from 192.168.99.1: icmp_seq=2 ttl=64 time=26.2 ms
```

## How it works...

The OpenVPN server allocates an IP address for the client, but that does not mean that the client interface actually needs to assign these addresses. The `example10-8-up.sh` script does exactly this.

Some older Linux kernels refuse to add a route without an address being assigned to an interface. Hence, we assign the address `0.0.0.0` to the `tun0` interface. To add the routes that are pushed by the server, a special `route-up` script is used, `example10-8-route-up.sh`, which brings up all the routes.

# There's more...

Please note the following when considering an IP-less setup.

## Point-to-point and TUN-style networks

This recipe can also be used in a point-to-point style environment, where static keys are used to connect two networks. Similarly, it can also be used in a TUN-style setup.

## Routing and firewalling

At first, this recipe might seem odd. The advantage of this setup is that the OpenVPN client itself is not reachable by other machines on the VPN. This is handy when connecting many clients to an OpenVPN server, but some clients are used as gateways to the networks behind them (for example, to connect a remote office to the OpenVPN server). By not assigning the remote office gateway an IP address, there is no risk of the gateway itself being attacked from the remote VPN side. Also, server-side firewalling and `iptables` rules can be slightly shorter in this scenario, as there will be no traffic coming from the OpenVPN client with the VPN source address. This is also the reason why the server configuration has an explicit route to the client-side network:

```
route 192.168.4.0 255.255.255.0 192.168.99.1
```

It also explains why this recipe will fail if the VPN client and server are on the same local area network. If the VPN client can contact the VPN server directly then the VPN server will not be able to determine which traffic needs to go inside the tunnel and which traffic needs to be sent directly to the client.

# Port sharing with an HTTPS server

A common OpenVPN setup to allow road warriors to reach the home office is to have OpenVPN listen on the secure web server (HTTPS) port `443`. The downside is that you can no longer use that port on the OpenVPN server to actually host a secure website. OpenVPN 2.1 introduces a new `port-sharing` directive, enabling dual use of a TCP port. All traffic that is detected as OpenVPN traffic is processed by the OpenVPN server itself, and all other traffic is forwarded to another (local) machine and/or port.

In this recipe, we will set up an OpenVPN server to share TCP port `443` with a web server and we will show that both OpenVPN and a web browser can successfully connect to this server.

## Getting ready

We will use the following network layout:

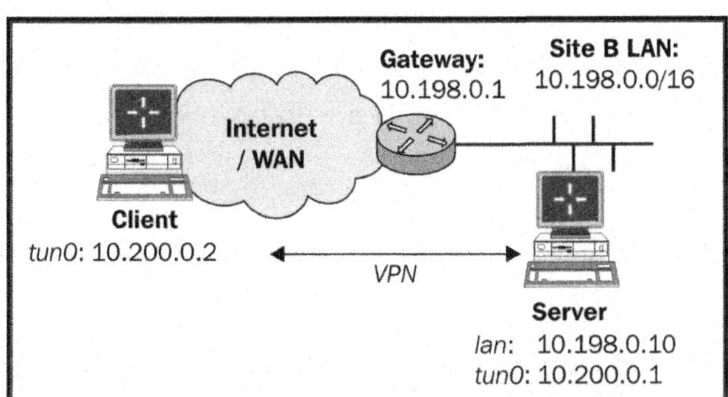


Set up the client and server certificates using the first recipe from `Chapter 2`, *Client-server IP-only Networks*. For this recipe, the server computer was running CentOS 6 Linux and OpenVPN 2.3.12. The client was running Windows 7 64 bit and OpenVPN 2.3.10. Keep the server configuration file, `example8-9-server.conf`, from the *Tuning TCP-based connections* recipe from `Chapter 8`, *Performance Tuning* at hand, as well as the client configuration file, `example8-9.ovpn`, from the same recipe.

On the server computer, a secure web server was running on port `8443`.

# How to do it...

1. Create the server configuration file by modifying the `example8-9-server.conf` file. Change the following line:

   ```
   port 1194
   ```

   Change it to the following:

   ```
   port 443
   port-share localhost 8443
   ```

   Save it as `example10-9-server.conf`.

2. Start the server:

   ```
   [root@server]# openvpn --config example10-9-server.conf
   ```

3. Next, modify the client configuration file, `example8-9.ovpn`, by also changing the port to `443`. Save the client configuration file as `example10-9.ovpn`.
4. Start the client and verify that the client can connect to the VPN server.
5. After the client has connected, start a web browser and browse to:

   ```
   https://openvpnserver.example.com
   ```

   The OpenVPN server log file will show lines similar to the following:

   ```
   ... Re-using SSL/TLS context
   ... TCP connection established with <client-ip>:53356
   ... TCPv4_SERVER link local: [undef]
   ... TCPv4_SERVER link remote: <client-ip>:53356
   ... <client-ip>:53356 Non-OpenVPN client protocol detected
   ```

# How it works...

When `port-share` is used, OpenVPN will inspect the incoming traffic on port `443`. If this traffic is a part of an OpenVPN session or if it is an initial OpenVPN handshake, then the OpenVPN server processes it by itself. If it is not recognizable as OpenVPN traffic, it is forwarded out to the host and port specified in the `port-share` directive.

Hence, it is the OpenVPN server process that is always listening on port `443`. The web server must be listening on a different host, interface, or port. With this setup, the same port can be used to offer two different services.

## There's more...

The web server that OpenVPN forwards its traffic to must be a secure (HTTPS) web server. This is due to the nature of the inbound SSL traffic on the OpenVPN server itself. It is not possible to forward the traffic to a regular (HTTP) web server. If the traffic is forwarded to port `80`, the Apache web server used in this recipe, the following error will appear in the web server error log file:

```
[error] [client 127.0.0.1] Invalid method in request \x16\x03\x01
```

### Alternatives

There are many alternatives available that can achieve the same functionality. One example tool that can distinguish between OpenVPN, SSL (HTTPS), and SSH traffic is the Linux-based `sslh` tool.

# Routing features – redirect-private, allow-pull-fqdn

Over the years, the routing features of OpenVPN have expanded. Most notably, there are quite a few options for the `redirect-gateway` directive, as well as several other less well-known routing directives:

- `redirect-private`: This option behaves very similar to the `redirect-gateway` directive, especially when the new parameters are used, but it does not alter the default gateway.
- `allow-pull-fqdn`: This allows the client to pull DNS names from the OpenVPN server. Previously, only IP addresses could be pushed or pulled. This option cannot be pushed and needs to be added to the client configuration itself.
- `route-nopull`: All the options are pulled by a client from the server, except for the routing options. This can be particularly handy when troubleshooting an OpenVPN setup.
- `max-routes n`: This defines the maximum number of routes that may be defined or pulled from a remote server.

In this recipe, we will focus on the `redirect-private` directive and its parameters, as well as the `allow-pull-fqdn` parameter.

# Getting ready

We will use the following network layout:

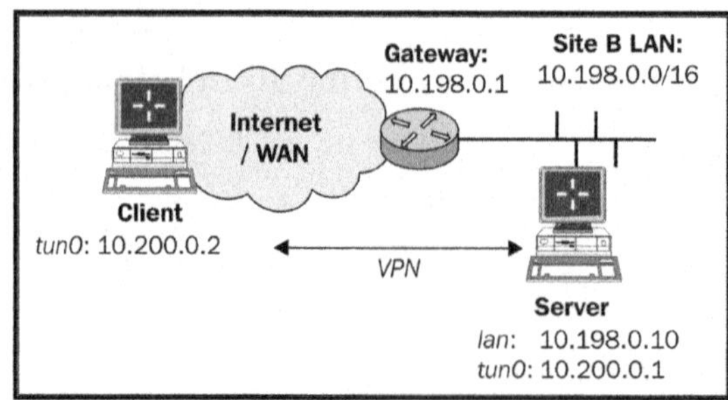


Set up the client and server certificates using the first recipe from `Chapter 2`, *Client-server IP-only Networks*. For this recipe, the server computer was running CentOS 6 Linux and OpenVPN 2.3.12. The client was running Windows 7 64 bit and OpenVPN 2.3.11. Keep the configuration file, `basic-udp-server.conf`, from the *Server-Side routing* recipe from `Chapter 2`, *Client-server IP-only Networks*, as well as the client configuration file, `basic-udp-client.ovpn`, from the *Using an ifconfig-pool block* recipe from `Chapter 2`, *Client-server IP-only Networks*.

# How to do it...

1. Append the following lines to the `basic-udp-server.conf` file:

```
push "redirect-private bypass-dhcp bypass-dns"
push "route server.example.com"
```

2. Save it as `example10-10-server.conf`.
3. Start the server:

```
[root@server]# openvpn --config example10-10-server.conf
```

4. Append the following line to the client configuration file, `basic-udp-client.ovpn`, and save it as `example10-10.ovpn`:

```
allow-pull-fqdn
```

5. Start the client:

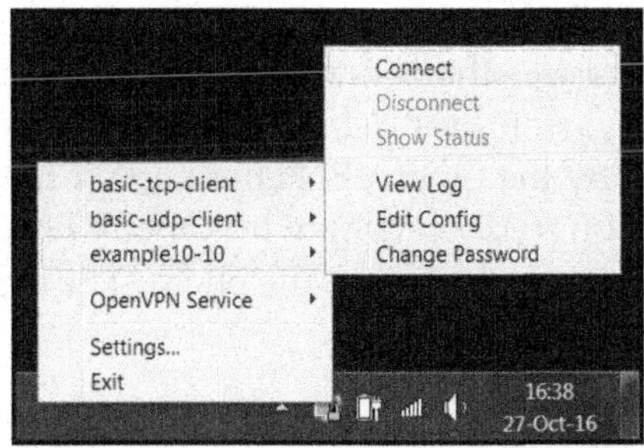


6. Watch the routing table after the connection has been established.

   If the DHCP or DNS server was on a different subnet than the client itself, then a new route will have been added. This is to ensure that DHCP requests still go to the local DHCP server and are not sent over the VPN tunnel.

   A route for the host `server.example.com` will have been added.

## How it works...

The `bypass-dhcp` and `bypass-dns` options for the directives, `redirect-gateway` and `redirect-private`, cause the OpenVPN client to add an extra route to the DHCP and DNS servers if they are on a different network. In large-scale networks, the DNS server is often not found on the local subnet that the client is connected to. If the route to this DNS server is altered to go through the VPN tunnel after the client has connected, this will cause at the very least a serious performance penalty. More likely, the entire DNS server will become unreachable.

The `allow-pull-fqdn` directive enables the use of a DNS name instead of an IP address when specifying a route. Especially, if a dedicated route to a host with a dynamic IP address needs to be made, this is very useful.

Note that the `allow-pull-fqdn` directive cannot be pushed from the server.

## There's more...

Apart from the directives explained in this recipe, there are more routing directives available to control if and how routes are added to the client.

### The route-nopull directive

The `route-nopull` directive causes the client to pull all the information from the server but not the routes. This can be very useful for debugging a faulty server setup. It does not mean that no routes are added at all by the OpenVPN client. Only the routes that are specified using `push "route"` will be ignored. Starting with OpenVPN 2.4, it is also possible to filter out options that are pushed from the server to the client. The next recipe will go into detail on this.

### The max-routes directive

The `max-routes` directive is introduced in OpenVPN 2.1, as version 2.1 allows an administrator to push many more routes when compared to OpenVPN 2.0. To prevent a client from being overloaded with routes, the option `max-routes n` is added, where `n` is the maximum number of routes that can be defined in the client configuration file and/or can pulled from the server.

The default value for this parameter is `100`.

## See also

- The next recipe in this chapter, where options that are pushed from the server to the client are filtered before they are applied

# Filtering out pushed options

Starting with OpenVPN 2.4, it is now possible to filter out options pushed from the OpenVPN server to the client. This allows users to have more control over the network routes and addresses that are pushed from the server.

This recipe will show how this new feature of OpenVPN works.

# Getting ready

We will use the following network layout:

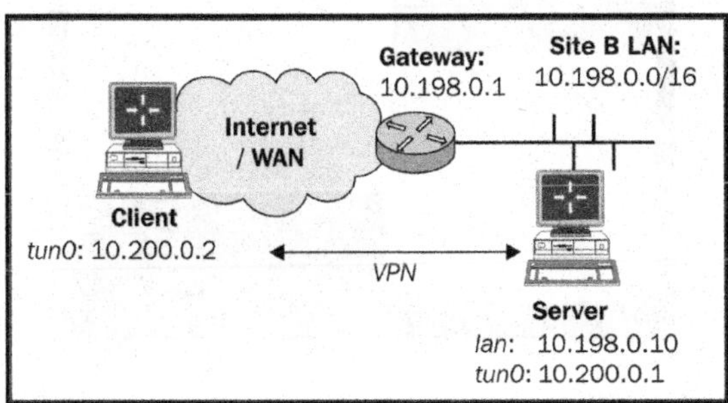


Set up the client and server certificates using the first recipe from `Chapter 2`, *Client-server IP-only Networks*. For this recipe, the server computer was running CentOS 6 Linux and OpenVPN 2.3.12. The client was running Windows 7 64 bit and OpenVPN 2.4_alpha2. For the server, keep the configuration file, `example9-2-server.conf`, from the *Linux – using pull-resolv-conf* recipe, from `Chapter 9`, *OS Integration* at hand. For the client, keep the configuration file, `basic-udp-client.ovpn`, from the *Using an ifconfig-pool block* recipe from `Chapter 2`, *Client-server IP-only Networks*.

# How to do it...

1. Start the server:

```
[root@server]# openvpn --config example9-2-server.conf
```

2. Append the following line to the client configuration file, `basic-udp-client.ovpn`, and save it as `example10-11.ovpn`:

```
pull-filter ignore "dhcp-option DNS"
```

3. Start the client:

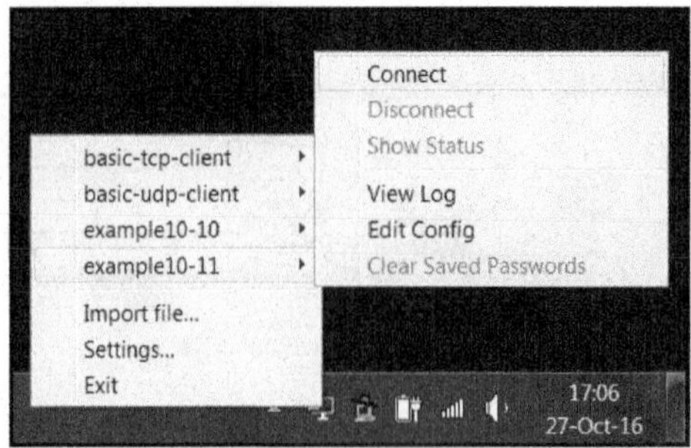


4. View the client log file by selecting `View Log` in the OpenVPN GUI. The log file will contain lines similar to the following:

```
PUSH: Received control message: 'PUSH_REPLY,dhcp-option DNS
192.168.3.1,route-gateway 10.200.0.1,topology subnet,ping
10,ping-restart 60,ifconfig 10.200.0.2 255.255.255.0'
Pushed option removed by filter: 'dhcp-option DNS 192.168.3.1'
```

5. Verify that the DNS settings on the client have not been altered using a tool such as `ipconfig /all`.

# How it works...

The `pull-filter` directive accepts several parameters:

- `accept t`: Accepts the pushed option `t` from the server
- `ignore t`: Ignores the pushed option `t` from the server, but doesn't abort the connection
- `reject t`: Rejects the pushed option `t` from the server and abort the VPN connection

Each option can be specified multiple times, with the last occurrence overriding earlier lines.

By adding the line `pull-filter ignore "dhcp-option DNS"` to the client configuration file, we ignore any pushed line that starts with `dhcp-option DNS`. Therefore, no DNS settings are accepted from the VPN server. This option can be applied to all options that are pushed from the server.

# Handing out the public IPs

With the `topology subnet` feature that OpenVPN offers, it becomes feasible to hand out public IP addresses to connecting clients. For this recipe, we will show how such a setup can be realized. We will re-use a technique from the *Proxy-ARP* recipe from `Chapter 2`, *Client-server IP-only Networks*, to make the VPN clients appear as if they are a part of the remote network. If a dedicated IP address block is available for the VPN clients, then this is not required. The advantage of using the `proxy-arp` method is that it allows us to use only part of an expensive public IP address block.

## Getting ready

For this recipe, the server computer was running CentOS 6 Linux and OpenVPN 2.3.12. The client computer was running Windows 7 64 bit and OpenVPN 2.3.11. Keep the client configuration file, `basic-udp-client.ovpn`, from the *Using an ifconfig-pool block* recipe from Chapter 2, *Client-Server IP-Only Networks*.

To test this recipe, a public IP address block of 16 addresses was used, but here, we will list a private address block instead (`10.0.0.0/255.255.255.240`). This block is used as follows:

- `10.0.0.18`: This is used for the server's VPN IP address
- `10.0.0.19`: Not available
- `10.0.0.20`–`10.0.0.25`: Available for VPN clients
- `10.0.0.26`: Not available
- `10.0.0.27`: The LAN address of the OpenVPN server itself
- `10.0.0.28`–`10.0.0.29`: Not available
- `10.0.0.30`: The router on the remote LAN

## How to do it...

1. Create the server configuration file:

```
mode server
tls-server
proto udp
port 1194
dev tun
```

```
ifconfig 10.0.0.18 255.255.255.240
ifconfig-pool 10.0.0.20 10.0.0.25
push "route 10.0.0.27 255.255.255.255 net_gateway"
push "route-gateway 10.0.0.30"
push "redirect-gateway def1"

tls-auth /etc/openvpn/cookbook/ta.key 0
ca       /etc/openvpn/cookbook/ca.crt
cert     /etc/openvpn/cookbook/server.crt
key      /etc/openvpn/cookbook/server.key
dh       /etc/openvpn/cookbook/dh2048.pem

persist-key
persist-tun
keepalive 10 60

topology subnet
push "topology subnet"

script-security 2
client-connect    /etc/openvpn/cookbook/proxyarp-connect.sh
client-disconnect /etc/openvpn/cookbook/proxyarp-disconnect.sh

#user  nobody
#group nobody

daemon
log-append /var/log/openvpn.log
```

Note that this server configuration cannot be run as user `nobody`. Save the configuration file as `example10-12-server.conf`.

2. Next, create the `proxyarp-connect.sh` script:

```
#!/bin/bash
/sbin/arp -i eth0  -Ds $ifconfig_pool_remote_ip eth0 pub
/sbin/ip route add ${ifconfig_pool_remote_ip}/32 dev tun0
```

3. Save it as `/etc/openvpn/cookbook/proxyarp-connect.sh`.
4. Similarly, create the `proxyarp-disconnect.sh` script:

```
#!/bin/bash
/sbin/arp -i eth0  -d $ifconfig_pool_remote_ip
/sbin/ip route del ${ifconfig_pool_remote_ip}/32 dev tun0
```

5. Save it as `/etc/openvpn/cookbook/proxyarp-disconnect.sh`.

6. Make sure that both the scripts are executable, then start the server:

```
[root@server]# cd /etc/openvpn/cookbook
[root@server]# chmod 755 proxy-connect.sh proxy-disconnect.sh
[root@server]# openvpn --config example10-12-server.conf
```

7. Next, start the client. The IP address assigned to the client should be `10.0.0.20`.
8. Use the client to browse the Internet and check its IP address by surfing, for example, to `http://www.whatismyip.com`.

# How it works...

Some notes on the server configuration file, the directives:

```
ifconfig 10.0.0.18 255.255.255.240
ifconfig-pool 10.0.0.20 10.0.0.25
```

Set up a pool of (public) IP address for the clients to use. Because not all of these addresses are available in the `/28` block, we cannot simply use:

```
server 10.0.0.18 255.255.255.240
```

The next statement is to ensure that the VPN server itself is reached via the regular network and not via the VPN tunnel itself:

```
push "route 10.0.0.27 255.255.255.255 net_gateway"
```

In order to redirect all traffic via the VPN tunnel, we need to explicitly state the new default gateway and `redirect-gateway`:

```
push "route-gateway 10.0.0.30"
push "redirect-gateway def1"
```

Normally, the following statement will also cause the topology setting to be pushed to the VPN clients:

```
topology subnet
```

But, as we're not using the `server` directive, this does not happen automatically. By explicitly pushing the topology, we ensure that the clients will also use the correct settings.

The `client-connect` and `client-disconnect` scripts are very similar to the ones used in the *Proxy-ARP* recipe from `Chapter 2`, *Client-server IP-only Networks*. By using a handy feature of the Linux `arp` command, we can make the remote clients appear to be part of the local network.

# There's more...

The `topology subnet` feature was introduced in OpenVPN 2.1 and is essential to making this recipe practical. Without this feature, each client would be handed out a miniature `/30` network, which means that each client would use up to four public IP addresses. This made the deployment of handing out public IP addresses to VPN clients very expensive.

# See also

- The *Proxy-ARP* recipe from `Chapter 2`, *Client-server IP-only Networks*, which explains in more detail how the Linux/UNIX Proxy-ARP feature works

# Index

## D



## E



## F



## H



## I

## K



## L



## M



## N



## O

## T



## U



## V



## W

CPSIA information can be obtained
at www.ICGtesting.com
Printed in the USA
BVOW03s0935240317
479291BV00002B/10/P

9 781786 463128